Bartered brides is a detailed study of marriage among the Maduzai, a tribal society in Afghan Turkistan. It is the first study of the area which looks in depth at both the domestic aspects of marriage and its relation to the productive and reproductive activities of women, as well as marriage as a means of managing political and economic conflict and competition. The fieldwork was carried out in the early 1970s before the 1978 coup and Soviet invasion. In this respect the book offers a unique account of a world that has disappeared.

Cambridge Studies in Social and Cultural Anthropology
Editors: Jack Goody, Stephen Gudeman, Michael Herzfeld,
Jonathan Parry

74
Bartered brides

A list of books in the series will be found at the end of the volume.

Five women of a Maduzai household

BARTERED BRIDES

*Politics, gender and marriage
in an Afghan tribal society*

NANCY TAPPER
School of Oriental and African Studies, London

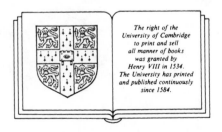

The right of the
University of Cambridge
to print and sell
all manner of books
was granted by
Henry VIII in 1534.
The University has printed
and published continuously
since 1584.

CAMBRIDGE UNIVERSITY PRESS

Cambridge

New York   Port Chester

Melbourne   Sydney

Published by the Press Syndicate of the University of Cambridge
The Pitt Building, Trumpington Street, Cambridge CB2 1RP
40 West 20th Street, New York, NY 10011, USA
10 Stamford Road, Oakleigh, Melbourne 3166, Australia

© Cambridge University Press 1991

First published 1991

Printed in Great Britain at the University Press, Cambridge

British Library cataloguing in publication data

Tapper, Nancy
Bartered brides: politics, gender and marriage in an
Afghan tribal society. (Cambridge studies in social
anthropology)
1. Afghanistan. Pathans; marriage.
I. Title
306.8108991593

Library of Congress cataloguing in publication data

Tapper, Nancy.
Bartered brides: politics, gender and marriage in an Afghan
tribal society / Nancy Tapper.
    p.   cm. – (Cambridge studies in social anthropology: 74)
Includes bibliographical references.
ISBN 0 521 38158 4
1. Durrani (Afghanistan people) – Marriage customs and rites.
2. Family – Afghanistan. 3. Women – Afghanistan. 4. Afghanistan –
Social life and customs. I. Title. II. Series: Cambridge studies
in social anthropology: no. 74.
DS354.58.T37 1990
306.81 – dc20   89–71323 CIP

ISBN 0 521 38158 4 hardback

For Richard

Contents

Illustrations

Plates

Figures

Tables

Case studies

Preface

Marriage – its ideology and associated practices – is the key to many societies around the world, not least in the Muslim Middle East. Not merely the central mechanism for social reproduction, marriage is also the main focus of social production. The choice of partners, the political circumstances behind a match, the negotiations between the two sides, the accumulation and exchange of the various customary gifts, the conduct and evaluation of the wedding ceremonies, the relations between affines and the eventual fruitfulness of the marriage – all these matters are the constant concern of all members of any community, so that any ethnographic account of culture or social relations in such a community that fails to recognize and examine the importance of marriage is necessarily incomplete.

In the Muslim Middle East, there is an additional problem for the investigator. The notorious seclusion and segregation of women has meant that the few recent studies of marriage are one-sided. Either they have adopted a 'male' perspective, treating marriage arrangements as a means whereby political and economic conflict and competition in the wider society are negotiated and managed, or they have concentrated more narrowly on the domestic aspects of marriage and its relation to the productive and reproductive activities of women. These are of course two sides of the same coin, but there have been few detailed studies of sufficient breadth to encompass both and to put the marriage system thus described into its wider theoretical context.

This book is a social anthropological analysis of marriage in an Afghan tribal society, drawing on both male and female perspectives, extended case studies, and historical and statistical materials. Central concepts concerning gender, kinship and affinity, and inequality and equality are examined, while the key values of honour and shame and responsibility are investigated through breach cases which reveal both the structure of competition and conflict for the control of political and economic resources and the role of the individual in the processes of social change.

The study is based on fieldwork done jointly with my husband, Richard Tapper (RLT), in the early 1970s in Afghan Turkistan among the Maduzai, a sub-tribe of the Ishaqzai, one of the major tribes of the Durrani Pashtuns. Although the Durrani people produced the rulers of Afghanistan from the founding of that nation until 1978, little has been written about Durrani culture or social organization. Tragically, since the 1978 coup and the Soviet invasion of Afghanistan, this study has become a memorial; the Maduzai have, so far as we know, been forced to flee Afghan Turkistan, and their way of life as we knew it is almost certainly gone forever. As an ethnographic and historical record, the book offers an account of a world that has disappeared.

Nonetheless, I have chosen to use the ethnographic present tense to describe conversations, events and social activities at the time of fieldwork and I have suggested areas in which the society was changing at that time. Ironically, such discussions have an anthropological interest even though they concern processes which have been made irrelevant by the terrible war which has overtaken the Maduzai and their countrymen. My choice of tense is not meant to disguise or deny the dreadful content of their recent experiences; rather, it is meant to give an immediacy to my account of the Maduzai and their views then of themselves, their history and environment. It is one way of trying to share with the reader something of their vitality, toughness and humour which were so much a part of our experience with them in the then independent Afghanistan.

The Maduzai live in Afghan Turkistan, a region which is ethnically very mixed and where members of many different tribal and language groups are in fierce competition for scarce resources. One thread of the book is the relation between the increasing political and economic competition in the region, the political manipulation of marriage, and changing constructions of Durrani identity. Historical materials – related to the Maduzai arrival in Afghan Turkistan from their southern Afghan homeland from 1915 onwards, the murderous feud which arose among them in the 1930s and the gradual shift from pastoral nomadism to a settled mixed agricultural economy – are used to analyse the changing role of marriage in the intensification of inter-ethnic conflict, and in the recent shift from subsistence production towards cash-cropping and from tribal identities to social class.

All aspects of identity among Durrani are defined by ideals and practices relating to marriage and the control of women. Durrani ethnicity and tribal identity are constructed in terms of religion (Sunni Islam), language (Pashtu) and a patrilineal pedigree which links them with the founding Pashtun ancestor. However, these criteria of identity often operate retrospectively, to rationalize changes of ethnic identity which are ratified through marriage.

The most explicit rule defining Durrani identity is that a Durrani woman should never marry a non-Durrani man. In practice, the ambiguities implicit within this marriage rule, and in the related form of exchange marriage, offer scope for both creating 'new' Durrani when allies are needed and redefining the status of other weaker Durrani who are exploited as workers and servants or even denied Durrani identity and political support altogether. Among themselves Durrani use exchange marriage as a device for resolving serious disputes and confirming social equality; over time, however, these same exchange marriages often become an excuse for conflicts which reflect and define the changing circumstances of former equals.

Durrani households and household identity are constructed in terms of a second explicit rule – that each household should form an autonomous unit whose head independently manages all household resources, including the behaviour of household women. One of the most salient indicators of the relative economic and political standing of a household is the marriages its members make. Economic success and political standing in the community may be expressed through the choice of spouses, the relative frequency of exchange and brideprice marriages, the scale of brideprice payments, the time and expense devoted to the marriage ceremonies and the numbers of people who attend and are feasted. But such public statements are open to interpretation and comparison and may also be seen to indicate a household's weakness and vulnerability.

Durrani discuss the control of resources in the language of honour and shame. A man's prestige – that is, his honour – depends on his ability to manage and defend human and material resources. Though a man's control of resources is expressed in absolute terms and includes, for instance, his power of life or death over the women of his household, the subordination of women to men is qualified in an important way. Where male prestige is heavily dependent on women, women have the ability to undermine male ambition and damage male prestige. This covert, subversive power of women is a second thread which runs through the book.

Much of the time, a woman's interests coincide with those of the household in which she lives. Where they diverge, her efforts to express and defend her own interests are usually hidden from public view, either behind a diagnosis of spirit possession or by the domestic secrecy which surrounds illicit love affairs. *In extremis*, however, a woman may openly defy the ideal of male dominance and the strictures of the ideology of honour and shame and precipitate a public scandal. Such scandals reveal women's potential power and the limits of their subordination in this patriarchal system. They also reveal the dynamic relation between gender and marriage in Durrani constructions of identity.

The book is divided into four parts, the first of which is introductory. Chapter 1 is a personal account of the fieldwork in Afghanistan and the aims and methods of the study. In chapter 2, the reader is introduced to some of the comparative issues concerning marriage in the Muslim Middle East. Chapter 3 provides background information on the Saripul region of Afghan Turkistan and the social relations between the Durrani and other peoples in the area.

Part II of the book is a consideration of the extent to which the indigenous classification of social groups is variously reinforced, transformed or simply bypassed by Durrani marriage practices. In chapter 4 Durrani ethnicity is examined in terms of Durrani ideas of patriliny, endogamy and procreation. Chapter 5 is a discussion of the tribal system and of local communities, including an account of Maduzai migration to the region and the feud. Household autonomy, with respect to both marriage choice and economic self-sufficiency, is the subject of chapter 6.

The fluid and chimerical nature of social groups is explored further in the pivotal third part of the book, which is concerned with ideologies of equality and inequality. The seventh chapter describes the various marriage forms and contrasts marriage for brideprice with exchange marriage. Chapter 8 examines marriage procedures and ceremonies, in which prestations and ritual elaboration are a rich symbolic language for the articulation of status competition and differentiation. The topic of chapter 9 is the choice of partners in marriage; it includes discussions of widow inheritance, polygyny and variations in brideprice payments.

The final part of the book concerns a household's ability to control its resources, particularly in terms of successful marriage and the behaviour of women. Chapter 10 focuses on spirit possession and illicit sexual liaisons, the loss of social control and the downward mobility of a household. The parameters of the marriage system are revealed most clearly when individuals privilege their personal interests and in doing so redefine their own status and that of others. In chapter 11 the opposite perspective is examined in an extended case study of the marriage strategies of a wealthy household over fifty years in which the household's social position is created and confirmed through the medium of marriage. The case demonstrates the intrinsic connections between marriage and cooperation and competition with and between local groups, and the extent to which individual action may confirm or confound social ideals. Finally, chapter 12 summarizes marriage among the Durrani in theoretical terms as an example of a complex marriage system associated with non-exogamous lineage organization, and considers the wider implications of such Middle Eastern marriage systems.

Acknowledgements

My debts to Richard Tapper (RLT) are limitless, ranging from the knowledge that, had I been alone, the Afghan Government would not have given me permission to do the kind of fieldwork on which this study is based (indeed the very fact that I was 'accompanying' RLT initially made official support more difficult to obtain); to the fact that an important part of the argument I present here depends on economic and other data which were collected and collated by RLT; and to his assistance in many, smaller matters, including the translation of German texts. RLT and I have both written elsewhere about the Maduzai, independently and in a series of joint papers, many of which I have drawn on in various chapters of this book: I give complete references to these publications in the bibliography. Our collaboration much enriched our fieldwork in Afghanistan and deepened such understanding as we have of the Maduzai. RLT recognizes the Maduzai I have described here and his agreement with the final draft of this study has been of the utmost importance to me. Thanks go too to our sons, Ruard and Edward, for their enthusiasm and help in preparing the final manuscript; to Susan van de Ven for her editorial care and to RLT for reading the proofs.

The research for this study was made financially possible by the following grants and awards: in 1968, the Nuffield Foundation and the Central Research Fund of the University of London; in 1970–1972, the Social Science Research Council (Grant HR 1141/1) and the School of Oriental and African Studies, University of London. Thanks are also due to the support we had from members of the Afghan Foreign Ministry, particularly Abdul Ghafur Rawan Farhadi.

I must also warmly thank Adrian Mayer who, as the supervisor of the doctoral thesis from which this book derives, was unfailingly encouraging over a long time. I thank too Abner Cohen for his continuing interest and support. I am also grateful to Stefan Feuchtwang, Audrey Cantlie and Hamza Alavi who commented on early drafts of the thesis, and particularly to Michael Gilsenan and David Parkin who examined it. Neil MacKenzie was particularly patient in introducing us to Pashtu; I thank him as a teacher and a friend. And of course we have both benefited greatly from the comments of colleagues, students and friends in seminars, classrooms and elsewhere where we have discussed our work on the Maduzai.

I also thank the many friends with whom we shared our Afghan experience: among them members of the British legation and of the French, German and British Institutes of Afghan Studies in Kabul, and particularly, Jon Anderson, Veronica Doubleday and John Baily, Micheline Centlivres-Demont and Pierre Centlivres, Nancy and the late Louis Dupree, M. Hasan Kakar (the first Afghan I ever met, who has only recently been released after seven years in an Afghan prison for supporting academic freedom in his country), Laurence LeBrun and Pierre Lacombe, Pribislav Pitoeff, Greta and Mark Slobin.

Other Afghan friends and numerous people in Jouzjan and Faryab gave us assistance, but it would be inappropriate now to list their names; we remember them all with thanks.

As for the Maduzai: they often said that they liked our being with them because we afforded them an amusing way of passing the time. If this is what we gave them, it is so little compared with their warm friendship and the great trouble they took for us throughout our stay. We care very deeply for them. When we left them in 1972 we wished for them, as they did for us, that their land would always be green. Now, after the changes, losses and suffering they have experienced, we can only hope that they have preserved something of their cultural integrity and some degree of self-determination. This book is meant as a humble tribute to the Maduzai people and as a memorial to their way of life.

Note on transliteration

I have not attempted to be absolutely consistent in transliterating Persian and Pashtu terms or proper names. The main aim has been to enable the ordinary reader to reproduce the pronunciation approximately, while the expert should have no trouble identifying the terms and names recorded. There are no diacritical marks; there is no distinction made between long and short 'a', and the Pashtu 'shwa' (ə) has variously been rendered as 'a' or 'e'; no attempt has been made to distinguish certain other peculiarly Pashtu sounds, such as the different forms of 'sh', 'n', 'r', 'd', 't'. I should note only that the diphthong in the English word 'dye' has been transliterated as 'ay' (as in the name 'Payz'), while that in 'day' has been given as 'ey'; that in 'how' is given as 'au' (as in *qaum*), that in 'owe' as 'ou' (as in Jouzjan).

Abbreviations and symbols

Abbreviations
Pa.   Pashtu
Per.   Persian
Afs.   Afghanis (unit of currency)
j.   *jeribs* (unit of land)

Kinship abbreviations
M   mother
F   father
B   brother
Z   sister
S   son
D   daughter
$1/2$ half-sibling
Thus, FBS = patrilateral parallel cousin
MF$1/2$BS = mother's father's half-brother's son

Symbols
△   male
▲   deceased male
○   female
●   deceased female
≈   engagement
≉   broken engagement
=   marriage
≠   divorce

I. Contexts

1

Personal background

Aims and circumstances

The fieldwork on which this study is based began when RLT and I travelled in
western Afghan Turkistan for a month in 1968. When we returned to Afghanistan
in 1970–1972, our primary aims were ethnographic. The first was to describe a
people (the Durrani Pashtun) and an area (western Afghan Turkistan) little
known to anthropologists or other scholars (see Map 1).[1] I was keen to examine
further the role and organization of women in sexually segregated societies (see
N. Tapper 1968; 1978), while RLT was particularly interested in aspects of the
pastoral economy and in the forms and contexts of inter-ethnic contact between
the Pashtuns and others in the region. The present study reflects our initial intentions, and its focus – the construction and meaning of marriage – has proved one
way of uniting our interests in terms of an institution of central concern to the
Durrani Pashtuns themselves.

Late in 1970 we travelled overland to Kabul and soon acquired permits to
begin a one-month survey in Afghan Turkistan. Our object was to visit sections
of the Ishaqzai, who were politically and numerically the dominant Durrani tribe
in Jouzjan and Faryab provinces, with a view to finding one group with whom it
would be convenient (for us, for them and for the authorities) to settle. In due
course we decided to seek out one of the many Ishaqzai subtribes which conduct
a mixed economy, combining pastoral nomadism with settled agriculture, in the
Saripul region of Jouzjan. After meeting considerable objections from local
officials, by mid-March we had settled in a camp of the Maduzai subtribe of the
Ishaqzai, now in spring pastures some ten miles from their winter villages and
farmlands.

At the time of our fieldwork there was no doubt in the minds of the local
officials or others in Saripul about where and with whom we were staying. However, even in the best of times circumstances change, and we could all imagine
situations in which it would be prudent for the Maduzai to forget our visits.
'Maduzai' is not their real name; this, the names of the Maduzai settlements, and

Map 1 Sketch-map of Afghanistan

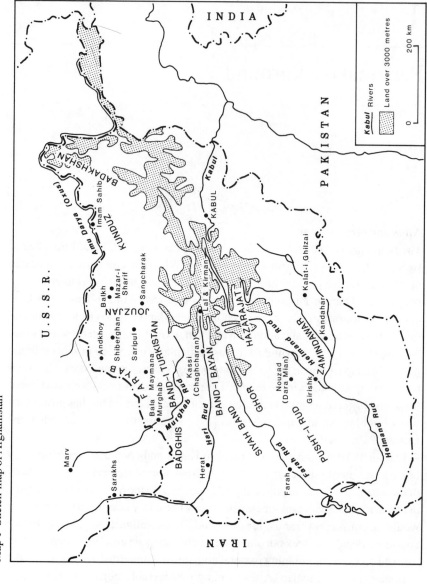

the names of their neighbours, are all pseudonyms. So too, of course, are all names of individual Maduzai and other local people. Maduzai fears concerned their relations as members of a subtribe with the Ishaqzai Khans and rapacious government officials about which I have said very little. Rather I have focused on matters largely internal to the subtribe which, they reckoned, other Afghans would find commonplace and of no great political concern. In the worst of times circumstances change beyond anyone's imaginings. This book is far less relevant to their present situation than any of us could possibly have known then. Its detail may, however, have an unexpected virtue: there is a great concern among Afghans now that, for the sake of their children, they recover all the materials they can about their lives and culture as they were before the Soviet invasion. I hope they will find this book a useful addition to the libraries they create.

The fieldwork
At the same time that we joined the Maduzai, we hired an assistant, Yusuf, an Uzbek from a prominent local family, whose knowledge of the area, acquaintance with the Maduzai, and connections in Saripul and elsewhere proved invaluable. Choosing an Uzbek assistant (and one who spoke Pashtu) was, to a degree, provocative – we justified our choice in terms of Yusuf's profession as a cook whose talents the Maduzai also appreciated. In fact the choice proved a splendid one: Yusuf helped us to expand our network of contacts far beyond the subtribe and, through him, we gained a perspective on ethnic relations in the region, and in the country as a whole, which was quite different from that which we learned from the Maduzai. Yusuf's presence, like our own, of course, had an impact on the people and the events I discuss. From the Maduzai point of view, however, in most contexts, Yusuf was simply assimilated to the category of non-Durrani servant, of whom there were many; our presence was far more anomalous.

During the first ten days of our stay with the Maduzai, Hajji Abdullah, the leading man of Section III of Lineage A (see p. 79f.), acting with the tacit approval of the Maduzai Khan, was our host. However the Khan soon began to fear that his enemies, in order to do him harm, would trouble us or our belongings. Once the Khan had declared us unwelcome, we had no alternative but to seek another group who might have us. While we were thus occupied, Hajji Abdullah's wife, Hajji Nanawor, perhaps the most influential Maduzai woman, who occupied a pivotal position between the two main Lineages (A and C) of the subtribe, mentioned our plight to her sister's son, Hajji Ibrahim, with whom she had just made the pilgrimage to Mecca. Hajji Ibrahim, leader of Lineage C, the headman of Sinjit village and the principal rival (not enemy) of the Maduzai Khan, seized the opportunity we presented to enhance his own prestige and reveal the Khan as weak and fearful. Declaring that he and his numerous sons could easily guarantee our safety, he offered to become our host; after one short visit to his camp we moved in to join him. Certainly this was a coup against the Khan, whose resentment of our presence showed itself intermittently throughout our stay. However, it would be a travesty to impute simply instrumental motives to Hajji Ibrahim; he and his family went to very great lengths to make our stay pleasant and productive. It is impossible to acknowledge adequately our debt to them.

Our hosts and their kin proved astonishingly willing informants and shared with us intimate details of their lives from the start. All men and nearly all women of the group were bilingual in Afghan Persian (Dari), the lingua franca of northern Afghanistan, and Pashtu, their mother tongue. The Maduzai used the former when talking with non-Pashtuns, including ourselves. As a consequence we tended to work in Persian, in which RLT already had fluency and I a rudimentary knowledge. Later, our understanding of Pashtu became reasonably competent, though we rarely conversed in the language. The Persian used by the Maduzai was strongly mixed with Pashtu syntax and vocabulary, and it proved relatively easy to identify Pashtu idioms, for which the Persian was often a literal translation. However, it must be said that the Maduzai's own fluency in Persian made us sometimes negligent about such linguistic cross-checking.

As the time of the spring migration to the mountains approached we wondered how we could cover both aspects of their dual economy, and we considered separating. However, this would have proved unacceptable to the authorities and, as we had permission from Kabul to go on the migration, we chose to do so and hoped to be able to study the villages and local agriculture some other time. In May, after further difficulties with the local authorities, Hajji Ibrahim took complete official responsibility for us and agreed to take us on the trek to the mountains of the Hazarajat. We moved daily for over twenty days, passing through the lands of many different ethnic groups.

Soon after our arrival in the mountain pastures, a most shocking breach of Durrani marriage rules occurred (see p. 61f.) and preoccupied our hosts and ourselves in the following weeks. This case confirmed my earlier decision to focus less on a study of women *per se* than on the topic of marriage. By this time it was clear that marriage formed a clearly delineated indigenous category; it was an institution of central importance to all aspects of social organization; and it was also the topic most likely to offer direct insights into gender constructs and relations.

In late July, the return migration began and a month later we were back in the Maduzai villages near Saripul, where we began a study of the social and agricultural activities there until our departure in September.

The following summer, in June 1972, we drove through the centre of the country from Herat to Kabul. We already knew of the disasters – a series of droughts and poor harvests aggravated by speculation and hoarding during the very severe winter. Pastoral nomads in the remote north and northwest of the country were starving (v. Barry 1972 and cf. Balland and Kieffer 1979) and no nomads from Turkistan had come to the summer pastures that year. Although official permission to travel to the disaster provinces, which included Jouzjan, was restricted, we were able to be in Saripul villages of the Maduzai by the last week in July.

We left the Maduzai in September 1972, never dreaming that we might not easily return again. We planned further research in Saripul town itself for 1979, but the political events of 1978–1979 precluded it. Since that time, we have been able to gather only the most meagre, general information on Saripul and its inhabitants. The Maduzai, like other Pashtuns from Turkistan, have left the area to become refugees: some have certainly gone to Pakistan, though it is likely that many others returned to their southern Afghan homeland after the Soviet invasion of their country. For us it is a personal tragedy to have lost all contact with the Maduzai and it is made much worse by the knowledge that this silence hides the far greater tragedies that they must have experienced.

For RLT and myself the Maduzai were an engaging people with whom it was easy to establish a considerable rapport. I think this was particularly related to two considerations: the security their Durrani identity then afforded them, and their experiences in a very heterogeneous ethnic milieu. This combination seems to have encouraged a good-natured tolerance of cultural differences which made them willing to accept both our account of ourselves and our work, and our foibles as they emerged in daily life.

Our contact with the Maduzai throughout the fieldwork was intense. To avoid becoming a serious economic liability to our hosts, we set up on our arrival a quasi-independent establishment managed by our Uzbek assistant. However, this consisted only of our 'guest-room' – a small canvas tent – and a two-person mountain tent for sleeping. When we were in the Maduzai village, we lived in Hajji Ibrahim's guest room within his compound. Sometimes during the migration, to avoid being conspicuous to his enemies, he insisted that we stay in his tent. In effect, in neither camps nor villages had we any privacy during our waking hours. Indeed, the cultural difference in attitudes to privacy was for us the most exhausting and stressful aspect of the fieldwork.

Throughout the fieldwork we maintained a standard of living similar to that of well-to-do Maduzai. Soon after our arrival our hosts asked us to don Durrani clothing, which we did, wearing it throughout our stay. On the migrations we travelled as did the Maduzai with horses and camels, but the Landrover we ran in the villages and spring pastures clearly set us apart. Indeed, in a limited way it afforded us a status comparable with the regional tribal leaders and helped us to gain access to this elite. The car also provided us with a most acceptable way, initially, of reciprocating the hospitality and friendship we were shown by the Maduzai: we fetched water for the camps and ferried friends from camp to camp and into Saripul town, and later we made regular trips to local and regional shrines as well. Apart from the car, we had little other paraphernalia: two tape-recorders, two cameras and a small medical kit.

Methods and materials
Our field materials were recorded in serial diary notebooks, maps, plans and genealogical charts, extensive tape-recordings and photographs. A constant ideal of our work was that we should manage a daily discussion of our activities, although we often did little more than share the most important tidbits of gossip picked up during the day. While neither of us spurned any information we could collect, in practice our respective areas of expertise soon became quite clear. I concentrated on issues concerning women, domestic organization and all aspects of marriage. I worked with both women and men but rarely left the camp or village. RLT, on the other hand, collected virtually all the material we have on pastoral and agricultural production and exchange, and on the wider political and ethnic relations of the Maduzai. He worked mostly with men and travelled much more widely throughout the region. There were important areas of overlap, both in terms of what we learned, particularly on the politics of the subtribe itself, and also in terms of the people who helped us most (see Tapper, N. and R. Tapper 1989).

Both of us relied heavily on our closest friends: both men and women of our host's own large household and the household of his brothers Agha Mohammad and Gul Mohammad, and those of his father's brothers, Sultan and Akhtar Mohammad; the Sinjit village 'headwoman' Kishmir and one of her nephews of Section II of Lineage C; Jumadar, a prominent man of the faction of Lineage C opposed to our host; the members of Anar Gul's household, permanent clients of Lineage C; in Chinar village my closest contacts were Hajji Nanawor, the leading woman of the village, and women close to her household, while RLT gained much information from her son and his close cousins, and from the eldest son of the leading man of Lineage D.

The picture of the Maduzai I draw here is, of course, a composite one; my ambition is to present marriage from as many perspectives as possible. To this end, I have tried to be scrupulous in cross-referencing the text to link case studies with other more formal discussions of, for example, household standing and Maduzai history, so that readers can themselves independently trace the differential materials from which this ethnographic collage has been fashioned.

The range and depth of information we collected was due to the willingness of the Maduzai to help us 'write a book' about them and their way of life. The contrast between fieldwork among the Maduzai and our earlier study of the taciturn Shahsevan nomads in Iran was striking (see R. Tapper 1979) and we have become convinced that, to a large extent, the Maduzai openness with us was related to features of their competitive and individualizing society. A person's ability to give a convincing account of him/herself was an important element in the management of social relations. The Maduzai valued articulateness and fluent, humorous conversation and they were well used to giving their own personal interpretations on all aspects of social life. We were an eager audience and they shared these interpretations with us – often competing with others to gain our sympathy and even support on particular issues.

Given that we had come to the Maduzai with a keen interest in the nature of political discourse, the situation we found ourselves in was something of a fieldworker's dream. Had we wanted on the other hand to collect detailed 'hard' data on household consumption patterns and nutrition, for example, the difficulties would have been virtually insurmountable. Equally, it should be said that we were so overwhelmed by the Maduzai willingness to talk about themselves that we were undoubtedly less sensitive than we might have been particularly to nonverbal areas of culture and action.

The Maduzai employ idioms of patrilineal descent and trace genealogical links as explicit devices to explain both social relations among themselves and with other Durrani groups, and residential patterns at all levels. In turn, residential patterns were a concrete expression of these idioms. Groups of close agnates often lived in adjacent houses in the villages and tent camps, while factional divisions within the subtribe were frequently expressed in terms of spatial divisions of the village settlements. The collection of genealogical and census materials on the subtribe was relatively easy and provided an organizational framework in terms of which we initially collected other materials.

However, as we shall see, patrilineal descent was only one of several idioms which the Maduzai used to discuss social relations. These alternative idioms – particularly those which referred to relations based on bilateral kinship, on the one hand, and to political action sets on the other – were of no less practical importance in Maduzai social life, but they were less consciously articulated as principles of social organization; rather, they were implicit in speech and action.

As outsiders remote from Maduzai struggles to control local resources, we were harmless and indeed became resources ourselves: our time and attention became one measure of the interest or importance of someone's views. At first, we did not understand that, although individuals sought to control information about themselves and their households, most of this information was already in the public domain. In fact, there were few if any real secrets: what was important was the presentation and interpretation of certain kinds of information. Within days of our arrival we learned of many major scandals, past and present, which were to preoccupy our hosts and us for the rest of our stay; only much later did we understand that these were not revelations at all, but attempts to preempt alternative interpretations of the same events.

The substantive information which we used to create the statistical bases of the study was, to a great extent, of the same order as the 'revelations' and treated in the same way by the Maduzai. Their own attitudes to the importance of certain

kinds of information made the collection of materials and comments on household wealth, for example, relatively easy. That is, although individuals tried to
keep details of the circumstances of their own household from others, members
of competing households were keen to discover and discuss those same details.
Moreover, field boundaries could be walked and sheep on a hillside counted,
while the sheep of a brideprice and the wealth of trousseaux were publicly displayed. In other words, estimates of household wealth were the stuff of everyday
life; our interest in such issues was not regarded as untoward, but natural, and
indeed, far less threatening than a similar interest expressed by a member of a
rival household. We collected accounts of household wealth directly from the
household members concerned only in the case of our closest friends. Otherwise,
the information came from others and is, as their information was, an interpretation of many different clues. In this respect, our estimates are probably comparable in accuracy to those made by the Maduzai themselves.

The collection of accounts of marriages involved similar interpretative licence
on the part of both our informants and ourselves, but it was easier, in large part
because of the importance of marriage among the Maduzai and the prominence
they gave to wedding rituals. Details of marriage arrangements, events at a
wedding and the people involved were readily recalled, and we learned to link
the dating of events, and, for instance, information on household composition, to
accounts of marriage. In fact, this strategy was successful enough for us to more
or less realize our ambition and solve the problem of defining statistical bases
for the study by collecting total samples of information – on the subtribe as a
whole for marriages, and on all the households of Lineage C for household composition, landowning and wealth.

There was virtually no disagreement among the Maduzai themselves concerning the areas where we collected such systematic material: there was little room
for debate about who married whom and when, or how many of the sheep of a
particular household had died, or been stolen or taken by wolves. What was
contested was the explanation of these facts – both their causes and their likely
consequences. In the book, a key concern has been to relate the available, agreed
upon, 'objective' information with the variety of interpretations which surrounded such facts, and with the significance the Maduzai attributed to them. I
have tried to look at things the other way round, and to consider whether or not
there were patterns in the interpretations the Maduzai offered, and whether or not
such patterns could be related to the uncontested facts, as the Maduzai saw them.

In this respect, it is notable that there were some aspects of daily life where the
Maduzai tolerated little interpretative licence. There were too many empirical
measures to allow much scope for bragging or deception about the various
indices of household wealth, or household composition, or the jobs people did.
Equally, there were other areas, particularly those related to religious discourse
and activities, where dissent and disagreement were strongly discouraged and

stigmatized. In these latter areas, there was often remarkable uniformity in people's comments, and alternative interpretations were stifled by pious references to the equality of all Durrani and the unknowable will of God. But there were yet other areas, particularly concerning the internal relations of households and the meaning of marriage prestations and forms, where self-presentations were constantly contested by others. Indeed, marriage ceremonies and the character of relations constructed through marriage were the principal arena of practical politics: they held the greatest fascination for the Maduzai and for me.

The importance of the household as an institution among the Maduzai also benefited us. Our intimate association with Hajji Ibrahim's household automatically created an identity for us and suggested the sympathies and insights we would have into the affairs of the subtribe, which the members of other households had an interest in either confirming or disputing according to their own relationship with Hajji Ibrahim. We were also lucky in that one aspect of our dependence on Hajji Ibrahim – which had considerable bearing on our fieldwork – was publicly defined in an incident concerning tape recordings which occurred only a few weeks after our arrival at his camp in the spring pastures.

Tape recorders were not, in the early 1970s, a standard item of household equipment: indeed, besides ours, there were none in the Maduzai settlements. We first introduced the tape recorders when I decided to see if it would be acceptable to record music at a wedding being held in our camp. The women at the wedding agreed to the idea with some delight. Then, quite unexpectedly, a heated row broke out between two of them, and was captured on tape. The women were very concerned that the swearing and personal comments would be heard by men, and I promised that I would not let this happen. However, children told the men what had occurred, and Hajji Ibrahim, among others, was greatly amused and curious to hear the recording. I refused and angered him greatly in doing so; RLT and I began seriously to fear that I had jeopardized our stay. Fortunately for us, the quarrel was allowed to pass when, after three very tense days, Hajji Ibrahim was called to mediate after a shooting incident in a nearby camp. Thereafter, because I had been able to keep my promise not to let anyone listen to the tapes without the speaker's permission, our tape recordings gained a privileged status and neither men nor women hesitated to make tapes for us on any subject. Much later, even Hajji Ibrahim laughed at my unintended challenge to his authority and praised us both as better Muslims than the Maduzai because, unlike them, he said, we always kept our word!

Indeed, the tapes took on an authority of their own. For instance, even a brief account of the 'brothel' in the village is on tape (see p. 236). It was made by friends who were quite determined to make us understand that we should not visit Majid the pimp and they insisted that we tape their story: it was their way of emphasizing its import and truthfulness – at the time we still believed the

Maduzai rhetoric of honour and shame and were incredulous that Majid, who was an excellent friend and informant, could behave in the way they described!

I have relied heavily on these tape recordings, but rarely identified their specific authors. Rather I have often drawn on several sources to summarize opinions and experiences, while treating particular viewpoints in my exegesis. In this respect, materials on the Maduzai feud (from both men and women, protagonists and others) were the most difficult to edit. The subject was a sensitive one, and although there was agreement about the sequence of events, there were, not surprisingly, considerable discrepancies in the interpretation of events as told by the members of the two factions concerned. I have chosen to present the feud story in the form of a continuous narrative. And, although I mention the discrepancies in my comments, I am well aware that the feud material could equally have been presented in a much more individualistic fashion. Perhaps such a task is for later; here the general outline of the feud is itself enough to provide an invaluable opportunity for looking at factionalism and marriage in a causal perspective.

We have some one-hundred hours of tape recordings; RLT is editing these rich materials into a more intimate portrait of the Maduzai than the one I present here. Of the tapes, perhaps two-thirds were done by men; women, while eager to make tapes, had far less leisure time to give to such activities. Although in general there are few differences in the style or content between men's and women's tapes, the latter are sometimes more personal and direct than those of the men. This reflects, I think, the women's determination to make every minute count: taping offered them an unusual opportunity and excuse to tell their own stories without interruption or fear of being indiscreet. In spite of their evident exhaustion in the evenings, and the fact that they would have to rise well before dawn, women often invited me to get out the tape recorder in their unlit rooms while the men were still out and the children asleep.

When I generalize about 'the Maduzai', I mean this usage to refer to the views expressed by both men and women; in verbal presentations particularly, these often coincided. However, where men and women expressed different points of view, these are identified as such, while the non-verbal discourses of subordinate men and women are treated explicitly in the analysis. There is no doubt that by labelling the shared and articulated views of men and women as the views of 'the Maduzai', I am privileging the dominant discourses of gender relations and of social inequality. The reader needs to be aware of this bias, while remembering that it is one which reflects real differences in social power within Maduzai society.

We also took many photographs. These were another way in which we repaid hospitality. Men and women were delighted to have pictures, especially portraits, of themselves and their families. We had many developed during our short visit in Kabul and brought back many more on our return in the summer of 1972. And, though it is of course impossible to be absolutely certain that the reproduction here of some photographs of women would be acceptable, I have few qualms about using them in this way. Maduzai pleasure in our photography during the fieldwork period was considerable and they did not share the attitude of some Uzbek friends, who surrounded with great secrecy the few photos I was asked to take of them and their families. Thus it was I, not the Maduzai friends I was with, who was surprised and shocked to see the photos of my closest Maduzai friend, Sheri, which I had given to her father after her tragic death in the summer of 1971, pinned on the wall of his guest room.

2

Comparative perspectives on marriage
in the Muslim Middle East

In general the ethnographic and theoretical treatment of marriage in the Muslim
Middle East is extremely uneven, making comparative study of a wide range of
topics very difficult. However, as Eickelman (1989) has made a systematic and
excellent critique of this corpus of materials, his survey does not need to be
repeated here. Rather, in this chapter, I want only to set the scene for the ethnographic inquiry which follows by suggesting that the institution of marriage, with
its central place in Middle Eastern societies, must be approached from both structural and interpretive perspectives and that the relation between these perspectives must be addressed in the analysis.

The starting point is a central problem in anthropology: the choice of terms that
can be used to analyse different cultures and bring them into a frame in which
they can be both explained and compared with each other. The futility of attempting universal definitions is now widely accepted; it is not so much that terms like
'family' or 'religion' can have only a loose analytical value as 'polythetic
classes' but that they do not translate any significant categories in many cultures,
they have no 'meaning' and distort or disregard indigenous categories that do.

The problem is essentially one of translation, but it is impossible to ignore the
fact that numerous cultures do include categories that translate easily into
English terms once favoured as analytical concepts. This ease is of course decep-
tive and brings its own difficulties as may be seen in the anthropological treatment of 'marriage' in the Muslim Middle East.

Unlike some parts of the world (cf. Needham 1971: 6–7), in the Muslim
Middle East 'marriage' is an indigenous concept and institution of great importance, whose organizational potential is often explicitly recognized by Muslims.
It is based on the Islamic marriage contract, and one bias in the anthropological/
orientalist literature is to treat the contract as the key to the institution as a whole.
This contract is formally understood as between only the bride and groom, but
clearly many other people, men and women, are involved in bringing it about and
interested in the consequences.

The central problem for a given family is the divided and changing loyalties of a daughter, once she is married and raising sons for her husband's family. Here, an understanding not only of marital ties, but also of romantic liaisons, illicit unions and illegitimacy, turns on the rights and responsibilities a woman's own closest agnatic kin have towards her, and the extent to which these are transferred to her husband at marriage. The issue of the male control of women before and after marriage leads directly to questions of economic and political organization.

A brief look at Islamic family law reveals great scope for alternative interpretations of the legal status of women in marriage (see Tapper, R. and N. Tapper, Forthcoming a). The idioms in which these ambiguities are typically discussed throughout the Middle East are those of responsibility and honour and shame on which there is now a well-known literature.

One weakness in this literature has been the tendency to reify the indigenous notions which are translated as 'honour' and 'shame', rather than to treat them as idioms which articulate an ideology of control. As Pitt-Rivers has shown (1977: 1–17), this ideology is so structured that the outsider can distinguish two quite opposed modes of thought which meet and are merged in the actors' notions of prestige or honour. In one, 'honour' is constructed in a competitive sense: this mode of thought is relevant to this-worldly relations and is based on a recognition of inequality. In the other mode, altruism and generosity are central and honour is constructed in a religious sense, where relations are based on an ideal of equality, seen ultimately as equality before God. In this system, no relationship is ever articulated exclusively in one mode or the other; the same linguistic idioms and conceptual framework are used for both aspects of every relationship. The system is compelling because it appears to resolve a fundamental contradiction between ideals of social equality, rooted in absolute religious precepts, and strategic considerations which refer to, explain and contribute to the social inequality inherent in the control and exploitation of resources. Both passivity and competitiveness, both equality and inequality, can be explained and justified. The fascinating sleight of mind this involves has been documented by a number of authors; see, for example, the recent work of Abu-Lughod (1986), Gilmore (1987) and the Josephs (1987).

Less often does the literature come to grips with the fact that the primary and constant referents of notions of honour and shame are gender and sexual differentiation. Here a notion of responsibility is of particular importance. Though a number of authors have discussed the indigenous notion of *ʿaql*, which is usually translated as 'reason' or 'rationality' (cf., e.g., Anderson 1982a, 1985; Rosen 1984: 31ff.; Abu Lughod 1986: 90–91; Eickelman 1989: 172, 205, 242–244), its wider implications of social responsibility have been little explored. In this ethnography, I translate the Durrani term *akl* as 'responsibility' throughout; my concern is to understand it as an idiom to discuss both the management and control of resources and the differences between men and women in 'natural' terms.

Thus, *akl* is used to explain the subordination of women in terms of their 'natural' weaknesses. It is this system of classification associated with the notion of *akl* which forms the basis on which the notions of honour and shame are elaborated. Together, notions of responsibility and honour and shame constitute an ideology of control that embraces relations of both production and reproduction: it applies to the control of all resources, including the sexuality, reproductive capacity and labour of women.

Models of Middle Eastern marriage

One of the main problems with the literature on Middle Eastern and Islamic marriage practices is a confusion based on the unspoken assumption that the social organization of Arabs, particularly nomads or villagers in the Eastern Mediterranean area, can be regarded as prototypical of all Islamic Middle Eastern communities. This confusion has been particularly evident in the now extensive literature on the FBD marriage 'problem' on which Holy (1989) has offered a particularly interesting new perspective concerning the symbolic and practical solidarity it fosters. RLT and I have also been advocating an alternative approach to the study and analysis of marriage in the Muslim Middle East for some time (see N. Tapper 1979: 28ff., 1981; R. Tapper 1979a: 291; Tapper, R. and N. Tapper, forthcoming a; cf. also Meeker 1976; Abu Lughod 1986: 159). We suggest that the 'Arab model' should be played down, and two contrasting models considered, with implications for a wide variety of differences of behaviour and organization among the societies depicted. These two models of Middle Eastern marriage establish a framework in which the intimate connections between the issues of marriage and group identity, equality and inequality, and relations between men and women can be investigated.

The basic difference between the two models is that in model A the rights transferred to the husband at marriage are less complete than in B. In model A, a woman remains the responsibility of her male agnates (brothers and father) after marriage, at least until she has grown-up sons. If she misbehaves, it is up to them to punish her. As a corollary, she may return to her natal home and receive protection and maintenance during the course of her marriage. Men's honour depends on the behaviour of their female agnates, and is formally unaffected by that of wives from outside the group. A woman's sexual modesty, and a man's honour as it resides in the women for whom he is responsible, is a quality which is determined by agnation, and is not transferable.

Following the Leach (1957)/Fallers (1957)/Lewis (1962) hypothesis concerning the determinants of marriage stability, one expects marriage ties in societies conforming to model A to be unstable, since agnatic ties of men and women are comparable in strength. In practice, in the Middle Eastern literature, there is an unfortunate lack of data on marriage stability, whether the incidence of divorce or of separation; but in those societies which in other respects seem to be best understood in terms of Model A, it is frequently reported that there is no particular stigma attached to divorce, which often follows simple domestic quarrels or personality clashes between spouses or co-wives, while more serious offences such as adultery by the wife may lead to divorce or to her death at the hands of agnates.

In model B, a married woman's behaviour is primarily the concern of her husband and his agnates. A man's honour is affected by the behaviour of his unmarried sisters and daughters, his mother and his wife. Indigenous terms which may best be translated as 'honour' or 'responsibility' refer to a man's ability to guard his honour by controlling these women, and also to the women's own reputation; it seems to be a quality attached to the woman herself, vested in her sex and not her agnation, and can be and usually is transferred along with her person at marriage. Responsibility for a daughter or sister is almost entirely transferred to the husband and his agnates at marriage, and the expectation is of more stable bonds. In such cases ethnographers usually draw a contrast between a married woman's emotional ties with her agnates and the jural transfer of rights in her. The main difference with model A is the overriding responsibility of the husband for controlling his wife's behaviour, although this may to some extent be shared with her agnates.

In these societies, divorce is rare, shameful, and only most occasionally arises from domestic disputes, incompatibility of spouses, or even from the inability of a woman to bear children. A wife who misbehaves or is accused of adultery should ideally be killed rather than divorced, and the responsibility for such action rests with her husband before her agnates. The most extreme statement comes from the Swat Pathans, of whom Barth reports:

Since the husband has absolute authority over his wife, to divorce her is to admit defeat and no advantage is gained other than the simple economic saving from discontinuing her support – at the cost of her labour. There is thus, in a sense, no reason for divorce among the Pathan, and very good reasons against it (Barth 1959: 40; cf. also Lindholm 1982: 111).

Indeed, divorce is almost unknown. A similar strong abhorrence or disapproval of divorce is found among the Durrani, who are the focus of this study.

This brief discussion suggests something of the potential of the two models; they are also relevant to an understanding of patterns of marriage choice, the character of affinal and matrilateral relations, the amounts of brideprice and other marriage payments, the symbolism and complexity of wedding and other marriage ceremonies, and other areas of social organization. Elsewhere RLT (1983) and I (1980; and Tapper, R. and N. Tapper, forthcoming a) have tried to tackle such comparative issues. In the ethnography that follows, I use this discussion of the two models as a background against which to develop the implications of model B as it applies to the Maduzai. Thus, with respect to marriage choice, we shall see that Durrani sometimes express a preference for close kin marriage, but the meaning of this preference lies in the construction of their notion of 'closeness' which is an idiom used to define and manage all social relations and is only indirectly related to genealogical distance. And, more widely, it is within this framework that I address the changes over the last fifty years which have resulted in men's increasing control of women in marriage.

The centrality of the institution of marriage

As the two models suggest, the centrality and complexity of the institution of marriage derive from two sources, the possibility of marrying close relatives, and the ambiguities of the ideology of control as it relates to productive and reproductive resources. Though he is not concerned with the manipulation of an ideology of control *per se*, Comaroff has recently implied that in systems which are characterized by close kin marriage the relation between the two issues is intrinsic (1980: 39) and he notes that social management in such a 'fluid and enigmatic social environment, in which categorical linkages overlap and entail normative contradictions' (1980: 40) is very complicated. He adds, 'the marriage process itself actualizes complex configurations of overlapping relations, . . . established theoretical paradigms have had so much difficulty comprehending such arrangements' (1980: 40).

Thus, the institution of marriage may be seen to structure all aspects of political and economic relations in such societies, but the framework within which it does so is, because of the nature of close kin marriage, as Comaroff suggests, individualistic and competitive. One way of approaching the complexities of this configuration is via the systematic elucidation of the underlying principles of the institution: the criteria on which classifications of marriage forms are based, the meaning of marriage payments in the exchange system as a whole, the ways in which persons and things are conceptualized in such exchanges, and the ambiguities and contradictions inherent in these principles – that is, the areas open to manipulation and political negotiation.

It follows that a basic problem is how to deal with the choices such a system presents to actors, and the consequences of these choices. Various anthropologists have come to see that the 'system' must be viewed as a complex one: patterns of marriage choice are only partly determined by preferences and ideals, while the consequences of choice are best explained in processual terms, through the analysis of political and economic strategies (cf. Seddon 1976: 185–186).

There have been in recent years several important studies which have, implicitly or explicitly, employed a processual analysis, among them those by Cohen (1965, 1970), Marx (1967), Aswad (1971), Peters (various articles), Bourdieu (1977), Jamous (1981), Bradburd (1984), Donnan (1985, 1988), Wright (1985). Though each of these studies is quite distinctive, all recommend the diachronic study of social institutions such as kinship and marriage in terms of the social processes by which resources are controlled and status is defined and reckoned. However, the ambitions of such processual analyses are difficult to realize both because of the finely grained quality of the historical as well as contemporary data which are required to describe adequately the contexts of particular marriage choices and the context of the alliances marriages are held to create, and because of the inherent problems of generalizing from the minutiae of particular case studies. That is, successful processual analyses depend on data of considerable detail and depth drawn from a wide variety of contexts. This in itself would seem to demand that the anthropologist treat materials from the point of view of both the actors themselves and the outside observer.

The emphasis on the parameters of the actors' discourse in different contexts and different times has been the salient characteristic of the interpretive (and semantic and reflexive) anthropologies of the post-structuralist era; a number of these have had an ethnographic focus in the Muslim Middle East, cf. Rabinow (1977), Geertz (1979), Rosen (1984) and the Josephs (1987). These anthropologies have been important in correcting the excesses of both structural-functional and structuralist views of human society, but, because they focus on actors' accounts of their society, rather than their actions or the wider social contexts or institutional frameworks within which these actions take place, they complement, but do not displace, other styles of anthropological inquiry.

Indeed, I would argue that an emphasis on interpretation which focuses on those who are most articulate in a society is limiting: not only must verbal and non-verbal discourse (and silence) be related to institutional forms, but so too are both historical and cross-cultural comparative studies necessary to reveal further the specificity of any particular society. For instance, I suspect that certain kinds of important questions are simply not asked if one focuses on individual negotiation and interpretation and if historical change is treated, often implicitly, as simply the cumulative effect of individual decisions. Such perspectives are inadequate both as a means of treating people's own perceptions of social change, and for discussing objective changes in the wider environment of those same people.

Thus, I shall not hesitate to talk of the relationship between demography and resources in Turkistan and to suggest that, as this relation has changed during the fifty years of Maduzai presence in the area, so too have Maduzai interpretations of their culture and the stratagems they have adopted. As the population has grown and available resources have declined relative to the number of individuals competing for their control, so too the meaning of notions of equality and the meaning of brideprice and exchange marriage forms have changed. These changes are reflected in decisions whose consequences are structural: for example, the development of institutions which allow for more comprehensive control over the transfer of women in marriage. By the same token, if I were to concentrate in the Maduzai ethnography only on actors' interpretations, I would fail to see both the way in which women's involvement in spirit possession or illicit sexual liaisons is socially patterned as well as the connections between these activities and the increasing competition for resources in the wider environment.

Equally we can not ignore or dismiss questions concerning the status of the outsider's perception of regularly patterned actions. Indeed, it seems to me incumbent on anthropologists today to ask, for instance, about the meaning of the incidence of divorce in a society. That is, so long as there exists some notion of 'divorce' and actions which are so described, then the consequences of these actions for social relations – and indeed, the very meaning of the indigenous notion itself – cannot be understood without considering the incidence of divorce. Certainly the actual numbers, status and activities of women without men, and vice versa, and the population of remarriageable people, cannot be irrelevant to an individual's interpretation and use of such a notion of 'divorce'.

And, if such a strategy can lead to a deeper understanding of any one society, it makes equal sense to attempt comparisons; not because they have some 'objective' value, but because they are a tool for asking further questions about an institution such as marriage and the range of meanings and actions it has cross-culturally.

Gender and marriage and power

Feminists and anthropologists have very properly raised doubts about the universality of female subordination and pointed to the relation of such constructions of gender relations to an intrinsic Western bias towards models of inequality and hierarchy. However, as RLT and I have argued elsewhere (1987 and 1988), such biases also exist in many societies of the Muslim Middle East whose culture and history are closely related to our own. In this respect, Middle Eastern material on gender is not remote or exotic, as the common stereotypes suggest.

This is particularly evident in one of the most conspicuous paradoxes in many studies of marriage in the Muslim Middle East: the almost incidental or marginal ethnographic treatment of women in spite of the great ideological significance of gender and the importance of the control of women as resources in such systems. Two biases have doubly excluded women from anthropological discourse: Western sexist perspectives in which it is usual for men's ideals, beliefs and actions to be privileged above those of women have reproduced and reinforced a comparable indigenous bias in Muslim cultural traditions. Together these biases have served to create a conceptual and social dichotomy between women and men and have been used either to excuse students from investigating what is a difficult area of inquiry in many Muslim societies or implicitly to justify accounts which rely exclusively on only male or only female informants.

In this book I am concerned to avoid the now conventional treatment of the activities and beliefs of women as though they constitute a legitimate, separate unit of study. The subordination of women to men remains an important theme in the ethnography, but my focus on the economic and political concomitants of gender relations requires a consideration of the nature of dependence of men on men, as well as women on men, and women on women. In other words, I am particularly interested in the relation between gender and the structure of *de facto* social inequality generally.

Thus, we have seen how the social configurations of marriage patterns summarized in terms of Model A and B are treated indigenously in terms of notions of responsibility, honour and shame, patriarchy, male dominance and the passivity of women; but this is only part of the story. The two models have other implications which also deserve systematic treatment.

Each model encompasses a normative discourse which relates the institution of marriage to other key institutions in the society – the household, named kinship groups, local communities and ethnic and sectarian divisions. Typically, this discourse is directly related to the creation and maintenance of the social order and to the stability and continuity of social forms. It is perhaps most frequently articulated by men, who thereby expound a point of view which associates their personal interests with the wider society, though women too may use this discourse in their accounts of marriage and other aspects of social life (cf. Bourdieu 1977: 164–165).

However, in the Muslim Middle East, as elsewhere, there is an alternative discourse which is expressed more often in action than in words and more often by women than by men. The alternative perspective is one which allows for the expression of the interests of individual women and men where these diverge from those which define key values and social identities. Though there is a clear relation between gender differences and personal autonomy to act and to manage the interpretation of one's choices, both men and women contravene social norms for their personal ends. Not surprisingly, the tension between what is judged to be for the social good and what are deemed anti-social expressions of private interest emerges most frequently and dramatically in the context of marriage. And, in terms of the male-dominated discourse on marriage, when women in particular do display a degree of autonomy *vis-à-vis* men, their activities and implicit power are often construed as subversive.

I use the term 'subversive' to describe certain possibilities for women's action which, while they are implicit in the dominant ideologies of gender espoused by both men and women, nonetheless are constructed in opposition to the ideals of male dominance which they contradict. Women who exercise the power implicit in such contradictions can upset or overturn accepted relations between the sexes, and in practice can, to a degree, escape men's control of their behaviour. However, when I use the term 'subversive' to describe, for example, women's illicit sexual activities among Durrani Pashtuns, I do not mean to imply that these actions (which the outsider can see as both patterned and far-reaching) are understood systematically or even necessarily intended by individual women.

Subversive women

In all societies gender distinctions are of intrinsic relevance to a study of cultural constructions of sexuality, marriage, reproduction, the socialization of children and domestic roles. Ortner and Whitehead have suggested that 'the structures of greatest import for the cultural construction of gender in any given society are the structures of prestige' and that 'the cultural construction of sex and gender tends everywhere to be stamped by the prestige considerations of socially dominant male actors' (1981: 12). A corollary of this argument is that where male prestige is heavily dependent on women, whether in terms of female productive or reproductive labour, or women's general comportment, women have a capacity to undermine male ambitions and damage male prestige, and this potential power of women is often elaborated about women as polluting and threatening to men (1981: 20, 21).

Rogers' model of gender relations in peasant societies (1977) elaborates a similar point. She suggests that the informal power of women and a 'myth of male dominance' are likely to be particularly prominent in societies where women are associated with the domestic sphere, where their activities are an essential complement to those of men outside the house, and where the household is of central importance socially to the community as a whole.

These ideas are an appropriate starting point for the study of gender constructions among Durrani Pashtuns (and elsewhere in the Muslim Middle East) where the household is a social unit of great importance and where there is a marked asymmetry of gender constructions articulated through the far-reaching idioms of responsibility and honour and shame.

Both Meeker and Papanek comment on the ways in which men make status claims through the control of women. Their comments are particularly relevant to those societies and cultures which are best understood in terms of Model B.

Meeker's discussion of *namus*, a term which is widely used in the northern tier of the Middle East to refer to women's 'shame', and men's honour as it relates to women, provides a neat summary of the central issues. He writes,

Namus ... implies a common measure which applies to all men and reflects a state of each man. Male 'control' of a woman's sexuality is appropriate for such a universal measure ... [and the] customs concerning the control of women can become almost the very definition of community and a means of differentiation of one community from another (1976: 267, 268; cf. Papanek 1973: 317).

Women act as status demonstrators for the men who 'control' them; but there is another side to their dependence:

Feminine power is not overt, but, due to their participation in the familial honour (as the repositories of its moral and sacred aspects) women hold in their hands the power not merely to put pressure on their menfolk but actually to 'ruin' them . . . It is only too easy to understand then that men, conscious and resentful of their vulnerability through the actions of their womenfolk, should be eager to credit them with . . . faults which justify their exclusion from the political sphere and the authority of their menfolk over them (Pitt-Rivers 1977: 80).

In short, women's potential power over men is part of the logic of the ideology of control and the practical management of Middle Eastern gender constructions by men and women. In the Maduzai ethnography the most important areas for women's 'subversive' action concern spirit possession and illicit sexual relations. However, other topics, which do not figure importantly or at all among Durrani Pashtun women's concerns and activities, properly belong in a wider discussion of 'subversive' women in the Muslim Middle East: for example, institutionalized elopement (Bates 1974) or prostitution (Jansen 1987), lesbianism (Shepherd 1987) or the importance to women of magic and sorcery as widely reported in North African societies.

In N. Tapper (forthcoming b) I discuss the associations between, on the one hand, the incidence and character of the muted, 'subversive' discourses of spirit possession and illicit liaisons and, on the other, the variety of structural elements implicit in the dominant ideologies of control which RLT and I have discussed in terms of models A and B. This more wide-ranging inquiry suggests that such variations be understood in terms of 'alternative ideologies' and their relation to social change. Salzman's articles (1978a, 1978b), which focus on Middle Eastern tribal societies, discuss several ways in which the alternative values contained within a single ideology may be maintained as 'social structures in reserve'. He does not describe a system in which there is the continuous interplay of alternative values that characterizes the Durrani ideology of control as it is expressed through marriage and other exchanges. However, the Durrani example does seem to suggest a further type of value maintenance of comparable importance. Historical evidence shows the institution of marriage and the exchange system as a whole to be responsive to social and environmental changes, while cross-culturally, different Pashtun peoples from Swat to Sistan would seem to use the same ideology of control to define and support ostensibly very different social structures.

With this declaration of my commitment to the comparative enterprise, we must now proceed to an ethnographic account which I have endeavoured to present through materials and interpretations which can be used later in such comparisons. I understand marriage in a Middle Eastern society as a system involving choices among a number of alternative forms, each of which has symbolic meanings in the context of economic and political values and activities. The ethnography is specific and concerns a particular Afghan community. My method is not new: it is an anthropological commonplace to suggest that there is an intrinsic relation between, on the one hand, the conceptual framework and meanings understood and managed by actors, and, on the other, aspects of social structure documented by statistical and other methods by the anthropologist as outsider; and that both be examined in the light of detailed ethnography of some historical depth. My analysis concerns the intimate connections between public and domestic domains, discourses and structures; my wider concern is to show that the study of marriage in the Muslim Middle East need no longer be related merely to the parochial concerns of regional ethnography, but can contribute usefully to wider anthropological studies of marriage, politics and gender.

3

The regional background: the Durrani of Saripul

The western part of Afghan Turkistan, falling within the two provinces of Faryab and Jouzjan, is both fertile and ethnically diverse (see Map 2).[1] Taken together these two features are of crucial importance to an understanding of the Maduzai ethnography which I present here. Maduzai social life takes place against a background of fierce inter-ethnic competition for the control of productive land; in turn, of course, this competition has had a direct effect on Maduzai beliefs and practices, especially those related to gender and the institution of marriage. Thus, as we shall see, among Durrani Pashtuns – including the Maduzai – the control of women's behaviour and their exchange in marriage are perhaps the most important criteria used to define their ethnic identity.

In this respect the geography and the social milieux of Afghan Turkistan are of direct relevance to this study, but as the wider contexts of Durrani ethnicity and other questions of social identity have already been discussed by RLT (1983, 1984b, 1988 and forthcoming a and b) and myself (1979, 1982), my concern here is to describe social identity and ethnicity from the Durrani point of view and to relate these to the ideology and practices of marriage as found within the Maduzai subtribe. Nonetheless, to realize adequately even this more limited ambition, a certain amount of background information is necessary: particularly on the ethnic cast of characters, the history and nature of the Pashtun presence in the region and the crucial interface between the Durrani leaders, other ethnic groups and the government. The Maduzai subtribe is also introduced in this chapter.

The social geography of Afghan Turkistan

From the steppes and sandy deserts of low elevation near the Soviet frontier, the land rises in loess hills southwards towards the Band-i Turkistan mountains, the northwest spur of the Hindu Kush, rising to nearly 3,500 m. Higher mountain chains lie further to the south in the provinces of Bamyan and Ghor. Springs and snow run-off from these ranges feed streams and rivers flowing north, which cut deep, spectacular gorges across the mountains and then disappear soon after reaching the Turkistan steppes. Summers and winters in Turkistan are extreme; in the mountains the summers are pleasant but short, snow often lying in the valleys for over six months of the year.

In the mountain valleys at 1,500–2,000 m, a limited amount of wheat and barley can be irrigated by the fast-flowing streams, while precarious crops of wheat are raised on the slopes above. Otherwise the slopes above 3,000 m provide good if rocky pasturage after the snows melt, and flocks of hardy mountain sheep can be raised locally so long as much of the irrigated valley land is devoted to fodder crops for use in the long winter. In the scattered settlements, houses are closely packed for protection against the extreme cold.

As the mountain ranges and valleys decrease in altitude towards the north, the climate becomes less harsh and settlements are more frequent. Dry and irrigated cultivation are more productive, while the mountain slopes still offer good seasonal pastures. Closer to the urban market centres of Saripul, Sangcharak, Gurziwan, Belchiragh and Maymana, fruit orchards and vineyards predominate in the valleys, and dry-farming on the mountain slopes at up to 2,000 m. Still further north the mountains give way to rolling hills and slopes, fine winter and spring grazing; cultivation is normally restricted to the broad valleys of the Saripul, Shur Darya and Shirin Tagau rivers.

The steppes and foothills of Afghan Turkistan are traditionally the lands of the Uzbek Turks. Until the consolidation of Afghanistan under Amir Abd al-Rahman (1880–1901), the towns of the area (Maymana, Andkhoy, Aqcha, Shiberghan, Saripul) were seats of small semi-independent Uzbek Khanates, and the population surrounding them was primarily Turkic-speaking. Now the area is extremely heterogeneous: for instance, on the road between Saripul and Shiberghan, one passes in quick succession communities of the following ethnic groups: Uzbek, Durrani, Maliki, Durrani, Uzbek, Hazara, Durrani, Baluch, Arab, Sayyid, Durrani, Ghilzai, Durrani.

Many Uzbeks are village farmers, while in the towns craftsmen and tradesmen are predominantly Uzbek. In Saripul a number of powerful Uzbek families, descendants of former chiefs, are looked to by all local Uzbeks for political and religious guidance. There are small enclaves of other Turkic groups in the region, mostly refugees from the Soviet Union. Turkmens are numerous in the neighbouring districts of Shiberghan and Andkhoy, but few in Saripul.

The Arabs, who are mainly pastoralists, live in several scattered communities in the Saripul vicinity and have little political unity. They claim descent from Arab tribes of the original Islamic conquests, but they now speak Persian and have assimilated some features of both Uzbek and Turkmen cultures.

Moving south out of Turkistan and into the mountains, one finds discrete groups of Hazaras, Aymaks, and Tajiks. The Hazaras, who speak a distinct Persian dialect, long defended their independence in the Hazarajat mountains as a nation of a million or more people; the characteristic used most readily to distinguish them is that they are Shiᶜi Muslims, whereas the vast majority of Afghans are Sunnis. Since the conquest of the Hazarajat by Amir Abd al-Rahman in the 1890s, small groups of Hazaras have scattered over the country, several settling in the Saripul vicinity. Here they are industrious farmers and have a Khan

Map 2 Sketch-map of north-central Afghanistan

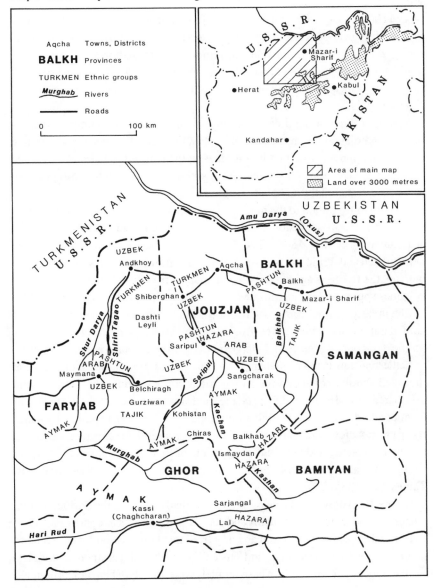

of some influence and maintain ties with their relatives in the Hazarajat mountains. The latter are still organized under powerful local Mirs.

The Tajiks in western Afghan Turkistan appear to be a residual category of Persian-speakers with no other tribal or ethnic affiliations. They are often confused – and confuse themselves – with Aymaks. In the Saripul region there are outposts of two of the main Chahar Aymak tribes of Western Afghanistan, the Firozkohi and the Taymani. Many of the Tajiks and Aymaks practice vertical nomadism and many of them move into tent camps in summer, not far from their villages.

The Hazaras, Aymaks and Tajiks are often quite isolated, two to three days' journey even in good weather from the nearest town or road. These mountaineers rarely leave their valleys, let alone the region; for information about the outside world they rely on military conscripts, on the few local men who travel to market, and on the nomads who pass through their lands in spring and summer.

Scattered through the area are several small distinct communities such as Sayyids, Khojas and Ishans, claimants to holy descent who for the most part live like their neighbours but get religious dues from them and sometimes specialize in religious education and services. Two kinds of gypsies, Jats and Jughis, are also found scattered throughout the region.

Pashtun immigration to the north began on a large scale with the pacification of the area and its inclusion within a unified Afghan state under Amir Abd al-Rahman in the late 1880s. The Amir was anxious to colonize the heavily depopulated and fertile tracts of Afghan Turkistan and the northwest, and also to bulwark the frontiers against possible incursions from Russia and Bokhara. For both these purposes he chose his own Pashtun tribespeople (cf. N. Tapper 1973).

The invasion came from two directions: first, members of the Ghilzai tribal confederation and other tribes from eastern Afghanistan, often the Amir's political opponents, were sent in large numbers from Kabul to exile in the north, to settle and farm; most of them were farmers by origin. Secondly, several thousand families of the Amir's own tribal confederation, the Durrani, and associated tribes from Kandahar and the southwest, were sent to the northwest as frontier guards. All of the Durrani immigrants were long-range pastoral nomads by origin, but they were granted land rights in favoured spots and given advances to help them settle and cultivate, though few of them did so at first. (For more details of Pashtu-speakers in the region, see N. Tapper 1979: 65ff.; R. Tapper 1984: 235–236.)

Before 1900 only small groups of Pashtuns had arrived in the Saripul region, where they occupied vacant lands and settled with little local opposition. Then large numbers of nomads began arriving from the west and southwest, some of them straight from Kandahar, and ousted the Arab and Turkmen pastoralists from the local grazing lands. These nomads were largely Ishaqzai Durrani, led by one small subtribe, the Nazarzai, which by 1910 had seized control of all vacant productive lands in Saripul and acquired tax-farming and other lucrative posts.

Criteria for maintaining ethnic boundaries vary with both the boundary and the group and their relevance changes according to context. In the political context, competition between groups over resources leads to major alignments, particularly that between Pashtuns and the rest, seen as 'Aughaniyya' versus 'Uzbekiyya' (see p. 39). On the other hand, in interpersonal exchanges of goods, services and information, ethnic barriers are normally lowered. Members of all groups meet in the Saripul marketplace, although even there, a tendency to localize exists; otherwise, although outsiders rarely venture into the mountains alone, in the Saripul vicinity there is considerable mobility of labour and trade between different ethnic groups. As for the Pashtun nomads, passing the length of the region, they maintain a complex chain of transactions involving goods and information. Most important, each nomad household has a series of 'friends' in Uzbek, Aymak and Hazara villages along the route, usually debtors who take cash advances, animals and wool from them, to be redeemed in local produce and fodder over a number of years. Nomads regard these friendships as important interest-bearing investments akin to the lands some of them own in the same villages; recently villagers have sometimes withheld their dues, but relations between the participants are cordial, in spite of latent tensions and backbiting.

Table 1 shows our rough estimates of the population of the different ethnic groups that Durrani identify in the Saripul subprovince (*woluswali*), though clearly each group has a different view of the ethnic complexity of the region and of its own role within it.

Late-twentieth-century changes

In the basic ecological, ethnic and political structure of the region, the main force of change during the twentieth century has probably been an increase in population. Until the 1950s, the region was underpopulated, while the writ of government did not extend far outside the administrative centres, being concerned mainly with the collection of taxes from the peasants. Farming was confined almost entirely to the irrigated river valleys, and many parts of these were uncultivated 'jungle'. However, public security has improved, taxation has lightened, the population has increased, and a land rush has occurred as a result.

Now the wide valleys immediately north and south of Saripul are fully cultivated; moreover, dry-farming of the steppe and mountain slopes has spread rapidly at the expense of pasture, although in many places this new farming strategy is a very risky enterprise. Like Afghanistan as a whole, the region now depends on a successful dry-farmed wheat crop for survival. In a good year, Saripul can export a surplus, but after a bad year, like 1970 or 1971, famine can threaten. The situation is one of population saturation in the region, given the

Table 1. *Main ethnic groups in the region ranked according to Durrani precepts*

Durrani label	Self identification	Sect	Language	Estimated population (households)	Percentage of total population
'Afghan'	1. Sayyid	Sunni	W. Pashtu	200	1
	2. Durrani	Sunni	W. Pashtu	2,500	10
'Parsiwan' (literally 'Persian-speaker')	3. (Non-Durrani Pashtuns) a. Ghilzai, Kabuli	Sunni	E. Pashtu	1,000	4
	(Customs and dialect differ from Durrani; accepted genealogies show them to be Durrani collaterals, but Durrani say they give daughters to Parsiwans)				

	b. Baluch,
	  Maliki,
	  Babi,
	  Lodin,
	  etc.
		Sunni	W. Pashtu	2,500	10

	(Share virtually all cultural features with Durrani, but are unable/unwilling to claim Durrani descent; Durrani say they give daughters to Uzbeks)				
'Uzbek'	4. (Non-Pashtuns) a. Uzbek	Sunni	Uzbeki ⎫	10,000	40
	b. Turkmen	Sunni	Turkmeni ⎭		
	c. Aymak, Tajik	Sunni	Persian	5,000	20
	d. Arab	Sunni	Persian	1,000	4
	5. (Non-Sunni) a. Hazara	Shiʿi	Persian	2,500	9
	b. Jat, Jugi	dubious Muslims	Persian	200	1
				c. 25,000	100

water resources available. However, both crafts and trades have expanded, as has employment in government service; there has also been a small amount of employment in new industry, particularly associated with Soviet gas and oil exploration, mainly in Mazar-i Sharif and Shiberghan, but also in the Saripul vicinity. Nonetheless there is continual emigration to the less crowded and developing northeastern provinces.

Ethnic and tribal identity (*qaumi*) provided, in the 1960s and early 1970s, the basic framework and language of social and political interaction in the region. However, a further reflection of the growth of population has been the emergence, by the early 1970s, of elements of class formation which cut across ethnic boundaries (cf. R. Tapper 1984; 1988).

The *qaumi* mode of association and of conducting political business contrasts with the *rasmi* (official) mode. 'Class' as a concept is not explicitly recognized except by newly educated urban youth. There is no term equivalent to 'class' in common speech, though other terms for collectivities and statuses had strong class connotations – for example, *khan* and *bey* (wealthy and influential men) and *rayat* (economic and political dependants of Khans and Beys). As we shall see, among Pashtun nomads and villagers the term *wolus* is in constant use to describe the power of united community effort, especially against the oppression of both Khans and the government. Maxims such as *da wolus zur da Khoday zur* ('The people's power is God's power' – or perhaps *vox populi vox Dei*) are commonly quoted to explain the success achieved when a community has collected a *lashkar* (army) to carry out its purposes.

By the 1970s the development of class formation could be discerned in a four-fold class structure: a traditional élite of landowners, tribal chiefs, wealthy merchants and other regional leaders; a 'bourgeoisie' of independent propertied tribesmen and peasants and established traders and artisans; a property-less and dependent rural and urban 'proletariat'; and a new 'intelligentsia' of young, educated townspeople, especially teachers and some officials (including some educated and even employed in Kabul). This class structure does not coincide with ethnic divisions, nor do standard local occupational categories have any ethnic implications – for example, *maldar* (pastoralist), *mulkdar* (landowner), *gharibkar* (labourer, usually casual), *dokandar* (shopkeeper), *dihqan* (farm-worker) – and ethnic and occupational groups are in the process of realigning themselves on new class lines. However, the redefinition of interests and political groups is barely beginning, and other kinds of changes, such as the possibility of interethnic marriage (see p. 60), remain unthinkable to both the Durrani élite and ordinary tribespeople.

The Ishaqzai of Saripul

As we shall see in chapter 4, the relation between the ideology of patrilineal descent and actual social groups is complicated. In the Saripul region nine recognized divisions of the Ishaqzai tribe are represented, one of them by four politically distinct branches (subtribes) which separated before leaving Kandahar, but which have yet to be recognized in the genealogies as separate tribal divisions. In other cases, local branches of a recognized tribal division have separated territorially since their arrival, but still maintain political unity as a subtribe. Additionally, as we shall see, a subtribe may include members of more than one recognized tribal division, united by residence and for political purposes.[2]

Some fourteen subtribes of the Ishaqzai Durrani Pashtuns have winter quarters and villages in Jouzjan province, mostly in the vicinity of Saripul town. These subtribes are social entities which, although based on an ideology of common descent, are essentially political groups with some territorial unity and potential for common action.

Apart from its name, most often that of a recognized Durrani tribal division, symbols to unify the subtribe are few and unimportant: there is often more than one leader; there are neither common property nor common rituals; common residence is not necessary for effective membership, which is both fluid and undefined. Each subtribe has a core of members who claim common patrilineal descent within the tribal division (*tayfa*) whose name the subtribe bears, but each subtribe has two kinds of secondary members: (a) members of the core descent group who happen to reside elsewhere, more or less temporarily (e.g. as herdsmen or labourers), but who maintain potential and often active membership in their subtribe of origin; and (b) members by residence, who bear the name of some other tribal division, or even another ethnic group; they may combine to maintain close links with their group of origin while participating in political affairs in their subtribe of residence (*wolus*). Members of the second category vary widely, from long term residents of holy descent (Sayyids, Aghas) or office (Mullahs), to seasonal labourers and shepherds, and to political and economic refugees from other regions. So also varies the extent to which their membership in the subtribe involves them in rights and duties properly confined to the descent group core. Local people most often refer to these 'subtribes' by their tribal names, but they may also refer to them by their geographical locality or by the names of their leaders. In practice, the 'subtribes' emerge as clearly recognized and recognizable entities.

The subtribe and its leaders

Among the Durrani, and other Pashtuns, the institution of the *jirga* or *maraka* assembly of household heads (sometimes including women household heads) enables them to form action-sets, *ad hoc* groups to deal with disputes and a wide range of social problems. An elder (*mesher*), greybeard (*spin zhirey*), or Hajji may convene an assembly whenever important internal matters need discussion or decision. Decisions are made, but rarely unanimously, and no elder can compel junior household heads to change their minds. Any particular *jirga* assembly will be made up of both the agnates of the principals as well as other householders of the *wolus* with which they are associated. However, the character of local *jirga* assemblies varies considerably depending on the issues to be debated and the status of the protagonists. The assemblies are not exclusive, and important elders of groups other than those principally concerned may be invited to attend, as may village headmen or the Ishaqzai Khans, whose authority will ensure that decisions are supported. Nonetheless, except in matters of extreme importance on which there is general agreement that some concerted action should follow immediately, *jirga* assemblies are essentially fora for the public expression of differences.

Jirga assemblies are important for the airing of views and the formation of public opinion. They also have an important symbolic role as the concrete expression of the ideal of the equality of all Durrani. However in all serious cases, political action depends ultimately on the Durrani leaders, who have many of the characteristics of the Melanesian 'Big Man' – charismatic personality and creative intelligence, persuasive articulateness and access to resources which can be used to recruit followers through the exchange of gifts and debt relationships. A man with such qualifications and a modicum of personal ambition may be drawn into the political arena almost by default, as members of his local descent group and others living nearby may persistently appeal to his skill in solving disputes. If he assumes a leadership role and through it increases his network of contacts and knowledge of the local government bureaucracy, his very success will serve to increase his following.

Some such leaders – those of considerable wealth – may assume, or may be accorded, the title of Khan and include a retinue of hired thugs among their following. The authority of such men is generally accepted and supported by other Durrani, in part out of fear, but mainly because of the Khans' political effectiveness in the region where their activities become a symbol of Durrani ethnic identity. Khans act as brokers in all serious dealings between fellow Durrani and members of other ethnic groups or representatives of the central government; a role which can be very lucrative.

Both the position of a Khan and that of a lesser leader may be formalized in the elective post of government headman (*qaryadar*) of a particular settlement, although such elections by acclaim are held only at lengthy and irregular intervals. Headmen may deal directly with government officials on formal and routine matters; their duties can be onerous, with no official rewards, but they may informally take dues or cuts for any of their activities. Headmen are responsible for ensuring that villagers are registered for census purposes and conscription, but deceits are regularly perpetrated, particularly with regard to the latter. Headmen are also responsible for organizing teams required by the local subgovernor as corvee labour, for example to fight locusts. Otherwise, the headman's duty is to provide information about villagers and village resources when this is required by the subgovernor or another official, and to contact villagers on behalf of officials if necessary. Only informally do the headmen have an obligation to present the villagers' point of view to local officials, a role that is undertaken only when it involves little personal risk and the possibility of political or financial gain. When in difficulty, the village headman will call on the expensive aid and superior resources of members of the Ishaqzai Khan family.

Relations between the local leaders, whether Khans or headmen, and government officials vary considerably and depend on the strength of character of the latter. In general the wealth and local knowledge of the Ishaqzai Durrani Khans and the leading men of other ethnic groups allow them to dominate local government affairs. However, the power of their Khans does not necessarily protect ordinary Durrani tribesmen from interference or depredations by local government officials. On the contrary, Durrani householders greatly fear becoming involved, however accidentally, in any affair in which local officials and thus also the Khans take an interest; both officials and Khans are felt to be only too ready to exploit any contact for the benefit of their own pockets.

The Nazarzai Ishaqzai Khans

The region as a whole is dominated economically and politically by members of the Nazarzai subtribe, leading members of which – the Khans – are near descendants of Seyf Akhundzada, whose sons, headed by the eldest, Ghulam Rasul Khan, led the Ishaqzai migration to the region at the turn of the century.

The Nazarzai Khans conduct extensive pastoral activities, but base their power partly on control of immense areas of farmland and partly on privileges granted them by successive Afghan governments. Ghulam Rasul Khan's son, 'Rais' Abdul Ghafur Khan, was for many years Subgovernor (*hakim*) at Saripul, and, until his death in 1969, directed a lucrative business in Mazar-e Sharif. In recent years the family has controlled regional affairs informally through the successive Hakims, now appointed from Kabul. In the 1965 and 1969 parliamentary elections, Kamaluddin, a brother of Abdul Ghafur Khan, managed by devious means to win the Saripul seat against the votes of the majority. Hajji Kheyr Mohammad Khan, son of Abdul Ghafur Khan and the present head of the Khan family, lives in Saripul town. Other branches of the family live on and supervise their estates, scattered throughout the region; some more or less close to the town and valley, but one each in Sangcharak, Shibarghan, and Ismaydan in the mountains.

Ishaqzai domination has not remained unopposed. In the first years after their arrival in the region, they oppressed the local Uzbek and Aymak population, as well as previous Pashtun arrivals, forcing many of these to emigrate from the region. In 1929–1930, during the Bacha-Saqaw revolution, the Uzbeks, Turkmens and Aymaks of Saripul rose against the Nazarzai Khans and drove them into the mountains, setting up a Saqawi supporter as Governor in the town.

The last Shah's father, Nadir Shah, terminated the revolt in 1930 and restored Durrani rule at Kabul. The Nazarzai Khans regained power in Saripul and commenced reprisals. They recovered their former lands and seized more, even lands belonging to the Hazaras and Arabs, the only local groups to have supported the Pashtuns against the Saqawis. However, as a result of complaints by leading Uzbeks, Ghulam Rasul Khan was placed under house arrest in Kabul, where he later died.

A number of other Nazarzai Khans were arrested and placed in temporary custody in the early 1930s, when government control was being re-established in Turkistan by Minister Muhammad Gul Khan Mohmand. Despite fiercely pro-Pashtun sentiments, Muhammad Gul Khan refused to countenance the oppression perpetrated by the Khans. He balanced the domination of Durrani from Kandahar by introducing many more eastern Pashtuns to the area (especially as landowners between Aqcha and Balkh), and he appears to have dealt fairly with petitions against the Nazarzai brought by Uzbeks and Aymaks from throughout the Saripul region and its hinterland.

During the following decades, however, local authorities turned a blind eye to

Pashtun oppression, in conformity with what was essentially a tacit central government policy of political and cultural discrimination against non-Pashtuns. Ethnic divisions were manipulated at both local and national levels. In the Saripul region there were numerous further revolts against the sons of Ghulam Rasul Khan. In the mountainous hinterland the Hazaras of Kashan and the Aymaks of Chiras and the upper Saripul river valleys drove out most of the Nazarzai Khans by abandoning their villages and lands or threatening to do so, appealing to the central government over the heads of local officials, and on occasion resorting to armed resistance; they tolerated only one or two Khans for what good they could do in the role of patrons.

Confrontations have also occurred in and around Saripul, usually between Uzbeks and Pashtuns. Typically one of the Khans would seize property (land or flocks) belonging to an Uzbek peasant (sometimes a village leader); the latter would complain to the government, but might then suffer violence – often murder – by agents of the Khan, whose complicity could not be proven. In one notorious case in 1970, a Khan personally shot dead seven Uzbek farmers who had come to his house to complain. He was said to have had their bodies desecrated. Subsequently he was arrested and sentenced to four years in jail, but after having served a few months in considerable comfort, he was released on payment of 100 *jeribs* (20 hectares) of land to each of the bereaved families. A public peace-making ceremony in Saripul followed, accompanied by a two-day *buzkashi* tournament. The outcome of this case was generally considered to be a victory for the Uzbeks and a dishonour for the Pashtun Khans. Many Pashtuns, however, maintained that by their standards the Uzbeks' acceptance of compensation was dishonourable. Nonetheless, the Uzbeks probably would not have achieved even this limited success if they had not been represented by their own powerful leaders. By the early 1970s Uzbeks, Hazaras, and Aymaks of the region had such leaders, often able to defend their followers' interests effectively when threatened.

The Ishaqzai subtribes of Saripul vary widely in situation and character (see N. Tapper 1979: 60). They fall into three main categories. First, pastoral nomads with winter tent-villages in the dry hill steppes west of Saripul. These are comparatively isolated from other ethnic groups and from administrative controls. The second category consists of similarly tent-dwelling nomads, but they camp most of the year beside the fertile Saripul river valley some miles north of the town. Few of them own any farmland in the valley, although they often dry-farm the neighbouring pastures. The third category is now semi-sedentary. Such people have winter settlements in or on the edge of the valley, own lands there, have mostly built mud houses, and half or less of the population make the summer transhumance to the central mountains, though all of them are in regular contact with members of a whole range of other ethnic groups. The Maduzai subtribe belongs to this last category.

The Maduzai subtribe

The Maduzai subtribe comprises 272 households (about 1,900 souls), based on two villages and several hamlets and tent-camps situated in the valley about 15 km north of Saripul. Over three-quarters of the households have built mud dwellings, although this in itself is not an index of sedentarization. The Maduzai are pastoral nomads by origin, preference and ideology, but the uncertainty of the national and world markets in Persian lambskins, their main pastoral product, has encouraged them to look elsewhere for economic security, while they have experienced the rapid population growth and land rush mentioned earlier as having affected the whole region.

The Maduzai were fortunate in that soon after their arrival in the north (c. 1917) they acquired very cheaply a large area of irrigated valley land. For many years this lay under-exploited, but now the Maduzai have opened their land to intensive cultivation. Nearly half the Maduzai households possess and benefit directly from shares in irrigated lands, totalling over 1,000 hectares: others also farm dry lands nearby. The landless Maduzai acquire essential agricultural produce by working for their landed neighbours, by trade or by the sale of pastoral produce.

A third of the population, including many of the landowners, have substantial holdings of animals, especially sheep. Between September and early May the flocks are kept in the hill-steppe pastures to the east of the valley. From early March until early May, while the lambs are born and the spring wool is shorn, about three-quarters of the Maduzai go out to camp in their pastures, to provide the additional labour required, to supervise the collection of lamb-skins, and also to get away from the villages and to enjoy the festive spring atmosphere and the best season in the pastures. By mid-May these pastures are scorched dry and the wells brackish or dried up, and the flocks are taken to the mountains, leaving the steppe to the wolves. Usually about a third of the households send tents to accompany the flocks on the 300 km migration to spend the early summer months in the central mountains; the rest return to the villages to supervise or take part in the summer's agricultural activities, which include mowing the dried steppe grasses for use as hay during the following winter.

The Maduzai subtribe is essentially a political unit. Although it is seen by its members as a local descent group, only 201 of the household heads actually claim descent from the ancestor Madu; of these, 177 belong to the four core lineages which dominate the subtribe politically and economically. A further 56 household heads, claiming descent within other Ishaqzai subtribes or Durrani tribes, are permanent residents with the subtribe and share rights and duties of membership with households belonging to the four core lineages, while a final 15 households, similarly associated with the subtribe, are non-Durrani by origin. The political unity of the Maduzai is accompanied by a certain autonomy, for they are

Table 2. *Composition of the Maduzai subtribe (c. 1920 and 1972)*

	c. 1920	1972
Core-lineage households		
Lineage A	24	77
Lineage B (5 households joined in c. 1925)		15
Lineage C (Torabi)	12	70
Lineage D	5	15
Client households		
Maduzai collaterals	14	24
Other Ishaqzai and Durrani	c. 5	56
Non-Durrani	c. 10	15
Totals	70	272

led by a man accorded the title 'Khan', which means that for many purposes he is the single intermediary between the tribespeople and the government, a function performed for most other subtribes by members of the Nazarzai Khan family.

The Maduzai differ from most other subtribes in the region not only in the degree of their political autonomy but also in the extent of their settlement. Although in many ways they remain pastoralists at heart, and the pastoral sector of the subtribe economy continues to be of great importance, it is nonetheless the case that they are basically settled, and most people spend most of the year in the winter villages in the Saripul river valley. In village life, the flexibility of movement and association – characteristic of camp-based nomads – has been lost, and conflict and competition among them has inevitably intensified, though population pressure is also a factor in this. Nonetheless it remains true that the two arenas – the village communities and the nomadic camps – form a single entity. For example, political and economic decisions made in the villages over agricultural concerns are likely to have a direct effect on relations in the pastoral arena, and vice versa. At the same time, the dual economy of the Maduzai affords them a wider range of solutions to political and economic problems than those available to other local groups which are more exclusively pastoral or agricultural. The Maduzai are well aware of this advantage and seemed likely at the time of fieldwork to continue their dual economy for the foreseeable future. Moreover, the wider economic and political choices available to the Maduzai have contributed to an elaboration of the institution of marriage among them. However, in their political and economic organization, the Maduzai differ in degree and not in kind from other local subtribes, and in their attitudes and decisions concerning marriage are representative of other local Durrani.

Durrani ethnic identity

Since the time of Ahmad Shah Durrani (1747–1772), the Durrani have constituted an interest group to which economic and political privileges (such as tax
concessions and freedom from conscription) accrued by virtue of descent.
Although legislation provides for the equality of all Afghan nationals, Durrani
domination still (up to the time of fieldwork) pervades all branches of political
and administrative life. If only for this reason, the poorest nomad or peasant who
can claim Durrani identity is able to maintain, at least in the eyes of fellow-
Durrani, a position of social superiority to members of all other ethnic groups.

The traditional rivalry central to the history of the Afghan state, between the
Durrani and the Ghilzai confederacy to the east, sharpened the boundary between
Durrani and all other Pashtu-speakers, including Ghilzai, in such a way that
'Pashtun', for Pashtu-speakers themselves, is a category which often has limited
cultural content. At the same time, their political history has led the Durrani to
place great value on the cultural unity of the confederation and to play down the
distinctivenesses of groups at lower levels of segmentation. Certainly in the
north, leaders of named tribal groups have numerous followers from others; subtribes, the primary political units, which are of the greatest relevance to everyday
life, are associated with named descent groups, but membership can be acquired
by outsiders with other Durrani descent ties.

Against this background it is perhaps not surprising that among groups in
Saripul it is the Durrani Pashtuns who use the most exclusive ethnic criteria to
define themselves. Durrani ideas of their superiority in the region arise first from
Durrani political domination at the national level, and second from local domination by Durrani Khans. Not only are the Durrani a small minority (about 10 per
cent) of the population of the region, but the same range of wealth is found among
Durrani as among other ethnic groups. Although the Khan family as a whole is
enormously wealthy and powerful, individual Khans are not greatly different
these days from chiefs of other ethnic groups. In fact, the 'superiority' of ordinary
Durrani tribesmen is only tenuously related to real economic or even political
status.

The major criteria which Saripul Durrani use to maintain their identity, and
which buttress their claims to status, are complex and confusing but quite
exclusive. To be accepted as a Durrani, at least in the Saripul region, a man must
claim membership by descent of a tribal group whose name ends in the Pashtu
suffix *-zai* (offspring of), practise Sunni Islam, speak Kandahari Pashtu as
mother-tongue and give his daughters only to Sayyids, the descendants of the
Prophet Mohammad, or other Durrani. These criteria in theory distinguish
Durrani from all other groups. Objectively they are often quite spurious and
untenable, in that they complicate rather than simplify the ethnic situation. Taken
in combination, however, they do define the parameters of Durrani identity and
accepted behaviour. The most decisive criterion for incorporation is ascription

by descent, from which the other features are held to follow: if a man cannot prove his descent claims he will be suspected of being, in private, a Persian-speaking Shi'i, while the most tangible grounds for exclusion is giving daughters to non-Durrani.

In most everyday contexts, Durrani call all non-Durrani Pashtuns 'Parsiwan' (or 'Farsiban'), literally 'Persian speakers'. All non-Pashtuns are called 'Uzbek', a category which Durrani use to refer to Sunni Persian-speakers of all sorts (Tajik, Aymak, Arab, etc.), Uzbeks and other Turkic-speakers, and Shi'i Hazaras. When pushed to be more precise, Durrani will narrow these terms considerably, but not always consistently.

The ostensive cultural similarities between Durrani and 'Parsiwan' and the competition for the same economic resources, make this ethnic boundary particularly sensitive for Durrani, and it is highly marked. In this respect the Parsiwans who pose the greatest threat to Durrani identity are the groups of diverse origins (Baluch, Khalili, Maliki, Moghol, etc.) who came with the Durrani from southwest Afghanistan. They are mainly Sunni Muslim and Pashtu-speaking, and share virtually all features of custom with the Durrani, but are unable (or unwilling) to claim descent within a recognized Durrani tribe. Durrani point out that the tribal names of these groups do not end in the suffix *-zai* and, more importantly, that they sometimes marry their daughters to non-Pashtuns.

Members of Ghilzai and other eastern Pashtun tribal groups live in small scattered communities in the Saripul region. They are Sunni Muslims and speak Pashtu, but their dialect and many of their customs are different from those of Durrani. The latter rarely refer to them as 'Pashtuns', saying that they are not 'real' (*asl*) ones; more often they are all termed 'Kabuli' as opposed to 'Kandahari' (i.e. Durrani). Some Durrani would call them Parsiwans, but others, particularly the more educated, argue that the accepted genealogies show Ghilzais and other Kabulis to be collaterals of the Durrani. Nonetheless, opinion is united that Durrani girls should not be given to them, as they are said to give their own daughters to Parsiwans.

The local political domination by Durrani, as well as Pashtun domination in the country as a whole, is reproduced in the use of tribal labels. Pashtu-speakers commonly call themselves 'Pashtun', while speakers of other languages in Afghanistan almost always call them 'Afghan' (colloquially 'Aughan') and their language 'Afghani' ('Aughani'). Although 'Afghan' is officially promoted as applying to all citizens of the Afghan state, in the north of the country it is often used for 'Pashtun' even by the Pashtu-speakers themselves, particularly when speaking Persian. To the Durrani tribespeople with whom we stayed, 'Durrani', 'Pashtun' and 'Afghan' are practically synonymous, and they use these words interchangeably to identify Durrani as opposed to all other groups, including non-Durrani Pashtu-speakers. For simplicity I shall not employ the term 'Afghan' in its local sense, but at the risk of confusion I shall sometimes follow the Durrani usage of 'Pashtun' to describe Durrani customs and identity.

Durrani sustain their claims to ethnic superiority by maintaining close contacts, and usually residing, with others who make similar claims and with whom they share common descent; and by strict adherence to the rules which define their identity and by which they justify their claims, particularly the ban on hypogamy. In everyday life they express their identity most often in terms of the concept *'Pashtu'*. *'Pashtu'* may be used to describe virtually all aspects of Durrani culture and it is a direct synonym of 'honour' in some of its senses (see p. 107). Thus, a particularly laudable action may be praised as 'Pashtu work', while a Durrani who fails to live up to some social expectation may be said to be 'without Pashtu' (*bi-Pashtu*). Durrani also support their claims to superiority by a folk etymology of their name: *dur-andishi* (paradoxically a Persian phrase) meaning 'far-thought'. That is, Durrani are those who remember and are generous in respecting the bonds of friendship, as opposed to non-Durrani who are *kota-fikr*, 'short-sighted', and hence quick to take offence against relatives and friends.

Though religious distinctions are not a major feature of relations between different Sunni ethnic groups, certain cultural differences are given a religious flavour in the attitudes of one group towards another. Thus, Durrani are proud that by local standards at least, their women are not segregated or veiled at home: they say it is not Pashtun custom and not demanded by Islam, and they ridicule the whole idea of cloistered women as Uzbek nonsense, praise the Hazaras for being in this respect like themselves, and upbraid any Durrani family whose women are so cloistered as being 'without-*Pashtu*'.

To be a Durrani means more than just being a Sunni; it indicates the ability to trace unbroken descent to a recognized Durrani ancestor and through him via the accepted genealogies to the ancestor of all Pashtuns, Qais Abd al-Rashid, who is said to have been among the first voluntary converts to Islam. Thus descent gives Durrani, and in theory other Pashtuns, a claim to religious superiority over all groups other than Sayyids. Moreover, in the Durrani view, all Pashtun custom is hallowed because it conforms strictly with religious prescriptions; they rarely make a distinction between custom and religious law and frequently are unable to do so. Things Pashtun and things Muslim are identical. As a buttress for their notions of their own religious superiority, Durrani form a separate religious community and have slight interest in the teachings of religious leaders of other ethnic groups. Each Durrani group sees to the education of its own mullahs, while other formal religious leaders are either Durrani or members of local Pashtu-speaking Sayyid lineages. Important in their religious life are visits from members of the Qadiriyya brotherhood, who conduct Sufi rituals and exorcise spirits among their followers, men and women, who are numerous in Pashtun settlements.

Durrani ethnic identity and their ideals of status equality depend on claims to religious privilege and pure descent. In particular, the integrity of the entire Durrani ethnic group depends on the maintenance of the absolute prohibition on the marriage of Durrani women to men who are not Durrani but of some 'lower' ethnic status, and breaches of this rule are dealt with collectively and with great ferocity. In this fashion, much interethnic competition is disguised from Durrani, whose attention is directed away from the political and economic factors in interethnic confrontations and focused on their assumed hereditary rights to superior status.

II. Social groups and marriage

4

Patrilineality, gender and endogamy

Durrani insist that they transmit property and status through the male line and that nothing is inherited or passed on through women, whose only claim on their father's estate is the trousseau provided for their first marriage. Nor has a widow any claim other than a provision for her maintenance which is administered by her husband's heirs. In most contexts Durrani men and women discuss issues which might be analysed under the heading of agnation as if it were only applicable to men. From this point of view patrilineal descent is a fundamental principle of Durrani social organization and underlies all their concepts of social grouping. Not only is the male role in procreation held to be primary, but descent is considered to be unalterable and to determine tribal membership. As they put it, 'Descent (*nasab*) makes a tribe (*tayfa*)'; and queries about descent demand an answer in terms of a named tribal group.

Social groups, agnatic and affinal ties

The Durrani confederacy is divided into a more or less fixed configuration of recognized tribes and tribal divisions. The names of these and their genealogical relation to each other are perpetuated by written Durrani and local histories originating in their southwestern homeland. Learned tribesmen in the north have knowledge, and sometimes copies, of versions of these histories. Though the configuration of tribes is by no means agreed in detail, it is held to have a permanent reality overriding temporary political groupings. However, while a Durrani must be able to demonstrate his descent from recognized Durrani ancestors, it is not so important to trace one's exact connection with fellow members of a subtribe.

In each subtribe a small number of individuals know pedigrees and skeleton genealogies extending some six to ten generations back to recognized Durrani tribal ancestors, but normally there is little call for this kind of information and little interest in it, and in fact few individuals know their own pedigrees further than two or three generations back (see N. Tapper 1979: 101). Clearly this lack of genealogical interest is consistent with the fact that descent ideology is formally relevant to Durrani only at the level of the ethnic group where it defines their equality and determines marriage choice and political allegiance, and it is consistent, in practice, with the scatter of Durrani communities and their mobility throughout the country.

While the actual names of Durrani subtribes are often of importance only in relations with the Ishaqzai Khans or government officials, the constitution of these subtribes is of the greatest concern to those who see themselves as members of such a named group. The principles which are used to define subtribe membership and activities are complex.

The Saripul Durrani use a variety of terms interchangeably for groups of various kinds and at various levels – a lack of precision which may perplex the ethnographer but has many advantages for the actors. If they are to be understood adequately, one crucial aspect of the ambiguity of the indigenous terms must be mentioned. A variety of different indigenous terms for social groupings may be used to refer to the same, or more or less the same, group of people. However these terms are not necessarily used synonymously. Most often they describe nuances of social structure and/or organization, but because their referents may be the same grouping on the ground, the terms themselves are polysemous. For this reason, for example, ethnographers who find patrilineality, with its elegant simplicity, an adequate explanatory device, of course find their view confirmed. In virtually all cases imaginable, actual social groups can be seen to be constituted in terms of a combination of organizational principles, the three most important of which are patrilineality, affinity and residential propinquity.

The complexity of indigenous usage is suggested in the following examples. Among the Durrani, phrases using the term *aulad* (from the Arabic, meaning 'offspring of'), the suffix *-zai* (Pa. offspring of) or the term *plar* (Pa. father) specifically refer to groups of agnatic descendants of a particular ancestor, though these groups may be of any size, from children of a living man, to putative descent groups as large as the primary ethnic groups (Afghan, Uzbek, etc.), to all human beings who are the children of Adam. A subtribe is a group whose name should end in the suffix *-zai* and whose members can also be described as the *aulad* of the apical ancestor and as the people of one father (*plar*).

Three other terms, which also have descent connotations, may also be used to refer to social groups at different levels. Thus tribes and tribal divisions may be termed *tayfa* (from the Arabic, meaning clan, tribe, family), a word which may also be used to refer to recognized divisions of any larger category of animate creatures such as insects or jinns. More often the term *qaum* (from the Arabic, meaning people, nation, tribe, group, family, sect) is used for human groupings of all kinds. Frequently *qaum* is modified by the name of some living or dead individual, man or woman, and, in context, this device precisely locates the group referred to by the speaker. The related term *qaumi* means 'people of the same *qaum*', and also mutual support between such people (see N. Tapper 1979: 105 and n. 5). A third term, *wolus* (from the Turkish *ulus*, meaning people, nation, tribe) is used to imply the political nature of social groups at a variety of levels. *Wolusi* is any concerted action taken by such a group. One of the main types of social grouping designated by these three terms is the subtribe.

As the gloss on the meaning of *wolus* suggests, though it may be used to refer to a group organized at least in part on the basis of descent, it actually denotes other aspects of group identity and behaviour. In this respect the terms *wolus*, *tayfa* and *qaum* differ in a very basic way from those terms, such as *aulad* or *plar*, whose meanings derive explicitly from the principle of patrilineality. Though all three terms have descent connotations, each one primarily denotes other organizational principles. *Wolus* is associated with political action. The term *tayfa* contains an historicity and when it is used of a social group the term emphasizes its particular location in time and space; in other words, it suggests a certain territoriality and implies external relations with other *tayfa*. Finally, the term *qaum*, by contrast, refers to a social group in terms of the mutual support of group members and the desirability of intermarriage between them. This latter preference is a key aspect of social grouping.

Common patrilineal descent establishes the equality of all Durrani and their superiority *vis-à-vis* others. The use of the term *qaum* adds a further important dimension: a *qaum* is ideally endogamous and the term thereby defines all Durrani as equally eligible as affines. Thus a man may use the term *qaum* to refer to any descent group to which he belongs and, as long as he marries a Durrani (but not any other Pashtun), he may claim that he has married within his *qaum*. Conversely, it is said that 'A good girl will always marry into her own *qaum*'; however, because of the term's sliding range of referents, as long as she marries another Durrani, a woman both fulfills this ideal and demonstrates that she is a 'good woman' and a credit to her natal family. In effect, conformity with the ideal of endogamy (which is often expressed independently of its association with *qaum*) does not require distinctions to be made between fellow Durrani. The usage of *qaum* itself allows the ideal to be achieved quite easily without any bounded marriage isolates being formed among Durrani.

Given the prevalence of the use of the terms *tayfa*, *qaum* and *wolus* to refer to social groups (see N. Tapper 1979: 178, n. 4) which, in other contexts, may also be described in terms of descent, it is not surprising that rights and duties related to specified degrees of kinship or affinity are very few and rarely invoked in practice. Only in matters of extreme importance which call into question the ethnic identity of a specifically related group of agnates (an *aulad*, or 'the households of one father (*plar*)'), are they likely to mobilize into a politically effective group (*wolus*).

Membership of a local descent group or a subtribe is an issue which is brought into the open in cases of conflict and commonly resolved by some form of marriage. The Durrani traditionally recognize certain principles of collective responsibility, rules of blood compensation and the validity of the use of exchange marriage both to reconcile disputing kinsmen and to recognize the status equality (or common *qaum* identity) of strangers. For example, the Saripul Durrani say that if a man is killed, his *qaum* have the right in religious law to seven women in compensation. In practice, they say, the killer may give two girls in marriage and then take a Koran to the victim's house and ask to be freed of the obligation to give more. The killer's *qaum*, from among whom the girls given in feud marriages will be found, will also be expected to pay any cash compensation the victim's family, or the government, may demand.

For a man who has been wounded, at least one woman must be given. Because there are likely to have been killings and woundings on both sides, people say,

Those involved must take girls from each other and make peace, so that the feud (*badi*) will leave their hearts. If their hearts are not full, they will become bad again; but if their hearts have become close, there will be no more killing.

They insist, however, that if a Durrani kills a Parsiwan he will give only money, never women, in compensation. Maduzai history, summarized below, offers examples of both exchange marriages of reconciliation and recognition, and feud marriages; their wider significance is discussed in chapter 8.

Thirty-five years ago, when the Maduzai feud occurred, the rules of agnatic co-responsibility and blood compensation were in operation. When talking of those events today, which they do with reluctance, Maduzai express a combination of regret and relief that such a succession of killings would be almost impossible now. Violence occurs, but 'There are two things the government will not now tolerate: sheep theft and homicide', and revenge killings are nowadays very rare in the Saripul area.

There are still occasions when agnates may help one of their number, and crises when tribal loyalties, if forcefully invoked by leaders, can unite large groups in order to collect cash contributions for a common cause such as compensation or litigation (see Case 2). In other circumstances agnates rarely co-operate or unite except when they are also affines or neighbours, while disputes between closely related household heads are the principal cause of divisions within a local descent group.

The rights and duties involved in agnatic kinship of itself are nowadays few and rarely invoked in practice. There is a fairly strong ideal that descendants of a common ancestor should be neighbours and politically united, and the strength of this ideal is greater the closer the ancestor. However, 'closeness' fosters conflict as well as co-operation, and people continually express regret at the degeneration of the times, such that nowadays even one's agnates cannot be relied on, brother fights brother, father fights son – all, moreover, regarded as signs of the impending end of the world.

It is of course impossible to be sure that the Saripul Durrani did not always have this attitude to agnatic relations (see N. Tapper 1979: 179, n. 7), but the evidence does suggest that in practice the strength of agnatic ties is not what it was. On the one hand, agnates have less need to unite nowadays – increased government intervention has reduced the possibility of interethnic warfare, the consequent demands for *qaum* solidarity, and the need for migrating nomads to move together in large, lineage-based groups. On the other hand, there are new sources of conflict between agnates. For instance, settlement has deprived groups like the Maduzai of the flexibility of camp association which they had as nomads and which enabled them literally to move away from disputes. Additionally, individual ownership of, and now pressure on, agricultural land has led to widening inequalities among close agnates and provided them, as they are well aware, with new grounds for quarrelling.

Affinal ties
Unlike agnates, disputes between affines are unlikely over property once the brideprice is paid and marriage completed, and any co-operation between them is construed as voluntary.

There are no formal or necessary obligations inherent in the affinal relationship and, except in extreme circumstances, a married woman's agnates have no formal rights in or duties towards her. Though affective ties may be strong, in everyday life they will not be allowed to take precedence over the rights and duties of the husband and his kin. This in itself is an indication of the equality of the affinal relationship. Nonetheless affinal ties are held to be irrevocable and, given the absence of divorce and the practice of widow inheritance, are held to endure until the woman dies. As one Maduzai man put it,

Once ties of affinity (*kheshi*) are made, they cannot be severed; I can never say 'I am finished with my affine'. If we have one hundred fights or one hundred killings, then for one month or one year we will be unhappy with one another, but in the end we will be reconciled, because of our friendship (*dosti*). That is, my daughter or sister is over there and I am forced to go to her, to see her, to bring her visiting, and in the end we will make up. A grey-beard will make peace between us and there will be a feast. However hard you try you cannot cut a relationship of *kheshi*, for the women would still visit back and forth – it is really to do with women (cf. Evans-von Krbek 1977: 203ff., 237).

A woman's children have a permanent tie with their *mama*, primarily their mother's brother, but by extension all the mother's male agnates and the group that they form, the *mamakhel*. Like agnatic ties outside the household and ties to affines, those with one's *mamakhel* are optative to the extent that they imply no specific rights and duties, nor do they necessarily define the character of social relationships, though they are all distinguished from relations with strangers by ideals of fellowship, affection and cooperation.

A further ambiguity in the usage of *qaum* assimilates relations of affinity to those of agnation. Through marriage people of different groups (*aulad* or *tayfa*) may 'become *qaum*' while retaining their separate membership of different named tribal divisions. This is reflected generally in the use of the Persian term *qaum-o-khish* for 'relatives'. Where marriage is deliberately used to unite separate kin groups for reasons of political expediency, the ambiguities created by the juxtaposition of the term *qaum* with its near synonyms, *aulad*, *tayfa* and *wolus*, are of considerable importance. In effect, agnatic and affinal ties are equally unformalized; the essentially bilateral character of Durrani kinship terminology bears this out (see N. Tapper 1979: App. 1).

Like the term *qaum-o-khish* for relatives, the term *khpalwan*, 'one's own people', has a broad range of possible applications but refers, essentially, to an ego-centred group. It is a term most often used for what Marx has called the 'effective kinship circle' (1967: 162–169), including cognates to the third degree and, in the Durrani case, some other families of immediate neighbours as well. Durrani consider that general norms of friendship and support should apply automatically within this range of people. Respect for one's *khpalwan* is marked by formal visiting on the two most important religious festivals celebrated by the Maduzai, the Ids of Ramazan (known as *Kuchney Akhtar*) and Qorban (known as *Loy Akhtar*) and it is they who gather for tasks involving reciprocal labour arrangements (e.g. sheep-shearing for men, felt-making for women) and for many small formal gatherings, such as the *push* associated with marriage (see p. 165).

While temporary and small-scale dependence on kin of one's effective network is part of the on-going social system and debts thus incurred will be reciprocated in kind, people may clearly distinguish between agnates and affines within this network. Thus a poor man may seek influential affines with the expectation that if his agnatic kin fail him (as they may well do if he is poor), he may be able to join the former as a client and be supported by them. Any family may benefit from its affines, particularly if the two families live at a distance from each other such that either may provide economic or political contacts or refuge for the other. While seasonal and annual weather conditions in Turkistan can vary widely, these variations are often localized, and a family with affines living at some distance may turn to them for access to seasonal pasturage, for jobs, or for simple charity in times of real distress. It is not uncommon to find a series of marriages between families of different subtribes; with each successful marriage, the next becomes easier. In general, the security and influence of a household rests on the number and kinds of connections that it is seen to have made and their potential for action; an ambitious household must, in making marriages, maintain a calculated balance between extending its range of affinal ties as widely as possible and consolidating its existing agnatic and affinal links by further marriages.

If agnation and affinity of themselves impose few specific rights and obligations to economic and political support, such support (*qaumi*) and common action (*wolusi*) are automatically consequent upon common residence and allegiance to particular local leaders. One may 'do *qaumi*' and act kindly and generously, acknowledging the moral bonds and economic and political responsibilities of common descent. For example, one may ask for a lower brideprice from *qaumi*, or collect money for, or donate land to, impoverished *qaumi*. Perhaps most importantly, it is believed that groups of individuals who find themselves involved in a political confrontation with outsiders, however defined, will gain their end if they have *qaumi*: thus it was said of a man jailed for his part in a murder, 'Men without *qaumi* will be imprisoned for life; those who have *qaumi* will be released'.

By the same token, fundamental to the idea of *wolus* is that all its members should stand together in confrontations with outsiders. As mentioned above, Maduzai often say, 'The people's strength is God's strength (Pa. *da wolus zor da khuday zor*); one person, however clever, can do nothing if the *wolus* stands together.' This power of a *wolus* stems not only from its potential as a fighting unit, but also from its ability to collect large sums of money for the bribery of officials, compensation for injury or other expenses. A *wolus* is defined by locality and by political effectiveness, which is in turn determined by size, wealth and charismatic leadership.

Clearly the way the concepts *aulad*, *tayfa*, *qaum* and *wolus* combine to express all levels of social grouping among Durrani creates and supports the ideal of the unity of the ethnic group as a whole and the equality of all its members. Given the multiplicity of referents for these terms, it is not surprising that Durrani insist that, within the ethnic group, there is complete freedom of marriage choice and that named subdivisions (e.g. tribes and subtribes) are considered simply irrelevant for the purposes of marriage.

Such notions are reinforced by the wider cultural background, which includes the Durrani understanding of the Islamic precept of the status equality of partners to a marriage, and by other aspects of Durrani culture. Particularly important among these is the Durrani use of the concepts 'near' (Pa. *nazhde*) and 'far' (Pa. *lare*) to discuss social distance (see also pp. 94, and 193). Thus two parties may be near or distant *qaum*, or these adjectives may refer to differences in custom or wealth or to the geographical distance between them. The many kinds of distance subsumed in the term 'far' ultimately imply each party's ignorance of the other's circumstances, which may jeopardize both the spouses' and their agnates' relations with each other. People who are judged distant are unlikely to be given women in marriage (indeed, a woman married into a geographically and socially distant group may even be said to be 'without *qaum*') and, in practice, as we shall see, there is a strong tendency to local group endogamy.

At the local level, the notions of *aulad*, *qaum* and *wolus* are used to characterize the empirical grouping of Durrani into subtribes; however the unity of a subtribe is not of a moral or corporate nature but contextual and transactional. One of the striking features of Durrani social organization is the strong ideal of the independence and self-sufficiency of households and the very real degree of competition between them. The constant competition between households of kin and neighbours focuses on the successful demonstration of control of women as objects of exchange and as reproductive resources. It is the nature of women's agnatic ties and their role in procreation which defines many aspects of this control.

Gender stereotypes, women's agnation and the ban on hypogamy

Among Durrani, gender roles are not seen as discrete or complementary, and both men and women emphasize the superiority of men over women (see also p. 209). Generally men are said to be 'authentic' and noble (*asl*) while women are imitations (*badal*) or imperfect (*kam asl*), though occasionally men and women remark with some surprise of some particularly, strong, resourceful woman that she is an *asl* woman. This dominant model and the consequent right of men to control women is justified almost entirely on religious grounds.

Both men and women describe women as foolish (without *akl*, see pp. 15, 209) and their supposed helplessness and fearful attitude to life are explicitly thought to be disabling, while their bodily functions make them unclean. Such stereotypes are the stuff of everyday conversation: they are reinforced by a variety of beliefs in the unnatural and demonic potential of women and by taboos which associate women's possession by jinn spirits with the power to kill young children and animals. For all these reasons women are said to be 'without religion'; this is particularly evident in sexual matters where women, because they are inhabited by devils and evil spirits, are both temptresses and easily tempted. Though women may pray in private, they are excluded from the mosque and virtually all other orthodox religious activities – a fact which is accepted by both men and women as a consequence of their ungodly nature. As women are held to be naturally inferior to men, so the statuses they occupy are dependent on men. Such ideas are used to justify the literal powers of life and death a household head has over the women of that household as well as to debar women from all formal control of produce and capital goods.

However this view of women, which is consistent with Durrani insistence that all property and status are transmitted patrilineally, is modified by considerations which relate to women as agnates. In practical terms this aspect of women's status is very limited, but it is sufficient to account for the ban on hypogamy (cf. Barth 1962: 138).

Though affective ties may continue, a woman's agnates relinquish virtually all practical rights and responsibilities towards her after her marriage to such an extent that even ideal statements about the residual rights and duties of agnates are extremely vague and contradictory. However, such ideal statements suggest that a woman's agnates may bear some responsibility for her behaviour, for example if she commits murder, but only by default, because at such a juncture her husband can in theory simply divorce her. Equally some Durrani hold that a woman's agnates have some right to compensation if she herself is murdered by her husband or his kin. However, such evidence as we have suggests that such residual responsibility and right to compensation are only very rarely, if ever, exercised in practice. Rather, in such extreme cases the response of a woman's agnates will be guided by expediency and their actions based on the notion that a woman's life is worth less than a man's and that the latter should never be jeopardized by the former.

In effect a man is responsible for the behaviour of his unmarried sisters and daughters, his mother and his wife, rather than his married sisters and daughters. *Namus* is the term often used to refer to a man's ability to control these women, while a variety of other terms from the vocabulary of honour and shame refer to the woman's own reputation: a woman's honour seems to be a quality attached to the woman herself, vested in gender and not agnation, and is transferred with her at marriage.

However, a woman's connections with her agnatic kin are never completely severed. After marriage her tribal identity continues to be that of her natal group and, after her death, it is the right of her closest kin to repossess her body for burial. This latter right is at first puzzling, particularly as there are no compelling affective or religious reasons why a woman should be buried beside her own agnates rather than with her children. Rather, it is best understood as the final ritual episode of a marriage (Barth 1959: 39; cf. Bourne 1966).

The ascendancy of wife-takers is a possible interpretation of all brideprice marriages, an interpretation which is reinforced by the absence of divorce, the practice of virilocality, and the fact that wife-takers are in a much stronger position than wife-givers to ignore the affinal links between them because they have no affective ties with members of the other household. Nonetheless in marriages between Durrani households, the inequality implicit in brideprice marriages (which account for 80 per cent of all marriages) is contradicted by the general idea of Durrani equality. The contradiction, which is used to determine the relative position of households within a community, is formally resolved, and equality between the two households is restored, when a woman's closest agnates reassert their control over her and reclaim her body. In other words, though the practical importance of the agnatic ties of a woman is minimized after her marriage, the notion of patrilineal descent remains unambiguous and ascriptive and women, like men, are born and die members of a named agnatic group.

A further aspect of the status of Durrani women is that they are superior to both men and women of other ethnic groups. For Durrani the most cogent demonstration of this point is their refusal to give women in marriage as compensation for the Durrani murder of a non-Durrani man. Since patrilineality is a fundamental principle determining tribal identity (and underwriting the assertion of the equality of all Durrani) a man who gave his daughter to a non-Durrani would place her and himself in an inferior position *vis-à-vis* his non-Durrani affines and he would thus automatically bring into question Durrani assertions of the superiority of the ethnic group as a whole. It follows that hypogamy is severely proscribed and in theory collective sanctions should serve to remove any offenders from the Durrani community: the woman should be killed and her family ostracized and expelled. The ban on hypogamy is very nearly realized in practice. However, while all the few breach cases we heard of caused great consternation, these sanctions were not uniformly applied (see p. 222).

The ban on hypogamy resolves two practical issues also related to the agnatic ties of women which would threaten Durrani control of productive resources. Women cannot dispose of any produce or capital goods of the household in which they are living, including items from their trousseau. Moreover, though a woman's right in Islamic law to inherit as a daughter and a wife is acknowledged, women do not exercise their right, nor do the men (normally brothers or sons) who inherit in their place feel any debt to them. In effect women cannot directly alienate resources from their families of either birth or marriage. And yet Durrani are well aware that this is contrary to the religious precepts accepted by rival ethnic groups and upheld in local courts.

This situation constitutes both an ideological and a practical dilemma for which no simple resolution is possible. But, by defining the ethnic boundary in terms of the control of women, Durrani partly resolve the problem. The existence and rare use of severe collective sanctions, and the frequent and emphatic insistence by both men and women that Durrani never give daughters or sisters to men of other ethnic groups, make literally unthinkable the fact that if Durrani women did marry such men then their husbands could gain control of property legally due to the women.

The procreative role of women
Alongside Durrani notions of patrilineality and the male role in procreation there exists an alternative set of ideas which ascribe importance to the procreative role of women. These ideas are a key to Durrani attitudes to hypergamy; they also play a part in the practical reactions of Durrani to breaches of the ban on hypogamy.

Durrani men and women admit that some personal traits may be transmitted through women: indeed, it is sometimes said, 'women are the source of descent (*nasab*)'. The exact nature of the procreative roles of both women and men is undefined and there is little elaboration of a biological model for either. The men's role is associated with semen, the 'seed' of the child, and also with the transmission of identity through the blood of the veins (*rag*). The woman's contribution is based largely on ideas of propinquity. Indeed, Durrani consider that the woman who carries a child in her womb for nine months has a far greater part in forming its personality than the father whose brief role in intercourse cannot, they argue, be of great significance in this respect. And women also stress their role in the socialization of children. However, women too may transmit certain characteristics and personality traits through the blood of the veins (see p. 57). The only other means by which women are considered to transmit status is through their milk. This idea is related to the Islamic proscription of marriage between 'milk-siblings', but we learned of only one case in which the notion was used to explain the social identity and position of a Durrani individual (see p. 70).

In practice, the male role in procreation is always assumed to be primary and ideas of the woman's role exist almost entirely as a secondary elaboration to cater for inequalities between male agnates. Women become scapegoats for the failings of men and only rarely is their role associated with a man's or a household's success. However this latter association remains a possibility (there are a number of aphorisms and moral tales told about how a household's survival and success depend on the quality of its women) and makes ideas about the role of women in procreation plausible. The way and the extent to which women pass on personal traits to their offspring affect marriage choice both within the ethnic group and between ethnic groups.

In theory, the patrilineal principle and religious ideals make all Durrani equally acceptable as marriage partners. Actual choices are made in terms of the personal characteristics of the principals as well as the social distance between their households. However, only the wealthiest and most powerful men can afford to choose and win for themselves or members of their household wives who approximate ideal standards. Only if a man has made several satisfactory marriages for members of his household, and has sufficient means, will he be in a position to marry for love and take for himself an attractive woman regardless of the economic and political standing of her natal household.

The point of view of men marrying daughters is somewhat different and they aspire to find them spouses from households which are economically or politically equal or superior to their own. This generalized preference also includes the possibility of the marriage of Durrani women to men of local Pashtu-speaking Sayyid lineages – the only acceptable marriage for Durrani women outside the ethnic group. With all such marriages a man hopes to secure his daughter's personal happiness and to form a useful and prestigious relationship with his affines.

Poor households are least likely to conform to these two ideal perspectives on marriage choice. The very poorest people in the community are often refugees from other regions who lack any 'close' relations locally with kin or others; not only do they give their women to 'strangers' in the hope of making friends of these affines and achieving some economic and political equality with them, but they also marry only the least attractive of neighbouring women.

The usual attitude of participants to any marriage is that it is the most advantageous transaction they can manage at the time. Though the parties to a marriage between Durrani households are ideally (and, in so far as the affinal ties are imbued with any importance, in practice) in a relation of equality, because participants on either side of any marriage focus on its positive advantages for them, all marriages can also be seen as 'hypergamous'.

Thus a poor man who takes an unattractive wife for the sake of potential ties with his affines emphasizes these latter aspects of the marriage and will ignore the risk that his children may suffer from traits inherited from their mother. His point of view is considered realistic given the importance of progeny and the relative unimportance of the traits which may be passed on by a woman. Equally, a wealthy man who marries an attractive woman from a poor household will disregard the claims his affines may try to make on him and emphasize the importance of having a good woman in his household. Again his point of view is considered reasonable; it is not difficult for a wealthy man to take a very cavalier attitude to his affines or, indeed, to disregard them totally. The Durrani attitude to the marriage of Durrani women to men of established families of Sayyids is seen simply as an extension of the criteria related to marriage choice within the ethnic group. The high religious status of the Sayyids will be entered into the equation along with other relevant considerations of social distance, including that determined by relative wealth, and the personal characteristics of the principals. In other words, the marriage of a Durrani woman to a Sayyid is treated as of the same order as a marriage within the group. All Durrani households aspire to marry their women to superiors, but superiority is judged in such a way that the ethnic superiority of Sayyids is not seen by the Durrani as in itself a sufficient reason for giving women to Sayyids.

Participants will view the choice of marriage partner as the best possible arrangement at the time. For outsiders, however, the fact of the marriage itself, and all the elements it involves, may say a great deal about the standing and future prospects of the households concerned, both *vis-à-vis* each other and *vis-à-vis* other households in the community. Marriage is itself perhaps the most significant factor in the upwards or downwards mobility of a household as well as the most important signal of changes in household status related to other areas of social life.

The implications of hypergamy

The nature of women's role in procreation has the same implications for 'hypergamy' within the group as for marriages between Durrani men and women of 'inferior' ethnic groups. First, simply because they are agnatic members of non-Durrani groups, such women are automatically held to be inferior to Durrani women. It is assumed that marriage with a non-Durrani woman will be injurious to a man's posterity. Ideally a Durrani man who is reasonably well-off will never marry a non-Durrani woman who might 'ruin his pedigree' (*pusht*, literally, 'back'); though the practice, which accounts for 10 per cent of all men's marriages, is rationalized in individual cases by the desire of a man to marry and father sons and his inability to find a suitable Durrani bride. A man 'forced' to take a non-Durrani bride may lose status as a consequence, but there are no collective sanctions against his action. He jeopardizes only the character of his direct descendants, and that only to a degree, since the importance of patrilineality in determining social identity takes precedence over all other considerations.

Children of such a union are not ordinarily stigmatized – their social identity is unambiguously that of their Durrani father, but it said they are liable to be quarrelsome, and to behave in the 'short-sighted' way typical of non-Durrani. If they are this way, people will laugh and say, 'After all, the mother was not Durrani; one vein is fallen.' Or, the children of mixed marriages may be described as hybrids (*du-raga*, literally, 'two-veined', the term used for hybrid animals as well), and sometimes a whole lineage descended from a union between a Durrani man and a non-Durrani woman may be so characterized. Such explanations are usually offered only when a household or larger group of agnates descended from such a union is, for whatever reason, weak and becoming weaker.

The degree to which the rule of endogamy is observed by the Maduzai is shown in Table 3. Ninety per cent of marriages made by core-lineage men were with women of Durrani or equal (Sayyid) status; 98 per cent of marriages of core-lineage women were with men of Durrani or equal status. The table also shows that in Lineage C, the group studied most intensively, the rate of Durrani endogamy has not changed significantly over the last generation: for men from 84 per cent to 86 per cent, for women from 99 per cent of 97 per cent.

Though hypergamy does occur in 10 to 15 per cent of men's marriages, the circumstances are such that the ethnic boundary is not blurred. Many of the practical consequences of hypergamous marriages can be avoided. I have mentioned that it is easy for the wife-taker to eschew all affinal ties; this is particularly true when a Durrani marries hypergamously, for he almost invariably takes a woman from a household of low socio-economic standing both within its own group and in comparison with his own. Only very rarely do economic or political advantages derive from an association with non-Durrani affines; most often such links are only tenuously maintained by Durrani and certainly involve no more than the immediate families in any social contacts. Moreover Durrani suppress as completely as possible the culture of the non-Durrani bride in favour of Durrani values, life-style and Pashtu language.

Table 3. *Durrani endogamy among the Maduzai*

	Marriages of men		Marriages of women	
	Number	Per cent	Number	Per cent
All core-lineages, 1972				
With Durranis or equals	223	89.6	204	98.1
With non-Durranis	26	10.4	4	1.9
Totals	249	100	208	100
Lineage C, 1950				
With Durranis or equals	61	83.6	68	98.6
With non-Durranis	12	16.4	1	1.4
Totals	73	100	69	100
Lineage C, 1972				
With Durranis or equals	94	86.2	91	96.8
With non-Durranis	15	13.8	3	3.2
Totals	109	100	94	100

The 1972 figures are for a total sample of all extant, completed marriages made by men and women belonging to the 177 households of the four Maduzai core-lineages. Data on marriages made by members of the other 95 households of the Maduzai subtribe are too few and scattered to be of any statistical use, but their omission makes the picture given in this and following tables slightly biased towards the kinds of marriages made by wealthier, more successful households. For Lineage C, the 1950 figures are again for a total sample of all marriages then extant and completed.

Men may marry hypergamously for a variety of reasons, not least the cheapness of non-Pashtun brides, but such marriages are sometimes quoted as further evidence of Durrani superiority; the circular argument probably reflects the constant need to re-assert, at least in their own eyes, their superior ethnic status. The ban on hypogamy, on the other hand, is almost completely effective.

An origin myth

The assumptions which lie behind the normative rules related to inter-ethnic marriage are rarely elaborated by the Durrani but are most often simply stated as categorical absolutes. Contradictions implicit in the structure of these rules are not explored but simply illustrated by supposedly contemporary anecdotes of the doings of remote Durrani groups. There is no consistency sought between the different and often contradictory morals of these stories (see N. Tapper 1979: 430ff.). However, one story about inter-ethnic marriage was of a rather different order and had the character of a brief origin myth. It is exceptional and of particular interest not only because it allows certain subtribes of the Ishaqzai Durrani tribe to claim quasi-Sayyid descent, but because of its bearing on Durrani ideas on hypogamy and the role of women in descent.

Our informant, a prominent Khan of the Babakzai subtribe, traced his own pedigree through ten generations until he reached his Sayyid ancestor, Sayyid Abu Muslim-i Bukhari.

Sayyid Abu Muslim was one of the Quraish Arabs who lived in Bukhara until the rule of the tyrant king Hujaj. As a result of a deadly quarrel with the king, Abu Muslim fled south to Kandahar with many of his kinsmen. Soon after this a Durrani tribesman in Kandahar named Ishaq quarrelled with his own wife Hawa and swore that he would divorce her if he did not find another wife by sundown. At dusk it seemed that he had failed to make another marriage, when Mandin, one of the Sayyid women, came to Ishaq and said that, to prevent him divorcing Hawa, she would marry him but that she would not sleep with him. Ishaq married Mandin but when, in spite of her wish, he tried to sleep with her, he found himself impotent, for she was one of the Prophet's descendants. Some time after this, Ishaq gave two granddaughters, the children of Hawa's son Idi, to the sons of Abu Muslim's own grandson, Sayyid Joghadar. It is from these unions that the Mandinzai branch of the Ishaqzai tribe descend. The Mandinzai are Ishaqzai through their mothers, but Sayyid on their father's side, while the Hawazai branch of the tribe are Ishaqzai on both sides.

The story of Mandinzai origins is particularly telling in the way it deals with (a) the status of Sayyids *vis-à-vis* Durrani; (b) the ideals and practices regarding hypogamous marriage; and (c) the question of the mother's role in a system based on the principle of strict patrilineal descent. In mythic fashion the story seems to attempt a resolution of these various issues. In spite of the higher status of the

Figure 1 An origin myth

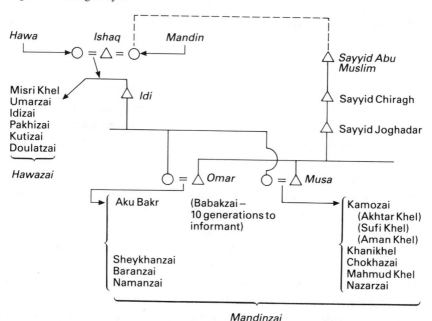

Sayyids, it is one of them, Mandin, who initiates contact with 'the Ishaqzai' and it is her name which is commemorated in the Durrani tribal lists. The Sayyid Mandin marries the Durrani Ishaq hypogamously to prevent a divorce – divorce being a most reprehensible act in religious terms. The marriage is not consummated because of Mandin's Sayyid origin, and two Durrani women are given to re-establish the hierarchical relation between the groups. Yet an equality between them is also recognized: the descendants of Sayyid Joghadar forego their right to claim Sayyid status, presumably because true Sayyids can only descend from a marriage of a Sayyid man *and* a Sayyid woman, and trace nominal descent to Ishaq, who is thus compensated for his barren marriage to Mandin. The Mandinzai are not Sayyids, but, compared with other Ishaqzai, they can claim a kind of special religious status. The story also implies a political dependence of the Sayyids on the Ishaqzai, which in practice is not unusual given the scattering of Sayyid households throughout Durrani territory; it also suggests the possibility of an historical assimilation via uxorilocal marriage of Sayyid migrants to the Ishaqzai polity in Kandahar.

Hypogamy

The origin myth suggests indirectly something of the contradiction between ascribed religious status and patrilineality on the one hand and the economic and political realities of inter-ethnic relations on the other; the theoretical importance of a woman's status and role in the resolution of such a contradiction is also clear. However, the kinds of resolutions which are effected in practice are best illustrated by contemporary case histories. Only four of the 208 extant marriages of the women of the core lineages of the Maduzai are hypogamous. Because these cases are unusual, both in their statistical rarity and in the extent to which they diverge from the strongly expressed ban on such unions, they are presented in some detail.

The first case, that of Kaftar's elopement with a Shi'i Hazara, was wholly exceptional and, as far as other Durrani men and women were concerned, represented an incomprehensible breach of the absolute rule which defined Durrani identity. The elopement provoked an extreme reaction among the Maduzai and provided us with a clear demonstration of the point beyond which Durrani will not compromise on issues of ethnicity.

By contrast, in none of the other three cases was there, in the first instance, any deliberate decision taken to marry a woman hypogamously. Rather each marriage occurred in the aftermath of a scandal and served, at the cost of dishonouring the woman's guardian, to resolve a dispute between agnates. These latter three cases say perhaps less about the ban on hypogamy among the Durrani than they do about the extreme consequences of household weakness and the loss of control of household women to near agnates. This complex relationship between hypogamy and the strength and weakness of agnates is clear from the two cases presented in chapter 10 (see p. 228f.); details of the fourth case, Padshah and the Lodins, are given in detail in Tapper, N. & R. Tapper 1982.

Taken together the four cases reveal the extent to which the normative rules relating to ethnic boundaries are regarded as inviolate and unalterable or may be modified by pragmatic considerations such that there is an osmosis of personnel across them. They also illustrate two other important themes which will be discussed at greater length later on: the importance of treating any Durrani marriage as part of an historical sequence, and the need to understand the part played by both men and women in marriage choice. Thus, all four cases clearly illustrate the extent to which each marriage is determined both by those that have preceded it and by the anticipation of others to come. That is, each marriage is embedded in the particular social, and especially marital, histories of the households concerned. The four cases also illustrate the independent and sometimes 'subversive' role that Durrani women may play in the history of a household's marriages: in each of the four cases women, directly and indirectly, play active roles in precipitating the marriages which occur. In the case of Kaftar, her marriage was a result of her own deliberate choice and actions. In the case of Laljan, a young girl risked involvement in an illicit romance with an agnatic cousin which was discovered and eventually led to her marriage to an outsider. In the other two cases, women other than the ones who are eventually married hypogamously act in ways which their agnates and others deem scandalous and, ironically the Maduzai would say, one of the consequences of their behaviour is the marriage of some other Maduzai woman to a Parsiwan.

Case 1: Kaftar's elopement

In the summer of 1971 there took place a scandal which confirmed all the Maduzai's worst fears both about the nature of women and about the Shiʿi Hazaras, the most despised of ethnic groups. The Maduzai reaction to Kaftar's elopement, which was as swift and forceful as they could make, revealed in a most dramatic way the importance to them of the ban on hypogamy. In their comments and discussions at the time they expressed a great horror of all hypogamous marriage; however, as the other three case histories suggest, the intensity of the Durrani reaction to Kaftar's elopement seems to have been an expression of the particularly great social divide between the Durrani and those whom they called 'Uzbeks', and of the extent to which Kaftar's action revealed Durrani weakness *vis-à-vis* such people (see p. 90f.).

Toryaley, a wealthy man of Lineage A, was in the summer pastures in the Hazarajat with the other Maduzai camps when his former servant Sipahi, an Hazara, rode up from Saripul ostensibly to visit some of his relatives in the mountains. He stopped for a few nights with his former employer, then left. Toryaley's daughter Kaftar followed him that evening, wearing the Hazara clothing he had brought for her and taking with her a large amount of her father's money. In his shame Toryaley spent the next two days searching unsuccessfully for the runaways before he informed the Maduzai Khan and asked for help. The Khan was appalled, and at once mobilized fourteen armed and mounted men, who went off in pairs in all directions to search for the girl.

The Hazaras recognized the tremendous blow that had been scored against the Durrani and put as many obstacles as they could in the way of the search parties. For a month there was no definite news, then the couple, now properly married, were run to ground in the distant castle of an Hazara chief. The Maduzai negotiators would accept no compensation – four girls and some four lacs (400,000) of Afghanis (£2000) were said to have been offered – but demanded the return of Kaftar. They now claimed that she was already engaged to her FBS (a lie) and therefore by both Shiʿi and Sunni precepts she must be returned. Eventually bribes persuaded the chief to hand the couple over to the local gendarme Commandant, but the Hazara people would not allow it and attacked the party as they left the castle. The girl was recovered by the Hazaras, and the Commandant severely wounded; the case now went to Kabul. Throughout the winter the Maduzai leaders, including the Khan, stayed in the capital trying to negotiate government action to secure the girl's return.

While all the Saripul Durrani felt themselves threatened by the elopement, none gave the Maduzai more than moral support, and actual financial help and political action were left to the Maduzai subtribe alone. The Maduzai talked of rousing all the Durrani in a general war against the Hazaras, but this was much less realistic than reports that the Hazaras had raised enormous amounts of money, far more than the Maduzai could hope to match alone, in order to secure government non-intervention in the case. Whatever happened in the short term, the Maduzai insisted that ultimately they would get Kaftar back. When they did so, they said, they would make an example of her by shooting her in front of all the women of the subtribe. Meanwhile, almost as soon as news of Kaftar's elopement broke, men of the subtribe, afraid for their own honour, began to marry off their engaged daughters and to seek engagements for the rest.

Toryaley remained in Kabul throughout the winter, returning home only to collect more funds to pursue the case. People said that by the summer of 1972 he had got through two brideprices (two lacs of Afghanis) and that he had sold all his sheep and mortgaged his land. As one young man said: 'People have been shamed. And Toryaley has eaten much shame and his name has become bad. He cannot even look a small boy in the face. The big camel has fallen down.'

People said that, though Toryaley's household will not be forced to leave the subtribe, nonetheless, even if Kaftar is recovered, the family has been ruined and may leave the area out of shame. A year after the elopement Toryaley's household remained completely incommunicado, even to the extent that they had failed to recover loans of domestic goods. We were told,

Now if a person is a long way from their tent, and if the women see that person from a long distance, they will put down the flaps of the tent from shame. People laugh at them and say, 'Look at that daughter of Toryaley, she ran off with an Hazara.' An Afghan [Durrani] is lost on account of her; she should have taken an Afghan husband, was the Afghan bad? Didn't the Afghans have enough wealth? If she is an Afghan she should have taken an Afghan. Were the Afghans so few? She has gone, gone with an Hazara. In this way it is very, very bad. Only the poorest man would marry one of Toryaley's remaining daughters. No one else. Everyone would ridicule him endlessly, saying 'Your sister-in-law has fled, and tomorrow your wife will be off with someone else.'

In fact a youth from one of the poorest households of the subtribe did marry one of Toryaley's remaining five daughters in the spring of 1972. I was told that the wedding was a very small one and that the guests laughed when the groom, snatching the bridal veil from his wife's face as she left her father's house, said 'How dare you have shame?'

Toryaley was widely condemned – by other Sunnis as well as by the Durrani. For example, he was much criticized for allowing his daughters to reach puberty unengaged. And Kaftar, who had, incomprehensibly, run away with a Shiᶜite Hazara, was also damned. People could understand, though not condone, the depth of Toryaley's shame which caused him to delay two valuable days before summoning help in his search. And even the Maduzai acknowledged that if Sipahi had been an Aymak or an Uzbek it would not have been so bad. They noted that at least such people are Sunnis, co-religionists of the Maduzai, and that, per-haps, compensation in women and money might have been made acceptable from them. In any case, people observed, such ethnic groups would not have been able to put up such a show of force as had the Hazaras. Durrani were forced to accept that the Hazara treated the elopement as a coup against Durrani hegemony and had effectively united to thwart Durrani action. To this end it was even said that the Hazara in Afghanistan had received large sums of money from Shiᶜite sympathizers in Iran.

Discussions of the case often ended with the wry observation that Sipahi not only spoke fluent Pashtu, but he even looked just like a Durrani and could be mis-taken for one by anyone who did not know better. The irony of Sipahi's fluency in Pashtu and his Pashtun appearance was one of the only areas of ambiguity in the case of Kaftar's elopement. Sipahi's personal qualities notwithstanding, the moral issues of the case were, for Durrani, clearcut and not open to compromise of any kind.

By contrast, the other three case histories, while still embarrassing to Maduzai informants, suggest ways in which the Durrani perception of the ethnic boundary between themselves and Parsiwans can, by dint of *ex post facto* argument, be fudged for reasons of political expediency. In this respect these cases tell us a great deal about the nature of interethnic politics in Afghan Turkistan and the political role of marriage among Durrani themselves. They also suggest the structural amnesia at work: the women given in 'hypogamous' marriages were socially disregarded by the Maduzai and their marriages were well on the way to being literally forgotten. I have no doubt that the history of other such marriages has been lost in the same way.

The limits of ethnic tolerance

Ideologically, the ban on hypogamy is very important. Nonetheless, it is of considerable interest that in the three extant cases of marriage between Maduzai women and Parsiwan men, the application of sanctions against the offenders was tempered by pragmatic considerations of an economic and political kind. As suggested in chapter 3, the economic and cultural similarities between Parsiwans and Durrani virtually preclude the establishment of an ascriptive boundary between them on grounds other than descent and marriage. But equally, their very similarity means that competition between them for the control of resources is likely to involve women, not least because marriage expenses are a major factor in the economic calculations of both groups and both use the idioms of brideprice and sister exchange to express relationships of status equality and inequality. Thus for the Durrani, marriages with Parsiwans are a real possibility and it is against this possibility that the symbolic barrier of proscription – the ban on hypogamy – is most intense. A few such marriages occur, but almost inadvertently by way of resolving problems which concern Durrani alone. In such cases, intra-ethnic issues are given priority over inter-ethnic ones.

It is also the case that other ethnic groups in the area are much more remote from the Durrani culturally than are the Parsiwans, and though the ban on marriage with 'Uzbeks' was fundamental from the Durrani point of view, it was, until the extraordinary case of Kaftar's elopement, simply taken for granted. Indeed, such a ban was made more or less irrelevant in this context by the 'Uzbeks'' own conception of the institution of marriage. Marriage does not appear to have the same economic importance for most people of the 'Uzbek' groups as it does for Durrani (and Parsiwan): brideprices are considerably lower (both absolutely and in relation to wealth); a woman is not so completely alienated from her natal family at marriage, she commonly takes her share of the patrimony; and her agnates retain residual rights in, for example, her remarriage as a widow. Moreover, though 'Uzbeks' too prefer to marry endogamously, they do not have the same strongly sanctioned ban on the inter-ethnic marriage of women as do Durrani. Thus, for a variety of reasons, marriage is not apparently used by 'Uzbeks' as a major idiom of political competition. When Durrani find themselves involved in a confrontation with 'Uzbeks' (a rare occurrence for ordinary Durrani tribesmen), its resolution is most unlikely to involve Durrani women or to cause one of them to be married hypogamously. 'Uzbek' values themselves, and the Durrani stereotypes of the various ethnic groups they subsume under this label, include so many major points of difference that it is more or less inconceivable that a Durrani woman would marry an 'Uzbek' man.

The cases of Maduzai hypogamy make it clear that marriage is an integral part of on-going political relations at all levels of social organization from the household to the ethnic group, and that marriage and political activity are inextricably linked in Durrani thought.

Where competition for productive resources is severe, symbolic arguments are likely to proliferate. However, for Muslims there are few legitimate criteria which can be used to create and support inequality. Thus the equality of all Muslims is a fundamental tenet of Islam generally and as it is understood locally in northern Afghanistan. Taken alone, it clearly cannot be used to differentiate ethnic groups in the area. However, Durrani, like Muslims elsewhere, elaborate three further basic elements in Islam which contradict the first and create a hierarchy of believers. These three are 1) the sectarian differences between Sunni and Shi'i Muslims and the various kinds of formal distinctions made between Muslim believers and non-Muslims; 2) the metonymy of a sacred genealogy; and 3) distinctions based on gender categories. The Durrani have elaborated all three of these elements to create and legitimize their perception of a hierarchy of ethnic groups, and to facilitate their own ethnic unity and its concomitant political advantages. Thus, distinctions based on religious status and patrilineality establish all Durrani as equals and as superior to members of other ethnic groups except Sayyids, descendants of the Prophet. Distinctions based on gender establish women as naturally inferior to men and subject to their control. The first two of these elements define the Durrani group, but they make no allowance for the unequal control of resources among Durrani, nor can they be used to manage the economic and political competition between Durrani and members of other ethnic groups. It is the third element, the set of ideas relating to the agnatic control of women and women's role in procreation, which offers a means by which Durrani men may create and express inequality among themselves and also a means by which the boundary between the Durrani ethnic group and others may be adjusted to fit economic and political realities.

As we have seen, Durrani ethnic identity is defined principally in terms of ascription by descent and the observance of the ban on hypogamy. Within the Durrani ethnic group, on the other hand, there is an absence of formal differentiation by descent or marriage rules. A strong egalitarian ethic pervades Durrani social organization, corresponding with religious ideals. No intrinsic social differences are admitted among Durrani, who are all held to be equal by virtue of common descent. 'We are Durrani, one people between whom women are exchanged.' And Durrani will not admit to a preference for any social category of bride or groom other than 'Durrani'.

For many Durrani in Saripul their ability to approximate these ideals has changed dramatically in recent decades. Settlement and the increasing importance of the control of farmland have led directly to the development of class divisions, while the expansion of the local government bureaucracy and the increasing influence of Khans over the settlers have made political inequality an established fact of life. Strong tendencies to endogamy are evinced by lineages, local groups and socio-economic strata, while the egalitarian ethic has been transformed into ideals of household independence and self-sufficiency, adherence to which is expressed at the local level through marriage and in a highly competitive form of *laissez-faire* capitalist political economy.

5

The Maduzai subtribe

Most disputes within a subtribe are economic in origin, but contested claims and political competition for the control of resources most often emerge in the context of marriage. The central role of marriage becomes clear in the following account of the history and social organization of the Maduzai subtribe. This discussion provides the necessary background for a detailed discussion of the subtribe and patterns of marriage choice.

The history of the Maduzai subtribe
Today the Maduzai subtribe occupies two substantial village settlements known as Chinar and Sinjit, and various smaller scattered hamlets and camps, of which the largest is Naju (see Map 3 and Table 4). The settlements are some fifteen kilometres north of Saripul on tracks to the east of the main dirt road between Shiberghan and Saripul. Officially the whole collection is called Chinar, comprising Upper Chinar, Middle Chinar and Lower Chinar. Maduzai themselves refer to these settlements as Chinar, Sinjit and Naju respectively and I will use these latter names here – not only are they less confusing but they are indicative of divisions within the subtribe which are ignored in the official village names. The Maduzai Khan, Purdil, lives in Chinar and is the official headman of that village and Naju; Sinjit has its own official headman, Hajji Ibrahim.

The Maduzai subtribe is of heterogeneous composition. A census taken in the summer of 1972 showed a total of 272 households (about 1,900 souls) living in the Maduzai settlements acknowledging the Khan's leadership, but only 92 household heads (of Lineages A and B) are generally recognized to be the descendants of Madu. Another 85 household heads (those of Lineages C and D) are generally suspected to be of other origins, but they claim to be a part of the Maduzai core with equal rights to those of Lineages A and B. The remaining 95 households come from a wide variety of tribal and ethnic divisions. The whole subtribe, in most contexts and especially in confrontations with outsiders, is

Table 4. *Maduzai residence (see also Table 2)*

	Chinar			Sinjit	Naju	Sarwar Khel	Lodin	Other	Totals
	(A)	(Tutizai)	(D)						
Core lineage households									
Lineage A	49	0	0	0	13	8	7	0	77
Lineage B	0	15	0	0	0	0	0	0	15
Lineage C	1	0	0	63	5	0	0	1	70
Lineage D	0	0	7	5	3	0	0	0	15
Client households									
Collateral Maduzai	10	0	1	1	10	0	1	1	24
Other Durrani	16	0	2	11	26	0	1	0	56
Non-Durrani	2	0	1	6	6	0	0	0	15
Totals	78	15	11	86	64	8	9	2	272
		104							

termed a *wolus*; at the same time, the two major settlements tend to be known respectively as the Chinar *wolus* and the Sinjit *wolus* (see also p. 000).

Early history

In the nineteenth century, the Maduzai lived in Nauzad, Bagni and Dara Mian in the region of Kandahar, where they seem to have operated a dual economy, being pastoralists themselves but owning some agricultural land. Around the middle of the century, they suffered a severe drought: both parts of the economy were disrupted when the underground irrigation channels dried up, and it was then, people say, that the Maduzai became scattered. Members of Lineage C claim that at this time they were separated from the main group of the Maduzai and became clients of the Khan Khel or chiefly clan of the Ishaqzai tribe. This separation, if indeed it occurred, threw doubt on the later Lineage C claims to Maduzai ancestry: others suspect the lineage of Parsiwan origins, saying they were actually servants of the Ishaqzai chiefs who rewarded their loyal service by 'making them Durrani'. Behind their backs they are referred to as 'the Torabi', a name which (lacking a -*zai* suffix) strongly resembles those of many Parsiwan groups; in fact, they too use the name privately among themselves.

Certainly either the Torabi alone, or possibly a larger group of Maduzai, were closely identified with the Ishaqzai Khan Khel in the latter decades of the last century, and in this way became acquainted with Taju Khan Ishaqzai, the man directly responsible for the organization of the first Durrani migration to Turkistan in 1888. Later, around 1900, one of Taju Khan's affines, Seyf Akhundzada of the Nazarzai branch of the Ishaqzai tribe, settled in the Saripul area. The present-day Ishaqzai Khans of Saripul are his descendants. Maduzai today say that before his own move northward Seyf Akhundzada had acted as Mullah to one of the leading men of the Maduzai *tayfa*, a collateral kinsman of the Lineage A ancestors. Through these connections the Saripul area became known to the Maduzai, and when, in the early years of the twentieth century,

Map 3 Maduzai settlements in the Saripul valley

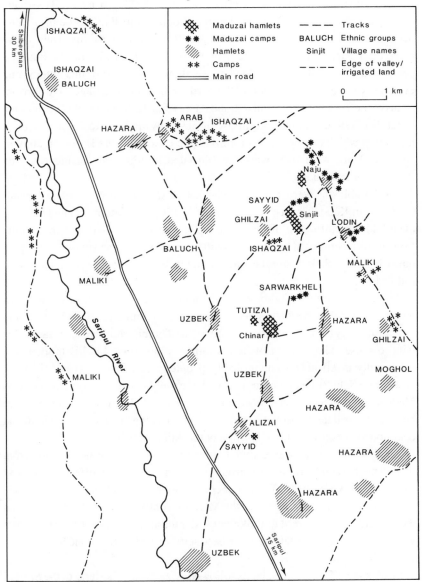

another drought struck their homeland and famine conditions prevailed, some of the Maduzai were persuaded to try their luck in the north.

Around 1913 Afzal Khan, paternal uncle of the present Maduzai Khan, visited the Saripul area; he returned home to Dara Mian intent on leading a Maduzai migration to the north. In the end his plan attracted followers from among the hardest hit of a number of different groups. Some 24 households of Lineage A and several households of their distant collaterals decided to follow Afzal Khan.

Then, to gain further followers for his expedition, Afzal Khan reunited his agnates with the Torabi group. To effect this end, Afzal Khan arranged two pairs of exchange marriages between the two groups, who thus 'through affinity became *qaum*'. In one of these exchanges, Afzal Khan gave his sister to and received a wife from one of the senior Torabi men, while for the other he persuaded some collaterals to do likewise, though only part of this latter group eventually joined the migration to the north. With these marriages, the Durrani status of the Torabi was recognized, and Afzal Khan further dispelled ideas of the Torabi's possible Parsiwan origins by successfully applying to the courts for an injunction which exempted them from the taxes which were levied on all non-Durrani. Thus the Torabi were (re-?)instated as Maduzai, an identity they strongly insist on today.

The Torabi, who were then twelve households, apparently owned no agricultural land in Kandahar (see N. Tapper 1979: 180, n. 10 and n. 11) and some of them had turned to long-distance trading to supplement their meagre income from pastoralism. Afzal Khan's proposition offered them security and the opportunity to revive their pastoral economy and it seems that all of them elected to follow him.

Associated with the Torabi were five households whose origins were even more dubious; they were the sons of Salu, who is admitted to have been 'found in a mosque' by the father of the ancestor of the Torabi, who gave the infant to his wife to nurse. The identity of Salu's father is unknown, but his mother was supposedly an Alizai Durrani; probably, people say, his father was an Alizai too. At any rate Salu 'became Durrani through the milk' and his *aulad* came north as Maduzai, and their descendants are now Lineage D. There were no marriages between these latter households and Afzal Khan's own lineage, though both had common affines in a group of Durrani of the Alikozai tribe.

Afzal Khan's party was completed by some twenty-five households from other Ishaqzai and Durrani tribal groups and from at least two different Parsiwan tribes, all of whom had affinal connections with the Maduzai. Some of their descendants continue to live near the Maduzai subtribe today, others continued their migration northward to Balkh but still intermarry with the Maduzai, while yet others only recently left the subtribe to settle on agricultural land in the north-east of the country.

In all, some 65 to 70 households followed Afzal Khan via Herat to the Saripul area and some 55 to 60 households remained under his leadership, forming a single settlement (cf. Table 4 and Figure 2). Some five years later, another leading man of Lineage A, Anwar, and his sons, joined the main group in Saripul, accompanied by some ten households and yet other distant collaterals. The latter are said to have been landless troublemakers, and after a murder about twenty

Figure 2 Skeleton genealogy of the Maduzai subtribe, c. 1920

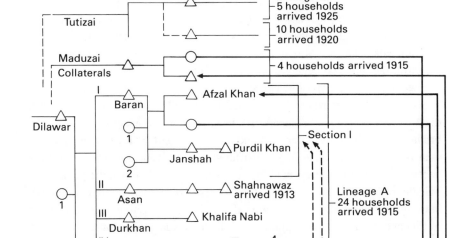

- - - Two pairs of exchange marriages within Lineage A.
——— Key marriages with Lineage C.c.1920.

years ago some of them fled the Saripul region. The four remaining households of this group nowadays call themselves Tutizai, although this identity is not recognized by the Tutizai of Lineage B and they are generally known as the *qaum* of Sadiq, their leading man.

Settlement in Turkistan

The first winter was spent near Imam Sahib Jafar, the settlement of Seyf Akhundzada's son Ghulam Rasul Khan, who was already established in 1907 as the official leader of the Saripul Durranis. Next year the group wintered near the present Maduzai valley lands, about 25 km southeast of Imam Sahib. These were then an uncultivated wilderness (*jangal*) abundant in thorn, while the nearby steppe pastures had been used only by a few Arab shepherds who fled from the new arrivals. The area was underpopulated, and land, water and food were plentiful: the Maduzai began to prosper. For many summers they continued to migrate to their former pastures in Band-i Bayan.

Soon after the Maduzai had established a pastoral base in the area, Afzal Khan died and was succeeded as head of Lineage A and the Maduzai by his half-brother, Janshah. In 1917 Janshah and his counterpart, Soleyman, the leading man of Lineage C (Torabi), were offered, very cheaply, 3,000 *jeribs* (600 hectares) of arable valley land by an Alizai Durrani remembered as 'the Tahsildar' (literally, the tax collector) who wished to return to Kandahar. Though initially there was little interest in this offer, Soleyman, together with Shahnawaz of Lineage A, urged its acceptance, and the land was bought for less than two Afghanis per *jerib*. With this land came rights in water from canals run from the Saripul River.

The Tahsildar provided deeds (*qawala*) for the land. These were reissued by Amir Amanullah's government in 1926–1927 and remain the basis of Maduzai landholding today. Of the 3,000 *jeribs*, the Tahsildar stipulated that 150 *jeribs* remain in the hands of the Uzbek farmers of a nearby hamlet who had treated him well when he had worked as their watermaster. The remaining 2,850 *jeribs* were divided into five equal shares of land and water rights and were distributed among five of the leading men of Lineages A and C. The five shares were each further divided and eventually parcels were distributed to all the households of Lineages A and C (see Table 5). Lineage D too received a quarter portion of one of the Lineage C shares, but none of the distant collaterals of Lineage A took part in the division, nor did any of the non-Maduzai members of the *wolus*.

This original land purchase and its distribution played a crucial role in defining relations within the subtribe. In essence, members of the *qaum* became landed proprietors while all others of the *wolus* became, to a greater or lesser degree, their clients (*hamsaya*). Further, incipient cleavages within the *qaum*, both between Lineage A and Lineages C and D, and also within Lineages A and C, were reified. Even more fundamentally, the tribesmen recognize the major difference as having come from the fact of landowning itself. As one man put it: 'In the old days there were no Khans and no inequality; such leaders as there were were called *malik* and were *khan bi-sterkhan* [literally Khans without cloths on which meals are served; that is, wealth and lavish hospitality played no part in the relations between a leader and his followers]. It was before people had land, and a man's opportunities were the same as his father's. Now land enters the question, and inheritance and power and wealth pass from father to son.'

Later other migrants joined the subtribe, and a number of large parcels of land elsewhere have since been acquired by individual Maduzai. Of the migrants, two more important groups were recruited by Janshah, who followed Afzal Khan's precedent of using exchange marriages to reunite distant kinsmen to gain supporters. This tactic has had a prominent place in the history of the subtribe and indeed is the principal means by which a leader may quickly increase the number of his followers. Leading men seek out and maintain contact with distant kin who might be amenable to such invitations offered for political reasons. Thus, even with the current over-population in the area, it is still considered possible that the households of Lineage A's collaterals who fled after a murder might be brought back to Saripul by the current Khan.

Earlier the same strategy was used to assimilate Lineage B to the Maduzai *wolus*. Lineage B are Tutizai, an established Maduzai branch, most members of which stayed in Kandahar. However, the five households who did come north arrived some time before the other Maduzai and lived for a number of years with Baluch nomads in the steppe west of the Saripul valley. In the 1920s Janshah sought out these distant kin and more or less forcibly persuaded them to settle in Chinar. To cement the alliance he arranged a pair of exchange marriages between his own closest agnates in Lineage A and members of Lineage B. Then, around 1930 other migrants arrived from the south: four households of the descendants of Osman, a half-brother of the founders of the agnatic groups which composed Lineage A (see Figure 4). This group is now known as Sarwar Khel after their leading man. Again exchange marriages with Janshah's own family were arranged, but in this case they were never completed and for many years the two groups quarrelled and several times the newcomers left the Saripul area. The complicated story of the political consequences of these exchange marriages is examined in detail elsewhere (see N. Tapper 1979: 348ff.), though it may be remarked here that the intransigent attitude of Sarwar Khel during this quarrel was said by the members of Lineage A to be the legacy of their Hazara ancestress, Dilawar's second wife.

Apart from the Saqawi Revolt in 1929, which in Saripul took the form of an interethnic war (see p. 34), the two decades following the Maduzai arrival in Turkistan were relatively uneventful. The traditional Maduzai summer pastures in the Band-i Bayan were abandoned for more accessible grazing, first in Kirman and then in Lal-o-Sarjangal; the Maduzai learned *karakul* sheep husbandry and in general their pastoral enterprises thrived in the conditions of abundant grazing which seem then to have existed.

Meanwhile, and at a pace which coincided with the increase in population in the Saripul area, the Maduzai began to farm their rich valley lands and to learn the techniques of intensive irrigated agriculture. Though Janshah had earlier occupied the Uzbek-style house (*gombad*) of the Alizai Tahsildar, only in the early 1930s were the first fixed dwellings built in the winter quarters by the same two men who had much earlier urged the purchase of the Tahsildar's land: first by Soleyman of Lineage C in what is now Sinjit and then by Shahnawaz of Lineage A in the present Chinar.

The Maduzai feud (*badi*)

In the spring of 1936 or 1937, as the Maduzai caravans were climbing towards the summer pastures in the Hazarajat, a quarrel erupted between shepherds whose flocks had become mixed in a narrow river gorge. The brothers Zahir and Qadir of Lineage A fought with the young Rishmin of Lineage C (see Figure 3). The latter was slightly injured and badly shaken. To make amends, the brothers carried Rishmin on one of the household camels to the next camping ground at Chiras.

Three of the Maduzai leaders, Rishmin's father's brother Adam, Zahir's own father Gulnur, and Janshah, the acknowledged head of all the Maduzai, were away on pilgrimage to Mecca. In their absence, Rishmin's father, Soleyman, was the only important leader present in camp. Soleyman wanted the whole matter settled peacefully, but his wife, a 'short-sighted woman of Parsiwan descent', called to her nephew Sherali: 'My son has been beaten and guns have been fired; it is women's work not to retaliate.' The hot-tempered Sherali, shamed by her cry, took his father's gun and mare, rode straight to where Zahir and his brothers were setting up camp and shot and wounded Qadir. Qadir's brothers soon recovered from their shock and tried to wrest Sherali's gun from his hands. Then someone hit him, and as he fell Zahir shot him dead.

Sultan, Sherali's elder brother, buried him while Lineage A moved their tents into a side valley some way from those of Lineage C. Then Sultan sent news to other households of Lineage C who were several migration stages away, but they were most reluctant to come. By the time they had arrived, Jallat Khan, one of the leading Ishaqzai Khans of Saripul, was already there.

Jallat Khan arranged that Sadozi, a sister of Zahir, be given to Ibrahim, Sherali's eldest son, and that Rabiya, the eldest daughter of Sherali's brother Sultan, should go to the wounded Qadir. Sadozi was married that same night. Her brother took her, with a few pieces of bedding, to Sultan's tent and the *nikah* marriage ceremony was performed for both girls, though Rabiya was still a small child and continued to live in her father's house.

Figure 3 Principals in the Maduzai feud

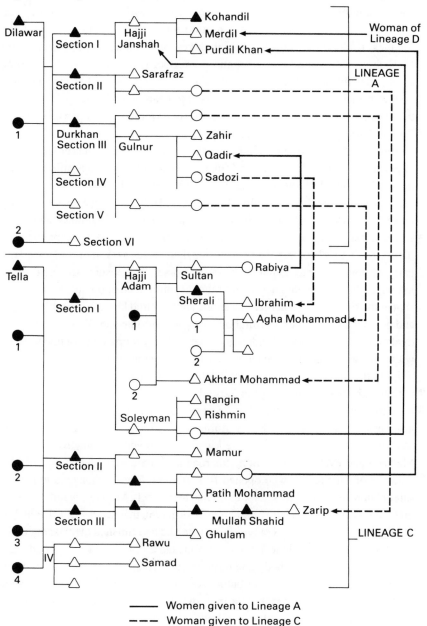

——— Women given to Lineage A
– – – Woman given to Lineage C

While the Maduzai were in the mountains the pilgrims returned from Mecca and were grief-stricken by what had occurred. Soleyman, angry that they had received only one woman in compensation for Sherali's death, insisted to the Maduzai leader, now Hajji Janshah, that they be given a second woman. Hajji Janshah in fact is said to have promised a further two women who were to be given when the nomads returned to the Saripul valley. When they arrived back, however, men of Lineage C were incensed to hear men of Lineage A boasting that they had killed a man and had paid only one woman in compensation to the Torabi 'Parsiwans' of Lineage C.

Sultan then spoke to some of his agnates and among other things promised one of his sisters in marriage to Patih Mohammad, a strong and determined young man, if he would kill Sherali's murderer, Zahir. Patih Mohammad agreed to do this and also swore that he would kill the sons of Hajji Janshah who were among those boasting most loudly. Some time later, Patih Mohammad and three cousins, Rangin, Ghulam and Samad, set off at night for a wedding party given for one of Zahir's brothers. They disguised themselves as women and joined the party, slipping out later to untie the guests' horses. The ensuing disturbance, as intended, drew the male guests out of the reception tent, and Patih Mohammad shot at the first man to emerge. The single shot he fired killed Kohandil outright and wounded his brother Merdil, both sons of Hajji Janshah. This action effectively united Lineage A behind their leader and they prepared for a major battle with Lineage C, although the latter were now more numerous.

Early the following morning, Mullah Shahid of Lineage C set out from Sinjit with his kinsman Mamur for the Saripul bazaar. A man of Lineage B warned them that late the night before there had been another killing, but they had heard nothing of it and disregarded the warning, saying that it was none of their business anyway as none of their close kin were involved. As they rode past the Maduzai graveyard halfway along the road to Chinar, they were ambushed by Sarafraz of Lineage A, who opened fire on them. Mamur managed to ride to safety but Mullah Shahid's horse stumbled and he fell. Mullah Shahid had been hit twice but he pleaded with Sarafraz not to kill him, that he was still alright, but Sarafraz told him to say his prayers and, when he had finished them, shot him in cold blood. With this all the members of Lineage C closed ranks: they collected Mullah Shahid's bloody body and posted guards round the tents of the lineage. Both sides prepared for a major battle. Abdul Ghafur Khan, the Ishaqzai chief who was at the time Governor of Saripul, swiftly intervened; on arrival at Chinar he arrested a large number of men of both sides and held them in prison until he had organized a *jirga* assembly of leading Pashtuns of the province some two months later.

Eight marriages were arranged between the two groups: in theory, one woman was given for each man wounded and two for each man killed, though in fact the following women were given (see Figure 3):

Lineage A (Qadir and Merdil wounded; Kohandil killed) received: Rabiya, brother's daughter of Sherali, for Qadir; a daughter of Soleyman for Hajji Janshah; a brother's daughter of Patih Mohammad for Purdil and a woman of Lineage D for Merdil, sons of Hajji Janshah.

Lineage C (Sherali and Mullah Shahid killed) received: Sadozi, a sister of Zahir for Ibrahim, the eldest son of Sherali; a father's brother's daughter of Zahir for Agha Mohammad, the second son of Sherali; a father's brother's daughter of Zahir for Akhtar Mohammad, a half-brother of Sherali; and a brother's daughter of Sarafraz for the young son of Mullah Shahid.

The circumstances of the feud marriages prefigured the subsequent relations between the two lineages. These marriages also provide clear examples of how marriage forms are manipulated for political ends.

As has been mentioned, the first two women were married the very night of Sherali's killing, but though one bride, Sadozi, was taken straightaway to live with her new husband, the other, Rabiya, was felt to be too young to move into her husband's household. The fact that such a young girl was married when there were a number of older and more eligible girls available was certainly calculated: the kin of Sherali were given a woman immediately for his death, while the wounded Qadir in effect accepted a smaller amount in compensation by agreeing to take a girl whom he was not to bring home for several years.

After two years of marriage Sadozi bore the first of many sons. She now insists that her marriage was an exchange with Sultan's daughter, Rabiya, who married her brother. This fiction is supported by the style of Rabiya's marriage. When Rabiya reached puberty, Qadir courted her and came to *bazi* and was well treated by Rabiya's mother who was anxious to help her daughter and reduce the bitterness between the two households. Moreover, Qadir's brothers put together a respectable brideprice of some 5,000 Afs. for her, and her own family prepared a trousseau (neither of which is normal for a 'feud-marriage'); the wedding itself was quite large 'with enough food for the dogs to eat'. Rabiya too was fertile, but like Sadozi she endured a loveless marriage. Both men, as soon as they were able, married second wives for love, and Rabiya suffered the further insult of being forced to share her living quarters with her co-wife.

After the further pair of killings in the valley, six more women were given in compensation. All three of the women given to Hajji Janshah's household, for the death and wounding of his sons, were married and taken to their husband's home on the night of the settlement itself. I know few details of the fate of these three women, though I think they were little happier than their counterparts married into Lineage C and, indeed, I was told that the nine-year-old son of one of them was accidentally killed by his father in a fury somehow connected with the feud.

Lineage C eventually received three women for Sherali's death. Sherali's sons were young at his death: his eldest son was still a boy when he married Sadozi;

the second son was only five or six years old, while the third son was not yet born. In the event, Sherali's second son and one of his young, unmarried brothers received the other two women in compensation, but their weddings did not occur until some years later. Their wives, like all the other women, were given 'free' in the feud, but, because it is shaming for any household to have to give a daughter 'for nothing', Sultan offered to pay brideprices for the two girls in hopes of reconciling all parties to the marriages. For one of them he paid some 7,000 Afs. to cover the cost of a respectable trousseau. In the second case, the husband had been courting and gone to *bazi* with his wife and she had become pregnant before the wedding; her father insisted that a *babirey* compensation be paid before he would let her go to her husband's house: Sultan paid some 5,000 Afs. in brideprice and gave her father an expensive gun worth a further 3,000 Afs. as *babirey* (see p. 164).

The last girl to be married was the only one given in compensation for Mullah Shahid's death. Apart from an infant son, Zarip, Mullah Shahid in fact left no close male agnates and there was no one willing to insist on the right of his son to further compensation: a sum of money if not another woman. The orphaned boy was brought up by his FFBS who had married his widowed mother. This man usurped all the child's patrimony. Some sixteen or seventeen years later, when the young man wanted to collect his bride, her kinsmen made extravagant brideprice demands for her, and not until after a considerable struggle, when the leading man of Zarip's section of Lineage C agreed to pay the 30,000 Afs brideprice himself, was the wedding held. The brideprice was demanded of Zarip because of his weak position, and his agnates assumed, rightly, that he would be quite unable to enforce his undeniable right to marry the girl. In fact Zarip was so oppressed by his agnates that after the wedding he sought refuge with his wife's family, where he continues to live and where he has recently been given building land for a house.

The killings occurred some thirty-five years ago, and it was difficult to get detailed information on the background to the events. Everyone we spoke to stated that there was no precedent for violence at all, and that Soleyman's initial wish to avoid any retaliation after his son's beating was honourable; in any case, at that stage other members of Lineage C were unlikely to wish to become involved. The matter was taken out of Soleyman's hands by Sherali, however, for motives which no one can now explain as other than foolhardiness. In fact, men and women on both sides simply blamed Rishmin's Parsiwan mother for causing the entire affair.

Even after Sherali's death things might have ended peaceably if Lineage A had offered their kinsmen another woman right away. But when it was learned that they had no intention of making any further compensation because of Lineage C's imputed Parsiwan status, this slur united all the members of Lineage C and provoked agnates distant from the original dispute to further violence. Even then, the poor Mullah Shahid failed to see that the killings implicated him in any way. Unlike Patih Mohammad and the other powerful men who went to the wedding party with the intention to kill, such a man could hardly expect to gain from involvement in a feud and was indeed more likely to lose what little he had. In the event, Mullah Shahid was killed and his son received, after considerable difficulty, only one woman in compensation. Of the graves of those dead in the feud, only that of Mullah Shahid became a martyr's shrine.

The few households of Lineage D also tried to dissociate themselves from Lineage C and the feud, declaring that they were Alizai, not Ishaqzai, at all. The Ishaqzai Khan was angered by this, and however much the leader of Lineage D protested that they were not *qaum*, the Khan insisted they were and he eventually forced them to give a woman to the son of Hajji Janshah. However, when it came to collecting the 3,000 Afs. to pay off the Khan, Soleyman took pity on Lineage D, who were at the time in effect clients of Lineage C, and paid their share.

The commitment of the whole of Lineage A followed Hajji Janshah's involvement, and when it became clear that a major confrontation was imminent it was Sarafraz, a member of a section hitherto uncommitted, who killed Mullah Shahid. Only one section of the lineage did not become directly implicated in the feud: the descendants of Dilawar's fourth son, who came rather later than the others and were by this time settled in Naju as close neighbours of Lineage C in Sinjit. (Section VI of Lineage A, Sarwar Khel, were not in fact living with the Maduzai in Saripul at the time.)

Once the feud had begun the Maduzai lineages camped apart, and the separate winter settlements of Chinar and Sinjit also date from that time. The hostility between the two groups is never far from the surface. Indeed, in the early 1960s, a quarrel over some land led to men from both sides facing each other with loaded guns on the land between the two villages. However, a respected leader of another Ishaqzai subtribe settled nearby came between the opponents carrying a Koran in his hands – the traditional gesture of the mediator and peacemaker. The people of Lineage C say that the men of Lineage A then retreated to Chinar but later were persuaded to come to the mosque in Sinjit where they ate and prayed together. 'It wasn't the sort of feud where killings took place, only bruises, so no money or women were exchanged. The Koran was brought between us in time'. Then the Sinjit men in turn went to the mosque in Chinar: 'After all, we are *qaum*; we visit each other. Since the feud, relations between us have always been somewhat uneasy, but we are all one.'

The Maduzai today
Lineage A

The 77 households of Lineage A (known variously as the *aulad* of Dilawar, or Janshah *Khel* after the present Khan's father, or as the *qaum* of Purdil Khan after the present Khan himself) claim descent from the six sons of Dilawar, who is two to three generations removed from senior living men of the group. Five of Dilawar's sons were by his first wife, a Durrani, the sixth being one of apparently several sons by his second wife, a non-Durrani woman and possibly even a Hazara. In general, details of the upper levels of the lineage genealogy are of little interest to members of the group, most of whom know little more than the name of the son of Dilawar from whom they descend. Figure 4 represents the current version of the genealogy which finds widest consensus, particularly among the leading men of the subtribe and their families.

When Maduzai want to differentiate among members of Lineage A, they do so by 'fathers' (*plar*), i.e. sons of Dilawar. The sections so formed are often called the *aulad* of the 'father' from whom they descend, or the *qaum* or *khel* of their present or recent leading man. Members of each of these sections are conscious of common interests; they tend to live close to each other and will act collectively in certain circumstances.

The genealogy suggests the relative independence of each section, though they vary considerably in size – particularly Section III, which is much the largest largely because Durkhan had twelve sons, whose descendants all came to the north. The present Khan is said to be descended from Dilawar's eldest son, but the birth order of the other sons is left in considerable doubt.

Of great importance to contemporary political relations within the subtribe is the fact that all those descended from Dilawar's five sons by his first wife are long established in the Saripul area, having arrived more or less contemporaneously with the migration led by Afzal Khan. Lineage A's three shares of the rich valley land bought soon after the migration were divided (unequally) among these five sections, most of whose members continue as landowners today (see Table 5; for further details of the land division, see N. Tapper, 1979: 141ff.).

> The initial recipients of the Lineage A lands (Janshah, Shahnawaz and Khalifa Nabi) were the leading men of the lineage. Their position as lineage leaders has been perpetuated by their immediate heirs.
>
> Section I: Among this second generation of lineage leaders, the Maduzai Khan, Purdil, is unusual in also having acquired a great deal of land elsewhere in the Saripul region.
>
> Section II, which has increased slowly, remains very prosperous on the original holding.
>
> In Section III, the principal heir of Khalifa Nabi is the section's wealthiest member and leader, though others have been able to augment their land holdings through purchase elsewhere. This is the largest section of Lineage A and remains relatively prosperous today.
>
> Section IV consists of the descendants of Anwar, who arrived after the main migration and apparently after the original lands were bought, yet

managed himself to acquire a share, though at the farthest end of irrigation on the edge of the steppe. They settled near their land, forming the Naju hamlet, now often known by the name of their leading man, Guljan, though some of them have bought more farmland some kilometres south of Chinar. A distance of almost four kilometres separates the Naju hamlet from the Khan at Chinar, enabling the households of Section IV to avoid

Figure 4 Skeleton genealogy of Lineage A

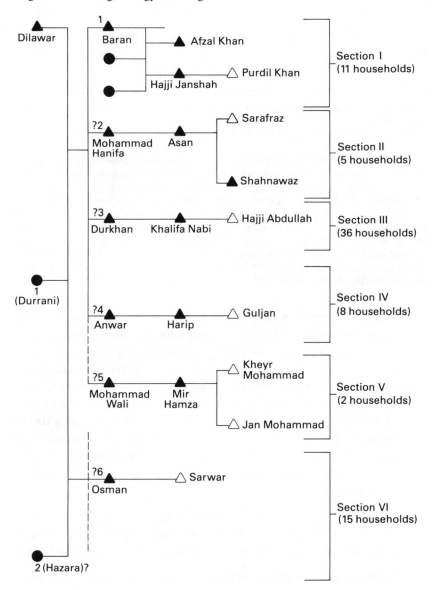

Table 5. *Maduzai core-lineages and land division*

Lineage A

528j. – Janshah				528j. – Shahnawaz	528j. – Khalifa Nabi			
264j.	264j./4			484j.	264j.	88j.	88j.	88j.
Jahanshah	I	V	IV	II	Khalifa Nabi	III		

Lineage C

528j. – Soleyman			528j. – Abdul Manan				
132j.	132j.	264j.	132j.	132j.	88j.	88j.	88j.
Soleyman	Adam	Teymur	Abdul Manan				Lineage D
I		IV	III			II	

3,000 *jeribs* of land bought from the Alizal Tahsildar
- <u>150 *jeribs*</u> to the Uzbeks
2,850 (sic – 2,640 *jeribs*); 2,640 *jeribs* divided into 5 shares, of which 3 (1,584 *jeribs*)
    went to Lineage A.

It is very likely that discrepancies between the principle of division into equal ploughlands and the real amounts of land included in each unit existed. But quite apart from this, accounts which refer only to the principles on which the division was based are not themselves consistent. Thus, the Uzbeks are said to have received 150 *jeribs* of the 3,000 *jeribs*, leaving 2,850 *jeribs* to be divided between the five leading men of Lineages A and C; and yet, the terms of this five-fold division into 6 ploughlands each implies that there were only 2,640 *jeribs* left for the Maduzai to share out. There is no way to discover the exact amounts of land involved in the division, though there is no reason to think that the shares shown here mask any major discrepancies between the sections in terms of what they received in principle and in practice.[1]

direct involvement in the day-to-day affairs of Lineage A. Among other things, these households form a separate religious congregation, using the mosque constructed by one of the Section's leading men. Besides their physical and social distance from their agnates, Section IV is held in low opinion by the latter, who say its members were always quarrelsome troublemakers. This bad reputation was forever confirmed in the summer of 1971 by the elopement of Kaftar, a girl of the section, with a Hazara youth (see p. 61f.). Nor have they been viewed much more favourably by their neighbours, Lineage C of Sinjit, but in this case, proximity and common opposition to the residents of Chinar have created certain sympathies between them.

Section V comprises only two households, led by Kheyr Mohammad, who, as a close henchman of the most prominent Ishaqzai Khan in Saripul, acts as a strategic link between Purdil Khan and the regional tribal leaders.

Section VI, the descendants of Dilawar's second wife, came from Kandahar much later and took no part in the original land division. Only in the last few years have some of them begun to install themselves as permanent residents in the area, while others, who only rejoined the subtribe in 1972, live in tents on the edge of the Saripul valley.

Further internal divisions do exist within Lineage A, but these are to an extent muted by the fact that the Khan is one of their number: the Maduzai are very conscious that lesser men need to make themselves close to men of power and wealth. The unity of the lineage is evident at the mosque which the Khan maintains near his compound, the congregation of which is drawn from all Lineage A householders living in Chinar.

The strength of faction loyalties in the lineage has not been seriously tested, though ironically our presence in the field did provoke a series of confrontations along these lines. During most of the fieldwork our host was Hajji Ibrahim, the leader of Lineage C, headman of Sinjit and the principal rival of the Maduzai Khan. By the end of our stay, Purdil Khan and his supporters (his agnates of Section I and the few, but wealthy, members of Sections II and V) wished us well away from Chinar, while the opposing group in Lineage A (the numerous members of Section III) entreated us to visit.

Hajji Nanawor, the wife of Hajji Abdullah, leader of Section III, was the father's sister of Hajji Ibrahim, our host, but recently Hajji Abdullah had married a daughter to the Khan, while his eldest son, an able and literate young man, had become one of the Khan's closest lieutenants. (As mentioned earlier, Hajji Nanawor and her son were among our closest Maduzai friends.) The affinal connection between Purdil Khan and Hajji Abdullah had a moderating effect on the tension we provoked. The importance of these ties is not lost on other members of Lineage A, who consider them likely to benefit both the sections concerned and to minimize the incipient divisions in the lineage as a whole.

Lineage B
Lineage B joined the subtribe some years after their arrival in the north (see p. 73). Their fifteen households today have a self-conscious unity comparable to that of one of the sections of Lineage A. Usually they refer to themselves, and are referred to by others, by their *tayfa* name, Tutizai. They cannot trace direct connections with other Maduzai in Saripul and this genealogical distance has served to separate them socially as well, though they do form part of the congregation of the Khan's mosque. The Tutizai have the reputation of being steady and hard-working, and have, so far as I know, carefully avoided any trouble which would have tested the *wolus'* acceptance of their membership of the subtribe. All the households of this group live in a hamlet adjacent to Chinar where they very recently bought farmland from some Uzbeks of Saripul town.

Lineage C

Sixty-three of the 70 households of Lineage C live in or close to Sinjit village; another five have recently moved to the nearby Naju hamlet. One further household has traditionally lived at the head of the Maduzai settlements where the track through them joins the main road to Saripul. A final household is that of Mullah Shahid's son, who went to live with affines in Chinar after the feud (see p. 78). Lineage C is in many contexts accorded the status of an independent *wolus* under the leadership of Hajji Ibrahim, the official headman. It unites the principles of common descent and common residence with its proven willingness to act in concert in many different situations.

Though recognizing their common descent from Tella who is two to four generations removed from the senior living men, members of the lineage see themselves as the descendants of 'four fathers' or 'four houses'. These four sections have a character comparable to the sections of Lineage A.

The initial division of the land purchased around 1917 has had an impact on the internal politics of Lineage C similar to what happened in Lineage A. The two original shares were taken by Soleyman and Abdul Manan. Like the shares of Lineage A, these comprised six ploughlands each and were distributed as is shown on Table 5.

Only a few years after the original purchase, Adam's son Sultan bought another 64 *jerib*s of land and a mill at the head of the lands of the subtribe; he became by far the wealthiest man of Lineage C. Sultan, however, like his father, was not personally ambitious, and his father's brother Soleyman and Abdul Manan jointly exercised leadership in lineage affairs for some twenty-five to thirty years. Meanwhile the major cleavage in the lineage was forming between Soleyman, supported by Sections I, II and III, and Teymur and his agnates of Section IV. Though all the sections are in some contexts spoken of as *qaums*, these two larger factions are also so described.

Some time in the early 1920s, Teymur began to realize the value of agricultural land, and he complained to Soleyman that his share was too small. The dispute continued until finally a tribal *jirga* assembly was convened by one of the Ishaqzai Khans and the issue was settled: Soleyman gave Teymur more land, and a set of exchange marriages was arranged between their children (see p. 000). But for some reason Teymur again became angry, until, after many more years of bitterness, a further compromise was arranged by Wazir Mohammad Gul Khan Mohmand (see p. 34), and another set of exchange marriages was contracted (see pp. 249ff.).

The legacy of this quarrel is spatially evident in two ways. First, the residential pattern in Sinjit village reflects the division of the lineage into two factions. Though there is no natural boundary between them, the village is seen as consisting of two parts. Section IV live in the 'upper' part of the village nearer the canal head and Saripul town and include the households of Teymur's

descendants by his first wife and those of his brother Nurjan, while the households descending from his second wife recently moved to building land in Naju
hamlet, though they continue to identify closely with their agnates; the last
household claiming descent from the third brother, Badir, left the Saripul area in
1972. All but two of the other lineage households live in the 'lower' part of the

Figure 5 Skeleton genealogy of Lineage C

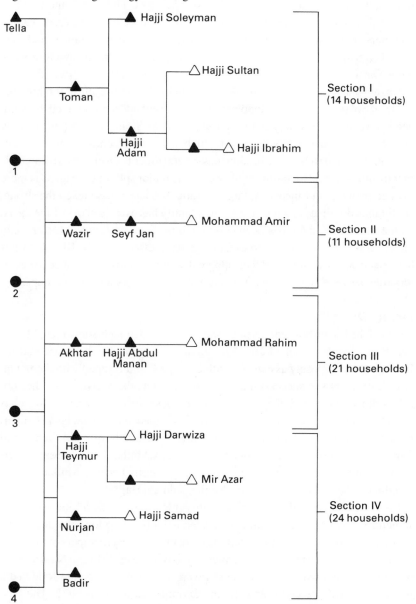

village. Secondly, there are two mosques in the village, originally established by Soleyman and Teymur respectively. Each has recently been rebuilt '*wolusi*', that is by the joint efforts and contributions of all the households living in the relevant half of the village. Those descendants of Teymur who now live in Naju continue to attend the mosque in Upper Sinjit if the weather is mild or the occasion important; otherwise they make use of the small mosque in Naju hamlet.

Though Soleyman and Abdul Manan (both of the Lower Sinjit faction) were informally accepted as the joint leaders of Lineage C until 1950, the first two official headmen of Sinjit, appointed soon after the feud, were in fact leading members of Section IV, the Upper Sinjit faction: first was Samad and then Darwiza. Samad was strong and apparently oppressed even his own followers, while Darwiza lacked the strength of personality necessary to confront the local Ishaqzai Khans and government officials, and in 1955 the youthful Ibrahim, the FFBS of Soleyman, won the appointment for himself and has remained the Sinjit headman ever since. Today all the households of the Sinjit *wolus* depend heavily on Ibrahim's leadership skills, a fact which is greatly resented by members of Section IV, not least because Ibrahim has several times been one of the principals in intra-lineage confrontations with them. The major split in Lineage C is more marked than that in Lineage A, largely I think because it has lacked the strong, continuous domination which the Khan's family has exercised over Lineage A. At the same time, there has been continuing pressure on Lineage C to remain united in the face of threats from Lineage A; in effect Section III, which lies between the two factions both genealogically and spatially, has played a mediatory role between them, not least because of its marriages with both groups.

Lineage D
Seven of the fifteen households of Lineage D live with their leading man, Mullah Daud, in a hamlet attached to Chinar village. Traditionally the households of Lineage D were closely associated with Lineage C and camped with them, but, after Lineage D's unsuccessful attempt to dissociate themselves from the sub-tribe following the feud, they began to build houses on their own land, which is in fact located close to Chinar. In spite of this, Lineage D's contacts in Chinar, particularly with members of Lineage A, are slight and they do not even attend Purdil Khan's mosque but use one maintained by Mullah Daud himself. Their association with Lineage C continues today, primarily because Mullah Daud's daughter is the favourite wife of the Sinjit headman, Hajji Ibrahim.

Five other households of Lineage D are settled in Sinjit with Lineage C who sometimes say of them that they have been neighbours so long that they have become like *qaum*, though their status is more that of client members of the Sinjit *wolus*. Finally, three impoverished households of Lineage D live in Naju hamlet, while two others whose circumstances were even more desperate followed a well-established precedent and left the Saripul area in 1971–1972. The land acquired by Lineage D in the original division was (unlike that of the other groups) formally distributed among the households and separate deeds issued. Because of this, other Maduzai observers say, their land was easily alienated from the lineage and indeed only Mullah Daud has much land left. This is considered to be a major factor in their declining numbers and increasing poverty in recent years.

Client households of the Maduzai subtribe
Ninety-five client households of a variety of Durrani tribal divisions (including Maduzai Ishaqzai) and other ethnic groups were also included in our 1972 census of the resident population of the Maduzai subtribe. Maduzai of the four core-lineages consistently refer to those I have called client households as *hamsaya* (literally neighbours); a degree of dependence invariably characterizes their status. It would seem that the relation between the core members of a local descent group and their clients has long been a feature of Durrani social organization (cf. *Gazetteer of Afghanistan* 1908: 78ff.). Nowadays, most individual client households become attached to a single core-lineage household, usually as economic dependants or subordinates, while those few wealthy client households which have come to be associated with the subtribe are likely to be politically dependent on one of the core-lineages or lineage sections. While the particular histories of these households differ greatly, there is one characteristic which these clients have in common: the lack of a strong agnatic support group. The Maduzai assert that without compelling reasons no one would willingly leave their own *qaum* to live with strangers. In some cases demographic factors lead directly to isolation, in others landlessness and poverty cause dispersal, while in yet others political difficulties force people to leave their agnates.

As will become clear, the figure of ninety-five households is, in a number of ways, arbitrary, but it is based on our own and informants' judgements about these households' contemporary and past involvement in the affairs of the subtribe. In this respect there is a continuum of such households, from those which have lived with the Maduzai for thirty years or more, have affinal ties with one or more of the four Maduzai core-lineages and are treated for many purposes as *qaum*, to households which I call 'transient' – those whose associations with the subtribe may amount to little more than squatting for a few weeks or months on unused land in the neighbourhood. Almost all of these households are very poor and depend on their labour for their livelihoods (see p. 117); most have fewer resources than many of the poorest Maduzai core households (of Quartile IV, see p. 118).

There is, finally, a fairly constant number of about ten households – 'part-time clients' as I have called them – which are associated with the subtribe on a more or less regular basis for only a part of each year, often to gain access to grazing at a particular point in the pastoral cycle. Of the seven such households we observed in 1971–1972 (not included in the census), four had affinal links with the sub-tribe, though only two of these were with one of the core-lineages.

Among the most committed to the subtribe are the Maduzai collaterals, who do not claim close common descent with the four core-lineages but may offer pedigrees plausibly tracing a common ancestor for themselves and Dilawar, the founder of Lineage A. Most of these collaterals were associated with the original Maduzai migration to the north; the rest seem to have arrived in the area later, but before the Saripul Maduzai's contacts with their southern kin became as inter-mittent as they are today.

The long-term residents on core-lineage land have the status of *wolus* mem-bers: on pain of being turned off the land, they are expected to contribute money (and sometimes men) to support subtribe concerns; in return, they may expect *wolus* support when they find themselves in some difficulty. In general, how-ever, the quality and quantity of this support is less than it is for households of the four core-lineages, but in either case the crucial factor is the wealth of a particular household. More is expected of the wealthier households of the *wolus*, whether kin or non-kin, and they, in return, will receive proportionately more help for their own affairs.

Long term residence alone does seem to lead to the inclusion of a household in the subtribe. Affinal ties may be used to this same end, regardless of the length of stay. Thus 71 of the 95 client households included in the census have been associ-ated with the subtribe for five or more years; and 38 of these 71 have formed affinal ties with one or more of the four lineages. However, 16 of the remaining 24 households which had more recently taken up residence with the Maduzai had either newly married with a lineage household, sometimes quite explicitly for the purpose of security and a place to stay, or had joined Maduzai affines of many years standing with the apparent intention of becoming permanent members of the subtribe.

Common descent can also determine the *wolus* membership of the client households, for if the members of one household find employment within the subtribe or marry into it, they may be joined by their own agnates who may settle more or less permanently with them. There are in fact 16 different groups of two or more households of close agnates (of which a group of 13 households is the largest); these account for 56 of the 95 client households.

Another factor is also relevant. Although my information on the marriages of the client households is incomplete, it is clear that they frequently intermarry. Certainly some groups of agnates are heavily intermarried, but marriage ties also exist between households who have only their association with the subtribe in common.

Finally, though people forced to reside apart from their own agnates prefer to live with their 'own people' (also *qaum*), the need for a common tribal or ethnic identity does not seem to be an important factor regulating the inclusion of client

Table 6. *Tribal and/or ethnic identity of client households of the Maduzai subtribe*

	Total	Resident for more than 5 years
Maduzai collaterals	24	24
Other Ishaqzai subtribes	25	17
Other Durrani tribes	31	20
Non-Durrani Pashtu-speakers (Ghilzai and Parsiwan)	12	7
Others	3	3
	95	71

households in the subtribe. Most of the Maduzai clients are from Pashtu-speaking groups, but apart from the ban on Durrani women marrying hypogamously, there is no apparent discrimination between Durrani and Parsiwan households. There were also three client households of Persian-speakers, two of Hazaras and one of Arabs.

The rate at which client households join or leave the subtribe seems quite high (see N. Tapper 1979: 181, n. 21). If households have no long-standing connections (e.g. affinal links) with the subtribe, their presence or absence is likely to pass unnoticed by all but their closest neighbours. Many client households are often not only socially invisible but also physically difficult to locate because they may take up residence, for example, in a room in one of the large house compounds. Unless the members of such a household eventually form more permanent ties with the subtribe, they have little impact on its affairs, though clearly as a pool of more or less impoverished labourers they are of considerable importance to the subtribe economy. It must often be the case that chance factors such as weather, specific labour requirements in the area, or the presence of a pretty, marriageable daughter, transform temporary residents into permanent associates of a core lineage and thus the subtribe.

Table 6 shows the tribal or ethnic identity of the client households of the subtribe, while Table 7 shows their affinal connections with households of the core-lineages. It is of interest that, though some of the non-Maduzai clients have not been resident with the subtribe for very long, rather more have affinal connections with the core-lineages than do the long-resident Maduzai collaterals. The former, lacking common descent with the core-lineages, perhaps have more reason to use or create ties of affinity with them. Thus, behind the diversity of origins and of motives for joining the subtribe, there lies a network of descent and marriage ties which unite all its households. Indeed, of the 95 client households, there were only 15 for which I could discover no agnatic or affinal ties with other households of the subtribe at the time of the census. Some of these 15 were long-term residents and had been joined at one time or another by their own agnates,

Table 7. *Intermarriage between Maduzai core-lineages and client households of the* wolus

	Total	Households without affines among the core lineages	Households with affines among the core lineages	Women (some now dead) given to core lineages	Women taken from core lineages
Maduzai collaterals	24	16 (67%)	8 (33%)	18	10
Other clients	71	42 (59%)	29 (41%)	15	17
	95				

while the rest could fairly be considered members of the subtribe for a variety of reasons: their known intentions to remain with the Maduzai; the situation of their patron, if any; the kind of work they had found within the subtribe and the extent to which they were known to be hard-working and hence employable; and the likelihood that they would in future contract a marriage with a household of the subtribe.

The subtribe as a *wolus*
There were many occasions during fieldwork when the strength of various ties to the *wolus* were tested. However, given the key role that gender concepts and marriage play in the constitution of the subtribe, it is perhaps not surprising that the way levies were collected to finance the search for the runaway girl Kaftar provides us with the clearest illustration of the nature of the *wolus* among the Maduzai.

Case 2: Kaftar (Part II)
Though there was never any real likelihood that the Maduzai, or any larger group of Durrani, would unite in a military confrontation with the Hazaras, money was collected to finance the search and the 'litigation' in Kabul. The girl's father, Toryaley, was himself of Section IV, Lineage A, and from the outset all members of Lineages A, B and C were involved.

At first, the subtribe leaders decided to levy 20,000 Afghanis (then about £100) each from the *aulad*s of seven fathers; five of Dilawar's sons (Lineage A: Section V being small was amalgamated with the Khan's family for this purpose); the Tutizai (Lineage B); and the Torabi (Lineage C). Lineage D were not involved, but would probably contribute to Lineage C's levy. Within Lineage C, the levy of 20,000 Afs. was to be divided equally (5,000 Afs. each) among the four sections ('four fathers'), though a contribution of 500 Afs. per household was also considered.

Later, when it was realized that expenses would be much heavier, the contributions from the five sections of Lineage A were raised to 50,000 Afs. each, while people talked of the sequestration of Toryaley's property to raise further funds. We unfortunately had to leave the field at this stage, and after our return the following summer were unable to work out exactly how the first collection of money was made, though people said it was done by the Maduzai Khan from the *qaum* alone and that strangers (i.e. clients) could choose to contribute or not.

A second collection was also made. This time the Khan collected 100 Afs. from every house belonging to his village of Chinar. This, people said, had nothing to do with *qaum*, and each household of Lineages B and D contributed, as did all the client households of the village; had any of the latter refused to pay they would have been told to move on. The Khan also asked the Sinjit villagers, who are not close patrikin of Toryaley, to give a further 10,000 Afs., and their collection was done again 'by father' – 2,500 Afs. from each of the four sections of Lineage C – though they in turn insisted that their respective clients contributed to their levy. Toryaley's own contribution to this second levy was put at 50,000 Afs. People agreed that the Khan had the right to demand this money from them, but, as the case continued to drag on in Kabul and the Khan and Toryaley failed to recover Kaftar, people grew dissatisfied. It was clear by the summer of 1972 that they would give no more. The strength and wealth of the Hazaras made it unlikely that the girl would ever be returned, and people were determined not to let the Khan 'eat' more of their money.

The Maduzai subtribe and marriage
The foregoing account of Maduzai history and social organization has shown the development of factional disputes at different levels of the subtribe and offered examples of the political use of marriage in the recruitment of distant agnates, the recognition of strangers, the reconciliation of disputants at various levels, and compensation for injury or death. The concluding discussion of this chapter summarizes the structure of political relations in the subtribe and considers the extent to which both political alliances and factions are revealed in the numerical tabulation of the subtribe marriage choices. The patterns which are revealed have themselves an intrinsic interest; their explanation clearly demonstrates the inadequacy of approaching the problem of marriage choice through statistics alone.

The three main levels of political alliance and confrontation are represented in Figure 6.

Level I
The main division within the subtribe is between its two main Lineages, A and C. The hostility between them is a legacy of the feud, but their mutual antipathy certainly began with the question of the identity and the (?re-)incorporation of

Lineage C into the subtribe at the time of the migration from Kandahar. It is perpetuated in their relative equality, in terms of manpower and wealth, and their
mutual dependence for protection from the depredations of the Ishaqzai Khans
and other tribal groups in the region. Relations between Lineages A and C are
couched in the idiom of ethnicity, which itself relies on the criterion of marriage-
ability between groups. As one man of Lineage A said,

In the beginning the Maduzai all lived together, but then, after the feud, the Torabi were
recognized as Parsiwans and our women are worth four of theirs.

Lineages A and C live in separate winter villages, each with its own powerful
leader. The subordination of all the Maduzai to the Khan (a member of Lineage
A) is of little importance in day-to-day affairs. Directly related to the major cleavage is the situation of the two smaller Lineages, B and D, both of which are resi-
dentially discrete but virtually all of whose associations are with Lineages A and
C respectively.

Level II

Within each of the two major lineages there are two genealogically defined factions. In Lineage A, Sections I, II and V stand in opposition to the much larger
Section III, while Sections IV and VI form two spatially discrete groups who side
with Section III against the Khan. Lineage C is riven by an even more marked
factionalism, again drawn on genealogical lines, which is also expressed
spatially. Sections I, II and III of Lower Sinjit stand in opposition to Section IV
of Upper Sinjit. Section III holds a mediatory position, as explained above.

The factional division within Lineage C is held to have begun with the unequal
distribution of original land holdings, but it is most clearly expressed nowadays
in terms of marriage. The members of Upper Sinjit deeply resent their
dependence on the Sinjit headman, Hajji Ibrahim, but the antagonism works both
ways. As one of the sons of Hajji Ibrahim said:

Those people of Upper Sinjit are not good people; they say all sorts of things. We don't
give women to them. We gave one of my sisters there and how much we regretted it. We
have not given any other women to those people, nor will we give any. Nor will we people
of Lower Sinjit take any of their women: before, we used to give and receive, but now it is
finished.

There is no special trouble between us, but is not good to marry them. For example, if
you [agreed to] take a girl from them for 10,000 Afs., they would swear it was 20,000 Afs.;
they are not good, they are always fighting with you. They give and take women among
themselves. You know the people of Chinar don't give women to the people of Upper
Sinjit. They have not given a single one, nor have they taken any from them. But the people
of Chinar, one of the Khan's group, give women to us and take women from us.

Unfortunately I did not record any detailed statement from Chinar making the
same point about marriage within Lineage A, but I know that factionalism there
is conceived of in the same way.

Level III

Disputes which follow genealogical lines also occur at the third level, between the households of a single lineage section. Here too, as is the case at the other two levels, marriages between opponents are discouraged in theory, but in practice they are used with some frequency in attempts to settle differences which threaten to get out of control, even though such marriages are as likely to exacerbate differences as to resolve them. However, given the more or less fixed land resources of the Maduzai, this pattern is likely to persist, if not intensify, in the future. In practice this is similar to the explicit hostility expected of first cousins among many eastern Pashtun groups where the term for FBS also means 'enemy'. Among the Maduzai neither does the term for FBS (*akazoy*) have this connotation (see N. Tapper 1979: 179, n. 7), nor is there any general recognition of a pattern of hostility between close agnates. It is possible that because of the well-recognized hostility at Levels I and II, it becomes necessary to focus on the harmony between closest agnates (Level III) in spite of much behaviour to the contrary.

The relation between marriage and political relations at each of the three levels is best shown through extended case histories of the kind to which chapter 11 is devoted. Here my concern is to examine to what extent patterns of alliance and conflict within the subtribe are reflected in the numerical analysis of marriage choices. As we shall see, such an analysis tells us little that has not already been discussed in historical and political terms. On the other hand, it does highlight

Figure 6 Principal levels of political confrontation within the Maduzai subtribe

Maduzai Subtribe (*tayfa, wolus*)

Level I (*wolus*)	Chinar *wolus* Leader = Purdil Khan Lineages A and B and clients		Sinjit *wolus* Leader = Hajji Ibrahim Lineages C and D and clients	
Level II factions = (*tol*)	Khan's faction Purdil Khan Sections I, II and V of Lineage A	Durkhan's faction Hajji Abdullah ✕ Sections III, IV and VI of Lineage A	Lower Sinjit Hajji Ibrahim Sections I, II and III of Lineage C	Upper Sinjit Sarwar ✕ Section IV of Lineage C
Level III independent households or clusters of households = closest agnates			e.g. Section I Hajji ✕ Hajji Ibrahim Sultan	

✕ = Hostility / Political opposition

Table 8. *Lineage C marriages – spatial distance between affines, 1972*

	Within subtribe settlements	Settlements adjacent to the Maduzai	Settlements 10–30 miles from the Maduzai	30+ miles	Totals
Men's marriages					
Within core lineages	67	0	0	0	67
Other Durrani	5	5	14	3	27
Hypergamous	3	2	2	8	15
Totals	75	7	16	11	109
Women's marriages					
Within core lineages	67	0	0	0	67
Other Durrani	5	9	9	1	24
Hypogamous	0	1	0	2	3
Totals	72	10	9	3	94

some of the subtlety and complexity of Durrani marriage: the ambiguity of the Durrani concept of 'closeness' as a way of expressing marriage preference, the ambiguities of the exchange marriage form, and the scale of the discrepancies between marriage preference and the political realities which dictate actual marriage choices. Indeed, the following statistical treatment of Maduzai marriages should serve as a salutory warning against the facile use of statistics to 'analyse' marriages in the Muslim Middle East generally.

'Closeness' and Maduzai marriages
I have noted that the Maduzai express no formal marriage preferences within the category 'Durrani', though there is a stated but imprecise preference for *qaum* endogamy. By implication, any classification of marriage choices as within or outside a specific group such as tribe, tribal division, subtribe, lineage or section bears little relation to the Maduzai conception of marriage choice, which is expressed in terms of 'closeness', an idiom which is used to define and manage all social relations, and is only indirectly related to genealogical distance (cf. H. Geertz 1979: 375ff., Rosen 1984: 19ff. as well as Anderson 1975, 1982a, Bradburd 1984, Donnan 1985 and Wright 1985 on societies from the northern tier).

'Closeness' derives from a detailed knowledge of background and present circumstances and leads to predictability (see pp. 51, 193). There is a general feeling that a 'close' bride is less likely to 'cause trouble', for example by publicizing the secrets of her marital home, or other shameless behaviour; similarly, to give one's daughter to someone who is close minimizes the risk of betrayal of family secrets, as well as ensuring some influence over her fate after marriage.

Table 8 shows that three-quarters of all of Lineage C's marriages are within

Table 9. *Maduzai marriages – social distance between affines, 1972*

Lineage	A No	A (Per cent)	B No	B (Per cent)	C (1950) No	C (1950) (Per cent)	C (1972) No	C (1972) (Per cent)	D No	D (Per cent)	Totals (1972) No	Totals (1972) (Per cent)
Men's marriages												
Within lineage	46	46	4	16	36	49	57	52	5	31	112	45
Between core-lineages of the subtribe	6	6	5	20	11	15	10	9	6	38	27	11
Among core-lineages	52	53	9	36	47	64	67	61	11	69	139	56
With other Durranis (or Sayyids)	40	40	13	52	14	19	27	25	4	25	84	34
Hypergamous	7	7	3	12	12	16	15	14	1	6	26	10
Totals	99	100	25	100	73	99	109	100	16	100	249	100
Women's marriages												
Within lineage	46	52	4	36	36	52	57	61	5	33	112	54
Between core-lineages	11	13	2	18	13	19	10	11	4	27	27	13
Among core-lineages	57	65	6	55	49	71	67	71	9	60	139	67
With other Durranis	30	34	5	45	19	28	24	26	6	40	65	31
Hypogamous	1	1	0	0	1	1	3	3	0	0	4	2
Totals	88	100	11	100	69	100	94	100	15	100	208	100

the subtribe settlements. Members of the subtribe, interconnected as they are by ties of agnation, affinity, neighbourhood and political and economic co-operation and competition, are indeed likely to be the people who are closest and hence most likely as marriage partners. However, for the purposes of marriage, as in virtually all other social contexts, the same criteria of closeness may be applied to anyone of Durrani or equal (i.e. Sayyid) status. By contrast, Table 8 also shows that women taken hypergamously by Lineage C men are much more likely to come from afar, often from quite different parts of Afghanistan. Sometimes Lineage C men themselves have sought out such women, while in other cases, the women's own agnates have brought them to Saripul to be married. Either way, normally there is virtually no contact with the women's families once the marriage has taken place.

Among the core lineages, as Table 9 shows, there is a general tendency to lineage endogamy, at 45 per cent of men's marriages and 54 per cent of women's marriages. Lineage C also shows an appreciable increase in endogamy over the last generation, particularly for women.

At the same time, a third of all marriages are with Durrani outside the four Maduzai core lineages. Most of these marriages too are considered 'close', and indeed, as Table 8 shows, most men take Durrani wives from households living within a radius of thirty miles of the Maduzai settlements, and, when Lineage C women are married to outsiders, they too marry within this distance. Though I have no figures to support this suggestion, from the Maduzai material it is likely that the rate of marriage with Durrani outsiders varies from subtribe to subtribe according to the composition of the local population: for the Maduzai it is

Table 10. *Maduzai men's exchange marriages, 1972*

	Intra-lineage	Maduzai lineages	Others	Totals	Percentage
A	8	1 (B)	5	14/99	14
B	1	1 (A)	2	4/25	16
C (1950)	13	1 (D)	4	18/73	25
C (1972)	27	0	5	32/109	29
D	0	1 (C)	1	2/16	13
Totals	36	3	13	52/249	21

relevant that there is in the Saripul area a considerable number of Durrani tribal divisions. The Maduzai are in regular and often close contact with other Durrani and, once a marriage has been successfully arranged, the next becomes easier and a whole succession of marriages is likely to follow. In this light it is perhaps not surprising that the Maduzai express little interest in or knowledge of the exact tribal origins and affiliations of Durrani spouses from outside the subtribe, who, except for occasional and insignificant teasing, are in no way stigmatized.

Maduzai exchange marriages
The figures presented so far can tell us nothing of the political significance of marriages, or of the form of marriage which each number represents. For example, 20 per cent, or one-fifth of all men's marriages, are exchanges, as is shown in Table 10. Here, as with the rates of lineage endogamy and marriages between core lineages, there is considerable variation between lineages; to explain this, each lineage's marriages must be examined more closely. The most comprehensive and reliable data are those on the marriages of Lineage C. As a detailed analysis suggests, though the high rate of exchange marriages in Lineage C may reflect the greater intensity of the factional division there than in Lineage A, it is just as likely to be a reflection of the highly ambiguous nature of many exchange marriages and my more informed understanding of the context of the exchange marriages made by the members of Lineage C. However with this warning in mind, it is nonetheless possible to discern a general relation between marriage choice and political alignment.

Lineage politics and marriage choice
Lineage A
In Lineage A, the factional divisions are clearly reflected in marriage patterns, as Table 11 shows. The Khan's faction have given no women to the opposing Durkhan faction, though they have taken six women from them, the most important being the daughter of Hajji Abdullah who was married to the Khan himself in 1969 for the very high brideprice of two lacs (200,000 Afs.). My information on

Table 11. *Marriages of Lineage A, 1972*

	Khan faction	Durkhan faction	Lineages			Other	Totals
			B	C	D		
Men's marriages							
Khan faction	11	6	0	0	0	13	30
Durkhan faction	0	29	2	4	0	34	69
Totals	11	35	2	4	0	47	99[a]
Women's marriages							
Khan faction	11	0	1	1	0	4	17
Durkhan faction	6	29	4	5	0	27	71
Totals	17	29	5	6	0	31	88

[a] 99 marriages made by 92 men.

the history of Lineage A's marriages is not so detailed as that concerning the marriages of Lineage C, but I suspect that, as in the latter case, these six marriages between factions are directly related to lineage politics both in their antecedents and in the extent to which they have caused or are likely to cause further division. The factional divisions within Lineage A are also clearly reflected by the tendency to faction endogamy.

A single, but important, marriage – that of the Khan's own daughter – links the Khan with Lineage B, while neither he nor others of his faction have made any marriages since the feud with Lineages C and D. By contrast, the Durkhan faction has links with both Lineages B and C and seven of the Durkhan faction's nine marriages with Lineage C post-date the feud settlement. The connection between the Durkhan faction and Lineage C is an important feature of subtribe politics: the leader of Lineage C, Hajji Ibrahim, the headman of Sinjit, stands in the relation of 'affine' and 'mother's brother's son' to members of the leading household of the Durkhan faction.

Lineage B

The marriages of Lineage B, the Tutizai, link them only with Lineage A of the subtribe (see Table 12). The Tutizai were persuaded to join the subtribe only at the insistence of its previous leader, the present Khan's father. Four marriages of political importance have taken place between them and the Khan's own household, though only one, involving the Khan's daughter, is still extant. The other six marriages between Lineages B and A are all with the Durkhan faction of Lineage A.

Lineage B's relationship with the Khan is one of political but not economic clientage and, to redress the balance in their relationship with Lineage A as a whole, they seem to have sought marriages with the faction opposing the Khan.

Table 12. *Marriages of Lineage B, 1972*

	Intra-Lineage	Lineage A (Khan's faction)	(Durkhan's faction)	C	D	Other	Totals
Men's marriages	4	1	4	0	0	16	25[a]
Women's marriages	4	0	2	0	0	5	11

[a]25 marriages made by 19 men.

Their long-standing connection with Lineage A has apparently precluded their close association with Lineages C and D, though the Tutizai justify their reluctance to become involved with the latter by referring to their own independent and authoritative Durrani pedigree, scorning the dubious background of the others.

Lineage C

The long-standing antipathy towards intermarriage between the two Lineage C factions was mentioned earlier. In fact, 16 of the men's 109 marriages extant in 1972 link the factions, as did 11 of the 73 marriages of 1950. A detailed examination of these marriages forms an important part of the extended case study of chapter 11. Here it is enough to say that virtually every one of these marriages rose directly out of the factionalism itself and has had an equally direct bearing on its intensification. Table 13 shows the marriages of Lineage C.

The imbalance in numbers of women given between factions (in 1972 the Ibrahim faction had given 11 and received only 5 women) is a source of considerable resentment among members of the Ibrahim faction. However, in terms of proportions of all women given, the Teymur faction have given nearly a quarter of their women (5 out of 22) to the Ibrahim faction, while the latter have returned only 15 per cent of their women (11 out of 72).

As mentioned above, in their marriages with the other Maduzai lineages, it is the Ibrahim faction which is linked to Lineage A and specifically to the Durkhan faction there. This both gives the Sinjit headman an important source of support within the Khan's own lineage and further fuels the anger of Ibrahim's rivals in Lineage C who dislike their political dependence on him.

Lineage D

Finally, Table 14 provides information on the marriages of members of Lineage D.

Lineage D have married only with Lineage C of the other Maduzai lineages and 7 of those 10 marriages are with the faction of Hajji Ibrahim. In this respect

Table 13. *Marriages of Lineage C, 1950 and 1972*

	Ibrahim faction	Teymur faction	A	B	D	Others	Totals
Men's marriages 1950							
Ibrahim faction	22	4	4	0	5	13	48
Teymur faction	7	3	0	0	2	13	25
Totals	29	7	4	0	7	26	73[a]
Women's marriages 1950							
Ibrahim faction	22	7	4	1	6	11	51
Teymur faction	4	3	0	0	2	9	18
Totals	26	10	4	1	8	20	69
Men's marriages 1972							
Ibrahim faction	33	5	6	0	2	24	70
Teymur faction	11	8	0	0	2	18	39
Totals	44	13	6	0	4	42	109[b]
Women's marriages 1972							
Ibrahim faction	33	11	3	0	5	20	72
Teymur faction	5	8	1	0	1	7	22
Totals	38	19	4	0	6	27	94

[a] 73 marriages made by 54 men.
[b] 109 marriages made by 97 men.

Table 14. *Marriages of Lineage D, 1972*

	Intra-lineage	A	B	C (Ibrahim faction)	C (Teymur faction)	Others	Totals
Men's marriages	5	0	0	5	1	5	16[a]
Women's marriages	5	0	0	2	2	6	15

[a] 16 marriages made by 14 men.

Lineage D's marriages are unlike the marriages made by Lineage A's wealthy clients, Lineage B, who have avoided marriage with their political patron, the Maduzai Khan, in favour of those with the rival Durkhan faction. Members of Lineage D in their weakness and poverty have sought association with the most powerful faction of Lineage C: they fully admit the importance of the marriage between their leader Mullah Daud's daughter and the Sinjit headman.

Political alignment and subtribe marriages

The patterns of political alignments and marriages within the Maduzai subtribe are summarized in Figure 7.

The major oppositions are between the two larger Maduzai lineages and between the factions within them. There is a strong tendency to faction endogamy which the Maduzai clearly recognize themselves, though the number of marriages between rival groups belies the general antipathy to such marriages, which are also seen in a positive light as a means of forestalling deeper factional division. There is also a strong preference for 'close' marriages, but as this concept is used to explain and describe most Maduzai marriages, its effect is to dissolve rather than to define recognized tribal divisions. 'Close' marriages facilitate political action and introduce a fluidity into Durrani social organization and structure which is hidden by their use of genealogical models. Because marriages across factional boundaries, and indeed marriages within the factions, are rarely a matter of free choice, but are most often part and parcel of political manoeuvres within and between these groups, many marriages among the Maduzai can only be satisfactorily understood by examining the specific circumstances of their arrangement. However, over time, both exchange marriages and the actual numbers of brideprice marriages between lineage groups become criteria for judging the state of political relations between them and determinants of future relations.

Figure 7 Marriage and social groups in the subtribe

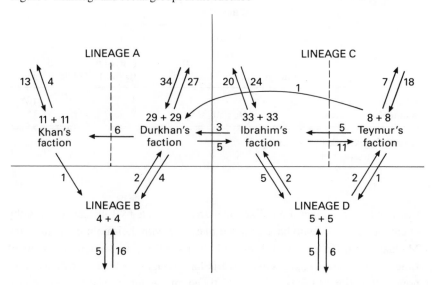

6

Household production and reproduction

One aim of this chapter is to outline the economic background of Maduzai marriage. The annual productive cycle, the character and amounts of capital resources controlled by households of the subtribe, and employment within the subtribe, will all be discussed, but the principal focus of this chapter is the relationship between marriage and household structure. The two are intrinsically linked, and the 'household' might also be defined as all those people who accept the decisions of the household head with regard to their marriages and those of their children and who allow the head to manage the raising of a brideprice or the disposal of a brideprice received. However, since household heads may not face such decisions for years or indeed at all during the period of their leadership, such a criterion is not sufficient for definitional purposes. Nonetheless, decisions about marriage remain the most important opportunity for household members to test the head's continuing dominance, and such decisions frequently become a pretext for household division, while the character of relationships between married members of a single household is viewed by Durrani as the ultimate determinant of household continuity or dispersal. Other factors are also relevant to a discussion of the developmental cycle of Durrani households, especially the number of marriages to be managed and their sequence, in terms of both the intervals between them and the sex of the principals. However, the discussion of these further considerations fits more appropriately in chapter 9 and will be treated in detail there.

The Maduzai household is ideally independent and self-sufficient: a residential, property-owning unit characterized by internal unity among all its members. In practice the tribesmen use two terms for household, *kor* and *kala*, almost synonymously. Pressed to make a distinction between them, they use *kor* more often for a nuclear family, *kala* for those people who pool their incomes, budget together and accept the economic decisions made by the acknowledged household head, *da kala mashar*. *Kor* also means both the trousseau of the bride and the platform at the back of a tent or room where the family keeps the bedding and other household items which were part of a woman's trousseau. In this sense, a *kala* may include two or more *kor* (see also R Tapper, forth-coming a).

Ideals of household unity

To the Maduzai the ideals of household unity (*entepak*) and self-sufficiency are inseparable (cf. Glatzer 1977: 154). This was explained to me by a Maduzai man in the following way:

> If you have a house of ten men and women, the women serve the house and collect things, while perhaps six men are out working – one as a servant, one as a sharecropper, one as a trader, another as a shopkeeper, while one will work their own land. And when they come home in the evening, none return empty-handed. When anyone says 'Bring back a stick', then six sticks appear. When these six men separate, they become six houses and the former household is ruined (*spera*). For instance, a man alone is not free to become a shepherd somewhere, leaving his wife alone; a man has friends and enemies, it won't do. But if we are six men in the same place, then if four of us go away to work and don't return for a year, there are still two of us here, to watch the house against thieves and so on. That is what household unity is like.

It is the ideal of unity against which the character of a particular household is assessed. Households with unity are much admired: for instance, it was said of the household of a man and his brother's son, 'They looked after each other well and with great fairness: they would have stood in the fire for each other.' If, on the other hand, a household is lacking in unity (*bi-entepak*), it will be a matter of common knowledge and a fact used by others to their own advantage. A household in complete disunity, for whatever reason, is said to be 'ruined' [Pa. *spera*, Per. *kharab*]: such ruin is the worst fear of every Durrani, and among the commonest opprobrious epithets are the synonymous Pashtu *kor-spera* and Persian *khana-kharab*, implying that so-and-so is completely worthless and his household is or soon will be ruined. Finally, it is said that no household separates unless its members have fought; following discord and division, 'the property becomes small and unmanageable and brothers get lost'.

Self-sufficiency in social terms is also of great importance and a household will be praised for neither interfering with (*gharaz kawal*) nor being interfered with by anyone else. Each household is held to have sole responsibility for its economic and political affairs and cannot automatically expect financial help or political support from even closest agnates. Sometimes help such as cash loans between households may be forthcoming, but just as often, a household in difficulty may find close agnates only too willing to prey on its weakness.

The economic advantages of self-sufficiency are explicitly recognized: tribesmen ask, why should they pay a servant wages when they can do a job themselves? In this sense self-sufficiency is directly related to the existence of an adequate labour force for household requirements, but it depends on more than economic independence. The fact that the household head controls all marriages made by its members has direct economic implications. Successful household budgeting often depends on success in marriage negotiations and the shrewd management of the large capital sums entering and leaving the household in brideprice marriages. Moreover, it is usual for brideprice payments to be made over several years, thereby requiring a long-term commitment of all household members to a marriage strategy. Junior married men within a joint household are particularly liable to resent the fact that their energy and earnings, far from benefiting their own wives and children directly, are used to finance the marriages of younger siblings or brothers' children. The allocation of resources for the marriages of household members is one of the most common precipitating causes of household division.

The Maduzai speak of household autonomy in terms of reputation or honour (*num*), that of each household being exclusive and unshared even by the households of closest agnates. The reputation of a household depends on success in the management of political and economic affairs, including of course marriages. Indeed the latter, because of their more public character, are often taken as signs of household viability or vulnerability. A household's success in the management of marriages depends on a number of related factors. Some are more purely economic – for example, the extent to which household members are hard-working and frugal, or the skill of the head at long-term budgeting. Others relate to his ability to control the behaviour of household members, both men and women, and to inspire their loyalty. The degree of respect, or honour, attributed to a household both by outsiders and by household members themselves is itself an important factor in social action. A household which has shown weakness in any context, whether in exchanges with outsiders or in disharmony among its members, is said to be shamed and becomes vulnerable to threats to its independence. A good reputation, on the other hand, creates a belief in a household's future: others are encouraged to seek its support and protection, and consequently, its strength and ability to protect itself are enhanced.

Gender, honour and the household

Households are competitive and their competition is couched in terms of honour, which in turn depends on the behaviour of household women and the control of the marriages of household members. In a sense it is women's *public* behaviour which is important and devices like seclusion and segregation are regarded as signs of a man's weakness and inability to manage the women of his household. Equally, household marriages are the means of both making public statements about household standing and judging the reputation of others.

As we shall see, women have very limited control of economic and political resources compared to men. In practice, they have the status of legal minors. A woman's guardian (*wakil*) – the father or other close agnate of an unmarried girl (*pegla*), and the husband or the husband's close agnate of a married woman (*shedza*) – have ultimate responsibility for all aspects of their behaviour. This inequality of status does not preclude able women from wielding considerable power within the household. Indeed, quite the contrary, since the construction of men's reputations makes them ultimately dependent on the loyalty and good behaviour of their womenfolk. Nonetheless, with respect to marriage arrangements, women are treated as little more than economic counters and part of household capital. Thus I was told of one man who had made the following bequests to his heirs just before he died:

> One of my daughters I have given in an exchange marriage with [my son] Mohammad Gul, so she is Mohammad Gul's. Another daughter is [my son] Mir Azar's. He already has a wife, but he still has a right to property from the estate so let him take the girl, whether to give her for brideprice or to exchange her for another wife for himself. A third daughter is for Bayak to exchange for a wife. And my fourth daughter is for my widow to do with as she will, whether to give her away for free or for brideprice, or whatever.

It is notable that the four daughters were treated as inherited property of exactly equal value (see also p. 199).

First marriages for women and men are arranged. Widow inheritance is approved of, and, though a widow with sons may choose not to remarry at all, she is very rarely able to choose a second husband by herself, while men control their own second and all subsequent marriages. Men have the right to divorce their wives at will, while the grounds on which a woman may initiate divorce are extremely limited. Divorce, however, is strongly disapproved of and virtually unknown. *De facto* separation does sometimes occur: men are sometimes forced to leave the region to find work and a few may simply abandon their wives, who have to return to their natal homes and find a living as best they can. More often, a post-menopausal woman leaves her marital home to join a married son in a separate household. Extra-marital sexual relations are difficult to pursue, but not particularly uncommon; as will be discussed in chapter 10, there is a clear relationship between the extent to which they become public knowledge and household weakness and discord.

Visiting among women, most often to the homes of close kin and affines, is common, though overnight absences from the marital home are usually short and strictly controlled by husbands. There is also a range of opportunities for women to meet in both festive and day-to-day contexts, but no clearly defined status hierarchy among women emerges and there are few opportunities for outstanding women to become recognized as women's leaders. In any case, a woman's chance of exercising any power beyond the household is extremely limited. She has no right or ability to dispose of any produce or capital goods of the household in which she is living, including items from her own trousseau, with the exception of a few economically insignificant goods bartered for small luxury items such as sweets or fruits. A woman's right to inherit as daughter and widow is recognized but not exercised. Finally, women hold no formal political positions in tribal society, though Kishmir, a woman of Sinjit village, is sometimes referred to as the women's *qaryadar* (Per. village headman; see p. 86; also N. Tapper 1979: 171, 357). She is a lively, intelligent widow, who is responsible for the organization of women's activities at marriage ceremonies and religious festivals. She also washes female corpses, a service for which she sometimes receives small gifts. The particular configuration of roles assumed by Kishmir is unique to herself, but among other Durrani and Persiwan groups in the vicinity there were a few other women of strong character also known as women's leaders.

The segregation of Durrani men and women is related to the division of labour by which women are confined to domestic activities, while economic and political decisions outside the domestic sphere are the prerogative of men. Veiling conventions are such that a Durrani woman normally does not cover her face to any man of any age or ethnic group while she is on her home ground – that is, in the villages or pastures associated with the household in which she lives. There is little sexual segregation in Durrani tent-households, and even in their village houses, where each married woman usually has her own room and where house compounds are surrounded by high mud walls, women are not segregated. These walls are more for defence against thieves than for privacy, and a man usually receives guests in his wife's private room and in her presence; where special guest-rooms exist, women of the household may visit them to gossip with the men there. Moreover a Durrani woman can and does receive male guests of her husband when no adult male is present or available to do so, and wives are able in their own right to entertain close male kin and affines.

In short, such segregation as Durrani women experience seems to be largely a practical consequence of the sexual division of labour and lacks strong normative supports. On a day-to-day basis, Durrani women's social interactions are with their families more than with other women. Women do not, as in some other Middle Eastern societies, operate in a more or less exclusive feminine milieu. Rather, there is a directness in male-female relations which, while valued in itself, nonetheless precludes the possibility of women constructing identities for themselves which are independent of those associated with the household and domestic roles.

Durrani women may converse in public with their husbands, and when they are free from domestic responsibilities they may, as long as they remain in their own or some close household, join men in conversation on any topic. Even on those formal occasions, such as weddings, when women do gather to the exclusion of men, all women and especially the female household heads are seen as household representatives, a circumstance which inhibits the development of structured relations of solidarity among women (cf. N. Tapper 1980: 69). Moreover, on such occasions when the host household will take the opportunity, in the food served or the items of trousseau displayed, to make statements about its standing in the community, women guests will make careful judgements about their success or failure.

Nonetheless, the celebrations associated with marriage offer virtually the only occasions when women together participate in activities which present an alternative version of gender relations. The women sing stereotyped *babulale* songs at weddings which can mock and castigate men's dominance, while women's dancing is identical in structure and form to that of men, suggesting a gender equality which is also expressed via the romantic lyrics of the dance tunes.

Within a neighbourhood, casual visiting among senior women or women from more powerful households is rare. Rather, such visiting is managed in more formal terms; for instance, women (as well as men) can invite women friends or kin to a meal. The absence of casual visiting among senior women may reflect their own secure personal position within their households, in which case they have little interest in cultivating outside friendships. It is often also a measure of the reluctance of other women to welcome a member of a competing household into their home; internal domestic arrangements are very exposed and visible to such visitors and can reveal a great deal about the condition of a household's internal relations. By contrast, junior married women do enjoy quite regular and more relaxed neighbourhood visiting, not least because much of the possible competitiveness between such women is deliberately suppressed. For instance, neighbour women are scorned if in everyday contexts they flaunt their good fortune – pretty clothing, rich diet, healthy children – before other women. And, there is the threat that braggarts will be stricken by the evil eye or jinn possession.

The lack of sexual segregation among Durrani, coupled with the rights men have to control all aspects of women's lives, leaves women very powerless indeed. However, as we shall see in chapter 10, there is an irony in men's ostensive power over women: because men's reputations and the relations between their households are construed in terms of their control of women's behaviour and the management of household marriages, women can ruin the reputation of a man and his household. However, in the same way that a household's success depends on the co-operation of both household men and women, so too household failure and dishonour are usually a consequence of mismanagement and misbehaviour on the part of various household members.

Household unity and honour

A man's reputation and that of his household are constructed in terms of the idiom of honour and shame. From an extensive vocabulary, the most widely used terms are *sharaf* (nobility, goodness), *gheyrat* (pride, self-respect), *nang* (honour), *izzat* (respect), *sharm* and *haya* (shame in both opposed senses), and *namus* (a man's honour derived from the morality of his womenfolk). There is a considerable degree of overlap between these terms; in essence they refer to the control of fertile resources (cf. Janata and Hassas 1975: 86). The concepts may also be subsumed in the more general notion of *num* (reputation, literally name, the big name or good name of a big man). Finally, the concept *'Pashtu'*, which directly associates honourable behaviour with ethnic identity, is used as a synonym for all or any of these facets of reputation.

The terms that are of particular relevance to relations between the sexes are *sharm* and its synonym *haya*, and *namus*. *Sharm*, shame in the sense of modesty and respect, is an appropriate sentiment for both men and women, though it also serves to underline the conceptual inferiority of women. Men are expected to show *sharm* before their elders and men of superior religious standing, while women are expected to defer to all men who have reached puberty and all women older than themselves or who are married to men who are their husband's seniors.

As with the English word 'shame', *sharm* in the opposite sense of 'disrepute' results from a lack of *sharm* (cf. Pitt Rivers 1965). Those who are 'shameless' (*bi-sharm, bi-haya*) are frightening and unpredictable and often get what they want in the short term at least, shaming others in doing so. Shamelessness may be spoken of as *badnami*, or *lachari*, or as being 'without Pashtu' (*bi-Pashtu*) or 'without *namus*' (*bi-namus*). Shameless behaviour is most often evaluated by the amount of public ridicule it excites: 'people's laughter' is a sanction of great force among the Maduzai. Such behaviour ranges from the unacceptable but essentially trivial to the most serious crimes the Maduzai can imagine. Kaftar, the Maduzai girl who eloped with the Hazara, was 'shameless' (*bi-sharma*) and also 'unveiled' (*bi-satra*): a *nighey* or shameless woman. Her father, whose reputation was ruined by her action, was said to 'eat shame'; he was *bi-namus*, 'father-accursed' (*pedar-nalat*); he was also called a 'bastard' (*bi-pedar*) and both a *daus* and *mordagau*, terms of general abuse meaning both cuckold and pimp. Both father and daughter were said to be 'not Pashtuns' or 'like gypsies'.

A man's *namus* depends on the propriety first of his mother, unmarried sisters and daughters and occasionally more distant female agnates, and second, his wife. To some extent a man continues to feel responsible for a married daughter or sister, particularly if he is closely related in some way to the husband. People sometimes say that a good wife increases the reputation of her husband alone, a bad one affects the reputation of her own agnates as well. In practice the husband's rights and obligations far outweigh those of the wife's patrikin. The extent to which a wife may be supported by her agnates is unpredictable and, indeed, they may effectively waive all responsibility by marrying her at a distance where they can neither control her subsequent behaviour nor be chastized for it.

Just as women are dominated by the men of the household in which they live, so too at a more abstract level the construction of gender roles may be seen to be dominated by considerations related to household structure and organization.

Paternal joint households

Large paternal joint households represent the ideal form and each man hopes in due course to head such a unit: the more descendants over whom he has direct authority, the greater his reputation and influence. The typical developmental cycle is as follows: a paternal joint household, at the death of the father, becomes a fraternal joint household if there are two or more married sons; half-brothers usually separate soon after their father's death, while full-brothers may stay together until their sons grow up; before these sons are married, the household is partitioned to form further incipient paternal joint households. Widows follow their favourite son at the partition of a fraternal joint household. Theoretically there are no limits on household size but households may divide prematurely for various reasons.

It would seem that the ideal household, and indeed actual practice, have changed in the last few decades. When the Maduzai were camp-dwelling nomads, and until they began to settle and take an interest in farmland, the main productive resource was the flocks, and fathers often gave a share in anticipatory inheritance to their sons at or soon after marriage. It was much more common, it seems, for sons to establish a measure of independence from their fathers. Father, sons and often other close agnates continued to co-operate in herding, but each nuclear family made independent decisions on many economic matters. In so far as agricultural land played a part, others were employed to work it, and the land-owner's shares of the plentiful produce and any income from it were amicably distributed at harvest time. Plots were not formally divided among the owners, and inheritance of land was not an issue in the organization of nomadic house-holds. More recently, as land has become the major resource and population in the valley has increased, plots have fragmented and economic independence for many households depends on access to land; there is considerable pressure among landowners to keep households –and patrimony – undivided at least until the father's death if not longer. Joint households now have major economic advantages as efficient farming units within which a flexible division of labour is possible. At the same time, there is still pressure for independence from young married men unwilling to contribute to the expenses of younger brothers' mar-riages, and wanting to control their own income and expenditure, whatever perils and economic costs they will face.

The distribution of household types and population among the four Maduzai core-lineages is shown in Table 15.

A single household may be subdivided into a number of separate cooking, eat-ing, dwelling or production units which may or may not coincide with each other at any one time. While such internal divisions may sometimes be signs of the incipient partition of the household, this is not necessarily the case and indeed the multiplicity of such units within one house may be seen as a source of pride, and proof of the good relations within it.

Table 15. *Household types and sizes, Maduzai core-lineages, 1972*

	Lineage A		Lineage B		Lineage C		Lineage D		Total		Total	
	No	Popu-lation	No	Popu-lation	No	Popu-lation	No	Popu-lation	No	Per cent	Popu-lation	Per cent
Household type												
Paternal joint	10	103	2	22	10	129	2	16	24	14	270	21
Fraternal joint	12	129	1	13	9	121	1	16	23	13	279	22
Simple	44	304	10	65	46	280	5	33	105	59	682	53
Fragmentary	11	23	2	9	5	16	7	15	25	14	63	5
Totals	77	559	15	109	70	546	15	80	177	100	1294	101
Household size	Lineage A		Lineage B		Lineage C		Lineage D		All Maduzai			
Mean	7		7		8		5		7			
Median	6		5		11–12		9		6–7			
Mode	4		3		5,7		1,5		4,6,7			
Range	1–27		3–13		1–22		1–16		1–27			

The 95 client households are not included, as census information is incomplete on them, so that the sample is probably slightly biased towards larger, wealthier, joint households.

A simple household is one containing a single married couple or a polygamous man and his wives and unmarried children. Engaged persons whose spouses live elsewhere are not counted as married for the purpose of the household census. A fragmentary household is one which contains no married couple. A paternal joint household includes a man and his wife or wives and at least one married son and his wife. A fraternal joint household contains at least two married brothers and their wives.

Men absent on military service or in prison are included in the figures. All single adults are counted with the households in which they are living; their presence or absence does not affect the categories used (but see below for more information on widows, widowers and other unmarried adults). There are undoubtedly some minor errors in the figures, particularly due to the difficulty of counting all small children; the most accurate figures are those relating to Lineage C.

In general, cooking and eating together are taken as a sign of unity within the household; in one notable case, a household of eleven adults (five married couples) and sixteen children was renowned for sharing one cooking-pot and bowl. However, meals are sometimes cooked at separate hearths for logistic reasons, or they may be cooked in one place but served in separate portions. Where such portions are given to men and women of the household respectively, this occasions no comment, but when it reflects a non-sexual division into eating units, the arrangement is likely to reflect tensions within the household. It is often women who feel that too many people eating from the same hearth is not a good thing: 'the food doesn't go round and the children fight'; but others consider it risible and shameful when members of a single household cook and eat separately, as was the case of one household in which bread was baked at three separate hearths each day.

The number of dwelling units (*kor*) of a household – tents, mud huts, or rooms in a large compound – can be multiplied to suit convenience and, unlike commensal units, provides no index of the internal relations within a household. In the winter settlements it is usual for each married woman to have her own room, while in the spring pastures a single household of, say, four married couples may live in the same tent, separate tents, or a combination of tents and mud huts. During the migrations and in the summer pastures, it is usual for all the members of a household to share a single tent. There is no concern to separate potentially marriageable children (e.g. FBS/FBD) into different households, as the matrifocal units within a single household are felt to be adequately segregated for this purpose; however, children living in the same household are almost never married to each other.

Finally, it may be noted that military service has little effect on household organization or any other aspect of the Maduzai economy or culture. Two years military service (*noukari*, *pushki*) is required of all able-bodied young men, but, because of the erratic way male births are registered, the order in which brothers are conscripted may be quite different from their birth order, while men whose ages differ by ten years or more may find themselves in the same levy. Some twenty Maduzai youths leave for military service each year but, because of the variety of their ages and the fact that they are not paid, it is, as the Maduzai themselves say, as if the conscripts are dead until their safe return proves otherwise.

The most radical type of subdivision within the household is that occasioned by the labour requirements demanded of households with a mixed economy – typified by the joint household which controls both flocks and farmland. The unity of such households lies in their joint property interests and in the fact that all income and expenditure are ultimately controlled by the household head. There are no formal rules about how the broader division of labour among household members is organized and what happens depends largely on the particular inclinations and skills of the individuals involved, though any arrangement will be directed or at least sanctioned by the household head.

Thus in some joint households couples may take turns, for a season or longer, living with the flocks or on the farmlands, while in others the division of labour may be semi-permanent. Women who are pregnant or nursing prefer to avoid the migration to the mountains, and illness or military service too may disrupt any emergent patterns. Especially for the summer season, children, even of four or five, may leave their parents' unit to reside with another couple of a joint household. In the case of older children, such arrangements are often designed to use their labour more fully. With smaller children, it is done to relieve the mother of child-care responsibilities: if she is making the migration to the mountains where she will be very busy, the children may stay behind, while a woman in the last stages of pregnancy who remains in the valley may send young children to the mountains for a season.

Maduzai regard the constituent units of a joint household as essentially interchangeable for the purpose of meeting labour requirements. Simple or fragmentary households which control both animals and agricultural land face similar labour requirements, and shortages are often resolved, however unsatisfactorily, by leaving either flocks or land in the care of others.

The division of labour between the sexes is as follows: men do all the work of agriculture and house construction, and tend, shear and butcher animals; they market produce and buy all foodstuffs and other supplies. Women rear young children, cook and clean, process milk, spin and weave. Other activities may involve the participation of both sexes: women milk while the men fix the sheep to head-ropes; the different stages of felt-making are divided between men and women; though women are held to be responsible for erecting the tents. Fetching water is done by either sex. Except in the case of butchering, which is forbidden for women, I know of no specific taboos prohibiting either sex from crossing the conventional boundaries, and indeed both widowers and widows may, though with considerable difficulty, manage a household single-handedly.

As we shall see, labour contracts between men are an important aspect of the economy. However, this should not obscure the fact that individual householders may also co-operate in economic activities of all kinds: in irrigation scheduling, in joining flocks into herding units, in reciprocal labour arrangements for harvesting, shearing and other economic activities such as marketing and trading expeditions. The fruits of men's production are partly consumed by the individual household, partly exchanged or sold on the market.

Women's involvement in co-operation outside the household is by contrast very limited. They may act as domestic servants for women in other households, but most often only as an incidental consequence of an economic contract between the husbands. The products of women's co-operation – principally felts – are primarily for domestic use, though some may become prestige items in daughters' trousseaux. The work is short-term, and almost always undertaken by unmarried girls, exchanged between households by mothers on a reciprocal basis. Otherwise, women's relations with other households involve few material exchanges and no active co-operation in any other domestic or child-rearing activities. In short the women's productive activities all take place within the domestic sphere and the fruits of their labour are destined almost entirely for domestic consumption or use.

Household property and resources
A household head administers both immovable and movable property. However, with immovable property (*mulk*) – rights in pasture, agricultural land and building land for houses – there is no necessary coincidence between the property-holding group and the household. The movable property (*mal*) of a household is usually in the form of animals and household goods, including those brought in by brides as trousseaux.

The household labour force is also managed by the head, and earnings which accrue to household members must be remitted to him. A man's first wife is not a gift: either he works for the household or, if he takes on herding or labouring jobs elsewhere, his earnings must all be put towards a brideprice – agnates living in other households do not help with brideprice payments. Though in some wealthier households a son may keep any earnings he receives from small jobs, in poorer households the luxury of any discretion in personal spending cannot be tolerated and income and produce from any source will be pooled. A woman who uses household resources such as wool, but works independently to make blankets or felts, will usually be allowed to keep these for her own use and they become the property of the couple alone. However, the status of such conjugal property, as of the much more important trousseau, is ambiguous; it can be alienated by the household head, though his action is likely to give rise to serious quarrels if it has not been done with at least the tacit agreement of the couple and the promise that they will eventually be given some kind of compensation.

The payment and receipt of brideprices for children of a household are also ambiguous. Maduzai say that not only has a father the sole right to decide whom his children shall marry, but he also has exclusive responsibility for seeing his sons married, while any brideprice he receives for his daughters is his alone. In other words, the household head has no formal authority in this sphere. In practice however the men of a joint household are expected to act in harmony: the household head arranges all marriages of its members – he is said to have been given this authority by the others – and directs the raising of all brideprices paid and the disposal of all those received. A man will refuse the household head such a role only if he intends to precipitate the partition of the household, for, as we shall see, brideprices figure so prominently in household budgeting that no other solution would be tolerable.

Pastures and pastoralism
In 1971 the Maduzai were still heavily involved in pastoralism. They owned around 10,000 ewes, and half the households had between twenty and several hundred head. Each herd of about 500 ewes and some goats is tended by a hired chief shepherd and a herding assistant, both of whom are sometimes from another ethnic group but just as often a poorer Durrani trying to amass enough money to marry. The Maduzai raise two breeds of sheep, *karakul* mainly for lambskins and *arabi* mainly for meat, the objective in both cases being market sales for cash and credit. Both breeds are shorn twice a year; the spring clip is sold or given to carpet-weavers on contract, but the Maduzai keep the summer clip for making felt and cloth. The sheep are milked from March until July, the products ghee (clarified butter) and dried whey-balls forming an essential part of most people's diet.

All pasture land in Afghanistan is formally state property (*sultani*), and only usufruct rights in it are officially recognized by the government. Rights to the steppe pastures bordering the Saripul valley were established when the Maduzai first arrived in the area, and they were officially recorded in the names of camp leaders around 1950. The Hazarajat mountain pastures used by the Saripul nomads and others in summer are customarily divided between tribal groups, and access to grazing is theoretically free. However tribal Khans and local Hazara chiefs maintain *de facto* control over most such pasture areas and they typically collect an illegal seasonal grazing fee (*alafchar*) for each herd using the land.

Typically a *yurt* (Pashtu *mena*), or area of winter/spring pasture, is shared between brothers or between father's brothers and brother's sons co-operating in herding their combined flocks of some 500 animals. If this agnatic corporation owns fewer than this number of animals, it may allow other households to join them as clients, and they may further look after the animals of households living elsewhere, sometimes for a remuneration in kind and in season, such as milk or wool. Thus the 'herding camp' (*khel* or *kaley*), a residential group, may be distinguished analytically from the 'herding unit', consisting of all those people owning animals which are herded jointly. The leader of the herding camp, the *sar khel*, assumes responsibility for the management of the herd, while the expenses of the joint herding venture are shared. The *sar khel*'s position is informal: in many cases he is no more than *primus inter pares*, and decisions affecting the camp and herding unit are reached by consultation among all the household heads.

Rights in the steppe pastures are held by fixed groups of close agnates, who are thereby constrained to co-operate in herding camps and herd management units, though they themselves may be joined by client households. These same constraints do not apply in the summer pastures, where agnates have no material interest in camping or herding together. By the end of the spring, tension between the households of close agnates is likely to be high; since the summer grazing system allows them to disperse, they do so with some alacrity, joining for the spring migration those households with which they hope to camp in the mountains.

The migration of some 300 kilometres to the mountain pastures is done as quickly as possible. The sheep travel separately over the mountain ranges to reach the summer pastures early, while the camel caravans, following the valleys, hurry along to rejoin the sheep and resume milking. In May the early mornings may be very cold, in places snow may still lie on the ground; campsites are narrow and, like fodder for the pack animals, are difficult to find because of the increasing grain cultivation by local mountain villagers. For this migration it is now usual for groups of no more than five or six households to move together.

In the summer pastures the camps are very small; sometimes a single household will live alone. For the women particularly this isolation is coupled with much hard work. For a month and a half, they milk, make ghee and then make felts. When these jobs are finished, the summer camps congregate for the return migration to Saripul in August, though the herds stay on a month or so with the shepherds, until the first frosts of autumn drive them back down to the steppes of Turkistan. The Maduzai say that the August migration is like a party: the hard work of the summer is finished, and they look forward to the reunion with the rest of their families in the valley. The leisurely pace of this migration coincides with their mood. The mountain villagers have harvested their crops and their hostility towards the nomads is consequently lessened; moreover there are now stubble fields where the nomads can camp and graze their pack animals. Larger groups move together now, sometimes consisting of twenty to twenty-five households, and when they camp near abundant water they are likely to stop for two or three days between stages.

Table 16 shows the number of households of the core-lineages which (in whole or in part) joined the herds in spring 1971, and the households which (in whole or in part) went to the mountains that summer. Most camps also included tents from Maduzai client households and often others from other subtribes. That was the second year of a severe drought in northern Afghanistan, affecting both pastures and crops. Many Maduzai suffered sheep losses and many who previously used to accompany the flocks to the mountains did not bother to do so, or (as indicated in parentheses in the table) sent only an unmarried son to supervise the flocks. The following winter was very severe and the flock losses were terrible; by the summer of 1972 many households had abandoned pastoralism, most of them temporarily, some of them perhaps for good. Few households joined the remaining animals in the spring pastures, and none went to the mountains.

The valley land

The land tenure system for farmland depends very much on the irrigation system. The towns and villages of Saripul and Shiberghan receive water from the same river on an eighteen-day cycle. In Saripul there are some forty canals, each of which waters the land of one or more villages according to a time schedule related to the size of individual holdings. In villages near the canal head, such as Chinar, most houses have domestic reservoirs filled every cycle; further down, where the canal water does not always reach – as in Sinjit and Naju – village households have thirty-metre wells to provide sweet water.

A Maduzai landowner wishing to cultivate his valley land opts for one of a number of possible arrangements, depending on his inputs of land, labour, water, seed, oxen and implements. If he has the labour he is likely to work the land himself; if not, he may hire a farmhand, find a sharecropper, or even rent his land to another farmer. Finally, if a landowner needs money, he may give his land in mortgage (*girau*) for a sum well below its market value, giving up all rights to cultivation and produce until he redeems it by paying back the same sum.

The fields are normally cultivated in a two-year rotation. The main crops are divided into 'white', winter-sown wheat and barley; 'green' summer crops such as melons, sesame, flax, beans, maize, alfalfa, tomatoes; and dry-farmed wheat, melons, sesame, and other crops. There are vineyards below Saripul, but the best grapes are grown above. In good years cotton has been widely cultivated as a cash crop, while in bad years maize is widely grown. The basis of diet among the Maduzai, as in most of the region, is wheat bread and animal ghee, supplemented

Table 16. *Maduzai core-lineage households which joined herding camps in spring and summer, 1971*

Lineage	Total households	Spring households	camps	Summer households	camps
A	77	58	22	17+(3)	11
B	15	15	6	2+(4)	2
C	70	49	14	16+(1)	8
D	15	2	1	(1)	—
Totals	177	124 (70%)	43	35+(9)= 44 (25%)	21

Numbers in brackets (but not percentages) indicate households who sent sheep to the mountains with shepherds.

on festive occasions, and in the houses of rich men, by rice and meat. The poor, particularly in lean years, replace wheat with poor quality rice, maize or millet; and animal ghee with sesame and linseed oil. Fruit (apricots, grapes, melons) is much eaten in season but vegetables are incidental and not highly regarded.

The locations of the lands originally acquired by the lineage heads were only vaguely noted on their deeds, though this did not prevent the further registration of these lands after they had been subdivided and transferred to other lineage members. It is usual for considerable discrepancies to exist between a deed-holder's entitlement and the area he and his agnates actually farm.

Almost all the Maduzai householders who own land are co-heirs to plots which are still registered in the name of a deceased agnate. Formal division of the land is avoided if at all possible. When it occurs, each parcener insists on receiving equal amounts of good and bad quality land, and is likely to end up with several small plots higher and lower on the canal, some of the latter receiving irrigation water only in rainy years. Another consideration which is never far from the villagers' minds is that, once divided and re-registered in the names of the individual heirs, the land may then be more easily alienated by them through sales to more distant agnates.

Security and the economies of size which are possible with joint ownership are clearly recognized and appreciated. In general, household division takes place without immediate reference to land tenure. Where the separating household has potential *de jure* rights to land, it may secure these by maintaining rights to cultivation and produce in one of two ways. Either, in the case of larger holdings, a *de facto* division of the land takes place, sometimes renewed each season, or, in the case of less extensive holdings, the land is managed jointly and shares in the produce are distributed at the harvest.

The Maduzai make a distinction between agricultural and residential land.

They hold that the latter must be sold outright, and never rented or mortgaged. Since all land sales are within the *qaum* (i.e. to other Maduzai of the core-lineages or with known connections with the core-lineages), the effect of this rule is to give all lineage houseowners a comparable interest in the village, while relegating all outsiders living there to a position of dependence as clients. When a household of the lineage, for whatever reasons, sells its own inherited house land, then, if household members or their descendants remain in the village, they too will have to assume a client status with regard to their dwelling place. Of the 70 households of Lineage C, 27 live on an agnate's house land, four live in houses belonging to their affines and one man has no house at all. However the consequences of dependence vary considerably for agnates as well as outsiders; a poor or weak dependent household may be very vulnerable to a landlord's whims, while a wealthier dependent household is not. The only exception to these kinds of residential arrangements is when house land has been ceded outright as a bequest (*waqf*) to a religious man who wishes to live in the village.

The relation between household partition and the division of house land parallels that regarding agricultural land. That is, a *de facto* division of the land typically coincides with household division, though any *de jure* settlement of hereditary claims may lag behind indefinitely. And, of course, *de facto* joint ownership of house land presents constraints similar to those associated with agricultural land: its outright sale becomes much more complicated and much less likely to take place.

Household wealth and income

The Maduzai subtribe as a whole operates in a surplus economy; that is, the grain grown on the irrigated valley lands owned by the subtribe is usually adequate for the needs of the total population; similarly the wool and meat produce of the Maduzai flocks are on the whole adequate for all the subtribe, while deficiencies in milk products and wheat are far more than made up by proceeds from the sale of lambskins and cash crops such as cotton. Such generalizations of course disguise the considerable inequalities in wealth and income that exist among the Maduzai, between those who own several hundred sheep and a hundred or more *jeribs* of land, and those who have no such capital at all but must depend on selling their labour.

I shall not attempt a full analysis of Maduzai production here, but some further indications of productivity and the rewards of labour must be given if the meaning of marriage payments and their place in the total economy are to be understood. Although the great seasonal and annual variation in conditions make talk of 'averages' somewhat pointless, it can be said that a flock of 60 ewes could produce meat and milk sufficient for the expected annual consumption of the average family of three adults and four children, while income from skins (about 10,000 Afs.) and fleeces (about 1,000 Afs.) would allow them the bare minimum of bought goods – flour, rice, fat and incidental items. Thus, 60 ewes (with a cash income of 11,000 Afs.) would seem the break-even point for the budget of the 'average' pastoral household if it owned no land. Ownership of 10 *jerib*s (about 2 hectares) of irrigated land would allow for similar consumption patterns in a household without flocks. This said, we must leave the hypothetical 'average' household. However, to put the following details in perspective, the reader should note that in Kabul in 1967–1972, £1 sterling fluctuated at around 200 Afs.

In 1972 a day labourer was paid 50 Afs. per day (800 Afs. per month), but employment was very seasonal. A domestic servant or herding assistant was given food and clothing for himself and paid a cash wage of 200–500 Afs. a month; even the maximum annual wages of 6,000 Afs. (£30) were insufficient to keep a family of two adults and two children, particularly in years of very high grain prices like 1970–1971. Such jobs are usually taken by men without dependants, who can save almost the full cash wages. Servants with dependants survive only on charity. A chief shepherd receives food and clothing and 10 per cent of pastoral produce: his average income is worth probably about 10,000 Afs., though it may range from nothing to more than 20,000 Afs. in a good year. A man who share-crops in the valley, providing his own labour, may gain produce worth more than 10,000 Afs., but even if the crop fails completely he is guaranteed around half a ton of wheat, on which a family of four could just live for a year.

As Table 17 suggests, within the subtribe the range between the rich and poor is wide, and while it would seem that such economic cleavages have always existed, the wealthy are more secure than before, now that their productive capital is the increasingly profitable resource of irrigated farmland. Twenty-five per cent of lineage households control 68 per cent of all capital assets, while another 25 per cent own virtually no capital resources at all. The range of capital holdings per household is between zero and 1400 units.

All Quartile I households in Table 17 had sheep and went to spring pastures, and their tents and flocks comprised the large majority of those going to the mountains. Most of Quartiles II and III had sheep and went to spring pastures, while most of Quartile IV also went, but without sheep. All Quartile I and II households had land, and so did most of Quartile III. Altogether 47 households had land, with holdings averaging over 20 *jerib*s; 42 households had sheep, with flocks averaging 100 head. Fourteen households had no capital at all, though some of them had expectations of inheriting land in due course.

A slightly different picture emerges if we consider household size in relation to wealth. There is in fact a clear correlation of household wealth, size and type: but it is striking that Quartiles I and II have roughly similar average holdings per person of valley land, while Quartile I households are distinguished by their much larger average flock; in flock sizes, on the other hand, Quartile II differs little from Quartile III, which has a much lower average land holding. This

Table 17. *Lineage C, household wealth and size*

	I (350+ units)	II (140–350 units)	III (40–140 units)	IV (0–40 units)	Totals
Number of households	16	17	17	17	67
Units of valley land					
(*jeribs* × 10)	5895 (16)[a]	3180 (17)	745 (14)	9	9820 (47)
Ewes owned	3560 (16)	635 (13)	414 (10)	54 (3)	4663 (42)
Other wealth	1490 (9)	150 (5)	0	0	1640 (14)
Total wealth	10945 (16)	3965 (17)	1159 (17)	54 (3)	16123 (53)
Average per household	684	233	68	3	241
Percentage of total wealth	67.9	24.6	7.2	0.3	100
Households with members employed outside	4	6	15	17	42
Households going (1971) all or part to *spring* pastures	16	12	10	11	49
to *summer* pastures	11	4	1	(1)[b]	16+ (1)
Population	217	130	109	84	540
Mean household size	13.56	7.65	6.41	4.94	8.05
Valley land units per person	27	24	7	0	18
Ewes per person	16	5	4	1	9
Household types					
Paternal joint	5	2	2	1	10
Fraternal joint	6	2	1	0	9
Simple	5	12	13	13	43
Fragmentary	0	1	1	3	5

For this table, 67 households of Lineage C have been put into quartiles according to wealth in land and animals (but not including pasture land used for grazing or dry-farmed, nor marriageable daughters). Wealth has been assessed in 'units', such that one *jerib* of irrigated land is equivalent to 10 units, and one ewe is one unit; in 1970 such a unit was worth somewhat less than 1,000 Afs. The value of mortgaged land has been divided, half assigned to the mortgagee and half to the mortgagor. Expectations of inheritance have not been included here.

   This assessment relates to 1971; 3 households elsewhere included within Lineage C have not been included here for the following reasons: one simple household resided with affines of Lineage A and we were unable to collect detailed information on the household economy; the second, a simple household, apparently supported themselves entirely by theft (see N. Tapper 1979: 204); while the third did not separate from a larger fraternal household until 1972. Information from other households of the subtribe indicates that generalizations made on the basis of Lineage C are broadly valid for core-lineage households, but not for the clients, whose households are likely to be both smaller and poorer.
[a]Numbers in brackets indicate numbers of households concerned.
[b]One household (1) kept its few sheep in the village in the summer of 1971.

suggests that large-scale pastoralism is now chiefly an enterprise for the wealthy household with labour in excess of agricultural requirements. Indeed, very few Maduzai households now depend exclusively, or even predominantly, on pastoralism alone.

   On the basis of expected income from capital holdings, all households of

Quartiles I and II are fundamentally prosperous. Such households are said to be 'full' (*sir, mor*), to have much property (*dunya*) and wealth (*doulat*); they are well-off and secure (*tayar*). This is certainly not the case for many households of Quartile III and all those of Quartile IV, many of which were described as 'hungry' (*ghwasha*), and some were literally so. Other terms for households without capital are 'poor" (*khwar, gharib*) and 'light-weight' (*spak*). In fact only 25 households depend entirely on production from their own land and/or flocks, so that 42 gain some or all of their income from various kinds of employment, ranging from the responsible position of water-master through independent enterprises of house-building to jobs of cowherd or field watchman, or by engaging in small-scale trading activities. Finally, one of the poor household heads went begging in a distant region of Afghanistan for a part of each year.

The authority of household heads
As the Maduzai put it, 'There are two sides to household headship, male and female': the man who takes decisions for the men is the *korwala*, or the senior or big man of the house (*da kala mashar*, or *da kala loy*). His female counterpart is known as *da kala mashara* or *da kala loya*. Both 'senior' and 'big' may be taken to mean 'eldest'. Finally, both the male and female household heads may be known by the title *ikhtiardar*, or decision-maker.

Ideally, and most often in practice, the male head has ultimate control over all household activities and personally directs those which take place outside the house, including herding, farming, buying and selling in the bazaar, and marriage negotiations. The female head directs the allocation of labour and consumption within the house and must also muster surplus resources for the entertainment of guests. It is however possible for the balance of power and authority between the two household heads to be reversed and for the female head to assume final responsibility for the management of the household. Such is also the case in those relatively rare households where a widow with sons refuses to remarry and herself maintains an independent establishment.

Neither age, marital status nor even gender are necessarily criteria used to determine household headship, and there are no formal rules about who in a household should hold the position. Usually overall headship is in the hands of the oldest man, but the Maduzai insist that this need not be the case and they refuse, even theoretically, to sacrifice economic and political expediency to the ideals which require respect and obedience to one's elders. Indeed, of the thirteen Lineage C households in which a father and grown son(s) lived together, in only eight was the father the overall head, though of the nine households where two or more grown brothers lived together after their father's death, in all but two the oldest was the overall head. Within a household, general competence alone is usually a sufficient criterion to determine who should be household head. And it is explicitly accepted that public recognition of ability plays an important role in the choice: the household flocks, land and house will become known by a man's name and he will become its acknowledged leader. In this way, they say, a man's name may disappear even before his death and his house may be known by that of his son or brother. But the converse is also true, and a dead man's name may linger and be used to refer to the household of his descendants for many years.

As is the case with the overall head, the Maduzai, both women and men, insist that there are no rules which determine *a priori* a woman's claims to the position of female household head, and they deny that particular statuses – e.g. the wife of the male household head or the mother-in-law in a paternal joint household – are inherently more compatible with headship than others. Again, they insist, a leader emerges from among the household women informally and her authority then becomes acknowledged more generally. Indeed the pattern of women's leadership was rather more varied than that of the overall headship: for example, in seven of the ten paternal joint households in Lineage C, the father was the head, but in only four of these seven was his only wife herself the female leader, while in one other paternal joint household the father's senior wife was the recognized headwoman, though her co-wife's eldest son was the male household head.

Like the overall head, the female head is expected to be a creditable representative of the household, and intelligence, conversational ability and general manner and appearance are as important to the efficiency of household management as are more prosaic domestic skills. However, the role is not at all clearly defined, and there are few external constraints to guarantee a certain standard of behaviour. The female headship may be expanded in scope and authority to allow a strong woman to become the *de facto* overall head, while it may amount to little more than a nominal status in the case of a weak woman who holds the position by default when there is no other woman in the household to take her place.

In spite of the fact that men and women agree that a household without adequate female leadership is without blessing (*bi-barakat*) and headed for ruin, sometimes a household may have two women who are both regarded as household heads, while in others each woman of the household is said to be 'her own head' (*pa khpal sar*). Bad relations between women of a household, however, are certainly not a sufficient cause of household partition, nor are good relations between them any guarantee of household unity. When men and women speak positively about unity, they focus on relations between men, yet when the subject of disharmony is broached, stereotypical explanations about quarrelling women are often mentioned. Women can and do agitate for household division but there does not seem to be a direct relation between women's quarrels and the blame which is attributed to them. Rather, since there is always likely to be some tension between women of a household, men can plausibly deflect public attention and perhaps private guilt from their failure to live up to the ideal of harmonious relations among close male agnates. I think it is likely that women accept this explanation partly because many of them will have experienced just such tension themselves, but primarily because they all subscribe so whole-heartedly to notions of their independence within a domestic unit and can empathize with those who have not achieved it.

Roles and relationships within the household

Expectations of marriage are fundamentally similar for both sexes: the relationship between the partners should grow to be based on mutual affection and respect and their union should be fertile.

Romantic love is celebrated in stereotypical stories, songs and poetry and it is the sentiment said to be behind the most colourful and dramatic attachments formed by the Maduzai, whether within a marriage or not. Notions of romantic love are associated with an idealization of physical qualities, and ideals of male and female beauty play a part in all social evaluations. However, thoughtfulness, generosity, intelligence and companionship are also seen by both men and women as essential components of a happy marriage (see N. Tapper: forthcoming b).

In marriages where there is respect and affection between spouses, this is not disguised or denied in public. Frank and entertaining conversation about all aspects of social life is valued and at the evening meal both partners are likely to recount their day's activities in the most amusing and informative manner possible. Other more general issues may be discussed and the couple will typically arrive at joint decisions on virtually all matters affecting their household directly. In other ways too a happy marriage is visible in the contact between spouses: a man may cut his wife's fringe for her or they may work side by side to complete some arduous task like preparing the camel loads during the migration. Indeed a close comradeship between husband and wife may be expressed not only in spontaneous displays of affection but also in the sexual satisfaction of both spouses (*pace* Vieille 1978: 161–8).

Nonetheless, it is women, rather than men, who put the highest premium on affection within a marriage. Though a man may be able to do little to extricate himself from an unhappy marriage, he may, unlike his wife, at least take comfort in his theoretical right to divorce her or to make another marriage for love. In any case, a man is always assumed to be the dominant partner in a marriage and if he is dissatisfied he may punish his wife physically or withdraw the material and emotional support on which she depends. Certainly men do strike their wives in anger, but a man who does so regularly is less likely to be admired than to be despised by outsiders as weak and ineffectual. Other members of the community will not normally intervene in a man's treatment of his wife even when, as in one extreme case, it leads to her death. But they are likely to take advantage of the lack of good sense and control that such a man reveals and to interfere with other activities of his household and manage or manipulate them to their own advantage.

More often, the loss of a husband's affection deprives a woman of the small luxuries she prizes – clothing, trinkets and the thoughtful purchase of domestic goods at the bazaar. Women who find themselves thus uncared for suffer continual embarrassment and deeply fear public laughter. Moreover, a woman's standing in both the household and the wider community depends in part on the character of her relationship with her husband. A woman whose words are unheard at home commands little consideration from others.

Women's attitudes toward men are fraught with ambivalence: men are to be pitied for the crushing responsibility of supporting a family, yet their control over women's lives is deeply resented. Men's attitudes toward women are also ambivalent. Women may be praised as resourceful, intelligent companions, but these very qualities are feared for they threaten both the theory and practice of male domination. The few kinds of love magic with which the Maduzai are familiar and claim to use add further insight into their complex gender stereotypes: those employed by men focus on the element of physical attraction in romantic love, while those sought by women are believed to make a husband affectionate and stay his bad temper. So too it is the women who believe that other men and women, jealous of a happily married couple, may use charms maliciously to break them apart.

Husbands' overwhelming formal superiority in marriage constrains wives to act with great circumspection. This helplessness of women is, I think, paradoxically reflected in the fact that, though the Maduzai insist that there is no divorce among them after the Islamic *nikah* ceremony has been performed (but see the exceptional case of Shekar, p. 233), the few times I heard divorce being discussed seriously were in terms of a judicial divorce for women. That is to say that the Maduzai only really become aware of the extent to which men control women's lives in extreme circumstances. Thus, women and men say that a woman whose husband is impotent has legitimate grounds for seeking a judicial divorce, though I learned of no cases among Durrani in which divorce on such grounds was obtained. Equally, Maduzai admit the possibility of a woman obtaining a judicial divorce in the case of persistent and severe maltreatment, though again I know of no such case where this occurred.

A woman would need the support of outsiders to her household to obtain such a judicial divorce, yet Maduzai almost never directly intervene in the domestic affairs of others. The limits of non-intervention are clear where married women in desperate circumstances have no kin available or willing to support them (see N. Tapper 1979: 390, 443ff., 459 n. 10).

Apart from a husband's impotence and extreme cruelty, there are no grounds on which the Maduzai consider a woman's right to seek divorce. For example, long absence of the husband, for whatever reasons, would not necessarily be considered grounds for divorce. Cases of the husband abandoning his wife are rare. However, when Maduzai comment on such cases, the woman's plight is often

treated as wholly irrelevant. Two cases illustrate this point; both were the consequence of the same crime. In the first, a young girl whose engagement had been
forced upon her family by her husband (see N. Tapper 1979: 424), was left
'sitting in her father's house' when her husband was sentenced to twelve years'
imprisonment for his part in robbery and murder. By the time of his release the
girl would be in her middle twenties, and yet it was said that her father would
never seek a divorce for her. As one man explained,

She won't be freed because they are Afghan [Durrani]. She will have to be asleep for
twelve years. They can't give her elsewhere.

In the second case, the engagement occurred only a week before the husband was
arrested and subsequently imprisoned for eighteen years. His father-in-law, a
poverty-stricken man, petitioned the government that either his daughter be
divorced or her brideprice be paid so that she could be married. The authorities
apparently sympathized with the loss of income his daughter's engagement
entailed and demanded that the groom make the choice himself. We left before
his answer was known, but it was clear that the outcome would not be affected by
any pity for the girl should the marriage be completed.

Children and the household

Men and women agree that the fertility of a union is the most important aspect of
a marriage; the image they use comes from the Koran: that children are like fruit,
and their parents like fruiting trees, blessed and pleasing to look at. Both men and
women are very demonstrative and indulgent with their young children, whom
they consider a great source of pleasure and entertainment. Discipline is minimal
and parents rarely adopt an authoritarian pose. Indeed, parents who react
severely to the misbehaviour of their child, even in brief moments of anger, are
likely to be publicly reprimanded by other adults, while the physical abuse of a
child is considered a heinous crime and appears to be rare (but see p. 252;
N. Tapper 1979: 285 n. 21, 443).

   Though the mother takes primary responsibility for the day-to-day care of her
children, she is often assisted by her husband in minor and more pleasant tasks,
and it is usual for a man to play with his children whenever he is present. Moreover, Maduzai expect that a child who is no longer nursing, and perhaps followed
by a new baby, will grow very close to its father and for a time ignore its mother
altogether. At this stage children of either sex often accompany their father on
errands.

   Children of both sexes are said to be the gift of God, but sons are incomparably
more welcome than daughters, for the continuity of a household depends on its
sons, while daughters are 'lost' at marriage. As one woman said,

Daughters are saddening; they are separated from their parents and the hearts of their
mothers and fathers burn for them, particularly if their husbands are poor or if they have

co-wives or their wombs are not always full. Sons never leave their parents and it doesn't matter if they are poor or have trouble, because they are all together.

The daughter's pitiable situation is reflected in infant feeding practices: to compensate her for the hardship to come, a mother may nurse her daughter for up to two and a half years, while a boy 'who will always be at home and have everything' may only be nursed until he is two. Similarly if a woman becomes pregnant while still nursing – an eventuality, known as being 'milk-to-milk', women dread – the older child, if a boy, may be weaned immediately, while this is less likely in the case of a girl. In all other respects the physical care of children of both sexes is similar and equally solicitous, though the cultural bias in favour of sons is expressed in the rituals associated with their birth and in other small ways (see N. Tapper 1979: 286). Early childhood is free of rigid sex typing. Children of both sexes play together, and boys will learn how to spin and make felts and may be expected on occasion to help with the milking, while girls sometimes herd near the house or act as watchmen for the 'green' summer crops. The division of labour associated with gender emerges only when children are around ten years old. At this time too, a man will quite deliberately alter his previously close, affectionate relationship with his daughters, as if this new remoteness will make it easier for him to marry them in a more calculating manner.

The rate of infant mortality among the Maduzai is very high. In a Tajik village some 100 miles to the east of Saripul, a thorough demographic study disclosed a rate of 153 deaths per thousand, among the highest in the world (CINAM 1973: vol. 2, 23ff.; see also UNICEF 1978; M. & R. Poulton 1979). While my information on child mortality among the Maduzai is incomplete, the figures I have on mortality before puberty suggest a comparability with the Tajik study. For the 39 women on whom I have complete reproductive histories and whose child-bearing period had ended (by death or menopause) at least fifteen years ago, an average of 6.5 children per woman were born alive: 48 per cent of all these children died before the age of fifteen. Six of these 39 women died in ways which other women associated with childbearing.

Women can and do joke about childlessness: either laughing at the nuisance of having intercourse and babies or joking that barren women are well-loved by their husbands because their vaginas are tight like a young girl's. However, failure to produce surviving male children is the greatest tragedy a woman may suffer. A woman who is childless regards herself as worthless; the prospect of her lonely and unsupported old age is terrifying. Any happiness in her marriage is likely to be destroyed if her husband takes a second wife, though if the couple are fond of each other this may not happen for as many as ten childless years. And though their behaviour belies it, women with daughters but no sons say their misery is as great as if they had no children at all. Male sterility is also recognized as a serious disability, but it less visible socially and arrangements which in part compensate for childlessness are available to men but not women. For example, one childless man married a widow whose children by a former marriage he was able to treat as his own, while another man, having no sons of his own, married his one daughter uxorilocally to form an unorthodox paternal joint household; I also strongly suspect that men who fear they are sterile encourage their wives to become pregnant through an adulterous liaison.

The need and desire for children and the very high rate of child mortality combine to put great pressure on the procreative abilities of both men and women, for there are no generally recognized cultural alternatives such as adoption or fostering to supplement biological inadequacy. A couple's overall standing in the community depends greatly on the number and sex of their surviving children, and effective marriage strategies may be seen as virtually the only, though often unsatisfactory, way of counteracting lack of control over reproduction.

Other domestic relationships

Only in the most limited way are parents felt to be responsible for the character of their grown children, and in general the Maduzai are tolerant of individual differences and accept personal foibles with a degree of fatalism. Though in practice men may be open, demonstrative and deeply affected by their emotional ties with their parents, siblings and children, women often claim a monopoly on such feelings. The difference, I think, is that, in their material and emotional dependence on others, women tend to offer their affection uncritically and without regard to wider political and economic issues, whereas men will, and often must, sacrifice affection for other concerns. For both these reasons, the content of relationships within a household varies considerably, depending on the personalities of the individuals involved and the extent to which household wealth and security makes it easy to be generous and thoughtful of others. Though there are, of course, normative rules about kinship status and role behaviour, these are few and of a very general kind (on kinship terminology, see N. Tapper 1979: App. I).

A grown son is expected to show respect for the authority of his father in all things, both because of the care his father has taken in raising him and because of the intrinsic wisdom of the older man. Moreover, father and son are expected to help each other throughout their lives, even if the son has separated from the father's household. Sons may bitterly disappoint their fathers if they are weak and unreliable, but only very rarely will the relationship of mutual support be completely severed. The relationship of a mother and her grown children involves even fewer explicit expectations: they should be loving and respectful, while she is likely to be almost wholly uncritical of them. Given her dependence on her sons' good will in her old age, it is hardly surprising that, within the household, she will almost invariably take their part in quarrels with their wives. In spite of a father's great fondness for his young daughters, he becomes emotionally distant from them once they are married, whereas for women, the ties between mother and daughter are often the strongest emotional bonds they know. However, there are no formal visiting rights between a mother and her married daughter and, in practice, a woman often can do little to help them, though, in one extreme case, I heard of a mother's stealing food and flour from her own household to support her child.

Relations between siblings are ideally supportive. This indeed is usually the case between sisters who, regardless of the circumstances in which they find themselves after marriage, are likely to remain close and loyal to one another throughout their lives. They are sometimes able to arrange marriages between their children and they say that a sister's child is regarded with the same affection as their own. Relations between brothers and sisters are far more ambivalent because of inequality in their respective statuses after marriage and the fact that a brother's relationship with his sister is then always mediated by her husband. Women say that a good brother is one who listens to whatever they have to say and helps them in any way he can, but there is often little he can do. To bring themselves closer to their brothers' support, sisters may press exceptionally hard for marriages between their own and their brothers' children, while, if a brother's household is in dire straits, a sister may be prepared to steal food or clothing for him from her own household.

Because of the nature of property holding and in spite of the ideals of fraternal love and support, relations between adult brothers are likely to be strained both as they approach household partition and even afterwards when they are established in independent households. Quarrels between brothers are regarded both as endemic and as a travesty of social norms; as a leading man remarked about one such long-running dispute: 'There is Afghanistan for you. A man loses his gun and the first person he accuses is his brother.'

Of affinal relations within a household, those of the daughter-in-law with her husband's kin are in many ways the most crucial. She is likely to have little personal contact with her husband's father, towards whom she is expected to be modest and demure. However, a young wife is very conscious of her father-in-law's social position. Her self-esteem as a bride is closely related to this and a lack of commitment to her marital household may reflect the discrepancies she perceives between her treatment and household wealth and power. A woman is expected to show deference to her mother-in-law in all things. In the same way that a father has a residual right to respect and support from a son even after the latter has established an independent household, so too does a mother. If widowed, she may join her son's household where, if she is a strong personality, she may reassert her control over her daughter-in-law and become the female household head. When a man's mother has been directly involved in the choice of his bride, she and her daughter-in-law are likely to get on reasonably well together. But if mother and daughter-in-law are at odds, the fault is almost invariably seen by outsiders to lie with the younger woman. Relations between women and their sons' wives may, in extreme cases, deteriorate from verbal battles to physical violence, the strain often increasing directly in proportion to the number of children the young woman has and the time she must spend caring for them. Relations between a bride and her husband's sisters are likely simply to reflect those with her mother-in-law.

A woman is expected to be reserved before her husband's brothers, though in fact, if they are younger than her husband, they may become her close companions and even her allies against him. Men say they treat their brothers' wives as sisters, but people are well aware of the ambivalent nature of this relationship, for if the husband dies they are likely to become man and wife. Men and women insist that such a change in their respective roles is easily managed, though in fact men sometimes refuse to marry a brother's widow because she is 'too close' (p. 185). One woman, however, admitted as a general principle that when a woman's husband is away (e.g. on military service) she may secretly sleep with his brother, though men, publicly at least, insist that such a relationship is utterly forbidden.

A man's relations with his wife's younger sisters have the same character as do a woman's relations with her husband's younger brothers, though they are never likely to be more than superficial. Relations between a man and his wife's brother are, once the marriage has been completed, ideally relaxed and supportive. Whatever content they have in practice, such relationships involve no formal obligations at all.

By contrast with the easy-going relations women are likely to have with their husband's brothers, their relations with the latter's wives are likely to be jealous. Such women are likely to be in direct competition for control of household resources on behalf of their respective husbands and children, though they may see their competition in terms of the strength and power each has over her own husband. Any differential treatment of the brides of a household by their husbands' parents is likely to exacerbate greatly the tension between such women, and the partition of a household is often blamed specifically on them.

Finally, co-wives too compete on behalf of their own children, whose interests are most directly forwarded by a wife's gaining and holding the affection of her husband. Men who marry a second wife for love are often grossly unfair to their first wife and her children. If the older woman is past menopause she may well choose to live with a married son in a separate household and will often be encouraged by her husband to do so. But men may marry polygynously for other reasons which do not so easily lead to the unequal treatment of their wives. Again there are virtually no rules governing relations between co-wives, bar the expectation that each will have separate sleeping quarters and that they will sleep with their husband on alternative nights (an important provision since each woman will want as many children as possible). Co-wives who are treated fairly by their husband often adjust to their relationship with a calm dignity, but women nonetheless regard giving their daughters in marriage as a man's second wife, or, conversely, 'having a co-wife put on her head', as great tragedies.

Inheritance and household partition

The division (*taraqa*, *taqsim*, *wesh*) of a patrimony (*miras*) occurs three days after a man's funeral; it must be preceded by the sacrificial distribution (*kheyrat*) of an animal. The division should take place before a mullah, with other big men to act as witnesses, and shares are supposed to be reckoned according to the Hanafi school of Sunni Islam, but property division or disputes are not taken to the courts (among other reasons because judges would insist on women's rights), and inheritance practices follow Pashtun custom.

After the payment of the funeral expenses, a widow's right to inherit an eighth share of her husband's estate is recognized in a provision for her maintenance: she is never allowed to alienate any property. There is a widespread feeling that sets of paternal half-siblings should inherit, *per stirpes*, equal shares of a father's estate, thus clearly reaffirming the ideal of equal treatment due to their mothers; but in practice an estate is usually divided among all brothers on a per capita basis in accordance with the Sharia rules. Daughters should get half a brother's share, but they are expected to give their shares to their brothers and the latter have no debt or obligation to their sisters for this gift. If a woman's parents die and she has no brothers, the estate will go to her father's brothers or even more distant agnates who must maintain her until she is married. As one man commented,

Even if she has no one at all – no *qaum*, nothing – she would find a man from somewhere and make him near to her, saying he is my *qaum*; then he would inherit.

In a few exceptional recent cases, women, usually encouraged by their husbands, have tried to claim their share of the patrimony, but the strong, unanimous reaction of other men, including the leaders of the subtribe, prevented this from happening. Even with increasing competition for land, it is unlikely that the traditional practice of disinheriting sisters will change; not only does the practice guarantee continuing agnatic control of property, but it is also a salient marker of Durrani ethnic identity: as one man said,

Sisters give their inheritance to the brother they like best or divide it between all their brothers: then everybody's heart is happy. A woman never takes it herself, to her husband; it is not the custom. Uzbeks do that, Parsiwans do it, but our people never do. If she took it to her husband, we would laugh.

Women are said to be able to leave small personal effects and their clothing to anyone they choose, but I suspect that, unless a woman manages to transfer such property secretly before her death, she has little hope that her wishes will be respected. Indeed it is normal for a dead woman's husband or sons to be deeply suspicious of the motives of men and women, particularly her own close female kin, who wish to visit her room or tent after her death and they are likely to put everything they can under lock and key. In effect a married woman has no personal property, and household effects, whether they were a part of the woman's trousseau or acquired later, belong to the husband or his heirs.

The developmental cycle of the household

The Maduzai recognize the inexorable movement of the developmental cycle of the household, and whatever the exact circumstances, the foundation of a new household is marked ritually. A woman explained,

When a household splits or one part separates off, a white-haired woman is brought along to dig out the new hearth. The hearth (*negharey*) is an important thing; it is weighty because both bread and rice are cooked on it. We don't count houses in terms of hearths, but everyone knows how many hearths a house has, and if they are separate. When the new one has been started by the old woman, a prayer is said for good luck and then women friends of the new house bring melons and raisins and mulberries and have a party and eat sweets so that the new house will be sweet.

A household head is always eager to keep the household together; the pressure for partition comes from married dependants, against whom the head has virtually no sanctions to prevent them from separating. The only structural supports he has to buttress his position are the strength of the ideal of household unity and the known risks faced by small independent households, but these will certainly be inadequate if he lacks the personal qualities needed to command respect among both outsiders and household members. If a man's claims to a wife are not recognized by the household head, he may threaten to leave the household and provoke a full division of the property unless he is satisfied. But unless he has some reason to think he can compel such a division, this strategy is of very dubious value. On the other hand, a household head has the right to expel household members at will, though it happens rarely, and usually only after grave provocation such as gambling with household property. However, I know of at least one case where an excess of male labour, compared with the few resources a household controlled, led to a married son's expulsion. The only sanction he could have used to keep himself within the household was that he would leave and force a division of the property but, as the household was so poor, the threat made little sense.

The main pressures influencing a man to separate from his father derive from a highly subjective equation involving the extent to which a married man's labour within the household is likely to increase his father's estate and hence his own patrimony, or whether he is likely to reap greater benefits from his own labour if he becomes independent. Earnings from outside employment are only rarely used for capital investment; most often they are used either to improve a household's immediate standard of living or to pay brideprices. However, separation from a father's household can be very risky: a bad year or an injury or death within the small separating household can spell disaster and near starvation, and there are a number of cases in which such households have been reabsorbed into the original joint household. On the other hand, if the paternal joint household has labour surplus to its requirements for the management of its own resources, an able young man who is likely to have to take outside employment anyway may well prefer to become independent rather than see his earnings administered by his father and used to buy wives for his younger brothers. It is most likely that the sons separating from their fathers are the oldest and thus usually the earliest married, while younger sons, or at least the youngest son, will remain with the father and occupy the family home – 'his father's hearth' – at the latter's death.

Given the absence of anticipatory inheritance, the degree of independence the household of a married son achieves while his father is still alive depends greatly on the respective personalities of father and son. In many cases, the independence is considerable; in other cases, the father is likely to interfere, not least because the departing son often lives in a dwelling provided and maintained by his father. Moreover, though the independent son is free to give his daughters in marriage where he wants, it is said to be good (and it is usual) to ask the father's opinion about all such marriages.

There is an ideal of fraternal solidarity, but actual co-operation and harmony between full brothers is often a reflection of hostilities between groups of half-brothers, traceable to disputes over patrimony after their father's death. Later, when a further division occurs between full brothers, relations between them too may deteriorate. Even after the partition of a household, efficient exploitation of joint or neighbouring shares in pasture of farmland may demand continued co-operation of brothers in herding units and agricultural combines. The tensions between independent households of close agnates generated by these circumstances are expressed in incessant backbiting between them.

The economic pressures on brothers to remain in a fraternal joint household are, in many respects, the exact opposites of those encouraging sons to separate from their father. First, an unmarried son will not separate before he has received a wife. Secondly, if a household has a shortage of male labour in proportion to the resources it controls, it is likely to remain together. In almost every household in which brothers are held together by labour shortages, relations between women of the household are strained and sometimes very poisonous indeed. But however strong the personal feelings of the women, they are not allowed to override the fundamental economic considerations which keep the household together. Finally, when fraternal joint households do divide, there is a clear tendency for younger brothers to separate from the oldest, who is often the household head. The latter is thus seen as remaining by the father's hearth.

So long as a household remains joint, all persons, men and women, who belong to it have a wide variety of common interests which are most often subsumed under the rubric of household honour. The ties men and women have to the household are constructed in fundamentally different ways. The men of a joint household form a corporate group, united by the ideals of agnatic solidarity but divided by their respective interests in the household property. Among women of a joint household, there are few ideals or issues which unite them and many considerations which lead them to see themselves as having rival interests in household resources.

Maduzai social life is characterized by a lack of specific rules relating to interpersonal behaviour. In this light, it is hardly surprising that where people between whom there are conflicts of interests must associate, and where there are few sanctions against the expression of these conflicts, quarrels are endemic. Certainly this is the case between the households of close agnates. So too is it the situation experienced by women living in a joint household. And, of course, the intensity of the quarrels in both cases is related to the length of time the enforced association is expected to continue and the degree to which interests diverge. Household unity, and indeed the perception of shared interests between the households of close agnates, is to a considerable extent created by the threat to prosperity and security posed by competing households and other groups of close agnates.

132

Plate 1 Examining items of a trousseau inside the bride's family tent

Plate 2 Displaying the trousseau outside the tent

Plate 3 Groom being dressed in new white clothes by the mullah

Plate 5 Bride being escorted to her marital home

Plates 6, 7 and 8   A married couple ask to have their picture taken

Plate 9 Maduzai children playing 'house': 'bride' and 'groom' dolls are asleep in the tent

Plate 10 A respected older woman

III. Ideologies of equality and inequality

7

Brideprice and direct exchange

A basic and explicit principle in Durrani marriage is that the exchange of women between two men indicates a mutual recognition of status equality, while the single transfer of a woman by one man to another for brideprice indicates the recognition by the wife-giver of the potential or actual status superiority of the wife-taker (see N. Tapper 1981: 405 n. 4). The ascendancy of wife-takers is thus a possible interpretation of all brideprice marriages, but, in such marriages between Durrani households, the implicit inequality is contradicted by the general ideal of Durrani equality.

The phrases most often used by Durrani to refer to the state of marriage derive from the verb 'to wed' (*wada kawel*). However, Durrani also frequently differentiate direct exchange marriage and marriages for brideprice or money. I have called these two distinct modes, respectively, the symmetrical and the asymmetrical. In fact, each of these modes comprises three forms, distinguished indigenously in the one case but only analytically in the other. Linguistic usage here seems to relate directly to the meaning of the two modes: symmetrical exchange marriages are the primary means of expressing social equality and uniformity and they are treated linguistically as uniform in their occurrence and impact, while marriages of the asymmetrical mode create and emphasize status differences and are themselves verbally differentiated.

All direct exchange marriages are known by the same generic term, *makhi*, which (like its synonyms, the Arabic *badal* and the Persian *alish*) is also a generic term for all kinds of direct exchanges. However it is useful analytically to distinguish three forms of direct exchange marriage, occurring in distinct contexts. These will be called the 'neutral' form of essentially apolitical exchanges made for convenience; exchanges of 'recognition'; and exchanges of 'reconciliation'. In the case of marriages of the asymmetrical model three different forms are distinguished by indigenous terms: two (*mahr-e kotara* and *mahr-e mosamma*) according to the type of brideprice contract made, while the third, qualified by the Maduzai as either as gratis (*muft*) or as a feud (*badi*) marriage, I call 'compensation' marriage.

The essential features of the system are summarized in Figure 8.

When brideprice marriages take place, as they usually do, between families of comparable socio-economic standing, the families concerned may explicitly assert their equality. Nonetheless, they are usually accompanied by a degree of tension and competition over just this question, and the reputation of both sides is felt to be at stake. The wife-givers must demonstrate their equality with the wife-takers, in spite of the loss of their daughter to another household for brideprice; the wife-takers may be content to maintain their equality and potential superiority, or they may take various opportunities to make political claims, either in terms of their position relative to the wife-givers, or in terms of their general standing in the community. The main idioms in which claims to status may be made can be divided into those associated with the mode of marriage itself, and those associated with the other prestations, rituals and ceremonies of marriage, which are the subject of chapter 8.

The asymmetrical mode of marriage

Durrani often talk of the marriage of a woman as a 'sale' and of the brideprice as a 'price', the words used being those appropriate to any economic transaction (see N. Tapper 1979: 401 n. 11), but they recognize, in theory at least, that a woman, as opposed to other forms of goods, can only once change hands for money (see p. 185). Brideprice payments are usually made in instalments over a period of several years, and must be completed before the wedding, when the bride leaves her natal home with her trousseau to join her husband. Among Durrani, the Islamic marriage rite, the *nikah* ceremony, performed for all marriages (including all exchanges) always includes the promise of or actual transfer from the groom to his bride of a small sum as *mahr*, the Islamic dower (see p. 167). This prestation is seen as quite independent of any others, including brideprice and trousseau. Once the wedding and the *nikah* and the *mahr* transaction have been performed, brideprices are not returnable in any circumstance; nor do Durrani, among whom divorce is virtually unknown, recognize that portion of the *mahr* known as the 'deferred dower' which is, elsewhere in the Islamic world, regarded as a woman's insurance against divorce.

A brideprice is customarily seen as the equivalent of one hundred sheep. The average value in cash, animals and other goods of the brideprices paid between 1967 and 1972 was 65,000 Afs., then worth about £325. There has been considerable general inflation in Afghanistan during the past fifty years, but it would seem that the ratio of the market values of sheep and irrigated land has hardly changed over that period. Men complain bitterly about the amount brideprices have become, but they are still held to be far lower than they might be, if one added up what was being sold.

Part of the brideprice will be returned to the groom's household in the form of a trousseau, but this rarely amounts to more than a third of the whole and the bride's father is likely to make a material profit on the transaction. This profit is recognized as such, and there is no pressure to convert it immediately into further brideprices, yet it is considered poor compensation for the expense a father has had in raising his daughter. One man calculated (with some exaggeration) that for fifteen years a daughter eats fifty *sir* of wheat at 50 Afs. and wears two suits of clothes at 2,500 Afs. – 'It works out at a lac (100,000 Afs.) before you have got rid of her'. Two sayings the Maduzai repeat with some frequency both make this point; they say, 'No one ever becomes rich when his daughters grow up' because 'Brideprice is a mountain of straw for the wind to blow away.' And of course, men with few or no sons talk of the brideprices they receive for their daughters as little consolation for the absence of male heirs.

When Maduzai discuss brideprice, they do so using a generic term (*walwar*), but they always recognize that a contract may be one of two kinds, the 'chopped-up' (*kotara*) or the 'named' (*mosamma*) – here they use the term *mahr* for the brideprice, though in other contexts this term is used in its legally proper sense for the dower. In the *kotara* contract the amount is fixed before witnesses at the engagement ceremony; once this sum has been paid, the groom or his guardian can insist the wedding be held. With the *mosamma* brideprice, the amount is not fixed at the engagement ceremony, rather the contract is open-ended and whatever the bride's guardian asks as brideprice must be paid before the wedding can be held.

Kotara brideprices

By fixing the amount of the brideprice at the outset, the *kotara* form requires less faith between the parties, either in their good intentions or in their intrinsic equality, and of course in practical terms it involves the groom's guardian in

Figure 8   Marriage modes and forms

Asymmetrical mode (The exchange of women for bride-price or blood)	*Symmetrical mode* (*Makhi:* the direct exchange of women for women)
I *Kotara* form: strictly economic transaction; wife-takers superior	Neutral form: conformity with egalitarian ideals of Islam, Durrani ethnicity
II *Mosamma* form: bride as 'pure gift', denial of inequality	Exchanges of recognition: strangers become Durrani
III *Muft* or *badi*, compensation form: women given gratis for blood spilt, to restore balance	Exchanges of reconciliation: disputants reconciled, assertion of basic equality

fewer financial risks. In short, the *kotara* contract encourages a narrowly economic view of marriage. Put another way, *kotara* brideprices are not about affinity but simply about finding spouses. For this reason the *kotara* form can be used to express highly individualistic claims to status. Three brief examples may be mentioned here; the social context of these cases is given in more detail in chapter 11.

In one instance, a leading man of Lineage C was determined to marry the daughter of his rival from Lineage A, though the latter demanded an unprecedentedly high *kotara* brideprice for her. This sum was duly paid and the rivals and their respective followings became political allies (see pp. 246, 275). In the second case, there was competition between Hajji Ibrahim, the leader of Lineage C, and the Maduzai Khan, to marry a girl from a politically unimportant household. Her father demanded and received a very high *kotara* brideprice from Hajji Ibrahim. Though the overall status of the bride's father was virtually unaltered by the marriage, the high brideprice, welcome in itself, protected his reputation as a kind of compensation for having allowed himself to be used as the vehicle for a political message directed elsewhere (see pp. 259, 275). These brideprices both deeply impressed and offended public opinion: partly because they were grossly inflationary and partly because the singularity of the *kotara* form was used so blatantly by the groom's side for their own political ends. As a final example, a leading family of Lineage C demanded a very high brideprice from an important member of the local Khan family: the Khan paid up and went on to celebrate the wedding in an extremely lavish manner (see p. 251).

I agree with the Maduzai conviction that the present predominance of the *kotara* contract, in terms of both the number of such agreements reached and the importance they have in people's thinking about marriage, reflects wider changes in the economic circumstances of the Durrani of Saripul and a concomitant change in the place of brideprice in the economic system, rather than any change in the essential meaning of brideprice. It is notable in this context that the Maduzai continually emphasize the importance of having senior men to witness a *kotara* agreement. If such witnesses are lacking, the *kotara* contract may not be binding and the bride's guardian may in practice claim the right, fundamental to the *mosamma* agreement, to demand what he wants from the groom. There is a basic acceptance of the practical strength of the bride's guardian during the engagement period and the likelihood that, unless forestalled by the groom, he may by threats or cunning transform a *kotara* contract in this way; I heard of many such cases, though in all of them the bride's guardian was regarded in a bad light.

The Maduzai say that in the past all brideprices were in effect *kotara*. Then, no formal engagement ceremony was held: the bride's guardian simply gave a thread (*tar*) from his turban to the groom or his guardian as a sign of his willingness to complete the verbal contract between them. The wedding was held whenever the agreed sum was paid. As one man put it, 'In the past people weren't so money-grubbing, there was lots of land and much money about, and people were naive', by which he meant that private arrangements over brideprice were always honoured. By contrast, I was often told that nowadays the economic climate 'is hard; the population has become great, brideprices expensive and people clever and sharp'. They prefer the *kotara* form to be explicitly stated before witnesses (*sharii*, according to the Sharia, i.e. before a mullah); if the contract is 'customary' (*urpi*), they fear it will not stick and the father of the bride will take anything he likes.

Though average *kotara* brideprices paid for a Maduzai girl over the last five years were valued at around 65,000 Afs., it would be a mistake to see this sum as having a fixed relation to other prices. It is common for half the total brideprice to be paid in cash, and half in sheep. The Maduzai treat the relation between cash and sheep as if it were a kind of algebraic equation based on 'thousands', literally 1000 Af. banknotes called *hazari*, which are used obligatorily whenever cash is given as part of a prestige exchange for productive or reproductive resources. Thus we have the formula: x *hazari* $+ 2x$ sheep $=$ 1 brideprice. For example: 30 *hazari* $+ 60$ sheep $=$ a brideprice of 60,000 Afghanis, if sheep are valued at 500 Afs.

However, the relationship between the amounts involved and other economic factors is complicated and the meaning of the various sums may be changed in a number of ways.

Durrani rank productive and reproductive resources for the purposes of exchange in such a way that four spheres of exchange are evident to the observer (these I discuss further below, p. 281). The elements which compose these spheres are, in descending order: men, women, productive resources and valuables, and produce, as well as the anomalous element of cash. They are manipulated by parties to a marriage in ways which serve to define their status *vis-à-vis* each other and the wider community. In general, the father of the bride is likely to insist on the full payment of the brideprice if he has any misgivings about the marriage, if the social distance between the parties is great, or if he simply wants the money and can wait. Conversely, fondness for the groom, or sufficient wealth to allow magnanimous gestures, may mean that the bride's father is informally prepared to accept substitutes within the third sphere of productive resources and valuables, or labour amounting to bride-service, which reduce the monetary value of the brideprice paid; or he may be willing to hold the wedding without receiving the full payment. If the bride's father himself is in financial difficulty, he may be forced, either by means of substitutions within the third sphere or, much more damagingly, from the fourth sphere of produce, to accept a smaller and less prestigious brideprice than was agreed.

For example, if sheep are accepted as part of a brideprice, it is usual for them to be ascribed a fixed cash value at the engagement ceremony which only indirectly relates to the market value of the animals. In recent years in Saripul young ewes have had a market value of between 200 Afs. (in the autumn of 1971 after two years of extreme drought) and 1500 Afs., but the average price has been around 1000 Afs. for *karakul* animals, while sheep included in a brideprice have most frequently been valued at 500 Afs. each. Thus a typical brideprice of 60,000 Afs. may be made up of 30,000 Afs. cash and 60 sheep. By valuing sheep for the purposes of brideprice at a rate fixed at the lowest likely market price, the bride's father affords the bridegroom an opportunity to benefit from an upturn in the market. That is, the groom is likely to give the sheep portion of the brideprice when the market value of the animals is relatively low, while when their market value is higher than their brideprice valuation, he may sell animals to pay off the cash portion. Clearly, during any single engagement period, market prices may not vary in a way advantageous to the groom, nonetheless a *kotara* brideprice agreed at 60,000 Afs. may be more or less in real terms depending on when the portions of sheep and cash are given.

Another and far more dramatic way in which the real value of a brideprice may be altered is by assigning a high relative value to the sheep at the time of the engagement ceremony, thus benefiting the groom directly. For instance, if sheep are valued at 1000 Afs. each instead of 500 Afs., then a *kotara* brideprice of 60,000 Afs. will be made up of 20,000 Afs. and 40 sheep and not 30,000 Afs. and 60 sheep. With such an arrangement, in effect the bride's guardian gives his ward for less than the usual amount involved in a brideprice of 60,000 Afs. *kotara*. This is one way in which the bride's guardian may aid a favoured groom, though in a few cases such an arrangement was a direct consequence of the bride's side having sought (even to the extent of offering the woman in marriage) and gained affines who were markedly their economic and political superiors; this is a device used by reasonably wealthy households to attach themselves to a powerful patron (cf. Glatzer 1977: 155–156).

The third way in which the real value of a brideprice may be altered is as follows. Often after a *kotara* brideprice (and the related value of sheep) has been fixed at the engagement, an informal substitution of animals or other items may take place, though it is more prestigious for both parties if the amounts are met in the manner first stipulated. Thus camels or other livestock may be given in place of the sheep or they may be assigned a cash value and given in place of the cash portion of the brideprice.

Other valuable household goods – such as guns, carpets, a fine horse or camel – may be treated in a like manner, though only a very poor man will accept grain or other produce as part of the exchange. Substitutions are made on the initiative of the groom or his guardian but may operate without undue loss to the bride's guardian: that is, a substituted item may be assigned its market value. But sometimes the substituted item may be over-valued (clearly the groom's side will not offer undervalued substitutes). Thus, for instance, a gun which would be worth

15,000 Afs. on the market might be valued at 25,000 Afs. and given in lieu of that amount of cash in the brideprice. Again this may be a way in which the bride's guardian can help a hard-pressed but favoured groom, but often it is indicative of an attempt on the part of the groom's side to reduce the amount in real terms: if the bride's guardian has an immediate need for cash, he may be forced to accept items as worth more than their market value. Indeed, the more desperate the bride's guardian, the more likely that such substitutions will be made and the more they will be over-valued. In such cases, the economic dependence of the bride's side on the groom's side is manifest.

Finally, it does sometimes happen that an impoverished young man in effect does bride service. That is, he goes to live with his father-in-law (at which time the *nikah* marriage ceremony may be performed) and works for him over a period of years. A household of any standing who let their son do such bride-service would be ridiculed mercilessly, as a young married man said:

If a young man goes and works a little for his father-in-law, helping him with small chores, this isn't bad and the young man may be excused some of the brideprice. What is bad is when a man goes to live with his father-in-law like a woman – as though he is a woman taken in marriage. People laugh and say, 'Other people marry off their daughters but so-and-so has married off his son.' It is not an Afghan [Durrani] custom.

However, poorer men may literally have no alternative if they are to marry at all. If the young man is attractive and industrious, he may even find a wealthy household lacking male labour which will welcome him as a son-in-law. This is among the most important ways for a poor but able man to become upwardly mobile. If they get on well, the young groom may, after several years, find his father-in-law happy to help him set up an independent household, though this does not always happen. Four of the 45 Lineage C men engaged between 1967 and 1972 were living with their fathers-in-law and working for them, though in only one case nad the *nikah* ceremony coincided with the onset of this arrangement.

Mosamma brideprices

Mosamma brideprice marriages differ fundamentally from the *kotara*. The *mosamma* contract means that the bride's father can ask whatever he wants for his daughter. *Mosamma* contracts are uncommon, accounting for 10–15 per cent of all brideprice marriages.

The Maduzai explicitly and emphatically associate this form of contract with the wish of the two parties to demonstrate publicly their mutual good will. In its ideal and formal aspects, it denies the superiority of the wife-takers implicit in brideprice marriages. The most important aspect of the *mosamma* form is that both parties ideally gain prestige by demonstrating the (literally) priceless nature of the woman who links them, and, by extension, of the affinal relationship. By agreeing to a *mahr-e mosamma*, which leaves him open to considerable financial loss, the groom's guardian declares his acceptance of the bride's guardian's formal advantage over him during the engagement and his trust in the latter's honour, but he is also proclaiming his own honour, as a man able and willing to produce any sum that may be demanded. In effect the contract involves both parties in a relationship which is broadly defined; ideally it demonstrates the depth of friendship between them.

In practice, however, the *mosamma* form often has quite a different meaning which contradicts the ideals with which it is associated. Usually both parties, while stating publicly at the engagement ceremony that the brideprice is *mosamma*, nonetheless agree privately to a specific, and often low, brideprice. By agreeing to a *mosamma* contract the individuals involved are, by definition, close, and the exact nature of their relationship may not be known publicly. Most often, however, it would seem that the bride's father is forced to accept the low brideprice because of some weakness *vis-à-vis* the groom's guardian, while the latter is prepared to agree to the *mosamma* form for the sake of a cheap bride gained without shaming a dependant into possible disloyalty. As the Maduzai note, all the material advantages in the *mosamma* contract lie with the bride's father, and it often happens that, once the contract has been agreed, he tries to remedy his status weakness *vis-à-vis* the groom's side by insisting on his right to demand whatever brideprice he wants. The friendship between the households involved in a *mosamma* contract may have been illusory in the first place, and even if genuine, it is as often thwarted as forwarded by the *mosamma* form itself. As one man said, 'Men's hearts don't become close with *mosamma*.'

Only three of the twenty-six brideprice marriages made by men of Lineage C in the last five years involved a *mosamma* contract, the rest were *kotara* (see p. 198). Two of these were within Lineage C and each exacerbated the conflict between the parties involved (see p. 270; N. Tapper 1979: 433ff.; 401 n. 13). In the third case, a man of Lineage C took the daughter of a close friend, a client neighbour and member of Lineage D, for his son for a secretly arranged *kotara* brideprice of 50,000 Afs.; the Lineage C household was wealthy (Quartile I), while the client household was not (Quartile III) (see (l), p. 203).

Compensation marriages

Apart from *kotara* and *mosamma* forms, there is a third variant of the asymmetrical mode – the giving of women in compensation for blood spilt by wounding or homicide. Ideally in such cases there is no brideprice at all: those who committed the violence give 'gratis' one woman to a wounded man, or two women to the closest kinsmen of a murdered man. The relation between wifegivers and wife-takers is again unequal. The offenders, by giving a woman, can only be equal or inferior to the victim's family; and yet the gift of a woman can never really compensate for the loss of a man; so, in this latter sense, the wifegivers are in fact superior to the wife-takers. Unlike some other Middle Eastern peoples (cf. Black-Michaud 1975: 92–93), the Durrani do not make any explicit connection between women given in a compensation marriage and the sons they may bear as replacements for the murdered man.

As with the *mosamma* form, there is a further paradox in the nature of compensation marriages: this time between the extreme inequality implied by the ideal and the notable equality which in practice exists between the two parties. Homicide does not lead to compensation marriages unless the fundamental equality of the two parties has been demonstrated by effective retaliation and vengeance. Marriages for compensation usually occur in pairs, each side giving women for injuries suffered by the other. Because such marriages are balanced, they look remarkably like direct exchange marriages. Indeed the confusion between the two modes allows those who wish to emphasize the end of hostilities to speak of them as exchange marriages, while those anxious to continue a dispute will insist on their unilateral character. Moreover, if a marriage is completed some time afterwards, it may be that a quasi-brideprice is given; this is said to 'help finance the trousseau' of the girl given in compensation, but its more important, and equally explicit, purpose is to reconcile the two sides further and to avoid the shame of appearing to give or take a woman 'gratis' (see pp. 77, 254).

The symmetrical mode of marriage

Direct exchange marriages account for twenty per cent of all Maduzai unions, and 75 per cent of these are sister exchange – the prototype. Other combinations involve a man receiving a bride in exchange for giving a daughter, brother's daughter, father's brother's daughter or father's sister – the only condition being that the pair involved in the exchange should be living in the same household at the time of the engagement. The exchange marriages made by members of the four lineages of the Maduzai subtribe are tabulated elsewhere (see p. 96); here it may be simply noted that in 1972, 52 of the 249 extant marriages made by men of the four lineages were parts of exchanges, 35 of which involved sisters (see N. Tapper 1981: 405 n. 1).

Women and men in an exchange refer to their counterparts as their *makhi* or *alishi*. People express a certain dislike for exchange marriages in terms of a man's control over his wife: unlike in brideprice marriages, where a husband has complete control and the wife's agnates will not interfere with his authority except in matters literally of life and death, in an exchange marriage a man is made to feel responsible for his married sister in everyday affairs and this he resents. If A beats or oppresses his own wife, then her brother B will in turn beat or trouble his wife, A's sister, however blameless she may be. Men admit that an exchange marriage would seem to be an excellent idea from the women's point of view, but in spite of this logic, the women agree with men in their dislike of the form: their affective loyalties are likely to be divided and they may be considered by members of their marital home to be somewhat untrustworthy, yet they can never return to their natal home and they gain no real protection from their agnates. However, from both men's and women's points of view, the issue of reciprocal treatment is something of a red herring and has only limited relevance if the exchange is arranged by the brides' fathers (as opposed to their brothers). So long as a woman's father lives, his superior status *vis-à-vis* his son-in-law effectively disguises the reciprocal aspects of the exchange.

A number of areas of uncertainty in exchange marriages have become regulated in recent decades and, where political alliance is not at issue, direct exchange is often viewed as the least problematic way of gaining a wife and by far the quickest. Thus a married man who has been suddenly widowed, but has an unmarried female relative in his household, often favours such a marriage, though if he is also unable through poverty to consider the possibility of a brideprice marriage, people will remark that he has been forced to arrange an exchange. Certainly the exchange of one marriageable woman for another is efficient compared with the difficulties inherent in brideprice marriages where the capital value represented by a woman to her natal family is converted into cash and animals which may then be used in turn to acquire a wife.

There are no important differences in the sequence of marriage rites between direct exchange and brideprice marriages. Normally both girls are engaged on the same day, though at two separate *tar* ceremonies, one at the home of each bride. It is now customary for the father of each bride to demand a full brideprice, which will be waived so long as the exchange is completed. As in marriage for brideprice, should a groom die or become disabled, his bride will simply be transferred to one of his agnates; however, should one of the girls die or become unmarriageable, her father will have to pay a brideprice for the second girl to ensure that the latter's family suffers no loss. To complete an exchange in such circumstances, the agnates of the dead girl may in fact offer another girl in lieu of the brideprice, but such an arrangement is not automatic, nor particularly common. In effect it involves a totally new marriage contract, so, should another girl be accepted as a replacement for the one who died, a separate engagement ceremony must be held.

Maduzai claim that only in the last fifteen or twenty years have brideprices been stipulated in exchanges marriages as 'good' and 'proper' (*pak*) in the religious sense. Another area of uncertainty has also become more controlled: the effect of discrepancies of age between the two brides. The predominance of brother/sister exchanges means that often the two grooms are close in age, as are the two brides. Large discrepancies in the men's ages are usually ignored, for the timing of the weddings depends on the puberty of the brides. Within a range of two or three years, the weddings may be held separately, but it is common for these, like the engagement ceremonies, to be held on the same day. This is of some symbolic importance and does also minimize expenses. When the weddings are held simultaneously or within a short time of each other, they are said to be 'head to head'.

If, however, the brides vary widely in age, as sometimes happens, the wedding of the older bride may be held many years before the younger one reaches puberty, so long as the former's father-in-law pays a *sar* (literally, head) for her, though this payment may be omitted if the households involved are close, or if the purpose of the exchange is to confirm a friendship. This use of the word *sar* conforms closely to its usual economic meaning: in any situation where men exchange goods of different kinds, a cash payment of the difference in value is called *sar* (and cf. the *sar* sometimes paid for widows, p. 187). In the case of exchange marriages, the *sar* restores the equality of the two families even though one of the marriages is completed, as it were, prematurely. A *sar* may be just a token payment, or as much as 20 per cent of a regular brideprice. Normally the *sar* is arranged before and mentioned during the engagement ceremony, though it may be fixed later on an *ad hoc* basis to reflect some change in the circumstances of one of the families.

In theory, then, exchange marriages represent a direct exchange of equal value: if, however, one man marries earlier than the other, the time factor introduces an imbalance which is redressed by means of the *sar* payment. Ideally the *sar* is repaid once the exchange has been completed by the delivery of the second bride, so that in effect the benefits of a man's earlier marriage are paid for by the loan of the capital sum which the *sar* represents. The exchange, though delayed, remains balanced.

The specific changes in the form of exchange marriage are, I believe, related to a wider set of changes which have fundamentally affected the institution of marriage among the Maduzai. As marriage has become increasingly the focus of political and economic competition, changes have been introduced which reduce the impact of chance factors (like the death of one of the brides in an exchange marriage) on the circumstances of the families involved.

Exchange marriages are used politically in two main contexts: in the recognition of previously unknown groups as having Durrani or equal status, and in the resolution of quarrels. As is clear from the use of women to compensate for homicide, these two contexts are opposite sides of the same coin. Durrani give women only to those who are of the same kind as themselves, while all other people are seen as potential enemies, with whom violent quarrels are considered insoluble, if only because women cannot be exchanged. There is no expectation that exchange marriages between households will be repeated. Even in explicitly political contexts, a single pair of exchange marriages (that is, two marriages) is usually adequate to demonstrate the equality of the two sides, such that any later marriages between them may be of either mode.

Exchange marriages of 'recognition' and 'reconciliation'
When exchange marriages are used to establish status equality between previously unconnected groups, these exchanges of 'recognition', as they may be

called, involve the exchange not only of women but of important, if unquantifiable, economic and political resources. It is not unusual for strangers to seek the prestige, security and possible material benefits which association with or membership in a recognized Durrani tribe bring; but outsiders do not approach the Durrani group empty-handed – rather, the outsider group must be prepared to put manpower, material wealth or other resources at the disposal of the Durrani.

The practice of using direct exchange marriages to establish Durrani or equal identity and status depends on this function remaining ostensibly unrecognized. Thus the two sides must define themselves as Durrani before the marriage can be arranged. This they do using genealogical evidence which becomes irrelevant once the marriage has been completed. The fact that Durrani are both mobile and scattered means that the genealogical claims of strangers are plausible, and no doubt often valid, but it remains the case that such exchange marriages of 'recognition' do provide an effective means of incorporating non-Durrani into the ethnic group. The economic and political aspects of incorporation are well-understood and manipulated, sometimes explicitly, sometimes covertly, by both Durrani and others.

For the Maduzai the foremost examples of exchange marriages used to establish equal status were those which reunited Lineage A and Lineage C (the Torabi), in Kandahar shortly before the Maduzai migration to Turkistan. From these marriages stems the present political configuration of the subtribe. I was told by a Lineage C informant, 'We became affines, whereas we had not recognized each other before. We became one people (*qaum*) and they [Lineage A] brought us [Lineage C] north. We made *kheshi* with Chinar: we gave two women and got two women.'

Since that time exchange marriages of 'recognition' have occurred with some frequency among Durrani in the Saripul region, which has attracted migrants from all over the country. The following case is of particular interest.

Case 3: The Sinjit 'Sayyids'

A family of Pashtu-speakers, claiming to be Sayyids from a south-eastern part of the country, settled in Sinjit village around 1930. The head of the family took as a second wife a woman from Lineage D of the Maduzai, but when he later sought a wife for his son from Sultan, a leading man of Lineage C, Sultan was more cautious and agreed to give his sister only when he had himself been given a Sayyid wife, and an exchange marriage was successfully arranged (see also p. 255).

Later, however, when Sultan proposed to marry another of his sisters to the Sayyids for brideprice, his agnates protested that the relationship must be kept equal and that they should receive another woman in exchange for her. This was done, and later two marriages for brideprice were arranged between the two groups, with women being given each way. The Sayyids owned important tracts of land along the subtribe's route to the mountains. Through these marriages the Sayyids gained permanent association with the subtribe, while the members of Lineage C gained access to the land.

Then many years later a traveller from southern Afghanistan embarrassingly revealed the 'Sayyids' to be Parsiwans, 'inferior' non-Durrani Pashtuns by origin. One informant flatly stated that the real identity of the 'Sayyids' was always known to Sultan and the other Maduzai, but that they were prepared to ignore it for reasons of economic expediency. Today the authenticity of the 'Sayyids'' descent claims is stoutly maintained in public by members of Lineages C and D, who would otherwise be admitting breaches of the ban on hypogamy, though since in the last decade the 'Sayyid' families' wealth and importance have declined considerably, they are now often spoken of disparagingly as the clients of the Sinjit headman and his close agnates.

Exchange marriage is also a principal device for settling intra-group quarrels which seem likely to weaken the group to which the disputants belong and to make them vulnerable to outside interference. Quarrels amenable to the solution of exchange marriage cannot be identified *a priori*, for they do not form a category until settled, but those which end in such a compromise point to the equality of the disputing parties and their essential interdependence. The solution of an exchange marriage of 'reconciliation', as it may be called, is often proposed and sometimes even imposed by the leaders of a particular group or a *jirga* assembly of all its household heads.

The changing importance of exchange marriages
It is said that in the past exchange marriages were much more common, but that nowadays people have become 'clever and calculating' and exchange is not a good thing. Actually the two Lineage C samples of extant marriages do show an increase: 29 per cent of the 109 men's marriages extant in 1972 were exchanges, compared to 25 per cent of 73 men's marriages extant in 1950. But, more important than the uncertain meaning of that statistic is the Maduzai certainty that such exchanges are viewed differently now. This changed value of exchange marriages derives, I suspect, almost entirely from the use of exchange marriage in attempts to regulate the increasing competition and conflicts within the subtribe.

The possibilities of fostering group solidarity through exchange marriages are clear; the ties of affinity they create may facilitate the resumption of friendly relations between the two sides. But, just as often, because the marriages do not necessarily coincide with changes in the control of economic and political resources, the fundamental causes of a dispute remain unaltered, or even exacerbated, by the exchange marriage. The exchange marriages consequent on a number of intra-group disputes are discussed in detail in chapter 11 (see also N. Tapper 1979: 348ff. for an account of a convoluted series of marriage

154 *Ideologies of equality and inequality*

exchanges which explains the curious position of Section VI *vis-à-vis* the rest of Lineage A and the Maduzai Khan).

These cases serve to illustrate both the kinds of contexts in which exchange marriages may take place and the kinds of problems to which they can give rise when they are used politically to symbolize both equality and good relations between households or groups. They also illustrate how complicated a series of exchange marriages can become. Such complications alone can be a source of ambiguity and misunderstanding between both the parties involved and outsiders who are 'reading' the marriage arrangements for information about the political and economic strengths and weaknesses of particular households.

The Maduzai feel quite strongly that the exchange of women to settle a dispute should demonstrate and reinforce the underlying solidarity between the two sides; it is meant to prevent the outbreak of violence. As we have seen, when violence has already occurred, marriages arranged as blood compensation are not exchanges at all, for the fact of violence contradicts any notion of underlying unity. But since efforts to make peace are not likely to be successful until roughly the same number of casualties have been suffered by both sides, who have thus demonstrated their equality in combat at least, the marriages may seem like exchanges between the two sides and those involved may actually maintain that they are, thereby concealing their original cause.

Over time, there is often confusion between compensation marriages and true exchanges: they are similar in that women are received by both sides simultaneously, with little ceremony and no accompanying payments of animals or cash. Violent quarrels may be 'settled' when women are given in compensation, but quarrels over the same kinds of issues which have not resulted in serious physical injuries are often resolved by exchanges of 'reconciliation'.

The ideological use of these similarities has been mentioned; they are also important at a personal level and help to deal with the radical realignment of affections and loyalties which either kind of settlement entails. Thus, Sadozi, who had been given by her brothers to the son of a man they had killed during the Maduzai feud (pp. 74f., 252), steadfastly maintained that no women were given in compensation at all and that all the (feud) marriages were true exchanges. On hearing this remark, Sadozi's daughter-in-law, whose own close agnates had also been principals in the feud, but on the other side, flatly contradicted her mother-in-law and declared, 'Sadozi says it was all *makhi-makhi*, but no, it was during the feud that they were given: for everyone who was killed, they gave women.' I think that by denying this, and insisting that the marriages were made as exchanges, Sadozi was protecting herself from an admission that her brothers, to whom she remained much attached, were more or less responsible for her unhappy marriage: according to her sons, the hostility her husband showed her was directly associated with his continuing grief and anger at the murder of his own father 35 years before.

As we have seen, Durrani recognize two modes of marriage, each of which is composed of three forms, distinguished indigenously, in the case of marriages in the asymmetrical mode, but only analytically, in the case of marriages in the symmetrical mode.

In practice most marriages take either the *kotara* form of brideprice marriage or the neutral form of direct exchange marriage. The choice between them most often depends on a compromise based on the idiosyncracies of the two households involved, their respective abilities to manage the competitive elements of a marriage arrangement, and their convenience. Certain structural elements will also influence the choice: there is a tendency for households with many male children to seek inexpensive brideprice marriages for them, while those with many daughters prefer to arrange exchange marriages or expensive brideprice marriages for them.

But considerations of these kinds are of a different order from those in which the choice of the marriage form itself is used publicly to clarify political relations both between the parties to the marriage and between them and others. This is most obviously the case in exchange marriages of 'recognition', where the medium is the message, the status equality of the two sides being created and communicated by the very fact of the marriage itself. But even the meaning of this form is likely to be ambiguous in practice. Indeed, the rites, ceremonies and prestations of marriages of any form may be manipulated in many ways such that each one is open to a variety of conflicting interpretations. Such cases present intriguing puzzles for the ethnographer: for example, how does one make sense of conflicting claims about a marriage which may have been arranged either as compensation for a minor injury or as an exchange of 'reconciliation'? I know several cases (see chapter 11) in which the principals themselves believed from the beginning that a marriage belonged to two quite different forms – one side treating it as a long overdue completion of an exchange, the other as a marriage for brideprice. Such ambiguity clearly reveals my statistics on marriage forms to be, to a certain degree, arbitrary!

The ambiguities within and between marriage forms, and the multiple interpretations the system allows, are certainly an important element in its robustness and may account for both its geographical spread and continuity through time. However, when pressure on resources and competition between ethnic groups and Durrani households becomes severe, as has been the case in the Saripul region in recent years, certain elements in the marriage forms are liable to change. These changes have had the effect of either reducing the likelihood of usurpation or guaranteeing a man some security for his capital in women.

The most important change is the present insistence that every marriage be initiated by a formal engagement ceremony at which as many respected men as possible are assembled to witness the terms of the agreement. Another change reduces the area of ambiguity between parties to an exchange marriage: definite brideprices are now agreed on, so that should one girl die before her *nikah*, the exchange can still be completed in a quite straightforward way. Other changes have in effect increased the ways in which a man can benefit from a woman's marriage. Unlike in the past, when close kinsmen were said to have given women for free among themselves, nowadays there is no question but that a man must pay a proper brideprice if he marries a close cousin. Also relevant here are *sar* payments. In the context of an exchange marriage, the *sar* payment may compensate for any imbalance due to differences in the circumstances of the two girls; while in the case of widows, as we shall see (p. 187), a *sar* payment allows men to collect compensation for a widow they have inherited but whom they do not want to marry themselves. Nonetheless, in yet other areas uncertainty remains about the exact rights men have over women: in the repayment of brideprice in the case of the death of an engaged girl; in the status of unmarried widows; and perhaps most important, in the whole issue of female inheritance.

8

Ceremonies of Durrani marriage

The very complexity of Durrani marriage ceremonies sets marriage apart in a culture whose lack of ritual elaboration is otherwise notable. The basic uniformity of the ceremonial procedure also seems to be an expression of the fundamental and monolithic place of marriage in Durrani society. However, though the sequence of rites, ceremonies and prestations is similar for all marriages, these may be elaborated or attenuated for various reasons. Indeed, any marriage may be qualified in ritual terms, and the numerous opportunities for the manipulation of status claims add an important dimension to the meaning of any Durrani marriage. As the Durrani are well aware, the interpretation of such ambiguities is important both to the construction of the affinal relationship and to the standing of the two households in the community as a whole.

Both formal and private ceremonies emphasize an ideal balance and equality between affines, while there are certain areas, especially in feasting and entertainment, where the wife-takers can improve upon their position of inherent superiority and make public statements about their standing in the community as a whole. Opportunities also exist, though on a more limited scale, for the wife-givers to maintain publicly the equality which is also an accepted interpretation of any marriage between Durrani households.

Age of betrothal and marriage

Guardians arrange all first marriages for both men and women. Children may be engaged (and thus effectively married) from birth, but child betrothal is not common and the usual interval between the engagement contract (*kozda*) and wedding (*wada*) is two or three years. The Maduzai associate puberty with age of marriage, and a favourite aphorism runs 'a man is like wheat, a woman like barley' (wheat, the higher status grain, takes longer to mature than barley). Men wed for the first time anywhere between the ages of fifteen and thirty, depending to a great extent on the wealth of their households, but nowadays most wed at about twenty years of age. Girls (*pegla*) are said to be 'ripe' and to wed soon after puberty (*kamal*) at perhaps fourteen or fifteen years of age. However, biological age *per se* is of little importance to the Maduzai compared with social age as constructed by marriage. By contrast with the latitude allowed men, fathers who fail to ensure the marriage of their daughter soon after puberty are said to lack honour (*gheyrat*). While older girls are considered unattractive spouses, the pressure to engage a girl early stems largely from the fear that she will otherwise become embroiled in some illicit attachment.

Table 18 draws on the 1972 sample, and presents the approximate ages of all engaged members of Lineage C. The numbers are very small but it can be seen that the proportions of engagements with men and women outside the lineage are similar to those for completed marriages. The table suggests that very young girls are only given to lineage males and that, once a girl has reached puberty, a groom from outside will quickly complete a marriage, while delays after this time may be tolerated by a groom from the same lineage.

The Maduzai generally disapprove of both child betrothal and pre-pubertal weddings, especially the latter, which are considered 'against Islam' and a betrayal of parental responsibility. Objections to child betrothal, on the other hand, are couched in pragmatic rather than moral terms.

Most cases in which children are engaged well before puberty are exchanges in which one couple is markedly younger than the other. Often such exchanges are made to settle a quarrel between two families and the children chosen are the only ones available to stand as principals. In such cases age is disregarded and causes no adverse comment.

Child betrothal in other cases is seen as an issue concerning the girl; the age of the husband is of less importance, largely because it does not provide significant insight into the motives or character of the arrangement. That is, there is no advantage in marrying boys young, whereas girls represent a financial asset to their guardians which the latter may sometimes be forced to realize early. In doing so a man is likely to forgo the higher brideprice a girl would fetch if she were grown up for the immediate benefits which accrue from her early engagement.

From the point of view of the groom's kin, his engagement to a young girl is considered a risky procedure. As one man said,

The girl may be of one type, the woman of another. When a woman has grown, her qualities become known: the good ones command a good price, the bad ones a bad price. But if you have taken a girl when she was small, the arrangement stands however she turns out.

For this reason, men who actively seek to marry a young girl are usually those who anticipate difficulties and delays in amassing a brideprice. By marrying a child they allow themselves the years until their bride reaches puberty to accumulate the sum. Girls are given to such men when the latter are poor but

Table 18. *Current ages of engaged persons, Lineage C, 1972*

	0–4	5–9	10–14	15–19	20–24	Second or subsequent wives	Total
Boys							
Engaged to girls							
within the Lineage	0	3	2	9	5	6	25
Outside the Lineage	0	1	1	4	3	2	11
Total	9	4	3	13	8	8	36
Girls							
Engaged to boys							
within the Lineage	2	8	9	6	0		25
Outside the Lineage	0	1	5	0	0		6
Total	2	9	14	6	0		31

promising, and when the girl's father wishes to increase the male labour force he commands; though such men may not work directly for their fathers-in-law, they may act informally as retainers.

The boy's side should initiate a marriage proposal. Rarely, a girl's father may do so if he is in dire economic circumstances, but, as one man said, 'People will laugh; it is not an Afghan [Durrani] custom to press a man into accepting your daughter.' In virtually all such cases the girl is young, for, as the Maduzai note, mature girls do not lack for suitors. Thus a man's wife may die, and if he has small children, he must find a replacement quickly and may be forced to give a young daughter in an exchange marriage which allows him to remarry immediately. The dilemma faced by one Lineage C household illustrates other circumstances in which the engagement of a young girl may be sought by her father.

Case 4: Habibullah

In 1970, to avoid rapacious Government officials who alleged, almost certainly unjustly, that he had been involved in a homicide (the only recent such case to concern the Maduzai directly), Habibullah fled Sinjit village. He was a widower and the sole breadwinner of a small household comprising his elderly widowed mother, two sons and a six-year-old daughter. To find money, he was forced to sell his small landholding and his household thus became among the poorest of the lineage. Then, from a safe distance, Habibullah instructed that his daughter should be engaged to be married.

His sister and her daughter-in-law sought a suitable spouse for the girl, who was attractive and thought to take after her mother, who had been 'a good woman'. Eventually Habibullah's ZSW arranged the child's engagement to her own brother, a youth of fourteen. It was agreed that a high brideprice (80,000 Afs.) be paid in instalments of 10,000 Afs. a year until the girl reached puberty.

These payments were calculated to sustain the household in Habibullah's absence. So far, poverty has forced them to accept goods as part of the brideprice at much higher than their market value, so that the groom's guardian has made substantial savings on the arranged brideprice, while maintaining his affines' household. Meanwhile, in spite of his agnates' disapproval and while still in exile, Habibullah himself remarried hypergamously, taking an Hazara bride very, very cheaply.

The economic dependence of Habibullah's household on the groom's household typifies relations between parties to a marriage which has been sought by the bride's side. It provides firm support for Maduzai disapproval of such initiatives. Habibullah was considered not to have had any alternative. In general, Maduzai display a great deal of understanding for men who are forced to marry their daughters (as their only remaining resource) in the hope that the marriage and/or brideprice will enable them to recover from some desperate situation. Of course, such a strategy precludes any concern for the fate of the girl herself. However, Maduzai sympathies do not extend to other less desperate men who squander the potential wealth represented by their daughters (see N. Tapper 1979: 293). There are other difficulties inherent in the betrothal of children: some can result from the unformed character of the children, others may develop if serious changes occur in the relative economic circumstances of the two families during the engagement period (see N. Tapper 1979: 294ff.).

Siblings of the same sex may be married in any order, though it is usual for older children to be married first. Birth order is most often disregarded in the case of girls, mainly because their personal characteristics influence the suitors they attract and their guardian plays a more passive role in their engagement. And, in any case, as virtually all girls marry soon after they reach puberty, the exact order in which they do so is of little importance. By contrast a man must actively seek brides for his sons and it is considered that, to avoid dissension within the house-hold, the wise man will marry them according to their birth order. Nonetheless, sometimes a son may be married before his older brothers, especially if the father anticipates his particular support in running the paternal joint household which will result from the marriage. Most often, however, discrepancies occur in the marriages of half-siblings; with the encouragement of the favoured or perhaps only living wife, a man may seek brides for her sons first. Men who marry early gain undoubted economic and political advantages: they may father children ear-lier, and their affinal ties may offer them more opportunities for manoeuvre than would otherwise be the case.

Betrothal ceremonies
Although the boy's side should initiate a marriage proposal, men and women on both sides may discuss a possible match for some time before any formal pro-

posal is made. If the families are not well known to each other, women from the groom's family will visit the girl to consider her looks and demeanour, as well as the general character of her home. Only if they approve of the prospective bride will a formal proposal be made, while much of the bargaining over the brideprice will depend on their judgement. The girl's side too will take the opportunity of this visit to consider the suitability of the match, and if they disapprove, the suit is unlikely to proceed further.

Formal marriage guardians (*sahib*, *wakil*) of unmarried children are their father or, if he is dead, senior close male agnates; in practice the head of the household almost always acts in this capacity. Once the boy's guardian fixes on a particular girl he knows to be suitable and available, he will organize a delegation (*maraka*) of both men and women, senior people who are close to the household, to approach the girl's guardian. Once a suit has been mounted, no one else is supposed to tender another proposal for the girl until a decision on the first suit has been given, though gazumping sometimes occurs. If the suit is acceptable, and a brideprice can be agreed, the boy's family are expected quickly to organize an engagement party. They also thank the senior female matchmaker for her part in the success of the suit with a gift of a veil or some other small token.

Formerly, the girl's guardian might simply give a piece (*tar*) of his turban as his binding pledge to the boy's representative, and there was no public ceremony at all. But such an agreement could easily lead to dispute, even where deception was never intended. Nowadays marriages are so important, financially and otherwise, to a household's standing, that such risks are avoided and engagement ceremonies are almost always witnessed by a mullah and other senior men; the *tar* pledge has become three decorated handkerchiefs given to the groom's side.

The men and women who participate in the *tar* are specifically invited by the principals' guardians. Men of the groom's side, often thirty or more if the families are of some standing, arrive at the girl's house before noon and, after a meal, the formal betrothal ceremony takes place. The bride's guardian calls out the pre-arranged sum of the brideprice and the groom's representative must agree to it publicly. Then five or ten per cent of the sum will be handed over. Prayers are said over the *tar* handkerchiefs which have been brought in on top of trays of sweets, and the binding *nikah* contract is completed with the mullah's *fateha* prayer (see N. Tapper 1979: 298ff.). With this, the engagement is considered irrevocable.

From the *tar* onwards the boy and girl are regarded as married and are spoken of as husband (*mere*) and wife (*mayna*). Broken engagements, which are unusual, are formalized by the grooms' repetition of the Islamic divorce formula, but a 'divorce' in this context is viewed by the Maduzai as less serious than a divorce which follows the completion of the wedding ceremonial. Indeed, Maduzai insist that among Durrani, divorce does not occur after the bride goes to live with her husband, though, in practice, there are very rare exceptions to this rule (cf. Case 9, p. 233).

The *tar* ceremony is completed when the men fire off their guns and the party, including a young brother or brother's son of the groom wearing the ceremonial handkerchiefs in his turban, return to the groom's house where the men are sprinkled with water for good luck (*kheyr*). The handkerchiefs are then hung up in front of the groom's house where the women of his family and other well-wishers shower the *tar* with sweets. The *tar* is regarded as primarily a woman's party and sometimes more than a hundred women will have gathered for the festivities: they will be given a meal by the groom's guardian and may sing and dance until evening.

Soon after the *tar* an informal exchange of small personal items between the two sides is initiated by the groom's gift to the bride of a full set of clothes, *da nawe gul*, 'the bride's flower'. Thereafter she prepares small presents such as embroidered handkerchiefs for her new affines, both men and women. Whoever receives such a gift is obliged to return a small present – soap or a small piece of jewellery – at the time of the *push* (see p. 165).

The engagement period

Some time after the *tar*, the groom's guardian may arrange a *khoshey* (see N. Tapper 1979: 400 n. 5). The *khoshey* pledge and celebrations are in essence identical to those of the *tar*, though on a larger scale: for example, ten to thirty decorated handkerchiefs may be given by the bride's side, and may be accompanied not by trays of sweets, but by a *bani*, a silken cloth sewn to resemble a skin butterchurn filled with sweets which the men of the groom's side take home with them. In this respect, the *khoshey* presents an opportunity for conspicuous consumption and is usually held only when both parties want to make a display, or when the engagement has occurred many years earlier. Moreover, unlike the *tar*, the *khoshey* is regarded as a men's party. After the formal ceremony, the groom's guardian may organize professional musicians to accompany the men's dancing or an afternoon of *buzkashi*, the Afghan game played on horseback.

The *khoshey* may also signal the groom's wish to begin sleeping with his bride in her father's home, a custom known as *bazi* (the word literally means 'game' or 'deceit', see N. Tapper 1979: 400 n. 6). Depending on his inclinations and the approval of his mother-in-law, the groom may secretly begin to have sexual relations with his bride at any time after the *tar*, but this appears to be relatively unusual and generally disapproved; more often the groom will be formally 'taken to *bazi*' and his 'feet loosened' (*pshe khlase kri*) by his guardian and a party of his friends.

The groom's guardian will approach the bride's guardian, naming a day when he wishes to bring the young man to *bazi*. His request will not be granted until some further portion of the brideprice is paid. The bride's guardian may demand any amount he wants; depending on relations between the two sides, it may be as little as a single sheep, or as great as the remainder of the brideprice, the latter being tantamount to a refusal to permit *bazi* at all. The Maduzai speak of *bazi* as a relatively new custom which they learned from other ethnic groups in Turkistan. However, the custom is well known to Pashtuns throughout eastern Afghanistan (and see Elphinstone 1842: I, 240–241), and it is more likely that it is the relation between *bazi* and the control of brideprice payments which is new.

Once the portion has been paid, a small but high-spirited party of men, and sometimes the groom's sister or father's sisters, visit for an evening at the bride's house where her father will have gathered his sisters and a few other female relations. The male guests have their hands ceremonially washed and, after the meal, use the serving trays to send small cash gifts to the bride's mother and are given presents of handkerchiefs, hats or turbans in return. Then the bride's mother or another senior woman, in return for a few Afghanis, applies henna to the men's hands for good luck.

The visitors depart, leaving the groom behind. His hands are then also henna'ed by his mother-in-law, and after chatting with his affines he is intro-duced to his bride, with whom he spends the night. Before dawn he should depart, leaving a cash gift of some 500 to 1,000 Afs. under the mattress for his mother-in-law. For three nights he visits his bride, and on the third evening his father-in-law gives him a suit of clothes (also called *da nawe gul*). Thereafter he may visit the household at any time. During the day he will be entertained by his wife's family, her mother being especially solicitous 'for the bride's sake' (cf. Glatzer 1977: 151 and note; Evans-von Krbek 1977: 173, 235), though he should never talk publicly to his bride and must leave at nightfall before returning by stealth to join her.

Men and women agree that *bazi* is a splendid custom and couples avowedly in love with each other after many years of marriage recall the romance and excite-ment of *bazi* as the best time of their lives. One man called it 'God's blessing' and said that, even if it were possible to pay all the brideprice at once, payments would be prolonged so that the pleasures of *bazi* would not be missed. Not all couples, however, pass through this stage. The groom must initiate *bazi* and he may have other wives at home, or be so hard-pressed to collect money for the brideprice that he has no time for such frivolity. Or the marriage may have been arranged to settle a quarrel, in which case *bazi* may be out of place.

Among Maduzai, women before *bazi* are presumed to be virgins, but Maduzai have no interest in actual tests or proofs of virginity at the time of *bazi*. Once *bazi* has been initiated, sexual relations between a betrothed couple may become regular. No child may ever be born in its mother's natal home – should this happen it would be a sin (*'eyb*) and shame to both parties. As no contraceptive measures are taken, the usual way to prevent premature pregnancy is to postpone *bazi* until the end of the brideprice payments is in sight. Should the girl then become pregnant, she and her husband will strive to keep the fact secret and to secure an early wedding. If they fail in this, they may decide to abort the child, often with the complicity of the girl's mother who, unlike her father, is expected quickly to guess her condition (cf. Hunte 1985).

In fact, I heard of no case where a child was born before the parents' wedding, though some were born only days afterwards. What happens in case of an engaged girl's pregnancy varies with the relations between the two parties to the marriage. When these are amicable, the bride's father may strive to keep his daughter's condition secret and even agree to accept brideprice payments *after* the wedding has taken place; or, if the pregnancy has become public knowledge, he may ignore the gossip and simply ensure that the wedding proceeds with all due haste. But, if relations between the parties are already strained, the bride's father may use the pregnancy to demand a fine (*babirey*) additional to the brideprice.

Babirey payments were made in at least 4 of the 146 marriages in the 1972 Lineage C sample. The two sides may manage to compromise over the scale of the *babirey* payment but in two cases, when relations between the two parties were very bad, on the wedding day itself the bride's father publicly and provocatively announced his demand for a fine camel or an expensive gun. In both cases the father accused the groom, and the senior men of the groom's household, of having shamed him and blackened his name, and made dire threats on the groom's life; the *babirey* had to be paid before the wedding could proceed.

The custom of 'marriage to a gun' allows a marriage to be completed and the Islamic *nikah* to be performed even in the absence of the groom himself. Few men manage to visit their homes during the two-year period of military service, and shepherds or agricultural labourers may be obliged by their jobs to be away for long stretches during the year; if the girl should find herself pregnant after her fiancé's departure, a *nikah* by proxy ensures that she need not have her child in her father's house. Other cogent reasons for holding an early wedding day may also present themselves and be facilitated by a 'marriage to a gun' (see p. 272). The custom is sanctioned by the mullahs and said to be 'in the Book'; the procedure itself is apparently straightforward, the gun simply 'takes the groom's place' or 'is his representative (*wakil*)'.

The wedding
The formal contract of engagement gives a man sexual access to his bride, but he has the right to neither her labour nor any children she might have until she is brought into his home and the Islamic marriage ceremony is performed. This is done only when the full brideprice demanded by the bride's father has been paid. Then the groom may insist on holding the wedding (*wada*), though if relations between the two families are good he will postpone complete payment of the

brideprice until he knows that the girl's trousseau (*kor, da nawe kor*) has been assembled. On receipt of the last instalment of the brideprice, the bride's father should return one sheep, known as the 'head of the milking rope' (*sarwandarey*). The groom's side now prepare for the wedding, and he and his agnates may visit friends, agnates and affines (other than the new bride's family) to collect *nimouri*, or contributions towards the expenses.

These gifts, which are unlikely to total more than a few thousand Afghanis, are not obligatory, nor is there any formal expectation that they will be directly recipprocated later. On the whole, only the poor will ask for *nimouri*, households of any pretension to honour considering it shaming to do so. Indeed, a poor household may get by with spending little more than the sum collected as *nimouri*, while most people will probably spend in the region of 30,000 Afs. in all on engagement and wedding parties. However, the groom's side may spend as much as they like and some wealthy households may spend one lac (100,000 Afghanis) or more (cf. Glatzer 1977: 156–157).

Each night as the wedding approaches, young women will gather at the groom's home for singing and dancing. Meanwhile his mother will finish her preparations of clothing and other personal gifts for the bride, and one morning some ten or twenty women will be organized, often under the direction of a woman's leader, to take these to the bride's home. Both the gifts and the party at which they are presented are known as the *push* or 'the mother's *push*'. The women are given a mid-day meal, then senior women from the bride's side accept a token fee of a few Afghanis and display the bride's jewellery and clothes, including her white bridal veil. Further gifts of clothing are also presented to her mother and father. The number of suits of clothing given to the bride – up to twenty at an important marriage – contribute to her renown, though it is a matter of pride for both sides that the presents should be as generous as possible. Sweets are then distributed and the women of the groom's side give small cash sums (called *makh-kshata*) to each woman of the bride's side in exchange for heavily embroidered hats or other small articles of clothing. The groom's parents and sometimes other close relatives also receive gifts of clothing.

The evening before the wedding, camels loaded with foodstuffs and fuel and topped with bright handkerchiefs are sent from the groom's house to the bride's house. The uncertainty of relations between the two families before completion of the wedding is underlined by the fact that the groom's kinsman who accompanies these beasts announces his arrival aggressively with gunshots, and then he and the professional cook whom he has brought with him stay to guard the rice from theft by the bride's family, thus preventing their own consequent shame on the morrow. This same night, sometimes known as the 'night of the drum', a further party is held at the groom's house and men and women may dance, separately, late into the evening to the music of hired Jat professionals. Meanwhile the bride is bathed, her body-hair is removed and her hands are henna'ed by her closest kinswomen. The groom is once more brought to *bazi* by a party of friends, and he too has his hands henna'ed.

The cook begins his work before dawn. Then, soon after dawn, the musicians resume playing and all who hear the sound of the shawm and drum are welcome to attend the wedding. It is said that the poor could not survive the winter without such meals. They are held out of doors where everyone may gauge the character and scale of the celebrations and where it is easy for strangers to join in.

Meanwhile men and women of the groom's party are gathered by invitation for the procession to the bride's house. They may walk or, if the bride's house is far, the women will ride camels decorated in elaborate trappings, while the men accompany them on horseback. Along the road the women will sing and sometimes dance, and, as the two groups near the bride's house, they merge into a single throng, the men firing their guns to warn of their approach. Men and women of the bride's side will have already assembled, and they greet the new arrivals. Separate men's and women's dancing circles soon form and other men's entertainments may be organized: wrestling, target-shooting, quail-fighting and even *buzkashi* if the wedding is an important one. Meanwhile the bride remains behind a curtain where she is clothed in her wedding finery and her hair dressed. A close kinsman (her brother, father's brother's son or mother's brother's son) parts her hair and he is given a small sum of money (*sar wodey*); this parting, her reddened hands and her white veil are the only outward signs of her change of status. Unlike the ordinary veils women wear, the white bridal veil covers the bride's face completely – the only time a woman is ever thus hidden.

Around midday a meal of rice and meat palao is ready and men and women are fed separately and in relays. After the meal, the senior men of both sides will agitate for the 'good work' (*kar-e kheyr*) to begin. A chain of male agnates and their wives pass the trousseau out of the house item by item, starting with a Koran and a bowl of water. Meanwhile, women of the groom's side sing songs (*babulale*) of praise or ridicule depending on the quality and size of the trousseau; the men too take the greatest interest in the various household goods and articles of clothing, which are displayed as advantageously as possible before being loaded onto the waiting camels.

The groom remains hidden near or even in the bride's house until he is fetched and a Mullah dresses him publicly in a new suit of white clothes which has come out as part of the trousseau. He is then blessed by the mullah, kissed on the face and slapped three times on the back by his wife's father and friends before he flees in a shower of sweets and coins. Then the bride is brought out by her mother and other senior women and is mounted on the foremost of the camels carrying the trousseau. She puts her henna'ed hand out of the all-enveloping bridal veil, sprinkles her own head three times with water from the bowl which is held up for her, and then she in her turn is showered with sweets and coins as her camel is led away. The groom's women sing as they depart with the new bride, while the groom's men shoot off their guns in celebration. At the threshold of the groom's house, the bride refuses to dismount and enter until she has been promised a gift, 'the veil (*paruney*)', of an animal 'to loosen her feet'. She begins a three-day period of seclusion in the room or tent which she and her husband will share.

It is usual for the Islamic *nikah* to be 'tied' at the groom's house on the evening of the wedding day. After a meal provided by the groom's guardian, representatives (*wakil*) are chosen from among the few individuals present: the groom's guardian and and someone for the bride. If some of the bride's kin, her mother or sister, have accompanied her to her new home, one of them may act for her; if not, the bride may ask her mother-in-law or one of her husband's brothers to be her *wakil*. A bowl of sugar-water 'so that the bride and groom be sweet together' is covered with a white handkerchief and placed before the presiding mullah. The bride and groom are asked if they agree to their marriage and witnesses press towards them to catch their replies. Then their *wakils* engage in token bargaining over the Islamic *mahr*. Agreement is soon reached and a small sum commensurate with the wealth of the groom is fixed. The mullah picks up the handkerchief (which he keeps as his due), recites various prayers in Arabic and makes the bride 'a partner in the hearth (*negharey*)'. Then the sugar-water, with its merit (*suwab*), is passed round the men, who all have a sip. Once the *nikah* has been performed, the competition inherent in the marriage procedure ends: 'There can be no more fights or demands for money; only then can the husband's heart be easy'.

The *mahr* is a sum of cash (a few thousand Afghanis at most) which the groom promises to give his bride. It is an essential part of the Islamic marriage ceremony, without which the Maduzai claim the marriage would not be proper (*halal*) and the husband would be punished on Judgement Day. Women explain the *mahr* as payment for the trouble they undergo in marriage, for sleeping with their husbands and for chores like washing their clothes. In fact, the promised sum is never paid: usually women 'return it' as a free gift to their husbands, though some – the less wise, according to most women – treat it as a continuing debt owed them, against which they may ask for gifts of clothing or jewellery.

For two days after the *nikah* the bride remains formally secluded in her new home, though visited by women of the groom's side, who appraise her looks and modesty. On the morning of the third day, the bride's female kin and women from each household of her husband's relatives and neighbours are invited to the *takht-tolawi*, the lifting of the bridal bed, which has remained spread out during this time. The women bring gifts of bread and fruit, and after a lively party the most senior of the women guests on the groom's side is asked to raise the mattress, finding as she does so some small gift tucked under it for her. With this the bride's feet are again said to have been loosened and she is now free to visit the homes of those women who have come to the ceremony, though she will not do so until she has been specifically invited to a meal with them. In the following weeks she will receive many such invitations. Such visits are known as *paruney* (veil), since at each house she visits she will be presented with a veil (*paruney*) or some other ornament or cash gift of up to 500 Afghanis.

The final ceremony of a marriage, the *sofra* ('dining-cloth') takes place when the bride returns to her father's home for the first time after the wedding, sometimes after a year or more. For this visit her husband kills a sheep and the cooked meat (also known as *sofra*) is wrapped in bread and a dining-cloth and sent with her. The wife may stay a week or sometimes as long as a month in her natal home. At the end of her visit, her father too kills a sheep and returns a gift of cooked food which the bride then distributes among her husband's male agnates.

Marriage ceremonies and reputation

I have already touched on some of the ways in which claims to status may be made through the numerous ceremonies and prestations of marriage. Analytically, it is useful to distinguish two aspects of the ritual sequence: the formal ceremonies and prestations held at the bride's house which are private, more or less obligatory, and narrowly prescribed by custom; and the more informal parties and entertainments sponsored by the groom's side, which are public and allow considerable variation in scale and greater opportunity for conspicuous consumption. Even in the formal ceremonies there is certainly a degree of competition between the two sides, and any serious lapse on either side will soon become public knowledge; the quality or quantity of handkerchiefs, clothing and cash sums are all evaluated in terms of reputation (*num*) and honour (*nang, gheyrat*). Small delegations of young, insignificant persons, or any lack of generosity, will be ridiculed and the marriage guardians will be shamed. However, apart from the use which the bride's side may make of the trousseau and their ability to determine the timing of events, the structure of the exchanges which constitute the formal ceremonies itself limits competition. Basically, these rites are balanced and emphasize the ideal equality and independence of affines. However, this message may be contradicted during the more informal public celebrations in which the groom's side may choose to dramatize the superiority implicit in their position as wife-takers.

The overall balance in Maduzai marriage ceremonial is easily seen if the ceremonies and prestations are divided into six discrete phases, though the Maduzai themselves see the whole process as more or less continuous. Figure 9 summarizes these phases.

Phase I is constituted simply by the *maraka* delegation of proposal. Phase II includes two major ceremonies, the *tar* and the *khoshey*, which are virtually identical in content: in effect, the *khoshey* exists mainly for emphasis and it is sometimes omitted. The major ceremonies of Phase III, the *bazi* and *push*, are almost mirror images of each other in their various features, including their medial elements which bear the same name (*da nawe gul*). Phases II and III are

Figure 9 Formal marriage procedures

Phase	Formal rites and prestations		Festivities	Notes
	Bride's side	*Groom's side*		
I *maraka*	Delegation of proposal ◄———			
	Discussion of brideprice			
II *tar*	*fateha* engagement contract ◄—		Groom's side:	Up to
betrothal	handkerchiefs ———►		party for	10% of
	hospitality, sweets ———►		women	brideprice
				paid
da nawe gul	Clothes for bride ◄———			
	personal gifts			
	bride to affines ———►			
khoshey	*fateha* contract ◄———		Groom's side	(optional)
'happiness'	handkerchiefs ———►		party for	
	hospitality, sweets ———►		men	
III *bazi*	Groom to bride ◄———		Groom's side:	Half
groom's	henna, hospitality ———►		party for	brideprice
'feet loosened'	cash ◄———		men	paid
	clothing ———►			
da nawe gul	Cash ◄———			
	clothes for groom ———►			
	personal gifts			
	groom to affines ◄———			
push	Clothes for bride ◄———		Groom's side:	Brideprice
clothing	hospitality ———►		party for	paid
display	cash ◄———		women	
	hats ———►			
'night of	*sarwandarey* ———►		Groom's side:	
the drum'	food, fuel,		party	
	handkerchiefs ◄———		for men &	
	groom to bride ◄———		women	
IV *wada*	Preparation of bride		Both sides:	
wedding	hospitality ———►		party for	
	display of trousseau		men and	
	dressing of groom		women	
	departure of bride ———►			
V *paruney*	———► Bride arrives			
'veil', bride's	◄——— camel to bride			
'feet loosened'	bride secluded			
nikah	◄——— Hospitality			
Islamic	◄——— *mahr* to bride			
takht-tolawi	◄——— Hospitality		Groom's side:	
'bed-raising'	◄——— gifts to bride		parties for	
paruney	◄——— Hospitality		women	
'veil' bride's	◄——— gifts to bride			
'feet loosened'				
VI *sofra*	◄——— Cooked food			
'hospitality'	Cooked food ———►			

characterized by considerable tension between the two sides. Though balanced overall, the reciprocity which characterizes this period is delayed, often over a period of years.

Phases IV and V form a pair which is different from that of Phases II and III. Phase IV, the wedding, is the most public and variable of the ceremonies. Phase V, marking the bride's period of seclusion in her new home, includes the essential and most invariable elements of the marriage, the *nikah* and the *mahr*. The two phases together last a few days at most, and the prestations of these phases are direct and immediate. Another contrast with Phases II and III is that the groom's side becomes responsible for the meals which are an integral part of all the formal ceremonies – though at the wedding both sides participate in joint festivities as well as ritual.

It is notable that among Durrani, unlike other Middle Eastern peoples, the rituals of marriage do not include any focus on virginity nor the spilling of hymenal blood, though henna, which is often treated as 'symbolic blood' and marks the danger and uncertainty of transitional phases in rites of passage in many Middle Eastern societies, is also used by Durrani to mark changes in sexual status. Maduzai regard the sexual relations during *bazi* as somewhat anomalous – as unconventional and exciting; a game, as the literal meaning of *bazi* suggests – rather than dangerous. And, in spite of the risk of pregnancy, the *bazi* period is not hedged round with elaborate taboos; indeed, the use of henna is the only visible sign that a change of sexual status has taken place. It is applied to the groom's hands on the first and last nights of *bazi* and to the bride's hands for her wedding day, and is thus linked situationally first with the groom's quasi-illicit sexual contact with his bride during *bazi* and then with their legitimate sexual relations after marriage. In this respect, the use of henna also marks stages in the transfer of responsibility for the bride from her guardian to the groom: first with regard to her sexuality, then with regard to his rights over her procreative power and her labour.

The three occasions when 'feet are loosened' also coincide with times of radical alteration in the couple's personal relations with each other and with their respective kin. After the engagement, the couple are known as man and wife, but their relationship as individuals does not alter substantially; if, however, the pair have been well known to each other since childhood, they will now be expected to display 'shame' in each other's presence. Only with Phase III and the onset of *bazi* does their relationship change, often to one of easy, demonstrative friendship. *Bazi* begins when the groom's 'feet are untied', and his relationship to his wife's kin also changes radically: in effect he is given the freedom of their house.

Throughout the engagement period the bride is not allowed under any circumstances to enter her husband's home. The second occasion when 'feet are loosened' is when the bride receives the *paruney* gift before entering her new home. The bride then becomes a full member of her husband's household, but as such she also assumes a new set of responsibilities. Relations alter drastically, not only with her affines but also with her spouse. *Bazi* is a time free of cares for the young couple, while the *nikah* ceremony marks the onset of responsibilities they have to each other as man and wife. At this stage the couple will conform with the conventional division of labour between the sexes and their relationship may become more strained for this reason alone. That is, burdened with chores and, if lucky, with child-care as well, the couple will have less time with each other than during the *bazi* period, and they may also find numerous issues concerning the adequate performance of household tasks about which to quarrel.

The third occasion when a 'foot-loosening' takes place is when the bride emerges from seclusion. In the round of visiting that follows, she gains the freedom of her husband's local community, a freedom for women in which Durrani take much pride.

In effect, the bride's seclusion in Phase V mirrors the groom's situation in Phase III while he is going to *bazi*. And just as the groom is brought to *bazi* for the last time at the transition between Phases III and IV, and then is dressed in new clothes at the end of Phase IV, so too the bride is dressed in new clothes at the beginning of Phase IV and then transferred to her new home at the transition between Phases IV and V. (To complete the symmetry, either the groom's third night of *bazi*, or his last visit to *bazi* on the night before the wedding, should also be held to constitute 'foot-loosening'; but I have no record that this is so in either case.)

The two simple elements which constitute the final Phase VI – the *sofra*, a direct reciprocal exchange of cooked food – confirm that any differences have been resolved and an equivalence has been established between the two groups of affines. This marks the end of the marriage ceremonial and stands as a clear statement of the bride's integration into her husband's household and group: she is allowed to return to her natal home as a guest only when it is clear to her husband's family that she has accepted her status as one of them. In a sense the formal, obligatory relationship between the two groups terminates at this point: hereafter, they must choose to maintain the affinal ties between them.

The inequality and competition between the two sides to a marriage are thus denied by the formal structure of the ceremonies and transformed into a relation of equality. Most important, the formal ceremonies are not public, and only the participants can easily evaluate the quality of the gifts and the spirit in which they are offered. Moreover, the formal prestations and ceremonies are relatively standardized in scale, and the kinds of small gifts exchanged on these occasions (unlike the brideprice and the trousseau) are well defined by tradition and roughly balanced in number.

As has been mentioned, the Maduzai consider the Islamic marriage ceremony and the *mahr* payment associated with it to be the only essential parts of the marriage procedure, while other elements of the sequence may sometimes be omitted. However, apart from cases of widow inheritance, there seem to be only two kinds of situation in which a substantial attenuation of the rites and ceremonies is likely to take place. Thus, in three of the eight marriages arranged to settle the Maduzai feud (see pp. 77 ff.), women were taken to their husbands' homes on the very night of the settlement and the *nikah* ceremony was performed immediately, though I was told that in each case the sequence ended conventionally with the *sofra* exchange of cooked food. The other situation in which the marriage procedure is reduced to a minimum is when dependents living within their guardian's household marry: this seems to occur only in the case of orphaned children; I learned of no other occasions when kinspeople married while living in the same household. In such cases it would seem that only the rituals related to the altered personal status of the bride and groom are observed: *bazi*, some token celebration of the wedding day itself, the *nikah* and *mahr*, and the seclusion of the bride; all others are omitted as irrelevant.

Public festivities in marriage

The less formal and more public ceremonies associated with a marriage allow for the more overt expression of the competitive elements inherent in all Durrani marriages. The principals themselves manage and manipulate these ceremonies to promote their respective positions *vis-à-vis* each other; they will also be evaluated by others interested not only in that relationship but also in the comparative standing of the two households with others in the community. Interpretations of the ambiguities inherent in the symbolism of food and hospitality play a prominent part in these promotions and evaluations.

In the context of marriage, the evaluation and treatment of food are based on 'taste' (*khwand, mazza*) and can be characterized as essentially aesthetic and qualitative. The most expensive and prestigious foods are regarded by the Durrani as having both 'good taste' and 'strength'. What is significant is the extent to which political and aesthetic evaluations coincide, thus allowing relations of political inequality to be expressed despite the strongly egalitarian Islamic and tribal ideologies to which Durrani fervently subscribe.

Each stage in the marriage procedure provides at least one, and sometimes several, occasions when one side must offer hospitality (*melmastia*) to the other, or when an exchange of food is expected. The idiom of hospitality is complex. In general, in his language and solicitous behaviour the Durrani host humbles himself before his guest (it would be religiously forbidden (*haram*) to do otherwise), accepting that the guest has the right to demand and receive anything. The guest's apparent superiority is illusory, however, for by putting himself in a position to receive hospitality he too is humbled, for he honours his host and implicitly acknowledges the latter's ability to fulfil his every request.

It is important to note that such hospitality, though essentially private, is commensal: host and guest must eat from the same bowl. Both men and women offer hospitality to others. Parties (*melmani*) are held on many occasions: out of friend-ship, to thank members of a co-operative work-party, to welcome a new bride into her husband's community, and to mark the settlement of a dispute. In all cases, *melmani* express status relations of both equality and inequality. They include the assumption that the host-guest relationship may be reversed at a later date. In effect, *melmani* are treated as delayed reciprocal exchanges.

There are, however, other ways of expressing both equality and inequality through the symbolism of food. Gifts of uncooked food, among the commonest forms of charity, signify the giver's claim to political superiority over the receiver. In the marriage procedure, the only uncooked food is that brought by the groom's side to the bride's house, where it will be used for the feast on the wedding day. The presence of this food is certainly felt to be provocative and it may be stolen by the bride's family. It is notable that at this point the bride's family have not yet relinquished their control over her and thus have a certain practical power over their affines and would-be superiors. However, the challenge of the uncooked food is deflected by the fact that the bride's family do not consume it themselves but rather oversee its cooking and public distribution at the wedding; in doing this, they and the groom's family have, *de facto*, a joint role as wedding sponsors. It is far more shaming if the bride's family accept grain or other foodstuffs as part of the brideprice.

Only cooked food is acceptable as a gift between political equals or from an inferior to a superior. Cooked foods, particularly meat dishes, are said to 'taste' better. Mutton or lamb cooked in clarified butter and served with rice is the most prestigious meal one can offer; it is also the most expensive. There is also a clear notion that the amount of food served, and the numbers fed, indicate the status of the host. High status and lavish hospitality are closely linked. This is particularly so when a host feeds his guest but does not share the meal with them. At meals celebrating or representing the host-sponsor's achievement, boiled sweets are distributed to participants to allay envy and 'sweeten' their acceptance of their host's success, while on other occasions large quantities of sweets, as a luxury food, may be given to honour a superior.

As has already been suggested, all these elements are clear in the prestations and festivities associated with marriage. Rites of hospitality and the symbolism of food emphasize particularly the role marriage plays in political and economic relations between households, rather than, for example, aspects of gender relations.

At all those essentially private occasions when the participants in a marriage must meet to arrange the contract, a *melmani* meal is shared between them: at the formal proposal (*maraka*), the *fateha* engagement contract of the *tar* (repeated at the *khoshey*), when the groom comes to *bazi*, at the *push* when the bride's clothing is brought by the groom's female kin, at the 'raising of the bridal bed' and when the bride is welcomed and invited to share a *paruney* meal with households in her husband's community. And in the final exchange of the marriage, the bride carries cooked meat both ways between her agnates and affines; this transfer is to the undoubted detriment of the food, but 'people would laugh' if a live animal or raw meat were sent instead on this occasion. Such exchanges signify the equality between principals on both sides.

At the public festivities sponsored by the groom's side, however, both the quantities of food involved and the manner in which it is served are evaluated so as to differentiate between competing households. Though these occasions reflect the claims and aspirations of the groom's side, it is nonetheless true that a large, successful party adds to the impact of a particular marriage generally and thus may reflect on the importance of the bride's side as well.

Another dimension of differentiation is introduced in the structure of the feast. If they can afford it, the groom's side hires a specialist male cook, usually a non-Durrani. The meal is then served to men first, often in a series of sittings, the more important eating first. All guests at any sitting are treated quite uniformly. Sittings for women and children come after those of men but follow an identical pattern. What is distinctive about such feasts is that a stranger cooks the meal that is fed to guests, while the host and his family do not eat. In this respect the commensal aspect of the meal unites the guests but differentiates them from their host, the food-giver. Particularly in politically important marriages, guests are fed in return for their recognition, support or allegiance. Maduzai say that a big feast, which for the local Khans may involve feeding upwards of 2,000 people, 'tastes good'; it is also a clear sign of both economic and political success and is likely to bring yet further success in the future (see Tapper, R. and N. Tapper 1986: 69).

Marriage feasting and entertainment are most lavish and ostentatious in the case of politically important marriages, when the marriage itself represents a kind of test of equality. Paradoxically, in such marriages the public ceremonial provides an opportunity for the groom's side to assert ascendancy over their competitors on the bride's side. Conversely, the festivities are least ostentatious in marriages where there is no immediate or intense political or economic competition between the two sides, usually because they are already established friends and political allies whose relations have been confirmed by a marriage; or both sides to a marriage may be in such dependant positions as to be effectively outside the political arena altogether; or the groom's side may already be clearly superior, politically and economically, to that of the bride.

The Maduzai usually evaluate wedding festivities in one of four ways. First, the amount of palao may be measured by the number of cauldrons (*deg*) used to cook it: thus at one 'two-cauldron' wedding we attended, some 150–175 guests (men, women and children) were adequately, if not lavishly, fed. Alternatively, the dry weight of the rice bought for the celebrations may be known: for the same wedding, fifteen *sir* (about 100 kg) were bought, while I was told of one very large Maduzai wedding for over one thousand guests, for which some 90 *sir* (about 600 kg) were bought.

Second, a wedding may be remembered for the amount of meat in the palao, the numbers of incidental ingredients such as carrots or raisins it includes, and the type of oil in which the palao is cooked: animal ghee is the most prestigious, but sesame oil or, among the poorest people, even linseed oil may be used.

Third, weddings may be known by the number of professional musicians hired for the occasion. They may be 'without drum' (*bi-dul*) 'with drum alone' (*yeka dul*) but no shawm, or with a pair of musicians playing 'drum and shawn' (*dul au sorna*) in attendance. The most extravagant case I heard of among the Maduzai was one for which three pairs of musicians were hired; this was regarded as excessive and, in effect, inflationary: it brought curses on the heads of the organizers (see p. 259).

Fourth, a wedding may be remembered for the other entertainments provided, particularly whether or not the *buzkashi* game was played. As *buzkashi* competitions are not held until the ground has been softened by the first of the autumn rains and frost, the largest celebrations occur in late autumn, which is known as the wedding season: favourable weather conditions coincide with the slackest period in the productive cycle, when (except for the few households which remain with the sheep in the winter pastures) all the tribespeople congregate in the villages and can easily attend weddings, as can the inhabitants of nearby villages; sometimes five or more entire villages may be notified of a forthcoming celebration.

Dispersal and the economic pressures of spring and summer, and the bad weather of winter, cause the *khoshey*s and weddings to be much smaller then. Though the Maduzai consider it a very mean strategy to limit numbers, marriage celebrations may even be held during Ramazan, when fasting prevents the guests from being fed until nightfall.

Members of the bride's party, especially her father, explicitly concern themselves only with their affective loss, and participate in none of the public festivities except the wedding itself. Yet they can express their resentment at the loss of honour inherent in their giving up control of a daughter, by holding the groom's side to ransom. Initially the bride's father may ask anything he likes for his daughter, and even after the brideprice has been fixed at the engagement he may find ways of making other extortionate demands. Except in cases where the bride has become pregnant during *bazi*, the choice of when to hold the various ceremonies is completely open to the organizers themselves and it is usual for an amicable agreement to be reached between the two sides. In formal terms, however, the bride's guardian controls the timing of all celebrations. Especially at the two early stages – the *tar* and the onset of *bazi* – which are the most significant markers of the increasing and irrevocable alienation of his daughter, he may insist on receiving brideprice payments which often represent a substantial proportion of the total sum. Only when the entire brideprice has been paid may the groom insist that the wedding and *nikah* proceed. Regarding the timing of the wedding, the groom's side are liable to public ridicule: 'the girl's guardian has no worries, the worry is for the other side; they fear that people will laugh if the girl stays in her father's house and they don't arrange the wedding quickly'.

In general the stringency with which the bride's father insists on his rights depends on the same considerations which motivate the groom's side to hold grand entertainments. He will be most implacable if the two sides are political competitors and his status is likely to be brought into question by marrying his daughter for brideprice. If such rivalry does not exist between the two parties, the bride's father may be quite relaxed about the timing of the ceremonies. Whatever strategy he adopts, it is essentially a private matter between the principals and, once the *tar* has been performed, the bride's father has little room for manoeuvre: should he be too severe in his demands, these are likely to become public knowledge and he will be scorned for his lack of generosity, while if he is careless in the exercise of his rights he may be despised as a weak man who has made a free gift of his daughter.

Only in the trousseau has the bride's father any further scope for making a public statement about the standing of his household. Especially in politically important marriages, where the wife-takers have publicly claimed ascendancy through the festivities they have sponsored, the bride's father may reassert his equal status through the gift of a large, impressive trousseau.

Finally, in exceptional cases, the bride's side is the political and economic superior of the two parties, a blatant reversal of the conventional superiority of the wife-takers which is implicit in brideprice marriages. This happens most often when, during a lengthy engagement, the groom's side suffers a series of misfortunes from which it cannot recover. The bride's side does not gain from this reversal: on the contrary, they are likely to suffer a blow to their prestige, for they are not only benefiting another household by the gift of their daughter, but are actually giving her 'hypogamously'. In such cases, the rights accorded the bride's father in the marriage ceremonial will be most severely exercised: in an effort to recoup lost reputation he may delay the wedding indefinitely, or he may demand illicit increases in the brideprice; it is not surprising that most of the rare cases of broken engagements take place in such circumstances (see p. 268; N. Tapper 1979: 432ff.).

Trousseaux

Among the Maduzai, though a woman's right to inherit under Islamic law as both daughter and wife is ignored, and though she has no formal right to a trousseau (*kor*, literally 'house') at marriage, in practice women take with them to their marital homes either (following Goody 1973) a 'dowry' (in the case of an exchange marriage) or an 'indirect dowry' (in the case of a brideprice marriage), both of which I have referred to as trousseau.

The trousseau is made up of a fairly standard combination of clothing and jewellery for the bride and a wide range of household goods, their value being judged partly by quality, but mostly by quantity. A girl works on her own trousseau, directed by her mother and aided by other young girls and a range of kinswomen, all of whom are invited to party meals and given small presents for their help. It is usual to give items of the trousseau in sets, two of everything, three of everything, etc. A respectable trousseau, for a girl given for an average bride-price of 60 ewes and 30,000 Afs., included the items listed below. The list also gives a clear idea of the kinds of material possessions associated with a Durrani household, though in so far as it contains items connected with economic matters, these are related only to animal husbandry and not to agriculture. (The list was given to me by the bride and her mother in much the same form as I give it; the categories are conventional and the women omitted the odd spoon, for example, from their inventory.)

(a) Clothing for the bride:
     A bridal veil
     Ten complete suits of clothing (dresses and pantaloons), including veils, each wrapped in a scarf. Cloth for three suits came from the groom's side at the *push*, as did some of the jewellery and the mirror listed below; dress-making was done by women of the bride's side.
     Two hats and two pairs of shoes
     Various items of jewellery, including one hat ornament, one nose ornament, a pair of bracelets, a keychain and several rings
     A mirror
(b) Clothing for the groom:
     One suit of clothes (shirt and pantaloons), including a waistcoat, hat, turban cloth and a pair of shoes
     A razor and mirror
(c) Household items made by women:
     Four of each: woven kelims; felts (two black and two grey); dining cloths
     Three of each: large storage bags; skins for water; camel ropes
     Two of each: complete sets of bedding, including mattresses, blankets and bolsters; woven saddle-bags; small bags; horse nose-bags
     One of each: camel head-dress and complete set of camel-trappings, including bells; set of horse-trappings and decorations; sheep milking-rope; set of weaving tools; goat-skin butter-churn
(d) Household items purchased in the bazaar or elsewhere:
     One Koran

Three large pillows covered in highly decorated knotted cases
Two of each: serving trays; bowls, teapots and sets of glasses
One of each: a decorated trunk; hurricane lamp; cooking pot; water
jug; ewer

The economic relation between brideprice and trousseau varies. However, it is assumed that the bride's guardian will use the cash part of the brideprice to cover the trousseau and his other expenses during the engagement, which may total about 5,000 Afs. spent on entertainment and small gifts for the groom and his family. A high brideprice is felt to deserve a substantial trousseau, but the actual amount spent by the bride's father is up to him: he is under no formal obligation to provide her with a trousseau at all, though he almost always does. In the face of public disapproval, a miserly father may provide his daughter with only the bare necessities, while a man who spends all the cash from the brideprice, and then adds some from his own pocket, is much admired. But even an impressive trousseau is unlikely to cost more than 30,000–40,000 Afs. to assemble, and the bride's father still gains, in the form of sheep worth 30,000 Afs. or more.

The ratio of the expenses of brideprice and trousseau remain roughly the same in both marriage modes. However, the origin of the cash for a trousseau differs significantly – in brideprice marriages, as we have seen, it comes from the cash part of the brideprice itself, while in exchange marriages, it comes from each of the brides' natal households respectively. This difference is a further element which both creates and emphasizes the different meanings of the two marriage modes – the hierarchical relation between the two households implicit in marriages for brideprice and their relative equality in marriages which involve the exchange of women.

Thus in exchange marriages, the bulk of the trousseau of each bride, apart from a portion of the bride's clothes and personal effects contributed by the groom on the occasion of the *push*, is provided by the natal household. That is, in fact, the only occasion when the estate of a woman's natal household is diminished for her benefit. Trousseaux given at exchange marriages are comparable to female inheritance, and indeed, in cases where a father dies before the marriage of a daughter, a daughter's portion (half that of a son) of the estate will in theory be set apart for her trousseau. In practice her brothers or other male agnates, who hold it 'in trust' for her, convert it into the goods which make up a trousseau only if she is given in an exchange marriage.

There is no doubt that the Maduzai are well aware of the discrepancy between Durrani custom and Islamic law concerning female inheritance. Though in practice a woman's right to inherit is denied, any tension or guilt which this might generate seems to be dissipated by focusing on the trousseau as the women's portion. There is, in fact, no notion of the indebtedness of brothers to sisters over inheritance, and a generous father can stifle any of his daughter's or her son's resentment of his control of family property by endowing her with a lavish trousseau. By transferring property to women in the form of a 'dowry' rather than inheritance, the transfer can be unambiguously defined in terms of valuables, excluding the main productive resources completely. That is, the threat of uncontrolled alienation of household property (because the number of daughters is uncontrollable) is avoided, and the integrity of the household, and even of the wider agnatic group which often holds land in common, is preserved.

There is another aspect of the origin of a woman's trousseau in exchange marriage which is of importance – in this case, to the meaning of the exchange marriage form itself. Thus, there is a coincidence between the underlying message of exchange marriages – which depend on the high evaluation of women – and the fact that here, in terms of their relation to their natal household, women and men are evaluated more equally than on any other occasion. Moreover, those elements of formal Islam which concern the religious equality of the sexes are implicitly brought out in the context of this most 'Durrani' (sc. Pashtun, sc. Muslim) form of marriage. Though women and property are both apparently being transferred in the same direction, in exchange marriages not only is the net value of the trousseau which has left the household equal to that which comes in, but the status equivalence of the spouses and their families is a central issue.

Trousseaux in brideprice marriages are made up of a combination of (a) goods originally given to the bride by the groom's kin; (b) manufactured items for the bride bought by means of some or all of the cash part of the brideprice; and (c) items which have been made by the bride and her kinswomen from materials produced by her natal household. As is also the case with trousseaux given at exchange marriages, this last category is often of the greatest value, both monetarily and in terms of a woman's pride and prestige. Trousseaux given at brideprice marriages rarely cause any substantial economic dislocation of the bride's household. Rather, the gift of a large trousseau means that the bride's household gains prestige but makes a smaller economic profit on the marriage than it might otherwise have done – and incidentally, it means that they may have to restrict their own consumption of resources such as wool for rugs for some time. Also, as in the case of exchange marriages, the most important economic input in trousseaux is women's labour, which is never evaluated in real economic terms and cannot be converted into cash.

Though the dowry-like payments in exchange marriages imply a high evaluation of women, it is of more importance to individual women that large trousseaux are most often given with brideprice marriages, and indeed the higher the brideprice the larger the trousseau. Finally, since much of the money for the trousseau of a brideprice marriage comes from the groom, the return gift of a trousseau is at once an acknowledgement of the relatively high status of his household and an attempt on the part of the bride's household to establish an equivalent status for themselves. Here, then, trousseaux are used to redress the imbalance inherent in brideprice marriages. The Maduzai view is that any large trousseau (whether large in an absolute sense or in proportion to the amount of brideprice) is a source of prestige for the bride and her guardian, and can in fact be used (as the wedding songs of the women clearly show) to shame the groom and his party.

Because both the quality and the quantity of the trousseau depend greatly on the time and skill of women who are also foremost in its evaluation at weddings, it is this marriage transaction which women can manipulate to secure status recognition both for themselves and particularly for the bride in her marital home. Along with their treatment of the groom during the *bazi* courting period, women see the work they do on a trousseau as a way of making the bride even more attractive to her husband and as an investment in her future. Indeed, both bride and trousseau stand in a similar relationship to the groom and their incipiently independent household. All trousseaux among the Maduzai become a primary part of a conjugal fund, controlled by the husband. In fact, the trousseau alone among the property held by members of a joint household is not formally under the control of the household head if he is different from the husband. And there are no circumstances in which either trousseaux or brides are returnable to their natal households. The preparation of a trousseau involves balanced reciprocity between women of many different households: friends of the bride from neighbouring households, the bride's own agnatic kinswomen and the wives of her agnates. I would suggest that the willingness and skill with which this work is undertaken is explained by the fact that work on a trousseau offers Durrani women one of the few ways in which they can express their shared identity over their position in marriage, and generally *vis-à-vis* men.

9

Marriage choice

Most marriages are arranged by the household heads of the bride and groom, neither of whom have any great say in the choice which has been made for them. These choices can thus be discussed, as the Maduzai themselves do, in terms of the household standing of the principals. Equally, because the interests of both men and women are intimately tied to the success or failure of the household in which they live, men and women of a household are likely to agree in their accounts of marriage, whether they are discussing their own marriages in particular or commenting on the institution in general.

At one level, the Maduzai maintain that the choice of a spouse, as with everything else in life, is a question of fate (*qismat*): 'Whatever is written, that is your destiny (*takdir*).' Within the Durrani group, outside the range of relatives proscribed as partners by Islamic law, there are no preferred spouses. People accept that the choice of marriage partner and the brideprice paid are arrived at by juggling three sets of factors: the personal characteristics of the principals, the social distance between their families, and their wealth.

Behind the immediate calculations between these three factors involved in marriage is the cultural imperative for adult men to marry and remain married throughout their lives. This expectation has an important underlying influence on the overall character of Maduzai marriage patterns, because men of all ages and in all kinds of economic and political circumstances compete for the available marriageable women. Women, of course, also compete for marriageable men; unmarried women make themselves attractive, particularly at weddings, while married women use their matchmaking skills to try and secure good marriages for their daughters, sons and brothers. There are no rules, for example, precluding widowers from taking virgin brides, or virgin youths from marrying widows. Thus, the range of possible suitors any woman may have is wide and the factors governing the choice of a particular spouse are very complex.

Demography and choice

In practice, one of the ways in which the range of possible suitors is limited is by the chance factor of the sex ratio in sibling groups of a household. Because among the Maduzai brideprice can be accumulated by wage labour, profit from capital resources and so on, the sex ratio among siblings is less crucial than if such a high brideprice were to be made up of goods which constituted a separate sphere of exchange. In extreme cases, however, an unbalanced sex ratio is of considerable importance in its effect on marriage strategies; it is also an issue which is related to the general problem of the relation between marriage and social inequality.

A man with daughters but no sons is disadvantaged by lack of male labour, and above all else he and his wife will desire a son and heir to support them in their old age. The solution to the second issue is for the man to marry a second wife and hope to father a son by her: such polygyny is not stigmatized in the way that plural marriages are in other contexts, though its impact on relationships within a household can be very great. The general importance which Durrani place on the need for male heirs is evident in the absence of rules regulating either the uses of a daughter's brideprice or the partners of an exchange marriage. A man may give his daughter for a brideprice which he will use to take a second wife, and with even greater frequency men arrange exchange marriages in which they give a daughter in return for a wife.

The other issue – the lack of male labour in a household with only daughters – can to some extent be remedied by marriages which are informally uxorilocal. The circumstances leading to such marriages occur rarely, if only because a man with only daughters is unlikely to set up a separate household. In spite of the disapproval which attaches to what is, in effect, bride-service, it is an alternative acceptable to a poor man, who could not otherwise marry or marry so early. Though the extreme patrilineal ideology of the Durrani excludes the possibility of a daughter continuing the agnatic line, I have ample evidence to suggest that this can occur, though unrecognized by the Maduzai, as the eventual result of an uxorilocal marriage.

In less extreme circumstances, a surplus of daughters still predisposes a household to certain marriage strategies rather than others. Because it is persistently forced to give women in marriages, such a household is likely to be seen as weak, if not to suffer actual political disabilities, in spite of economic gains. In so far as there are men of the household who can marry, exchange marriages will be preferred, to break the otherwise inevitable sequence of giving women for brideprice. When such a household does give a woman for brideprice, every effort will be made to minimize the potential loss of honour by ensuring that the brideprice is as high as possible, that the affinal household is a strong and wealthy one, and that the trousseau the bride takes is particularly impressive. These three factors interact in a complex fashion, but it is likely that less than the full amount of a high brideprice will be accepted if the groom's household is politically superior to that of the bride. Moreover, if a large trousseau is given in an attempt to balance relations between the two households, no great material profit will derive from the brideprice received. In any case, without a number of men of the household to protect it, any additional wealth a wife-giving household gains will be vulnerable to usurpation by others.

The implications of a surplus of sons in a household are quite different. First, there is no particular reason to arrange exchange marriages, since the political equality if not superiority of the household *vis-à-vis* its affines is in any case established by being wife-takers. Indeed, for this reason, members of such a household need not scruple about seeking cheap brides from poorer households, even though male labour can usually be converted easily enough into the cash and goods necessary for brideprices. Usually households with many sons are able to gain materially both as wife-takers, for example by paying less for wives, and as wife-givers, when they can expect to receive high brideprices for their daughters. Finally, the ability of such a household to defend its rights and ensure the non-intervention of others in its marriages is of great importance.

In households with many sons, the biggest problem nowadays is not how to find brides for them but how to counteract the tendency to the fragmentation of the estate which is a product of the Islamic laws of inheritance. I have already mentioned the notional unity of agnates who were once members of a single household; they helped to amass brideprices for each other, one of the very few sources of corporate identity and shared if residual rights, though these are far too weak to counter the competitive isolation of each separate household. Attempts to resolve the inevitable tensions (over authority and inheritance) between men once of a single household often take the form of exchange marriages which they have been forced to arrange to settle quarrels. Such marriages, as we shall see in chapter 11, may in the short run exacerbate as often as allay disputes, but they do nonetheless so complicate close agnatic ties that these are rarely dominated by the issue of inheritance alone in any direct way. In effect, frequent marriage between close agnates often has the effect of reinforcing the ideal of agnatic solidarity, though only as it exists *vis-à-vis* outsiders.

The death of a spouse and widow inheritance

Those men and women whose spouses die early may have an opportunity for expressing personal authority in the choice of a replacement, but this is by no means necessarily the case. A man's chance of marrying a brother's widow depends on a demographic lottery, while the incidence of polygyny is related in part to wealth. In all cases, women have less power to influence the arrangement of their marriages than do men. However, widows with male children may refuse to be remarried and succeed in managing independent households on their own. The cases of such women are thus of some importance in revealing women's attitudes to marriage generally. They also reveal the personal strength of character, and the good luck, which is required for women to escape from dependent marital roles and gain a degree of personal autonomy.

It is convenient to discuss separately the impact of death before and after completion of marriage as they involve certain practical differences. Legally, a marriage is not complete until the Islamic *nikah* rite has been performed, but for the Maduzai the emphasis is elsewhere: the engagement is considered irreversible, and, should the couple survive, the *nikah* will follow inevitably. The procedure followed when an engagement is cut short by the death of either of the principals clearly underlines the indissoluble nature of the contract entered into at betrothal.

If the groom dies or is severely disabled during the engagement period, his bride is spoken of as 'his legacy' (*miras*) and she will be informally re-engaged at the direction of his marriage guardian. So long as the original brideprice continues to be paid, neither the bride nor her guardian will have any say in the matter. No ceremonies are performed to effect the transfer itself, and the ceremonial relationship with the bride's family is not disturbed.

In effect, the situation is treated as one of widow inheritance, though two of the attendant complications of the latter form are normally avoided if the *nikah* has not been performed. First, if the girl is re-engaged to one of the dead man's agnates who lives in another household, his erstwhile guardian will ask no *sar* payment for the girl, but will expect to be reimbursed for the amount he has already given in brideprice, though this may be subject to private negotiations between them. Second, a bride widowed during her engagement is not thought to have rights of inheritance in her dead partner's estate. Not only would the courts be unlikely to uphold such a claim, but, of more practical importance, few previously unmarried men have any personal property of much value. Should such property exist, among the first claims on the estate would be the outstanding brideprice itself.

If a girl is disabled or falls seriously ill during the engagement, the duties of the groom and his agnates towards her do not lapse, but they will probably be eager to relinquish their claims to the girl, as if she were dead. This issue may lead to her divorce during the engagement period, though such a course may not be followed in political exchange marriages (see N. Tapper 1979: 348).

If the girl dies during the engagement period, then the marriage contract is terminated and her husband has no expectation of receiving a second bride in her place. He may however recover a part or all of the brideprice already paid, though there seem to be no widely accepted rules governing such refunds. Some people considered that the groom or his guardian could expect the return of the full amount, provided he had not gone to *bazi* and started sexual relations with his bride; only half being returned if *bazi* had begun. Others declared that the respective portions returned would be half the sum if *bazi* had not been initiated and nothing if it had. I have reliable information on only two cases: in one, the first alternative was followed – the girl died before *bazi* and the full amount paid was refunded; in the second case too, the girl died before *bazi*, but her guardian returned only a third of the sum to the groom. Clearly, this is an area in which the outcome of a case is determined by the relative power of the two sides and the extent to which goodwill exists between them. Since the deaths of engaged persons are, mercifully, relatively rare, it is not surprising that this area of uncertainty and risk in the marriage procedure has been slow to be brought under control by mechanisms of formal agreement.

Should a man's wife die even a day after the *nikah* ceremony has taken place, he has no right to appeal to his affines to redress his loss. The Maduzai admit no obligation to replace the dead wife with another woman, even were a second brideprice paid in full; nor would they offer any return of the brideprice paid for the dead woman. By the same token, the dead woman's trousseau belongs entirely to her husband. The bride's family have only one claim on her husband after their kinswoman's death – the right to bury her – and this right they may or may not assert.

A widow is inherited by her husband's agnates. The share of her husband's property to which she is legally entitled is either divided among his heirs or held in trust for their sons if they have any; only a provision for her maintenance is made, and this is controlled by the head of the household in which she lives. Though the Maduzai say she has the right to refuse remarriage, the husband's agnates are almost always able to dispose of her in marriage as they will. Whatever happens, a widow will not return to live with her own agnates and the Maduzai laugh at what they take to be the bizarre 'Uzbek' custom whereby a widow returns to her natal home to be remarried again from there, but they are not above trying to recover control of a widowed kinswoman (see p. 256; N. Tapper 1979: 87, 422 for various attempts to usurp the rights of a dead man's agnates). In practice, however, such usurpation is very difficult, because a widow can so quickly be remarried to one of her dead husband's agnates.

Men vaguely acknowledge that it is better if a widow does not remarry, and there is in fact a certain repugnance for the idea of marrying a brother's widow. As one man put it, 'the Koran sanctions two unpleasant customs: widow inheritance and sororate'. He explained that a brother's wife and a wife's sister are like a man's own sisters to him, and he would be repelled by the idea of marrying either of them. One man who refused to marry a brother's widow for this reason elaborated on his repugnance by suggesting that 'a sister stands in the place of a mother'. Whatever the affective difficulties of such marriages, or perhaps because of them, the Maduzai frequently recall the following aphorism: 'If death is just, the legacy is permitted', meaning that a man's heirs have the right to marry his wives.

Women too feel that widows should not remarry, but their reasons are couched in the idiom of freedom from conjugal duties and a husband's authority. One elderly woman, only recently widowed, assented gleefully to the headwoman Kishmir's proposition that she had 'become her own boss (*pa khpal sar shu*)'. Kishmir then elaborated,

This means that when her husband was around, and she wanted to go somewhere, he could stop her; but now she can disappear anywhere she likes. Nor does she need the permission of her sons. She has become the Commandant of the Brigade.

In spite of these sentiments, most widows will remarry if they have not reached menopause, while elderly widows who remain unmarried will live with one of their sons, or occasionally a daughter, or, if they are childless, in the household of one of their husband's close agnates. I knew of only one case in which a woman lived with her own agnates: the woman was very old, crippled and childless, and her dead husband's agnates had left the Saripul area. She was taken in out of pity, and would have starved if it were not for this act of charity.

Young widows may attempt to assert their right to remain unmarried by approaching one of their husband's agnates or a senior woman among the husband's group, taking the man's shawl or the woman's veil and saying, 'I take your garment and I will go wherever you go, but I will not take a husband.' Such an act is regarded as 'right and proper', but only if the woman has sons is her plea for sanctuary likely to be acknowledged and protection offered. When this happens, and I know of only three contemporary cases in the subtribe as a whole, the widow and her children form a separate household, but their affairs are likely to remain under the general supervision of the late husband's agnates.

The relative independence of such widows is hardly recognized: partly because they often head relatively poor households which pose no threat to others in the community, and partly because they are often seen as ideally feminine, accepting personal privation to protect their children from the possible tyranny of an uncaring stepfather who might usurp their inheritance. Rarely, however, a widow like Kishmir (see p. 105) may be particularly successful as the head of an independent household. She is admired, perhaps by men even more than by other women, but the model she presents is one which few women would emulate. It is an option fraught with practical difficulties related to the inferior status of women and the sexual division of labour: none but the strongest-minded women would attempt it.

Though I learned of several cases of young widows without children who attempted to escape the control of their husband's agnates by elopement or in other ways (see p. 256; N. Tapper 1979: 87), it is almost always the case that if a widow has no sons, or having them nevertheless wants to remarry, then her in-laws will decide among themselves who should take her. Usually she will go to the eldest unmarried men of the household in which she lives; if all the men are already married, one of them may take her as a second wife. However, if none of these men want her, they may give her permission to marry elsewhere, in which case it is said she may marry whomever she wants, though her in-laws will ask for a *sar* payment for her. The *sar*, which is said to 'free' the widow, may amount to up to a quarter of the original brideprice; it is handed over at the *nikah* marriage ceremony and divided among the late husband's kin, or, if she has sons, it will be held in trust for them. When she leaves her dead husband's house, the widow will take only a set of bedding and a couple of suits of clothes, while her children will remain with their agnates.

Thirty-seven of the 161 living Maduzai women who married within the four core-lineages (see Table 20, p. 191), have buried one or more husbands, and 21 of those 37 widows remain unmarried. Twenty-one of the 249 marriages of Maduzai men extant in 1972 were with widows. In all but two of these 21, the widow was married to one of her late husband's agnates: 10 men inherited a brother's widow, 6 the widow of a father's brother, while in the other 3 cases a more distant agnate took the woman. In 14 of the 21 cases the widow was married as a man's first wife, and in one other case, the woman was taken as the only wife of a widower. In most cases the unmarried man closest to the dead husband took the widow, but there are no rules governing her disposition; what happens depends very much on context.

The *nikah* is obligatory in the remarriage of a widow but there are no other formalities or celebrations. Informants were very uncertain about the length of the *'idda* waiting period which must elapse after a husband's death before a widow can remarry, suggesting anything from three months to two years, though they insist that a woman with child before her husband's death will wait until after the birth before remarrying. I think the Maduzai lack of concern about the waiting period, which in Islamic law is meant to establish the paternity of a child the widow might be carrying, is related to the indeterminate status of any widow who is likely to remarry.

Thus, I learned of a number of cases in which a widow entered into a second marriage with one of her late husband's brothers after having continued to live in the household unmarried for some time: in one instance, the couple were said to have fallen in love suddenly over eight years after the first man's death, and only then did they marry. However long a widow remains single, her in-laws, whether her husband's brothers or her own sons, retain their right to see her married. Ultimately too, they are responsible for her behaviour, though on a day-to-day basis their control of her activities may be minimal. There is always a threat that the indeterminacy of the period in which a woman remains single may allow scope for her to form alternative attachments which may dishonour the men who are supposed to control her behaviour.

The theoretical right of a widow to decide whether she faces the future as a single or a married woman contradicts the presumption of her late husband's agnates that she is part of their inheritance with which they may do as they want.

This contradiction is not resolved at an ideological level, and, if the plans of the widow and those of her inheritors do not coincide, its resolution depends largely on the personalities of the main protagonists. A case illustrating this point is discussed in chapter 10 (see also N. Tapper 1979: 357ff.). In the end, if a woman is sufficiently intransigent and her affines are sufficiently malleable, she may remain unmarried or marry whomever she wants, but the converse is also true, and a woman's affines are far more likely to have their way.

Polygyny

A Muslim man may marry up to four wives simultaneously, but Maduzai consider that only those who are rich or who lack sons will exercise this right. Polygyny is not highly regarded by men and is violently disliked by women: members of both sexes repeat the Persian rhyme, 'Two wives, two worries' (*do zan kadi, do ghamm kadi*), rather understating their general disapproval of the institution.

In spite of the Pashtu saying, 'A man leaves women, a dog leaves money' (*da sari shedza patezhi, da spi dunya* – 'dog' connotes a miserly, cowardly or passive man), polygyny is not particularly used as an index of prestige or wealth among the Maduzai. Wealthy men who are happily married will not seek a second wife, nor is it always regarded as a matter of urgency for men with no sons by their first wife to seek a second. Rather polygyny is viewed as a practical option for men who judge their first marriages unsatisfactory and who have the means to compensate themselves by taking a second wife. Dissatisfaction in marriage, whether because of lack of children or incompatibility, is highly subjective, though it is certainly the case that a wealthy man may be less tolerant of an unhappy marriage because of the relative ease with which he can remedy it. Men and women often ridicule men they feel to have married polygynously without good reason.

In Lineage C, the circumstances of whose marriages I am most familiar with, 10 of the 97 married men had 2 or more wives at the time of the 1972 census. Certainly their motives for polygyny were complex, but the reasons for the 12 further marriages they had made can be categorized broadly as: desire for sons (3 cases), romance (6 cases), the opportunity to acquire a second wife cheaply, for example by marrying the widow of a close agnate (2 cases), and a single case which arose out of the resolution of a quarrel.

The Maduzai view sympathetically second marriages made in the hope of gaining male heirs, and it is notable that in all 3 such cases the senior wife retained her husband's affection even after the second marriage had taken place. By contrast, the men who had contracted polygynous marriages for romantic reasons were sometimes mocked with some ribaldry behind their backs, whether they had so married because their first marriage had been arranged in the poisoned atmosphere surrounding the settlement of a quarrel (2 cases), or simply because they wanted a younger woman in the household (3 cases), or because, as in one case, the man had become involved with a widow and was forced by her kinsmen 'to give her a good name'. In all these cases the senior wife lost all or a good measure of her husband's affection to the new bride, though the extent to which the latter also took over the direction of household affairs varied considerably. All such second marriages are generally resented as extravagant and irrational in economic terms.

Whatever the differences in attitudes towards these two types of motive, it remains true that 7 of the 9 men who contracted second marriages for these reasons were wealthy and headed households belonging to wealth Quartile I; the 2 exceptions, men of Quartiles II and III respectively, both arranged exchange marriages with a daughter. The circumstances which offer a man a chance to marry a second wife cheaply are not necessarily tied to household wealth, but only in rare cases does such an opportunity coincide with a stage in the household developmental cycle, when, for example, there are no unmarried men in a household waiting to marry a brother's widow.

The principal deterrent to polygyny is the capital required for a second bride-price: the expense involved in the equal treatment of two wives – basically only their installation in separate sleeping quarters – is of much less importance. Even when a man does command sufficient resources to contemplate a second marriage, he is nonetheless likely to meet considerable opposition from several quarters. If the household is a joint one, where there are as yet unmarried but marriageable youths, the prospect of household resources being squandered on a plural marriage is likely to cause much hostility.

However, if the man chooses to exchange one of his own daughters for a wife, his agnates are unlikely to be able to offer the same opposition. Whatever the feelings of men of the household towards the second marriage of one of their number, the women are likely to be firmly opposed to it. Women invariably view polygyny as a tragedy for their sex, even when they are not personally involved, and indeed they consider the most serious harm one woman can do to another is to be instrumental in arranging for her to have a co-wife. Moreover, they are well aware that they, and their children, may suffer from the misuse of household resources, and that they will also have to bear the brunt of any day-to-day quarrelling between the co-wives and their respective children.

Potential affines may also oppose a married man seeking a second wife. A mother's great sorrow is to see her daughter marry such a man, and fathers too will often refuse such suitors for their daughters, however attractive their proposal may be in other respects. So a virgin bride is likely to be very expensive for a man with one wife already, and as there are few widows not taken by their late husband's agnates, a prospective polygynist may not easily find an acceptable bride.

Though the Maduzai themselves were apparently not aware of it, there has been a substantial decline in the rate of polygyny in recent years. The change is

Table 19. *Polygyny*

Lineage	Number of men married	Number of wives			Total wives	Number of polygynous men	Percent-age	Wives per husband
		1	2	3				
C (1950)	54	32	19	1	73	20	37	1.35
C (1972)	97	87	8	2	109	10	10	1.12
A (1972)	92	85	7	0	99	7	8	1.07
B (1972)	19	14	4	1	25	5	26	1.32
D (1972)	14	12	2	0	16	2	14	1.14
Total (1972)	222`	198	21	3	249	24	11	1.12

I know too little about the specific circumstances of Lineage B's marriages to account for the high rate of polygyny among them, though the man with three wives was in fact sterile, while two other men had inherited widows as their second wives. The small size of this lineage and their relative wealth (see p. 78) may be associated with this high rate of polygyny, but I have no knowledge of the men's motives in so marrying. In any case, the small numbers involved make further speculation pointless.

evident in the different rates for men of Lineage C between the 1950 sample and that of 1972 (see Table 19). I do not think that people's attitudes towards such marriages have changed much from what they were in the past. Rather the difference seems to lie in the fact that today sons and brothers are able to demand brides earlier than before and to insist that surplus capital go on brideprices for their first wives, not on second wives for their fathers. These changes are certainly related to the greater stress on household unity which has arisen with the increasing competition between households of the subtribe. Anticipatory inheritance is no longer practised by the Maduzai and there is now a strong emphasis on the importance of a joint household; insuring the early marriage of the other men of a household is one way the household head can help to reconcile his brothers and sons to remain under his authority.

A rough idea of the greater numbers of marriages men make, as opposed to those made by women, can also be drawn from Table 21 which concerns completed individual marital histories, that is, those terminated by death.

Serial marriage

Maduzai view serial marriage quite differently from polygyny. A man must have a woman 'to cook his food'; all adult men are expected to marry and, if widowed, to find a replacement wife at the earliest opportunity; until they do so, their houses are said to be 'ruined' and 'desolate' (*ela*). There is close conformity to this ideal: though very poor men may be forced to remain unmarried for some years before they can afford to take another wife, only the very old or the seriously ill fail to remarry at all. Of the 236 men of the 4 Maduzai core-lineages who in 1972 were or had been married, only 14 were without wives (see Table 20), and at least 5 of these are young and may be expected to remarry.

Table 20. *Remarriage*

	Number once married	Total marriages	Number widowed	Spouses now dead	Number now married	Unmarried widow(er)s
Men	236	344	68	95	222	14
Women	161	180	37	41	139	22

The men are all those of the four Maduzai core-lineages alive in 1972. The women, how-ever, include only those living women of the four lineages who have married within those lineages, as I was unable to compile complete details on the number of surviving widows among those married outside.

I was able to collect very little reliable information on people's ages, certainly not enough to establish life expectancy for men and women. But the information in Table 20 does suggest that life expectancy for women is lower. If it were the same for both sexes, more marriages would end with the death of the husband, since men are about five years older at first marriage; in fact, the percentage of men's marriages terminated by the death of the wife (95/344 = 27.6%) is appreciably higher than the percentage of women's marriages terminated by the death of the husband (41/180 = 22.7%). Lower female life expectancy would accord with the high rates of infant mortality among the Maduzai (see p. 124), since at the very least these point to both unhygienic conditions of childbirth and maternal malnutrition. One important consequence of a differential life expectancy between men and women would be the increased competition between men for wives.

I have no evidence to suggest that the rate of serial polygyny has declined in recent years. The demographic factors involved seem to be as follows. Demand for wives comes from three sources: young unmarried men; widowers wanting replacements; and wealthy and/or childless men wanting to marry polygynously. It may well be that since the Maduzai have begun to settle, women's life con-ditions have deteriorated and led to a lowering, relatively or absolutely, of their life expectancy, but unfortunately there is no evidence either way. If we assume that women's life expectancy has fallen short of men's at a constant rate over the last 25 years, then there has been a constant shortage in the supply of wives. By the same token, we may also assume demand from widowers to have been constant, so that the main change for which there is evidence, the decline of simultaneous polygyny, must be directly related to an increase in demand from young men, who are now marrying at an earlier age. This is related in turn to the abandonment of the custom of anticipatory inheritance and the early separation of sons from fathers, as discussed in chapter 6. The strength of the increasing demand from young men is further shown in the fact that the number of married men of Lineage C now exceeds the number of married women (97:94), whereas in 1950 the reverse was true (54:69).

Personal characteristics and choice

The Maduzai, both men and women, are far more able and willing to catalogue those attributes which make an attractive bride than they are to list the assets

Table 21. *Remarriage – completed Lineage C marital histories*

	Numbers of spouses					Total completed marital histories	Total	Number of spouses
	1	2	3	4	5			
Men	27	23	4	3	1	58	102	58:102 = 1.17
Women	64	8	2	—	—	74	86	74:86 = 1.16

This table is unsatisfactory in two ways: first, because it is based on completed marital histories, there is a bias towards marriages made earlier in the century when it is likely that men's first marriages were made some years later than at present and when polygyny was more important than it is today. Secondly, I offer information only on Lineage C. Collecting information on the marital histories of deceased women who had married outside the subtribe was very difficult, and such material as I have on the women of the other Maduzai lineages is not sufficiently reliable or complete to use here. Indeed it is possible that I have missed a few second or subsequent marriages made by such Lineage C women, thus making the contrast between men and women's marital histories more dramatic than it might be.

which are important in a young man. Certainly in part this is because of the active role the groom's guardian must play in securing a bride for his ward.

Explicit assessments of beauty, and the associated, though generally implicit, sexual connotations, are part of the rhetoric of romance and are couched in literary clichés drawn ultimately from the literary tradition which includes *A Thousand and One Nights*. Ideals of feminine beauty focus on the face and head: long, thick black hair, black eyes, a straight, narrow nose; white teeth and very white skin are also admired. Body proportions are also appraised: a woman should be tall, long-necked, slim-waisted and of upright posture, but stature is more important in judging men than women. Men who are tall, well-built with heavy necks (implying great strength) are thought most handsome, so long as their features are regular and their eye and hair colouring reasonably dark. In addition to the grossly ugly, both men and women with blue eyes, dark skin or pug noses are most readily stigmatized, while the physically deformed or disabled may be given mocking nicknames which broadcast their infirmity.

However, as one man explained, physical attractiveness is only one of the qualities of a desirable bride:

Where there is a good girl, she has good colour and appearance and is pretty; she is well-mannered and thoughtful. With regard to work, she is a clean (*pakiza*) girl, and she is herself *hallal* and has a good reputation. It is also good if she is from a group whose women are famous for bearing sons; she should be a woman who laughs, a flower of a woman.

Attractiveness can also be understood by its opposite: no one wants a bride who is old (i.e. some years past puberty); who is ugly or sickly or slow-witted; or

who has a reputation for being loose, bad or dirty (*mundar*) or impure in a
religious sense (*haram*). However, among disabilities only total blindness seems
likely to prevent a girl from being married. The Maduzai often say they have
never seen a woman who remained unmarried: as one man crudely put it, 'even
a sewing needle with a hole won't lack for a husband'.

The personal characteristics of a young suitor are no less important to prospective affines than those of a marriageable girl, but here the criteria applied focus
more on his potential as a breadwinner than on his physical attractiveness – in
part because the bride and sometimes even her mother or other female kin have
little or no say in the matter. Women wish their husbands to be young and handsome and well-suited to them, but in the end a woman's well-being depends so
much on her husband's efficient management of household affairs that women's
preferences focus more on a man's intelligence, his ability to get along with
others, and his capacity for hard work.

Maduzai speak of 'cheap' and 'expensive' women, meaning those with or
without attractive personal qualities, just as they talk of cheap or expensive
marriages, meaning those in which the brideprice reflects such considerations. It
is notable that marriages are never said to be more or less expensive because of a
man's personal qualities, though these do affect the cost and kind of match he will
make. The less desirable he appears to his prospective affines, the more likely
they will demand a higher brideprice for their daughter, or demand payment in
full when they might otherwise have been willing to forego part of it. Close kin
may give an unattractive man an unattractive girl relatively cheaply out of sympathy, or poor people, anxious for the extra amount of brideprice they may get
from such a man, may accept him as a suitor, but if a young man is really quite
unacceptable he may only be able to find a bride from among strangers who do
not know his failings.

Social distance and marriage choice

Maduzai couch their discussions of social distance in terms of 'near' (*nazhde*)
and 'far' (*lare*) (see pp. 51, 94); these adjectives may refer to kinship distance, to
differences in custom, or to the physical distance between them. The social
distance between parties to a marriage is of considerable importance. The exact
criteria which the Maduzai use to judge social distance are complex and ambiguous, and the judgements they make are usually open to interpretation, but 'closeness' is an issue that is always considered.

Quite simply, people who are distant are unlikely to be given women in
marriage:

a good girl will always marry her own *qaum*, not from another *qaum*: if we give women to
others, we give them expensively; to our own (*khpalwan*) we give them five pence
cheaper. Among ourselves there is mutual regard (*mura^cat*): people say, if *qaum* is of no
use on such a day, when will it be? You are my *qaum*, you will help me.

'Closeness' in a relationship in fact works both ways. Not only may men expect to pay less for the daughters of those to whom they are near – the phrase *qaumi-walwar* is used either when the sum asked as brideprice is lower from the outset, or when the full payment is not demanded – but such people, 'for the sake of *qaumi*', may take a girl who is ugly or suffers some disability and who may not have attracted acceptable suitors from elsewhere. Finally, 'it is fit and proper to marry one's agnates, or, at the very least, they should be consulted about a marriage choice to prevent unhappiness.' Of a marriage between patrilateral parallel cousins in which a *qaumi-walwar* was given, I was told:

There is little money involved because the fathers are brothers. She is a good girl, but he wouldn't take any more. Her husband is a brother's son, and they are brothers of one mother and they wouldn't take from each other. If one of them had nothing and was hungry, then he wouldn't be sent away; brothers are this way, they don't examine or reckon up between themselves.

Few full-brothers are in practice so attuned to each other's needs, though the 'closeness' of agnates remains an ideal and marriages between close kin, including those between FBS/FBD, are valued also for the sake of the bride. As one man remarked of his son-in-law,

he is from the village of our people – our own (*khpalwan*), *qaum*, a brother's son – and if tomorrow my daughter has nothing and cries, or has some misfortune, then I can leave something for her and help her.

But agnatic kinsmen are not bound to help each other. Agnation implies no formal obligations with regard to marriage, and marriages between close kin are not necessarily preferred and certainly not prescribed. Indeed some people feel that patrilateral parallel cousins are so close as to be like siblings to each other, and I know of at least one man who refused to marry his first cousin for this reason (and, in this respect, compare the attitude of some Maduzai to marriage with a brother's widow, p. 185). More generally, members of an opposing faction may say scathingly of a group of kinsmen that they have to marry among themselves 'because other people don't like to give them women'.

The Maduzai express no preference for marriage specifically with their first agnatic cousins: such marriages are just one kind of 'close' marriage. The kinship terms which are used for such cousins (*akazoy*, *akalor*) are also used in a classificatory way to refer to even very remote paternal kin; for the Maduzai the category of 'close' marriages may include a whole range of agnates, and any analysis which distinguished actual first cousins from the rest would grossly misrepresent the Maduzai understanding of kinship and marriage choice (see N. Tapper 1979: 406 n. 34; cf. Barth 1959: 38, 40; Glatzer 1977: 148–149).

Moreover, 'close' relationships are not confined to agnates. Matrilateral kinsmen and even members of different tribal divisions may feel that they are close. For example, of one of the rare marriages between Lineage C and Lineage A, where a girl of Lineage C was married to her FBWBS, I was told, 'She was engaged a long time ago. Her husband is her *mama* [i.e. a matrilateral kinsman]; she was given a bit cheaper, as if they were *qaumi*.' A total lack of previous kinship connections need not prevent the development of a 'close' relationship and a marriage which reflects that closeness: thus, it is accepted that the personal friendships which develop between men away on military service may subsequently lead to marriages between their families. The families may be visited before a proposal is mooted, and, if they find each other acceptable, they may 'make friendship' (*dosti kawel*) through a marriage.

Finally, sheer geographic distance does not necessarily coincide with social distance. Indeed some of the marriages in which the parties are resident 75 km from each other are those between unrelated wealthy men who see themselves as political or economic allies. Such marriages are renowned for the character of the celebrations which usually accompany them; as one woman put it, 'the Afghan [Durrani] people much prefer a distant wedding; there are many sights to see, many competitions; it makes them happy'. However, another woman expressed her reservations about such 'close' marriages in which political considerations were uppermost and where the nature of the display at wedding festivities qualifies the closeness of the principals:

People say it is better to take one of our own women. Our fathers are one. Marriage with strangers causes a lot of trouble. The clothes and the presents have to be extra large. And there is a lot of *nang-o-jang* [literally, honour and fighting] between the two sides. If a marriage is with one's own, there is no worry about the clothes, whatever they take it is all right.

Marriages with literal strangers, that is, between households who were previously unknown to each other, are of quite a different kind. The Maduzai say that people may give a woman to a stranger only if they are poor and have nothing, or if the girl has been implicated in some scandal and has a bad reputation.

Poor men from southern Afghanistan have been known to bring marriageable daughters to the north where the brideprices are high, see them married and then abandon them and seek no further contact with them (see p. 268). Often where a marriage involves parties socially distant from each other, one of the households lacks strong kin ties elsewhere and for economic or political motives seeks to attach itself to some established household, though sometimes of course two poor and isolated households may, in the absence of more promising connections, arrange a marriage between themselves. Where strangers wish to attach themselves to an established household, unless an exchange marriage is arranged (see p. 203), it is they who give a woman, and indeed it may be the woman's guardian who initiates the proposal. Such people may be expected to yield a cheap bride, but as great social distance often coincides with the poverty of the strangers, it is often difficult to disentangle the main reasons for a low brideprice. From the strangers' point of view, anticipation of the benefits of affinity for both the bride and her guardian may lead to a reduction in the amount of brideprice they are prepared to accept. Of one such case I was told:

If a good girl is given to a good house, where they like the groom, they will give her a bit cheaper. They are happy and she will never go hungry. Such a house is in debt to on one. They are full and my daughter will be full. Maybe we will get something out of him. If we should get stuck for something our daughter will give us help or our affines will help us.

A household can find itself in desperate straits, when its only remaining resource is a marriageable woman. In such circumstances of ruthless calculation, the woman's fate may be of very little concern to her guardian indeed (see N. Tapper 1979: 443).

Clearly, where the woman's guardian does initiate the proposal, the accepted status distinction between wife-givers and wife-takers is accentuated, and a man who makes such an offer thus often accepts the status of permanent client to his affines. But it is not only destitute households who would consider giving a girl cheaply to make friends. A man may sacrifice reputation for economic and political security by offering a woman cheaply into the household of an important man, though, in all the cases of this kind which I knew, the offer of a bride came from men who, though not poor, occupied a marginal or anomalous position *vis-à-vis* the receiver's community: as one of the Sinjit headman Hajji Ibrahim's sons explained to me,

People want to be affines with the headman. He is a big man; if there is some trouble, whether in the town or within the *wolus*, whether with the government or in the pastures, then he will settle it. He is a good man and necessary to us in times of crisis. People try to make themselves close to him.

Household wealth and marriage choice

The complex relation between the three factors – the personal characteristics of the principals, the social distance between their families, and their wealth – is seen to determine not only whether a girl or youth is a likely candidate for a particular marriage, but also the amount of brideprice which will be required to complete the transaction. Indeed, choice and expense are inextricably linked in Maduzai considerations.

Of the three factors, the one most often mentioned by the Maduzai is the relative wealth of the families involved. As a married man from a large, wealthy household explained:

If a girl is beautiful, everyone will want her and she'll be taken expensively; if a girl is ugly or 'black', then only a poor person will take her – unless her manners are good, then people will take her for the sake of her industriousness and behaviour. And if an ugly girl has a rich father, people don't worry so much about her looks and take her. A man will do this in case one day his own father turns him out. He thinks, 'Then I could go to my father-in-law's house, he has lots of money and sheep and he will give me food'. However bad she is, she will be sold expensively. Someone will take her, either *qaumi*, or if her kin don't take her then the Tomanzai, or the Abdulzai, some one from far away will take her.

People may try to use marriage as a means of attaching themselves to the wealthy and powerful, while no one wants to take a woman from a poor household, whether the poverty is due to some sudden and unavoidable circumstance or is chronic and due, for example, to the shiftless character of the household head himself. Thus, as one man said, speaking of the amounts of Durrani brideprices in the region,

All other Durrani women in the valley are cheaper than those of the Maduzai villages; in the western steppe, before all their sheep died in the winter of 1972, [Durrani] women were more expensive than here; but now no one will marry them.

Degrees of poverty are of course distinguished. However, poverty on any scale is not a condition easily overcome and impoverished affines are not an asset to any household. If a marriage does take place between people of discrepant wealth, Maduzai assert that it is far better that they should be either close kin or very distant geographically.

The poor themselves are likely, in practice, to have few options about whom they marry. On the one hand, they are liable to give their own women cheaply: wealthier Maduzai insist that the marriage policies of the poor are dictated solely by hunger and that they give their daughters only to affines who will in some measure support them. On the other hand, poor men may marry unattractive women from wealthier households, that is, women who are ugly or have suspect reputations. Or the poor may simply marry among themselves.

At the same time, it is clear that only the wealthiest of men can afford to choose and expect to win for themselves or members of their family a spouse who approximates their ideal standards in terms of both personal characteristics and desirable affines. It is my impression that, among the leading families of the Ishaqzai Khan subtribe of Saripul, the women marry their own close agnates (there being no other Durrani of comparable wealth and power in the area) while the men, in so far as they marry outside the subtribe, choose women from moderately wealthy Durrani families who are, above all else, attractive in both appearance and manner.

For all but the very wealthy and the very poor, however, the complexity of relations between the factors underlying marriage choice makes it difficult to disentangle the priority ascribed to each and the means by which compromises are reached and marriages finally arranged.

In this context it is instructive to examine the reasons given for the failures, rather than the successes of marriage proposals. Such matters are, of course, a subject of some secrecy between the prospective groom and the woman's guardian, but the material I collected on recent suitors who have sought to marry Lineage C women provides some clues to the system of values employed.

It does seem to be the case, as was asserted by several knowledgeable men and women, that most women have only one declared suitor, the man whom they eventually marry. Certainly some marriages between close kin are tacitly agreed to years before, and the knowledge of such arrangements tends to preclude other suits. In other cases, quiet reconnaissance by women, and the suitor's own sense of the appropriateness of a proposal, seem to minimize the chances of an embarrassing refusal. I was told that most men are pleased to accept any reasonable proposal for their ward, and early engagements, which protect the girl's reputation and thus that of her guardian, are strongly favoured. And of course, the sooner a girl is engaged, the sooner her guardian may begin to collect brideprice for her.

Nonetheless it is not unusual for an attractive girl to be sought by a number of men. Etiquette dictates that their proposals occur in sequence, though this is not always observed and men may compete with each other to marry a girl (see p. 259). As might be imagined, the grounds on which suitors are turned down are various, but in effect all refusals demonstrate the need to balance concern for the woman's personal welfare with the overall standing of the would-be affines and the amount they are prepared to offer in brideprice (see N. Tapper 1979: 378ff.).

Social distance and brideprice

Some indication of the relative importance of the factors of wealth and social distance can be obtained from a tabulation of recent marriages contracted by members of Lineage C. In the following pages, the sample used is of all engagements arranged by Lineage C members between summer 1967 and summer 1972.

The basic similarity of the three upper Quartiles is illustrated by Table 22, which shows the rate of marriages contracted over the last five years by households in each Quartile. There is a direct and marked correlation of household wealth and number of marriages. In fact Quartile II has a higher rate of marriage per head of population than Quartile I, which does not differ very much from Quartile III. But although the rate of marriage per head varies little between these Quartiles, it is of considerable importance that the engagement period for men of poorer households is often much longer than for men of wealthier households. Equally, the sheer numbers of marriages in which the wealthier households are involved, though of course easily accounted for by the different sizes of the households in each Quartile, do have a considerable importance too. Just because wealthy households are regularly involved in marriage festivities, they are regularly in the public eye – for good or ill – and gain a certain aura of vitality from their activities.

Forty-five men were engaged, 30 to women of the lineage and 15 to outsiders; 14 Lineage C women were engaged to men from elsewhere. Eighteen of the 45 men's marriages were exchanges; 23 were for *kotara* brideprice, and 3 for *mahr-e mosamma*. One marriage was literally 'free': a wealthy man gave his infant daughter to his brother to correct a supposed injustice in the division of the

Table 22. *Household wealth and rate of men's marriage in Lineage C,*
1967–1972

| Wealth quartile | Households | | Number of marriages | Rate of marriages per population |
	Number	Population		
I	16	227	19	0.084
II	17	130	13	0.100
III	17	109	8	0.073
IV	17	84	5	0.060
Total	67	550	45	0.083

patrimony. He made this gesture 'so they would be close'; the little girl joined the brother's household and he was free to marry her to one of his own sons, or elsewhere as he wanted (see also p. 104). Twenty-three of the women's marriages too were for *kotara* brideprice. Clearly not all couples thus engaged had actually been wed before the end of the period; while one engagement and one marriage had already been terminated by the death of one partner. There are no cases of widow inheritance in this sample. All these marriages can be related to the wealth of the Lineage C households concerned.

The numbers are small – I do not have complete or wholly reliable data on household wealth for the other Maduzai lineages, or for the period earlier than 1967 in Lineage C – but case histories suggest that the Lineage C patterns of choice and expenditure are reasonably typical for the subtribe as a whole and are also relevant for the understanding of earlier marriages.

First, we can examine the *kotara* brideprice unions to see how far brideprices correspond with wealth and social distance. In the last five years Lineage C men have agreed to pay brideprices ranging from 30,000 Afs. to 85,000 Afs. for women of the lineage (13 cases, mean 61,538 Afs.), and from 10,000 Afs. to 90,000 Afs. for outsiders (10 cases, mean 64,000 Afs.). These variations reflect differences in social distance between the families, in their relative wealth and in the personal qualities of the bride. Differences of the latter kind depend on personal assessment and are clearly difficult to quantify, but they do without doubt give rise to variations in brideprice, independent of the relative wealth and standing of the natal households. For example, two Lineage C girls from very wealthy households married their closest agnatic cousins (their FBS and FFBS): one was pretty and vivacious and a *kotara* brideprice of 85,000 Afs. was agreed for her, while for the other, a dull, plain young woman, a grudging 60,000 Afs. was promised and paid.

Brideprice variations which reflect differences in wealth and social distance are easier to quantify. Table 23 shows that, on the whole, wealthier households both pay and receive higher brideprices, and also that brideprices are lower for

Table 23. *Lineage C brideprices, 1967–1972*

Men's marriages

Wealth quartile of groom's household	Bride from Lineage C		Bride from outside		Total	
	Number	Mean brideprice in Afs.	Number	Mean brideprice in Afs.	Number	Mean brideprice in Afs.
I	4	76,250	5	73,000	9	74,444
II	4	67,500	2	75,000	6	70,000
III	0	NA	3	41,667[a]	3	41,667
IV	5	45,000	0	NA	5	45,000
Total	13	61,538	10	64,000	23	62,609
I + II	8	71,875	7	73,571	15	72,667
III + IV	5	45,000	3	41,667	8	43,750

Women's marriages

Wealth quartile of bride's household	Groom from Lineage C		Groom from outside		Total	
	Number	Mean brideprice in Afs.	Number	Mean brideprice in Afs.	Number	Mean brideprice in Afs.
I	6	67,500	3	76,667	9	70,556
II	3	60,000	2	105,000[b]	5	78,000
III	2	65,000	2	65,000	4	65,000
IV	2	42,500	3	43,333	5	43,000
Total	13	61,538	10	70,000	23	65,217
I + II	9	65,000	5	88,000	14	73,214
III + IV	4	53,750	5	52,000	9	52,778

[a]This figure is unusually low. A widower in desperate straits (see Case 4) married (the *nikah* ceremony was performed immediately) a nine-year-old Hazara girl for 10,000 Afs., the smallest amount of brideprice paid during the five year period.

[b]The brideprices for these two women were unusually high. A lovely girl was married to a very elderly local stockowner from another subtribe anxious to remarry. Her father received 120,000 Afs. for her, the highest brideprice paid for a Lineage C woman during the five year period. Members of Sinjit village considered that this girl's father was literally a madman; this fact alone made him unlikely to find a husband for his daughter within the lineage, let alone get such a high brideprice for her. In the other case, Laljan was persuaded by the high brideprice of 90,000 Afs. he was offered for his dishonoured daughter to give her hypogamously to a family of local Parsiwans (see Case 8).

marriages within the lineage, though it is important to remember that the agreed brideprice may be reduced after the engagement. Accurate information on such reductions was hard to collect, but I believe they rarely amounted to more than 10,000 Afs. Usually reductions occur between close households, especially those of kinsmen, while in marriages between distant families brideprices are almost always paid in full. Thus, in terms of the actual sums paid, women of the same lineage are likely to be cheaper than outsiders as the Maduzai would indeed insist, but to a degree greater than the table suggests. As far as I know, however, reductions in the amounts agreed are not greater for the poor than for the rich.

Indeed, the most striking feature of the table is the lack of variation in bride-prices agreed in spite of the enormous wealth differences between households. Thus, the wealthiest Quartile own an average of 684 units per household, more than 200 times the average wealth of the poorest Quartile (3 units), yet the average brideprices paid by the former are less than twice as high as those paid by the latter (see also Table 17, p. 118). The contrast is far less striking if we relate bride-prices to household income (see p. 116f.). The average brideprice paid by house-holds of Quartile IV is four to five times their expected annual income; for Quartile III, it is two to three times expected income; for Quartile II it is one and a half to two times, while for Quartile I households the average brideprice prob-ably does not exceed annual income. But it remains the case that wealthier house-holds find it far easier to amass and pay a brideprice than poor households, who take far longer to do so.

'Exceptional' choices

As has been suggested, the beautiful daughter of a poor household may some-times command a higher price than the plain daughter of a Khan. But this does not mean a poor man can realistically hope to marry a rich man's daughter. A wealthy man will almost certainly refuse to give his daughter to any man who cannot keep her in the manner to which she is accustomed, while he is unlikely to want to marry a poor man's daughter unless he happens to fall in love with her. Generally, as people maintain, rich marry rich and poor marry poor, but other factors, especially the closeness of the parties, complicate this pattern.

'Exceptional' choices of marriage partners are often idiosyncratic and their explanation requires detailed accounts of the particular circumstances of each marriage. In this sense, the explanations of 'exceptional' choices reveal most clearly the complexity of this kind of marriage system and, indeed, a comprehen-sive analysis of such a marriage system requires an account of the 'exceptional' marriage choices. But though such explanations are crucial to understanding the system as a whole, they can be quite tedious and I offer only a brief summary of them here (for further details, see N. Tapper 1979: 386ff.).

The division of households into distinct wealth strata is somewhat arbitrary; moreover, during the five years of the sample the position of many households has been affected by the payment or receipt of instalments of brideprice. Bearing all this in mind, marriages between households of adjacent Quartiles are best regarded as just as isogamous as those between households of the same Quartile.

Table 24. *Intra-lineage marriage and household wealth in Lineage C, 1967–1972*

	Wealth quartiles	Bride's household				Total
		I	II	III	IV	
Groom's household	I	7	2	2ab	0	11
	II	4	2	3	0	9
	III	2ab	1	2	0	5
	IV	1c	2de	0	2	5
Total		14	7	7	2	30

The lower case letters refer to cases summarized in the text.

Such marriages, as Table 24 shows, constitute 23 of the 30 men's marriages within the lineage. It is the seven exceptions that need special explanation. They include two pairs of exchange marriages (a and b) and so involve only five pairs of households. The households in each of these five pairs belong to the same section – i.e. all of these seven exceptional marriages were between close agnates. All the principals in both pairs of exchange marriages were considered personally attractive, while in the other three marriages (d, e and c), where girls from a wealthy household went to men from Quartile IV, the girls were all very young and regarded as unattractive – (c) is the uxorilocal marriage mentioned in Case 9, p. 233.

The background of agnation in the seven exceptional cases suggests that closeness can override wealth differences between potential affines. Indeed 19 of the men's 45 marriages were with close agnates (girls from the same section) and a further eight from the same faction of the lineage. Only three marriages bridged the factions – and these are not hard to explain, for they are all examples of the way households involved in a financial crisis, and thus at least temporarily poor and desperate, are likely to be forced to marry their daughters 'far'. Two of the three were a pair of exchange marriages (f and g) arranged to settle a scandalous quarrel; the context of these marriages is discussed at length later (see Case 8, Laljan's daughters). The context of the other marriage (h) has already been discussed (see Case 4 – Habibullah; also note to Table 23). It should be added that this latter marriage was arranged by Habibullah's two sisters, one of whose sons (members of another Ishaqzai subtribe) was married into the opposing Lineage C faction. Habibullah did not let his own close agnates know of his plans for this marriage until the formal engagement ceremony had taken place. Though they disapproved of the marriage, it is unlikely that they either could or would have raised the funds he needed so urgently or have arranged to marry his very young daughter among themselves.

Marriage into non-lineage households

It was often difficult to estimate the wealth of outside households into which members of Lineage C were married, but it seems that all but one (a case of uxorilocal marriage) of the 15 men's marriages were with women from households poorer than their own – in eight cases considerably so – while six of the 14 women who married outside did so to less wealthy households, 5 of them considerably poorer.

Four of these eight exceptional men's marriages were with Maduzai households; of which three were deemed 'close': (i) and (j) were exchange marriages with the households of non-agnatic kin and (l) was between the children of close personal friends of long standing; the fourth, (k), was with an exceptionally beautiful girl. The remaining four marriages, all with outsiders to the subtribe, were all made 'from necessity', that is the households concerned could not easily find 'closer' brides: in three cases, (m), (n) and (o), because the householders were much disliked by those 'closer' to them, whereas (p) was an exchange which arose when a man and his son were both widowed in the same year. The household was wealthier than most (Quartile II), but the immediate need to find a wife for the widowed son caused the father to arrange an exchange marriage with a very poor family of refugees. I was told,

The young daughter of the household who was married was not very pretty, but the refugee did not mind taking her even though his own sister [given in exchange] was grown up. This way he had found himself a place to stay. He said, 'Let me become a client' and he did not ask for a *sar* payment, even though his sister was the older of the two women.

Three of the five exceptional women's marriages were with 'close' men of the subtribe; both the others were married to outsiders because of a combination of lack of alternatives and exceptionally high brideprice offers. Three of the five cases were exchange marriages and have already been mentioned above, see (i), (j) and (p). In (q) the Lineage C woman was given to a matrilateral kinsman (*mama*, actually FBWBS) of Lineage A. The agreed brideprice of 70,000 Afs. was reduced in various ways and outsiders commented that it was a *qaumi walwar* (cf. p. 194). Marriage (r) was between two households of Sinjit village, both of whose heads were regarded as unscrupulous by others – the marriage followed treachery to close kin on both their parts (see N. Tapper 1979: 433, 435).

In sum, marriage choices are determined by three main factors: the personal characteristics of the potential spouses, the social distance between them and the relative wealth of their households. There is a strong general ideal that girls should be married into households which are 'close' and equal in wealth to their own, and the statistics presented on recent marriage choices have shown that there is a reasonable conformity to this ideal. But there are plenty of cases where either exceptional closeness (close agnates bound by affective ties or issues of inheritance; or patrons and clients), or the exceptional qualities of the bride, override extreme differences of wealth; and others where men or women of defective reputation or appearance have to marry at a 'distance' into poorer households than their own.

Perhaps the main conclusion that should be drawn from the statistics of marriage is that, while they in general illustrate the interaction of the principles and constraints which form the ground rules of the marriage system, there are a large number of exceptions which can only be explained by the special circumstances of case histories. Indeed, marriages are not units of equal value and cannot be treated as such without badly distorting their importance. In a society in which the institution of marriage plays so central a role, and where there are so few prescriptions surrounding it, such differences cannot be reduced by statistical or other devices without frustrating the intention of the study.

The statistics are a necessary prelude to the further analysis of marriage. However they can only take us so far, after which we can learn more about the reasons for marriage choices, as indeed about the place of marriage in economic and political competitions, by considering each marriage in its historical context. This will be done in the following chapters.

IV. Case studies and structural implications

10

The power of shame

Maduzai conceptions of gender inequality and the inferiority of women are intimately related to their notions of honour and shame and responsibility. Together
the system of ideas and practices constitutes a more or less closed ideology of
control whose premises are unexamined and whose contradictions and anomalies are unnoticed. To the outsider, the contradictions and anomalies are particularly evident in relation to gender categories and roles.

As we have seen, Maduzai interpretations of honour and shame and Maduzai
social identity depend on a precarious balance between two things: first, the unity
of Durrani as an ethnic group which shares collective responsibility for maintaining their superiority through endogamy, and second, the ideal of the equality and
autonomy of each Durrani household which constantly competes for the control
of women as objects of exchange in marriage and as reproductive resources.

Thus, both the Durrani ethnic group as a whole and the Maduzai household are
defined explicitly in terms of marriage and the control of women. It follows then
that because these areas are central to the construction of Durrani identity and
society, women, who have so little autonomy or control over their lives or the
resources of the household in which they live, nonetheless have a certain power
to subvert the social order.

The reputation of a household is an active element in determining its future.
For a household to be successful, it must not only manage its affairs to ensure economic survival, but also create a belief in its ability to defend itself and its
resources against encroachment by other households. Pooling resources within
a household is an ideal which is often realized in practice, for internal dissension
is liable to weaken seriously the household's ability to compete and protect itself.
Household unity (*entepak*) is among the most valued of Maduzai ideals, while
they greatly fear the threat of household dishonour and ruin. The value Maduzai
give to household unity, coupled with their insistence on the inferiority of
women, creates further areas of ambiguity and an arena where women may act
subversively.

Of course, individual women have some leeway for personal interpretation and action within the framework of accepted norms, but they also have a limited degree of choice and control – to construct alternative views of their lives and follow alternative strategies in them – which are outside the framework of accepted gender relations. However, because the subordination of women to men is an axiomatic part of the ideology of control, this potential social power of women remains more or less unrecognized by the Maduzai. It is revealed when individual women act in ways which challenge the fundamental notions of female passivity and subordination to men. Such actions are not viewed as a threat to men, nor are they seen as having a positive value or meaning for women: rather, they are interpreted and rationalized within the framework of the ideology of control, which becomes circular and self-fulfilling.

As we shall see, stereotypes of women as unreliable and emotional are accepted by both men and women. In this respect men, who are in fact dependent on their own female 'dependants', do have reason to fear women's potentially subversive power. For women, the stereotypes also have other implications. The woman who threatens or actually engages in subversive activity may in fact gain a measure of control over her own destiny. However, in doing so, she is providing proof of the qualities which are used to justify her own and other women's inferiority. And yet, it is this very notion of inferiority which underwrites the sexual division of labour and places women and men of a household in what is in fact a complementary and interdependent relationship.

This chapter begins with a discussion of responsibility and gender. Then, I examine men's and women's differing experiences of social failure and the conflict between social goals and private interests, particularly with respect to households and marriage. Third, I discuss the extent of women's divergent interests, the ways in which they are expressed and their consequences for the wider society. Women's experience of spirit possession is informed by a covert model of gender which in fact perpetuates notions of female inferiority and dependance. By contrast, a woman's involvement in illicit sexual activity involves defying the stereotype of the weak woman and affords a woman the opportunity to express her personal interests in unilateral actions of sometimes a most drastic kind. Such unilateral actions may demonstrate both the degree of women's subversive power implicit in the ideologies of responsibility and honour and shame, and the limits of women's willingness to accept the constraints on personal identity and autonomy defined by these ideologies.

Gender stereotypes and responsibility

Durrani categories of the person (*tsok*) are not particularly clear-cut (see Tapper, R. and N. Tapper 1986; cf. Good 1977). Moreover, physical and spiritual dimensions of the self are intimately connected. One of the main terms Durrani use is *dzan*, whose meaning is 'self', but also both 'body' and 'soul'. Another term, *surat*, refers primarily to the physical body, while *ruh* and *nafas* (also 'breath') are the interchangeable main terms for both 'soul' and 'spirit' (which leave the body on death and are taken by angels to God's presence). And there is a further term, *sa*, which can mean 'breath', 'spirit', 'life-force', and 'blood'.

At this general level women's and men's bodies are similarly constituted. However, when Durrani consider the self in more detail, they focus first on the head and its associated gender differences. The head (*sar*) is the location of the brain (*maghza*) in which resides the supreme human faculty of *akl*. The Arabic term ʿ*aql* is usually translated as 'reason' (see pp, 15, 52), but I think that Maduzai usage suggests that 'responsibility' is more accurate: the Durrani notion of *akl* suggests agency, competence, the ability to predict and make rational, sensible decisions, but it also connotes a willingness to accept the consequences of action, self-control and discipline. As elsewhere in the Muslim world, Durrani men too are thought to have greater *akl* than women. Consequently, it is said, they are genuine (*asl*) and have both more duties and more privileges than women, who are, conversely, held to be only poor imitations or copies of men and are expected to be less able to control their emotions (*nafs*) and also to be more susceptible to disease.

Among Durrani there is relatively little elaboration of the physical or physiological differences between men and women; thus, women observe strict but minimal Islamic taboos regarding menstruation, during which they must avoid sexual intercourse and after which they wash thoroughly, as indeed both men and women must after intercourse; and childbirth, after which sexual intercourse must again be avoided until they bathe on the fortieth day. Moreover, women's sexuality is not associated particularly with death pollution, as is the case in many other societies (cf. Bloch and Parry 1982). Rather, it is elaborations of the contrast between 'rational, responsible men' and inadequate or inferior women which permeate everyday life and thinking. Here two brief examples must suffice. The context of the first of these we have encountered earlier (p. 40): when Durrani speak of ethnic differences they associate *akl*, 'thought' (*pikr*) and 'far-sightedness' (*dur-andishi*) with their own tribal identity, and compare themselves favourably in these respects with members of other ethnic groups whom they scorn as 'witless' (*bi-akl*), 'short-sighted' (*kota-pikr*), or 'shallow' (*spak*). Both men and women often use these latter characteristics to describe women as well.

Second, although devils (*sheytan*) exist independently of the self, and are sometimes said to be a type of usually malevolent spirit known as jinn, they do not come from outside but are thought to live more or less permanently inside every body. *Sheytan* can be controlled by *akl* and religious purity. The *sheytan*'s object is devilry: to cause quarrels and divert thought and emotions from the path of *hakk* (the right and just) to *nahakk* (wrong) and from *rawa* (permitted) to *narawa* (forbidden). One woman summarized her understanding of the condition of women, saying,

Why aren't women free? Because they have many devils, while men have few. In the beginning women went to the mosques but then one woman was obscene and insulted the Mullah, and the women were sent away. Men among themselves would not behave like this; women are corrupt, putrid. Women are not clean in the eyes of religion because they menstruate and bear children. If the women went to the mosque, then they and the men would desire each other, and if a devil messed up the prayers it would be blasphemous. And too, if women gathered in mosques, there would certainly be fighting; men don't fight even if there are twenty of them, but three women fight, and if there are twenty women, then there are twenty fights; this would be very bad with the prayers. Men fight about the government and so on, but it doesn't matter – they don't gossip.

Images of women as quarrelsome, sexually voracious and unclean as compared with men are reinforced by other beliefs, such as the local myth of the upturning of an original matriarchal order. The Durrani also believe in a particularly dreadful female jinn spirit known as the *mordazma* (literally, 'my mother') which aims to frighten its victims – always men – to death; some of the leading men among the Maduzai are supposed to have met and overcome the *mordazma*; not surprisingly, the stories told of such encounters emphasize these men's piety and legitimize their power.

Compared with the many cultural forms which express the supposed inferiority of women, there are very few constructions which admit a degree of gender equality. The three following examples are thus of some importance for they touch on areas in which the Durrani notions of female inferiority are modified, if only slightly and implicitly, to explain both the character of individual men and women and the role of women in defining Durrani ethnicity.

In Durrani symbolism of the body, women are often automatically, and disparagingly, associated with emotion (*nafs*), while men are associated with responsibility (*akl*). However, Durrani can draw on the more complex elements of the Galenic system to suggest that what is important is the achievement of some kind of personal equilibrium between rational responsibility and emotion. In such cases, the head (*sar*) is opposed to the body (*surat*). The main organ of the latter is *zra* (heart) which is the location not only of the *ruh* and *nafs* but also of the main human emotions such as courage, anger, fear, sorrow, love, hate and happiness. These emotions are thus recognized and given an intrinsic value, and women as well as men can achieve the ideal equilibrium state. However, because balance is achieved by controlling the expression of emotion with *akl*, Durrani judge that it is men, not women, who are more likely to gain such a state. Nonetheless, in this way the idiosyncracies of individual men and women can be recognized, and some individual women achieve a balance between *akl* and emotion which affords them greater wisdom than many men. As one woman explained,

If a woman works like a man, keeps her own counsel, and makes her own arrangements, this is good and she is a respected (*mutabar*) woman. Women who are upright in the eyes of religion, and not weak or silly, please people, and both men and women will approve of them and their work.

However, the qualities of reason, courage and piety are not expected in women, and one who displays them to an unusual degree is said to be 'like a man' or a 'man-woman' (*nar-shedza*). This term explicitly belies the categorical gender differences on which Durrani social order is founded; not surprisingly, it is only rarely used by either men or women, even of a successful, independent widow such as Kishmir (see N. Tapper 1989).

As with *zra*, the characterization of other bodily organs and physiology is complex and admits areas in which women as a category are important to Durrani identity. This is the case with certain aspects of their procreation theories which define the roles of men and women as complementary and both of positive value. For instance the blood (*wina*) a child is believed to inherit from its parents and to carry in its veins (*rag*) is crucial to its identity in terms of lineage and descent. Though both women and men may use such a notion to disparage and discredit the children of non-Durrani women, it is also the case that women, in particular, will boast of their children's superiority as it derives from their own patrilineage and not that to which both the child and its father belong. Similarly, the relation between blood and patrilineality is complemented by an association of the blood of childbirth which is linked with the key notion of homeland (*watan*) around which other important concepts of Durrani identity focus (cf. R. Tapper 1988).

Another aspect of body symbolism is the close association, physically and metaphorically, of the head (*sar*) and face (*makh*) with the maintenance of honour – and, in the context of marriage, with both *sar* and *makhi* institutions which create or confirm the equality, and thus equal honour, of the two sides. At one level, the idioms in which this relation is expressed emphasize the differences between men and women; on another level they are treated similarly, as both possessing honour whose bodily locus is the same. Thus, both men and women of honour are white of face, while the dishonour of either is revealed by a blackened or yellowed complexion, and by physical features, such as mouths or eyes, which are crooked or contorted. The cut and grooming of hair on the head and the style of head coverings (veils, caps and turbans) are important idioms for expressing the honourable status of individuals – child or adult, man or woman – and groups. Other garments too are, in a sense, part of the person, while the actual physical contact between clothing and the body serves to create a consonance of ideas of self and personhood.

Unity and disunity in marriage
Young men, like young girls, have little say about the marriages arranged for them by their parents. Once the wedding rituals have been completed, the couple

can expect to live together for the rest of their lives; among Durrani there is virtually no divorce. In this respect, a man and his wife share a common identity and are mutually dependent, whether as a conjugal unit within a large, joint household or as the male and female heads of their own; together they must seek prosperity and success or face failure and destitution. Their close co-operation, support and companionship are usual.

All adult Durrani are expected to be thoughtful and well-mannered. But men are expected to be more serious (*drund*) or mature (*pokh*) and to display courage in the measured defence of right against wrong. Such expectations focus crucially on the men's responsibility to protect their household's resources and weaker members against all threats. Women, by contrast, are expected to be honourable, but passive. Their inadequate constitution and their inferiority to men keeps them apart from the formal decision-making processes in the community; nor can women exercise any overt control over economic resources of any kind. Indeed, even the sexual division of labour precludes women from working outside the household: though they milk, they neither engage in other regular outside chores associated with the flocks, nor are they involved in any primary agricultural activities. Rather, women's key responsibilities concern child-bearing and raising children.

However, a woman's domestic authority and a degree of domestic autonomy are accepted and valued as part of her status as an adult. Each household is expected to have both a male and a female household head; though the female head is often the wife of the male head, there is some scope for an able junior woman to be accorded this position. The female head of a household is responsible for managing the internal division of labour among household women, and she may participate with the men in discussions of more far-reaching decisions about economic and political activities. For a household to compete successfully, all its adult members, men and women alike, need to be generally well-informed about Maduzai and regional affairs. They must also agree on household economic and political strategies.

Though a number of local aphorisms imply that a household may stand or fall according to the domestic skills of its women, gender stereotypes emphasize ultimate male dominance of the domestic sphere and the essential and complementary but ultimately subordinate status of women. Indeed, both men and women are liable to express the opinion that by far the greater burden falls on men, who must act in a wide range of public contexts. In spite of the importance of women's domestic roles, there is virtually no explicit recognition of the fact that women of a household have certain minimal expectations and rights which men must meet if they are to remain honourable and the household viable. The issue of women's conjugal rights is almost entirely hidden by both women's silence as dictated by their dependence and the requirements of household loyalty. As we shall see, it is also hidden by the system of beliefs and practices associated with spirit possession.

The idioms of responsibility and honour and shame constitute a male-dominated discourse and afford men many opportunities to expound a point of view in which they define themselves as responsible and their personal interests as honourable and in accord with those of the wider community. Indeed, there is far greater scope for men to define their interests as responsible and honourable – even when these diverge from the social norms which define key groups and identities – than there is for women to do so. Responsible, honourable women are those who passively accept roles defined in terms of their dependence on men. It is virtually impossible for a woman to justify, in terms which others would find plausible, any perception that she might have of personal experiences or interests which diverge from those of the household with which she is associated.

Maduzai women, disallowed either self-sufficiency or an equal role in the marital partnership, have virtually no sanctions to force a change in their marital situation and are often more or less helpless in the face of their husband's ill-will. Though unhappy wives do readily discuss problems of all kinds with a few close supporters, usually their own mother and sisters and one or two personal friends, even such discussions are not accepted as legitimate outlets for women's feelings and women often say that an intelligent wife should never express her dissatisfaction with her husband because this reveals disharmony and renders the household vulnerable to the machinations of outsiders. When a woman is in such a situation of extreme dependence, there are few alternatives if her husband is a man of strong character. There is a sad irony in the fact that, while women whose husbands are morally or physically weak have more chance of tailoring domestic relations to their advantage, they in fact despise such men, whose weakness also renders vulnerable the household as a whole.

A weak man may suffer continual verbal abuse from his wife. As we shall see, it is the most ineffectual men who are also likely to be cuckolded by wives who feel they have little to lose. I also learned of two Maduzai men who had been physically assaulted by their wives (indeed I bandaged one of them up!). More important, though, is the fact that the Maduzai believe that most of the hundred or so women prisoners in the provincial jail have been found guilty of the attempted, or indeed successful, murder (often by poison) of their husbands, often with the complicity of a lover. (The rest of the women in jail are said to be there because of violent crimes perpetrated against other women, e.g. co-wives.) While such beliefs have a kind of mythical status as affirmations of women's dangerous nature, there is perhaps some truth in them: I was told of a case in which the wife of a man murdered by Maduzai thieves was said to have brought the robbers to the door because she hated her husband (see N. Tapper 1979: 145), and it was widely known that another Maduzai woman attacked her father-in-law with a knife when he confronted her about her adulterous relations with a distant agnate (see p. 258).

In practice, there are few simple solutions to domestic discord for men either, but in theory a man can act unilaterally to improve the situation for himself. Men can, of course, take second wives, if their first is barren or if the couple are incompatible, but in practice their doing so depends on quite independent economic and other considerations. Equally, if a man is dissatisfied with his marriage, he may isolate his wife through uncompanionable behaviour, or he may even beat her, but persistent physical abuse seems rare: it is far too revealing, to other men and women, of a man's lack of *akl* and self-control. Moreover, though engagement contracts are occasionally broken for personal as well as political reasons, Maduzai insist that after the *nikah* marriage contract there is no divorce. Given the ease with which men could divorce their wives – all that is required is that the husband throw down three stones in the presence of witnesses – the absence of divorce is striking. Its absence, however, is comparable to that in other societies in which the control of women in marriage can also be understood in terms of the two models introduced in chapter 2 (p. 17; also see Tapper, R. and N Tapper forthcoming).

When the Maduzai admit, as they do with reluctance, that divorce after the *nikah* does sometimes occur, if not among themselves at least among other Durrani, it is invariably said to be caused by the immorality (*bad-kar*) of the woman. But even here, divorce is not the expected reaction: if a married woman behaves dishonourably, either the affair should be kept secret or, if that is impossible, she should be killed. Practice closely conforms with the ideal: women were certainly sometimes killed for sexual misconduct, and I suspect that many households had adulterous secrets to keep, but divorce was extremely rare.

Glatzer records a statement which well illustrates Pashtun pragmatism regarding divorce. One of his informants explained the discrepancy between the lack of divorce and the tribesmen's conviction that adultery was common:

We know that a man (*nar*) guards his woman so that she cannot commit adultery, or he kills the adulterers. But who can always be standing behind his wife? Who wants to bring on himself the enmity (*badi*) and the vendetta (*khun*) with the family of the killed lover of his wife, and who wants to lose the brideprice which he had paid for his faithless wife? That is why most men keep their wife's adultery secret. A shame (*badnami*) which nobody talks about is no shame (Glatzer 1977: 158).

Like the Saripul Durranis, the Pashtuns of Gharjistan reject divorce as an alternative in adultery cases; they say a cuckold can erase the shame of his wife's adultery only by killing her and her lover, and 'if he cannot manage this then he should divorce his faithless wife, but that doesn't free him from his shame. Divorce means for the man an admission that he wasn't man (*nar*) enough to prevent his wife's adultery and to kill the adulterers (Glatzer 1977: 157).

I know of only one case of divorce after the *nikah* among the Maduzai, and in its circumstances and timing it seems to be the exception which proves the general rule (Case 9 – Shekar, p. 233).

Spirit possession and women's irresponsibility

Private accusations of dishonourable or shameless behaviour are common among men and women. Their frequency in the form of abusive epithets must in part reflect the degree of competition between Durrani households. Such accusations are not necessarily particularly serious, and may indeed be expressions as much of admiration as condemnation for some ruthless action. Only people who are recognized as socially competent, independent individuals can be labelled either responsible or honourable, or irresponsible or dishonourable; those who are not full participants in the Durrani community are dismissed in quite other terms.

The inability of men and women to fulfil their social and moral expectations is explained, typically, in the case of men, in terms of 'insanity' (*lewantop*) and, in the case of women, in terms of possession by jinn spirits – supernatural, usually evil creatures that attack or possess people (or animals), causing illness or death. Suffering of all kinds may be attributed *ad hoc* to jinn when other explanations fail.

The fundamental difference between the afflictions of 'insanity' and 'jinn-possession' is the explicit association of responsibility with the former and not the latter. Women are defined as passive in the face of their misfortunes; men are not, and a man's 'honour' is understood to involve activity in the public domain (see Tapper, R. and N. Tapper, forthcoming b).

'Insanity' in boys and men refers to incompetence or a lack of sound judgement (*akl*), the main quality necessary for performing the male responsibility of providing for a household and defending its resources. In practice the term 'insanity' (*lewantop*) is applied to a broad range of behaviours that fail to conform with or which flout Durrani social conventions. Some men were labelled 'insane' when they proved simply unable (perhaps because of mental deficiency?) to perform expected household duties; other men, apparently intelligent, were called 'insane' after they had made a series of wrong decisions through, people said, a lack of judgement or reason.

Other men, who appeared to resent their social position and even to reject the system, were also known as 'insane'. One such man, apparently sound in mind and body, was the only survivor of an impoverished household and was socially weak and vulnerable, but he refused to accept unquestioningly the undignified role of labourer. It was said of him,

He is insane; he will spend five days with you (as a servant) for the sake of his belly, and the minute you say one thing against him he will get angry; he won't even ask for his wages but will just leave and go on to the next house for another five days.

The young man's marriage was jeopardized because of his 'insanity'. His father-in-law (a man known for usurping other people's rights) used the young man's refusal to accept his situation as an excuse to break off the engagement. He argued that if he gave his daughter to this young man, he would stay home five days, then spend a year away and his daughter would remain hungry: 'Why should I make her a troubled life – he can't care for her.' The young man resisted every effort to persuade him to 'divorce' the girl, until her father beat him and forced him to break the engagement and to state the divorce publicly (see N. Tapper 1979: 433).

An extreme form of such rebellion (though there were no cases in the village) is that of professional thugs who take to robbery and murder as a way of life, placing no value on their own or others' lives but putting them at risk in the pursuit of gain without honour. Such men too are labelled 'insane'.

The attribution of insanity to the activities of men who rebel is of considerable interest; as we shall see, it seems directly comparable to the social rebellion of some women which is hidden behind a label of jinn-possession. As with the diagnosis of men's 'insanity', diagnoses of jinn-possession among women are implicitly related to the expectations associated with gender identity. Thus, while unmarried girls are virtually never thus diagnosed, jinn-possession in married women is particularly associated with difficulties in performing female reproductive responsibilities.

Though victims of jinn possession are considered non-culpable, it is nonetheless the case that if a woman's reproductive difficulties persist, or if over time she fails to produce surviving children, her roles as wife and mistress of a household may well be usurped by a co-wife or some other woman of the household, significantly diminishing her status and domestic power. Women greatly fear and dread such a fate, which strikes randomly and serves to isolate individuals who, like 'insane' men, are rendered socially invisible.

In some respects, jinn possession among the Durrani shares many of the characteristics of the analytical category of what Lewis has called 'peripheral possession' (1986). Durrani ideas of spirit possession differ from the examples Lewis describes in the way that they both deny and disguise the relation between spirit possession and social grievance.

Though Durrani have a range of explanations for misfortune, and Durrani women and men do occasionally explain a woman's inability to fulfil her reproductive roles in terms of notions such as *eyb* or *gunah* (sin) which associate misfortunes with individual action, most often their explanations are in terms of jinn-possession. In many if not most social contexts, a woman's first responsibility as an adult is understood to be successful reproduction. This label not only excuses men from responsibility for reproductive success or failure, but also directs attention away from the social implications of a narrow definition of female gender roles. Moreover, because jinn possession is understood in physio-logical terms, Durrani are relieved of the need to consider further what are, to the outside observer, the quite obvious social concomitants of a woman's distress and helplessness in the face of circumstances which define her as a failure as wife, mother and household manager.

Personal biographies of women suggest that one in three married women in the community of the seventy households of Lineage C – the Maduzai whom we knew best – could expect to experience jinn-possession at some time during their lives. Possession is usually diagnosed in terms of a woman's illness during or after childbirth or when her children become ill or die. Possession trances or fits, in which an afflicted woman experiences a state of mental dissociation, are less frequent: fewer than half of the women said to be possessed by jinn spirits are likely to experience possession fits. It is notable that jinn possession in general is a diagnosis which falls randomly on women of the community, whereas those women who have experienced possession fits are almost invariably associated with large, often wealthy, paternal or fraternal joint households.

Durrani women never question the authenticity of jinn-possession and possession fits in other women. Possession offers women an implicit explanation for failure and the possibility of catharsis. There may also be a distinct element of self-acclaim in women's spirit possession (cf. Galt 1982). Moreover, because the aetiology of both possession and possession fits may centre on, for instance, a woman's attractiveness or some past action of hers known only to herself, such states allow Durrani women to define themselves as individuals in terms other than those of the explicit male-dominated ideology which concern only their reproductive activities and their domestic roles.

Unlike the women, Durrani men are particularly interested in the authenticity of women's possession experiences. Though they never raise questions of authenticity unless a possession fit has occurred, men label some of the posses-sion fit experiences of women as genuine (*asl*) and others as fake (*badal*).

Of the 94 married women in the 70 households of Lineage C, we knew fifteen who had experienced jinn possession fits. The twelve whose experiences were accepted by men as genuine were all strong-willed and intelligent. They were all women who, unusually, had fought openly and cogently to have their place in the household reassessed. These women may have had only limited success in this respect, but in doing so, each woman had actively promoted herself for a position to which she had no ascribed right: three of them were thought to dominate their husbands, eight others challenged the authority of the household headwoman, while the last was in a household where the women were unusually strictly seg-regated, which she resented.

One exceptional case is of particular note and suggests clearly that 'authentic' possession hides social rebellion.

Case 5: Shiri's 'insanity'

Shiri was a member of the large household of Hajji Ibrahim, the Sinjit headman, whose members we knew intimately. She was intelligent, witty and an excellent wife and mother of two sons and a daughter. She was nonetheless described to us, by her parents-in-law and by some of her husband's brothers, as insane (*lewaney*) as well as 'authentically' possessed by jinns. Almost certainly this was because she refused to be subservient to her parents-in-law and passionately campaigned for her husband's separation from his father's house. Her husband was Hajji Ibrahim's eldest son, and Shiri's campaign was unusual in its early timing and, particularly, because Shiri's own wealthy father was prepared to help the couple to become independent and improve his daughter's comfort. He was one of the leading men of the Sinjit faction opposed to Hajji Ibrahim, and his interest in his daughter's situation, though undoubtedly genuine, had many political overtones.

One of Shiri's brothers-in-law, who hoped also to separate from Hajji Ibrahim and join his eldest brother's new household, was sympathetic to Shiri's arguments and reported her to have said, 'My father-in-law has too many guests and I get tired of serving them. I want to look after my own children and my own husband – for us six or ten pieces of bread are enough for a day, why should I work so hard?' Shiri and her family did separate from Hajji Ibrahim's household but then Shiri herself tragically died, and the household was reabsorbed into the large paternal joint household.

It is notable that no one outside the household ever hinted that Shiri might be 'insane', which suggests that within the privacy of the household many more 'rebellious' women might also be thus labelled without such a label gaining public attention or currency. Not only would house members wish to keep instances of female rebellion from the public gaze, but should they become known the ideology of responsibility would preclude 'rebellion' as a plausible interpretation: if women are supposed to be controlled by men, they cannot themselves be responsible for deliberately failing to fulfil social obligations.

By contrast, three of the fifteen women who had experienced possession fits were said by men to have faked them. They explained that this was evidently so because they were women who, as they put it, 'were angry with the men of their household'. To us as outsiders, the salient difference between the two groups was certainly not the degree to which the fifteen women expressed their domestic distress in anger, but that the second group, whom men considered 'fakes', were women who, for whatever personal or structural reasons, were ineffectual and unable to influence their husbands or to persuade other members of their household to their point of view. Mabi's case is typical and, since Mabi was like Shiri married into Hajji Ibrahim's large household, the differing interpretations and reactions to their activities are particularly telling (see also p. 268).

Case 6: Mabi's 'fake' possession

Mabi had four small children – three sons and a daughter – and resented her mother-in-law Sadozi's claims on her labour. Mabi wanted her husband, Hajji Ibrahim's second-oldest son, to separate from his father's household, but her husband did not support her in this and indeed spoke disparagingly to outsiders of her looks and behaviour. Mabi became isolated within the household and increasingly embittered by her situation. She said of her mother-in-law, 'She also fought with my husband's brother's wife, Shiri; she is strong and does not like brides and she is pleased that my husband mistreats me.'

Sadozi had a younger co-wife, Molayem, who, with her children, was much favoured by Hajji Ibrahim. Everyone was aware of this and of the extent to which Molayem was given lovely clothes and so on. Mabi deeply resented Molayem's privileges and often said of herself, 'How people laugh to see me, the daughter-in-law of such an important man, without nice clothes to wear.' Willy-nilly, however, Mabi sided with Molayem against her husband's own mother, Sadozi, and Sadozi began to consider with some seriousness the question of finding a second wife for her son. Sadozi argued, 'Why shouldn't I saddle Mabi with a co-wife, she doesn't do any chores for me?' and outsiders to the household always sided with Sadozi, blaming Mabi for not helping her mother-in-law, who they said was too old to work the way she did.

After spending the terrible winter of 1971–1972 with her husband and children in the steppe pastures tending sheep in conditions of extreme privation, Mabi badly wanted recognition of her unhappy situation and she spoke indiscriminately with visitors and neighbours about her misery. She then became violently possessed with a jinn spirit in the sight of her powerful father-in-law. However, Hajji Ibrahim and his son, Mabi's husband, agreed that her fit was fake, and when she had recovered, they told her to pull herself together.

Certainly Mabi was a less confident woman than Shiri but, I suspect, other differences were equally important to an understanding of the way household members reacted to their efforts to gain recognition for their personal point of view. First, Mabi, unlike Shiri, did not have her husband's support in seeking to leave Hajji Ibrahim's household. And, moreover, other tensions between Mabi and her husband were given recognition by Sadozi's talk of saddling Mabi with a co-wife. The lack of agreement between Mabi and her husband made her both powerless and vulnerable; Shiri and her husband were said by all to be 'in love with each other' and certainly they saw their personal interests and those of the household as congruent.

The difference in power and wealth of the fathers of the two women must also be a factor in their treatment. Shiri's father, as we have seen, was a key figure in lineage politics and he was keen to help his son-in-law establish an independent household; Mabi's father, who I am sure had no less affection for his daughter, was not wealthy and, as a member of the lineage faction led by Hajji Ibrahim, was a political dependent of the latter and in no position to encourage Mabi's husband to separate from him (see also p. 259).

Women whose fits were labelled 'fake' were socially very weak indeed, while the category of 'authentically' possessed women included active, articulate domestic rebels. However, because such female rebels were 'known' to be possessed, the social significance of their rebellion was in effect publicly denied. This labelling of women's fits by men suggests the depth of men's fears of women as potentially dangerous and capable of subversive behaviour; it also upholds the principle of female irresponsibility and allows women's emotions and personal interests and ambitions to be ignored or dismissed as the work of jinn.

Thus, the ideology of possession, like that of honour and shame, leaves little room for social action by women. In this respect the fits, whether or not consciously faked, may reflect these women's recognition of their weakness as women and their inability to redefine female roles in a way acceptable both to them and to society at large. The only outlet for a possessed woman was to visit a shrine to seek exorcism, though, of course, the association of shrine pilgrimages with spirit possession serves to confirm beliefs in women's weakness in the first place.

Visits to local shrines (*ziyaret*) – the graves of martyrs or holy men or places remembered as having been visited by the heroes of Sunni Islam – are much enjoyed by women (cf. N. Tapper forthcoming a). The local Saripul shrine which the Maduzai consider to be the most important is a day-trip by horseback from the Maduzai valley lands, and a woman who has been given the rare permission to visit the shrine has indeed some cause to celebrate. As the women themselves say, such a visit is like a picnic for the small group of women who travel to the shrine, chaperoned only by a young boy. It is notable that the women who are able to free themselves from their domestic round for a day are most often women from larger, wealthy households, who are themselves relatively secure and loved. A shrine visit is, in practice, something of a very special privilege for 'authentically' possessed women who can find other women to look after their children and do their chores for a day, and whose menfolk trust them to be away at the shrine and allow them the use of a horse to get there. Shiri, but not Mabi, had visited the local shrine!

Given the desperate situation in which women, and sometimes men, can find themselves, it is perhaps surprising that suicide appears to be very rare among the Maduzai. Though it is by no means unknown (cf. Gobar 1970; Pehrson 1966: 66), Maduzai insist that suicide is a sin and, because it is forbidden by Islam, it never occurs. I feel certain that the stringency of their attitude to suicide is closely related to their understanding of responsibility. Thus, it is of interest, I think, that the only two cases I knew which might be interpreted as suicide are, in the

Maduzai telling of them, concerned with spirit possession and 'insanity': I was told that many years ago a woman of a poor household had died after having fallen into her cooking fire during a possession fit, while, more recently, a young unmarried man, who was usually described as both 'insane' and possessed by jinn, was said to have thrown himself off a roof to his death during a possession fit.

Weak men and subversive women

As I have suggested, because of the comprehensive rights which men have in women, a Durrani woman's own interests are often best served by unswerving loyalty to the household in which she is resident. However, the men who so completely control women in this society do have minimal responsibilities towards the women in their households, particularly in terms of maintenance and protection. Usually only when the men on whom women are dependent signally fail to live up to the expectations associated with the ideals of male dominance, may a woman act in her own self-interest to modify the terms of her dependence or, in some rare cases, to extricate herself entirely from a man's control.

Most often women manage this by deliberately involving themselves in some blatant sexual irregularity. Should they become public, such women's actions, like ideas of viricide (see above, p. 213), of course confirm Durrani stereotypes of women's irresponsible and dangerous nature, but this does not necessarily diminish the far-reaching consequences which such actions may have on men's political and economic status in the wider society: households may be 'ruined', political alliances restructured, and in some cases individuals or whole groups may alter their ethnic identity. Just as the dominant ideologies do not allow social responsibility to women, and channel domestic rebellion into behaviour that is attributed to jinn, so they lay the moral and social responsibility for women's more public rebellion squarely to the account of men. The ideal (but rarely carried out) action of such men – killing the offending woman – is regarded not as a punishment for moral error, but as a vindication of the man's honour.

Durrani feel that breaches of the rules governing sexual behaviour should be severely punished. The accepted sanction for incest, fornication and adultery (all of which are included in the single Islamic notion of *zina*) is death to both parties. However, both the incidence and responses to the various offences known as *zina* varied. I know of no cases of sexual relations between people who were forbidden to each other in marriage, though of course it is possible that such 'incestuous' relationships were kept very well hidden. For the Maduzai, such sexual relations are held to be a crime which marks the boundary between Muslims and non-Muslims: along with nakedness and cannibalism, only foreign men, particularly the godless Russians, have sexual relations with their mothers, sisters or daughters. Male homosexuality (*liwatat*) is practised in Afghan

Turkistan, but appears to be infrequent among Durrani men. Rather, such relations are a further expression of the inequality of ethnic relations within the region (see p. 238) – a recent notorious case of homosexual rape in the region had led to a murder as well. Lesbianism, so far as we know, is quite unknown among the Maduzai. Finally, a woman's sexual services are implicitly but so completely transferred to her husband at marriage that neither Maduzai men nor women could see any meaning to a notion such as 'marital rape'; in other circumstances among persons known to each other, rape does occur (see p. 236), while between strangers it is only known to the Maduzai in the context of the inter-ethnic warfare of the Saqawi Rebellion.

Though also classified as *zina*, other illicit sexual liaisons between women and men do occur, and their practical consequences for men and women vary considerably. Though it is more or less impossible to know how women perceive the personal risks they take, it is without doubt the case that on occasion women either initiate or willingly agree to an illicit liaison. The reasons why this should be so are clearly revealed in the most extreme cases. These cases also suggest that in many less dramatic ways the power of shame may allow women to threaten or force men into a degree of conformity, as well as hard work, to support the household. They also tacitly reveal an area of solidarity among women (cf. Boeson 1983: 122). Women are loyal to each other in the matter of love affairs – both in their silence and by colluding to offer a couple privacy. Indeed, in all the cases I learned of, when a scandal broke, it was said that a child had publicly revealed the liaison. Moreover, at such times it was clear that other women had sought strategies which would protect those involved (see, for example, Kishmir's action, p. 229).

In a household where a woman has access to a modicum of material goods and where her domestic status is duly respected, she will have little cause to jeopardize her own and the household's honour through sexual misconduct. Most importantly, a household economically and politically strong enough to meet the women's needs is also likely to be a household strong enough to punish severely any public betrayal of its standards. A woman's sexual misconduct in such circumstances can be tantamount to suicide.

Rather, illicit liaisons seem to occur when the household within which a woman lives is weak in the first place. Thus, a common pattern is one where a woman, having decided that the men of the household to which she belongs are inadequate providers or defenders of household resources and honour, attempts to escape the household via a romantic liaison. Whether the woman literally flees the household or not, a sexual liaison will, if it becomes known, shame the men of the household and threaten the viability of the unit as a whole. In such circumstances there are more options available to unengaged women than there are to engaged or married women; but, conversely, the risks to the unengaged woman are in many ways greater.

Romantic love and elopement

As elsewhere in the Muslim Middle East, there is among Durrani an oral tradition of songs and poetry which express notions of the equality and complementarity of men and women through the idiom of romantic love. Men and women seem to be equally familiar with this poetic corpus, but refer to it sparingly. Although, in many of the stories which were told as part of this tradition, the lovers meet with a dire fate, the idea of romantic love does offer an alternative model of behaviour for women and men – one in which they disregard their responsibilities to other members of their household and act according to their own personal inclinations and passions. While this alternative model certainly does not legitimize such actions in the eyes of others, it does at least render them comprehensible.

Sexual misconduct on the part of unengaged Maduzai girls, while uncommon, is not unknown. Thus at least two women in Lineage C had been involved in such cases between 1967–1972 (see Laljan's daughter (Case 8, p. 228; N. Tapper 1979: 419). Unmarried girls who have reached puberty are generally closely supervised by their parents, who fear public ridicule should they be less than conscientious in this respect. Though there are held to be severe religious penalties against bearing false witness, in fact gossip and rumours of romantic attachments between youths and maidens abound, but these are ignored unless the relationship is confirmed by subsequent events. Undoubtedly the greatest problem arises from pregnancies which occur in such circumstances, but I heard, and am fairly sure that the Maduzai themselves knew, of very few such cases. Contraception is never practised, leaving one to assume that abortions, for which the women follow a dangerous mechanical procedure, must occur with some frequency.

If a girl conceives a child before she is engaged and this becomes public knowledge, the shame falls on her father and brothers (see p. 226). Though an engaged girl continues to live under her father's custodial authority, ultimate responsibility for her conduct lies with her husband, who must acknowledge the paternity of any child conceived during this period. This is the import of the custom of the *babirey* compensation paid to her father in such circumstances (see p. 164). Clearly, the overlap of rights and duties at this time is likely to mean that the supervision of the girl is doubly intense, but the ambiguities of the situation can have the opposite result.

Particularly, the custom of *bazi* itself can provide a cover for an engaged girl's extra-marital affairs: on the one hand, the husband may come secretly to *bazi* before the formal 'foot-loosening' ceremony has been performed, and on the other, there are no tests of virginity at the time of that ceremony itself, so any pregnancy during the engagement can easily be attributed to the husband, regardless of his actual involvement. The Maduzai come to grips with the issue of responsibility at this stage in the marriage procedure only when particular cases arise. Then, as on other occasions, their attitude is likely to be pragmatic and their opinions to reflect the view that an engaged women represents a capital investment to both parties to the marriage and they should therefore treat her wisely.

Elopement *per se* is not regarded with great moral opprobrium by Durrani, but it is nonetheless rare between unmarried youths and girls. In the absence of anticipatory inheritance, a man continues even after his marriage to be dependent on the goodwill of his father, and I know of no unmarried man who dared to risk his father's anger and the possible financial and other losses by eloping with a Durrani woman. However, there were some unmarried men from very impoverished households who did elope with non-Durrani women who were themselves from very poor households as well: clearly, in such cases there was little risk of repercussions from either side. Only men from very poor households or wealthier men who are economically independent of their fathers will embark on such a course; in other words, these are men who are responsible for their own marriages. However, in practice, the responsibility for elopement is shifted to the woman: the men who elope are almost invariably described as having responded to the 'call' of a woman.

An unengaged woman may extricate herself from her guardian's household through the institution of 'calling out' (*nara kawel*) (cf. Glatzer 1977: 40). 'Calling out' is the one recognized means a woman has of rejecting her status as a pawn in the system of marriage and exercising the power implicit in her valuation for the purposes of marriage. In essence the custom is an elaboration of the religious prescription that all men and women should themselves have ultimate responsibility for their marriages, giving or withholding their approval of a particular match during the wedding ceremony.

Afghan family law recognizes this fundamental right of all Muslims, and, other things being equal, if a woman appears in court and states that a certain man is her husband, this will be officially recognized. To the Durrani, a woman who 'calls out' is making just such a public assertion, the presumption being that she is fully prepared to make a similar statement to a court. The man whose name she mentions would be dishonoured and shown to be a coward if he did not respond by taking her into his house and immediately arranging a wedding ceremony to be performed. Once a woman has entered her lover's house her guardian will make no attempt to force her to return. Rather, it is said, he is obliged to accept the marriage as a *fait accompli*, but he will however insist on compensation, his *jori*: this can consist of a brideprice or another woman given in exchange.

Women, unlike men, are not dependent on their fathers or guardians after marriage and they are thus not constrained from 'calling out' for this reason. Few women, however, would appear ready to jeopardize their relations with their natal families without grave cause, not least because if the man appealed to fails to marry her, for whatever reason, she is dishonoured and very vulnerable to punishment by her father or guardian (see p. 262). Thus, 'calling out' is a strategy likely to be successful only if the man involved both wants the woman and can bring more force to bear than can those men whose rights his response will infringe. Meanwhile, if the woman's guardian realizes she is considering 'calling out' for a man, he will try to forestall her at all costs. Ideally he can keep the whole business quiet and marry her off immediately, but he may judge that her life is not worth the dishonour she may bring him, and thus kill her. Few woman 'call out' for a man.

Given the extent to which the formal ideology of gender is male-dominated, the institution of 'calling out' may seem something of a puzzle, until one realizes how the institution tacitly affords the strongest and most powerful men of the community the opportunity to act as romantic heroes, to take often a second or subsequent wife at little cost to themselves and to display their power to intrude on and manipulate the marriage policies of other households (see N. Tapper 1979: 87, 421).

The value of a woman's life depends on the circumstances of the household in which she lives. For example, one local man was said to have murdered his daughter when she refused to agree to an engagement he had planned for her and sought to 'call out' for another youth: her father killed her before the lover could react (assuming he had intended to do so). In this case, though the father's drastic action conformed with ideals of honourable behaviour, other Durrani considered the man a fool who was too poor to afford such a gesture: he had lost his daughter and her brideprice and had gained precious little in return. The case is a sad exception to the rule that women normally take drastic steps to influence their lives only when the men of the household with which they are associated are too weak, politically, economically or in personal character, to take effective action against them.

In two other cases an unengaged woman and her lover successfully eloped, but the cases were very different in other respects and show clearly that a woman's worth to others in her household or in the community as a whole depends on the strength of the household with which she is associated.

In the first, the couple came from impoverished client households whose dependent and precarious economic and political status within the local community was hardly affected by the scandal the woman's father experienced. Indeed, as one of the wealthier men in the community commented when the girl's father pleaded with him to help recover her, 'it will cost more than 50,000 Afghanis in time and trouble [and bribes] to get her back. You would not have received that much in brideprice for her, so let her go. It is not important.'

The second case is one we have already met: Kaftar, the girl from a wealthy household who forsook her Durrani identity and eloped with Sipayi, the Hazara youth (see p. 61f., 90f.).

Case 7: Kaftar (Part III)

It will be remembered that the dishonour of Kaftar's elopement, which in this case was shared by all members of the local community, lay in the relation between her status as a member of one of the more important households in the community and her betrayal of the most basic rule of Durrani ethnicity, that no Durrani woman should have sexual relations with or marry a non-Durrani man. Quite simply, Kaftar's father Toryaley was blamed for his lack of control over his daughter and the subsequent ruin of his household. It is of interest that the secondary elaborations which served to confirm this judgement also attributed all responsibility to Toryaley. The Maduzai were not at all interested in the personal psychology or motivation of Kaftar. Rather, Maduzai explanations treated her actions as an extreme example of the stereotypically weak, lustful woman.

For instance, some notion of romantic love might have served to explain or dignify her actions. However, when we asked whether Kaftar had fallen in love with Sipahi, the Maduzai made it clear that this was hardly comprehensible: male servants and indeed virtually all men of other ethnic groups are so inferior and emasculated that no proper Durrani woman could find them attractive. This proved that Kaftar was even weaker and more foolish than other women.

Perhaps, we argued, Sipahi had fallen in love with Kaftar; but this argument too was deemed incomprehensible. After she had eloped, her shame was conceived in such a way that it completely distorted the memory of her physical appearance, and she was often described to us as if she were a monster or a freak: with a blackened face, a crooked mouth and speckled, shifty eyes. More likely, Maduzai said, Sipahi had eloped with her simply to shame the durrani and to damage them politically in the region.

The Maduzai offered other explanations which, while they added to the context of the case, left Kaftar's own personality a cypher. Thus, we learned (only after the elopement) that in 1970 another of Toryaley's unengaged daughters had become pregnant by her F1/2BS. The girl's condition was concealed, and later Toryaley took her to Mazar-e Sharif where the child was born and killed. When people heard what had happened, they scorned Toryaley as soft – he should have killed his daughter first. This episode was the beginning of a series of violent quarrels between Toryaley and his half-brother which culminated in Kaftar's elopement. Some people said, perhaps correctly, that it was her F1/2BS who encouraged Sipahi to elope with Kaftar in the first place. With hindsight, they suggested that Kaftar would never have run away if her father had made an example of her sister, and some added that the whole affair would have been forgotten if it had been Kaftar's sister who had eloped.

However, if one tries to consider the elopement from what might have been Kaftar's point of view, it may indeed be the case that her father was the cause of her disloyalty to her household and decision to run away. It seems that when an unmarried woman 'calls out' for a man it is because she utterly despairs of her guardian's ability or willingness to arrange a reasonable marriage for her. I suspect that Kaftar may well have felt trapped in this way.

At the time of her elopement her father had been involved for many years in a very bitter quarrel with his half-brother and other close relations, which had been very costly and shaming. Certainly by the spring of 1971, well before Kaftar's elopement, people had come to despise Toryaley as a persistent troublemaker to be avoided at all costs. By this time, it must have been quite clear to Kaftar that, because of her father's reputation, no attractive suitor would ever come forward to marry her, and that her prospects could only get worse: she was already 'old' (perhaps sixteen or seventeen) and her contemporaries were now married women with young families.

Of course, such an explanation tells us nothing of why Kaftar, unlike other Durrani women, was not prepared to tolerate the intolerable and accept her misfortune as God's will, or why she was prepared to risk her life, quite literally, to escape. However, such an explanation at least focuses on her motivation as an individual and as a woman and it gives some weight to the evidence (such as the theft of all her father's cash) which suggests her deliberate and calculated participation in the elopement.

Unmarried women and illicit sex
In spite of the severe sanctions for sexual misbehaviour, these are not uniformly applied. As already mentioned, 2 unengaged women of the 70 households were known to have been involved in recent illicit sexual liaisons; I learned of 8 other cases among the 94 married women of Lineage C. In other words, perhaps 10 per cent of married women had had a rather dubious past. These cases had a wide variety of outcomes: either the woman and her lover eloped; or they were married in the conventional way; or her guardian turned a blind eye to the affair while seeking a suitable spouse for the woman from elsewhere (often enlisting the help of her mother's kin (*mamakhel*) to do so); or, if the woman had 'called out' for a man, the very fact that her action was labelled this way meant that the man in question had accepted the political challenge to marry and protect her. In other words, only some of these cases became public scandals. When this occurred it of course confirmed the stereotypes of women as weak and treacherous, but from the woman's point of view it may have gained her a degree of material or emotional security.

Only four living women of Lineage C had married hypogamously. In the case of Padshah and the Lodins (see p. 125; Tapper, N. and R. Tapper 1982), the marriage was an almost irrelevant artefact of Padshah's rakish behaviour: because the girl's family were so weak as to be expendable members of the subtribe, her marriage proved an expedient means by which the Maduzai leaders could resolve an interethnic quarrel which had become embarrassing and costly. In every sense, Kaftar's case presents the opposite extreme: it is that of a woman from a wealthy household who completely disregarded Durrani ethnic precepts to gain her own ends and shamed the whole subtribe as a consequence. In spite of these two hypogamous marriages, the exclusive identity of Durrani is re-asserted: in the first case, because the girl's oppressed family themselves forsake their Durrani identity and leave the subtribe; and in Kaftar's case, because her own betrayal of Durrani identity puts her beyond the pale and deserving of death.

In the third and fourth cases, given below, the relation between hypogamous marriage and Durrani identity is more complex and ambiguous. This is particularly so because these marriages are in no sense provoked by non-Durrani outsiders, but arise out of the competition between households *within* Lineage C; moreover, a woman's intention to defy her weak guardian plays an important part in both cases. In the third case, the unengaged Zarur risked a romantic liaison with an agnate which, when discovered, eventually led to her own hypogamous marriage; while in the fourth case, the young widow, Zeytun, was married hypogamously after she refused to be remarried to one of her dead husband's brothers. In each of these cases the eventual outcome of the woman's subversive behaviour – a compromising hypogamous marriage – also subtly redefined the status of the household *vis-à-vis* other members of the lineage, of the subtribe and non-Durrani.

Case 8: Laljan's daughters' marriages: a household in decline

Laljan, of Section II of Lineage C, was once well off, with adequate land and a large flock of sheep. But he recently had become embroiled in quarrels over land with his own closest agnates, and had to sell his sheep and mortgage much of his land. Moreover, people say, he is badly served by his sons. 'There are more than twenty people in his household and yet they remain hungry and cannot feed themselves. If his eldest son gets some money, he gives it to his own wife, or buys clothes with it or hides it away for himself while if the other two grown sons come by any money, they give it to their affines to pay off their brideprices.' Indeed, this last is a source of amusement.

Four years before, one of Laljan's sons had been engaged to the daughter of one of the 'Sayyid' households attached to the subtribe (see p. 152). The girl was attractive but, as she was known to be ill and her family had no *qaum*, she was engaged cheaply. Even this brideprice was only half paid when, immediately after another son returned from military service, Laljan found a bride for him too, again from a lone household, this time of Ghilzais, also attached to the subtribe. People laughed at this behaviour, saying that Laljan was really very simple-minded to take a second bride before the brideprice for the first was paid. They say, 'if he were a man, it wouldn't have happened.'

The 'Sayyid' was not pressing for his daughter's marriage, but the Ghilzai father-in-law of the second son was, saying 'Since Laljan hasn't anything, he should send his son to work for me, and I would give him his bride.' So far Laljan has resisted this idea, fearing that by allowing his son to do bride-service, especially for a Ghilzai bride, he would make himself even more ridiculous in the eyes of his fellow villagers.

Then two years ago Zarur, one of Laljan's unengaged daughters, was discovered to be having an affair with a close cousin, as a result of which, to everyone's shame, the girl was married hypogamously.

Zarur and her unmarried second cousin (FFBDS), were discovered at a secret tryst by her younger brother, who promptly told their parents. News of the affair somehow became public and Zarur's name was 'blackened', especially as she and the young man were held to have involved themselves willingly in the affair with no intention of marrying. Intervention and punishment were seen as the sole responsibility of Zarur's father, but he chose to say nothing to the young man, hoping meanwhile to find a husband for his daughter. Zarur, however, though attractive, was said to have 'passed through the water and emerged on the other side' and people declared that no one could be expected to marry her unless for a much reduced brideprice. Laljan's house was in desperate circumstances when the incident occurred – a fact which accounts for his reluctance to chastise the culprits or to try and force the youth to marry Zarur – and he had little alternative but to seek a high brideprice for his daughter elsewhere.

The eleven households of Laljan's closest agnates offered him little support. Like Laljan, most of them were both poor and rather indecisive, and any direction they might have offered would most likely have come from his first cousins, including Kishmir, the 'women's headman' (see p. 105). But the support of these closest agnates was ruled out by the fact that it was Kishmir's youngest and favourite son who had compromised Laljan's daughter in the first place – and Kishmir was determined that her son should marry into a more affluent house than Laljan's. As the conflict thus lay between the leading figures of a lineage segment, other close agnates adopted a policy of non-interference, upholding the ideal of household independence and self-sufficiency, while avoiding the possibility of expensive commitments on one side or the other.

The crisis was eventually resolved by Kishmir herself. Through her own extensive local contacts she was able to arrange that Zarur marry the attractive and educated eldest son of the leading man of the few households of Babi Parsiwans who lived nearby. Laljan was prepared to accept this arrangement as the best alternative open to him. He had already been dishonoured by his daughter's behaviour, and the additional shame of her subsequent marriage to a Parsiwan was balanced by the large brideprice of nearly one lac of Afghanis that he was to receive for her.

The leading men of the lineage did try to dissuade Laljan from this marriage, but, as they were unable to find anyone prepared to offer a comparable brideprice for the girl, they failed, justifying their unwillingness to apply other sanctions by saying that if Laljan's closest agnates had refused to act, they had no right to interfere further. The wedding ceremonies were boycotted by members of the lineage and they speak of the marriage only with the greatest reluctance. The overall standing of Laljan's household and his agnates did not change dramatically thereafter, but this case revealed their inability to unite and settle their own affairs satisfactorily, and they became vulnerable to oppression and liable to further discredit.

It was said that Laljan married her to the Parsiwan to 'send away his sorrow' – both social and financial. He indeed collected a high brideprice from his non-Durrani affines, but this was quickly spent on land disputes and household expenses and, during the bad winter of 1971–1972, his family experienced real hunger. The following summer he (and his agnates) suffered several further grave setbacks, the most scandalous of which was the 'theft' of another of his daughters.

Majlun, an elderly widower from Section IV of Lineage C, had tried everywhere to find a new wife but had met with repeated rejections, partly because of his age, partly because of his bad character. He became interested in Laljan's daughter, Koreysh, but knew he would be refused her too; so, people said, he calculated that 'Laljan is poor, maybe if I do some trickery Laljan will have to give her to me.'

One morning in the summer of 1971 Majlun announced that the previous night two of Laljan's sons had come to steal wheat from his harvest pile. He said that he had fought with the boys and that one of them had knocked out his tooth. The loss of a tooth is a serious business, and the Maduzai say that a man has the right to one woman in compensation. However, everyone in Sinjit agreed that Majlun's tooth had fallen out long before, and that he had deliberately kept it for just such an occasion. And when Majlun began to demand Laljan's daughter Koreysh, the leading men of the village intervened, saying 'What you are doing to poor Laljan is unjust, he is a good Muslim, while you are lying and we shall not take your part.' At this Majlun went to the government to make trouble; he submitted a petition for Laljan's daughter, but Laljan mortgaged the rest of his land and paid some 10,000 Afs. in bribes and kept her.

However, Majlun persisted and even went to Kabul and petitioned the Ministry of the Interior, explaining how his tooth had been knocked out and that he had been promised a girl whom Laljan now refused to give. His petition met with little success, but Laljan became increasingly aware of how defenceless he was, and he even threatened to kill his own son and throw his body into Majlun's compound and say that Majlun had killed him. Laljan's threat was taken seriously, and at this point, fearing an escalation of the crisis and government intervention, the leading men among Laljan's agnates began to insist that Laljan marry the girl to Majlun. It was Hajji Ibrahim who suggested the exchange marriage to which Laljan finally agreed. Majlun paid a *sar* of 15,000 Afs. and a good camel to marry Koreysh, while one of Laljan's sons would marry Majlun's young granddaughter. The engagement ceremony was held in Hajji Ibrahim's compound, though even this was hardly neutral ground, since the lineage had split into the usual Upper Sinjit and Lower Sinjit factions over the affair. *Mahr-e mosamma* bride-prices were agreed for both the girls (in case of death), and in fact the *nikah* marriage ceremonies were performed at this time, so that there could be no more trickery or fighting, even though the girls were to remain at home for some time – Koreysh until a trousseau could be prepared and Majlun's granddaughter until she reached puberty.

It was well known that Koreysh was very unhappy about the marriage. She was young and he was old and treacherous. Several times she said she would 'call out' for some other man, but Kishmir, the headwoman, scolded her and Hajji Ibrahim threatened to kill her if she did any such thing. She had become a pawn in what could become an explosive lineage confrontation and her own interests were held to be quite irrelevant to the solution which was found.

So, by trickery and deceit a man of a rival agnatic faction of the lineage forced Laljan to give him a daughter in marriage. Laljan's expenses, spent on bribes to resist this oppression, were very great. In the end he had mortgaged or sold all the land he held. It was quite possible that his sons would eventually be forced to leave the subtribe: one was educated as a mullah and could gain a livelihood elsewhere, while the other two already had complicated relations of economic dependency on their non-Durrani affines.

Meanwhile, it was equally likely that the few wealthy Babi Parsiwan households, into which Laljan's daughter Zarur had married, would eventually join the subtribe and perhaps even be assimilated into it as Durrani. However, this is most unlikely to happen during Zarur's lifetime, for she, unusually, is now held to be responsible for her shameful marriage. After all, Maduzai say, long before the marriage took place, she had shown herself to be a weak, shameless woman. Though she is still secretly visited by the headwoman Kishmir, Zarur has been disowned completely by her own agnates.

However, from her point of view, she has not done badly: the Babi do not hold her earlier romance against her but treat her well, and her marriage into their wealthy household afforded her a degree of control over her life and some recognition of her individual worth which she was unlikely to have found otherwise. Moreover, it is possible that her children by the non-Durrani husband might be able surreptitiously to assume Durrani identity at a later date, a consideration which, while probably of no great importance to her, does matter to the Babi Parsiwans.

Members of Lineage C quietly conspired to hush up Zarur's marriage to a 'Parsiwan'. They rationalized the marriage to others, including us, by suggesting that breaking the rule against hypogamy was less terrible than keeping a 'bad' woman within the group. However, when they explained the circumstances of the case in detail, the overwhelming emphasis in their accounts was on the weakness of Zarur's father, Laljan.

The impression of Laljan's weakness built up gradually over a long period. After Zarur's marriage, which confirmed the disunity of the household and revealed how little support Laljan could expect from his close agnates, the household was oppressed still further and another of Laljan's daughters was then 'stolen' in marriage. Such 'thefts' of women, which is how the Maduzai speak of them, are a way of describing those occasions when a man forces a weaker man to agree to a marriage which is quite contrary to the latter's interests.

Married women and illicit sex

The absence of divorce among Durrani, and the fact that children of a marriage always remain in their father's home, mean that women who are unhappily married must nonetheless accept their marriage as a given. Jinn possession is one institution through which some unhappy women may gain a degree of personal consolation and support; others achieve some control over their own lives by involving themselves in illicit sexual liaisons.

A woman unhappy with her situation within a large, successful household headed by a man of character is most unlikely to risk involvement in an illicit liaison which might threaten their honour, quite simply because the men of such a household can and will respond in the most severe terms. They can afford to punish and replace women who besmirch their honour and they will be expected to do so. Ironically, it is married women associated with successful households who have the fewest alternative means of personal expression. As we have seen, it is the lively women of strong households who may experience possession fits: this is the situation of some fifteen per cent of married women in the community. I know of no way to account for the incidence of such possession fits except in terms of these women's recognized and unfulfilled expectations and rights.

However, other married women find relief from personal misery through illicit sexual liaisons. *Within* extended households, when a woman's husband is absent for a long time, illicit sexual relations may occur between her and one of the husband's own younger brothers. From a woman's point of view her relations with her husband's younger brothers are typically companionable and, I suspect, such sexual contact is often welcome. Such affairs do not disrupt a household's management of its women and do not, as far as I know, become the subject of public gossip or scandal. Equally, a husband who is impotent or infertile may accept, if not encourage, his wife in an affair with another man in the hope that she will become pregnant. However, again such affairs should be very discreet, if not actually within the household; I heard of one case in which one co-wife of a sterile man was widely known to be having an affair outside the household; publicly at least, she was despised by other women, while the other wife, who remained faithful but childless, was admired.

By contrast, a woman unhappy with her situation in a weak, impoverished household, whose menfolk are ineffectual and fail to support their women and children, may indeed be understood to suffer from jinn-possession (but not possession fits). She may also take a lover or even engage in covert prostitution for money and presents which she can dispose of as she wishes. I know that at least 6 of the 94 married women of Lineage C behaved in this way, while the men responsible for their control could not punish them with impunity. If was often wealthy local men who indulged in romantic affairs with these women or used them as prostitutes, and any confrontation with them was likely to leave the women's husbands public laughing-stocks at the very least. Whatever they did, they would be shamed for failing to control their wives in the first place. They were not likely to challenge their wife's lovers, and if they killed their wives, they would find themselves helpless to run their households alone and unlikely, unless they left the community altogether, ever to find another woman to marry.

The degree of autonomy which married women in weak households may have is illustrated, first, by the case of Shekar and her daughter, Zeytun, who was the fourth Maduzai woman to be married hypogamously; and secondly, by the account of the 'brothel' in one of the Maduzai villages. Each of these accounts also reveals the extent to which parties to a marriage contract must themselves be responsible for its enforcement. Maduzai recognize clearly that, particularly in the case of close-kin marriages, if the principals themselves lack the strength to enforce their rights, it is difficult to recruit outside support. They are much less aware of the personal choices individual women have when they are unwilling partners in a marriage with a weak man.

Case 9: Shekar's divorce and Zeytun's de facto independence

Shekar was first married to a man by whom she had a son and a daughter. Then about nineteen years ago, shortly after he had arranged the engagement of his infant daughter Zeytun to her first paternal cousin Dil (her F^1/$_2$BS), her husband died. Shekar remained in her brother-in-law's household, but he was poor and ineffectual; she did not immediately remarry, and rumour spread that she was 'not a good woman'.

Only a man desperate for a wife would have considered marrying this disreputable widow. But such was the situation of the elderly Khoshdil, who was widowed about a year after Shekar. He approached her brother-in-law and marriage guardian, who accepted his suit. Khoshdil paid a *sar* (see p. 151) of thirty sheep and 5,000 Afs., and the *nikah* marriage ceremony was performed. That night, however, Khoshdil discovered the truth of the rumours: Shekar was pregnant. At first she attempted to deny the fact, then she asked Khoshdil to accept the child as his own, but he ignored her pleas and divorced her and sent her from his house. It is said explicitly that she was not killed for fear of government intervention, though I doubt if the old man seriously considered that course.

Shamed, Shekar fled to her mother, a widow living with her own married son, and there she aborted the child. Khoshdil was too ashamed himself to ask for the return of the *sar* payment. Ironically Shekar's own brother, a poor man distressed by the fact that he suddenly had three more mouths to feed (Shekar had brought her two young children with her to Khoshdil's and thence to her brother's) claimed that as Khoshdil had divorced her she should get one eighth of all his property. This claim made the divorce public knowledge; people were appalled and Shekar's brother's attempt to benefit from her predicament gravely dishonoured him. The claim did not succeed. Shekar remained in her brother's house and there her children grew up.

Meanwhile, both Dil, the man to whom Shekar's daughter, Zeytun, had been engaged in infancy, and his father, Shekar's half-brother-in-law, died. Zeytun was then inherited as the fiancée of Yar Mohammad, her dead husband's heir and the older of his two younger brothers. At puberty, however, she refused to marry Yar Mohammad because of his poverty and she proclaimed herself a 'widow' with the right to remain single. She continued to live in her mother's brother's household and Yar Mohammad and his brother, who were Zeytun's guardians both as agnates and affines, were quite unable to force her to marry either of them. They gained no sympathy for their plight from Zeytun's mother's brother, while they had themselves only one close agnate, their uncle Lal Mohammad, who might have supported their claims had he not been impoverished himself. He was unwilling to involve himself in a quarrel which was likely only to reveal further his own weakness.

The continuing presence of these women in the village was felt to be an affront to Lineage C as a whole. Then, one day a Pashtu-speaker newly arrived from Kandahar approached the Sinjit headman and then the Maduzai Khan, explaining that he had heard about Shekar and her daughter and would like to marry the latter if it could be arranged. He was a widower and had a house in a village some miles from Chinar, and he said he would be prepared to take Shekar into his home as well. The Maduzai leaders were pleased with the prospect of being rid of the anomalous family, and they approached Zeytun's 'brothers-in-law' to 'free' her. These men were delighted with the offer of 20,000 Afs. *sar* which the Kandahari was willing to pay for Zeytun, and they accepted it immediately. Soon afterwards the Sinjit headman arranged an exchange marriage for Shekar's son and daughter. Zeytun married the Kandahari and her brother married his lame daughter, and they were forced to leave (Shekar with them) for the Kandahari's village.

It is clear that no close inquiry was conducted into the Kandahari's ethnic background. It seems fairly certain that he was a 'Parsiwan', but Maduzai uncertainty on this point gave him and them the benefit of the doubt. In any case, his origins were considered of little importance in the circumstances: it was most unlikely that any more respectable man would be found to take on these two women, and in doing so he performed a kind of public service for the village. Zeytun's marriage to the Parsiwan implicated no man's honour more than her own and her mother's own actions had already done. The marriage seemed on the way to being (deliberately?) forgotten by many people, but I was told by Kishmir, who cared for individuals more than principles, that Zeytun and her husband were well matched, they had children and some land and lived quite happily elsewhere in the Saripul valley.

Yar Mohammad and his brother were dishonoured by their inability to control Zeytun long before her marriage to the Kandahari, and in fact they stood to benefit from that marriage: they were paid a *sar* for ridding themselves of formal responsibility for her. Yar Mohammad died shortly after Zeytun's marriage to the Kandahari. His younger brother remains unmarried and the sole member of his household; he has tried several times to find a bride within the lineage, but so far without success. No one wishes to give their daughter to a man who is so poor (he owns no land or animals and works as a day labourer for members of the sub-tribe) and who has 'no *qaum*', that is, no close supportive agnates. His situation is such that he is likely to leave the subtribe and the area to try his luck elsewhere.

After they had been married a few years, the Kandahari's lame daughter died. Shekar's son was thus widowed and returned to Sinjit. In spite of all that had happened before, he personally was an attractive young man and his own identity as a lineage agnate was not in question; he was welcomed back by his kinspeople

Figure 10 Shekar's divorce and Zeytun's *de facto* independence

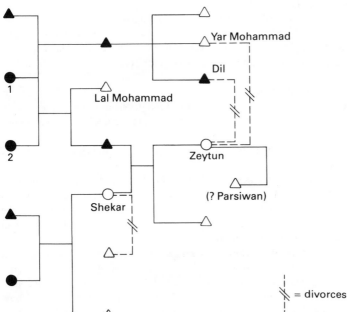

and offered, in return for bride-service, the infant daughter of his MZH, also an agnate.

Casual affairs, prostitution and household standing

Finally I turn to a description of the 'brothel' which operated in one of the Maduzai villages. This account underlines the full force of Maduzai pragmatism, and serves to illustrate some of the factors which lie behind the contradiction between their uncompromising ideals and their apparent tolerance of extra-marital affairs. As I mentioned in chapter 1, the man and wife who recorded the account for us were determined to make us understand that this kind of shameful behaviour did occur and that we should not allow ourselves to be associated with it by visiting the houses of those concerned. However, the couple were them-selves quite closely related through ties of agnation, affinity and neighbourhood to all those of whom they spoke. In their account of Majid's activities, their tone was of fascinated horror, but they were neither defensive about what they recounted nor personally shamed by it. They made it absolutely clear that in such affairs of honour each household stands alone: the shame of weak men is not contagious, nor do the strong feel any obligation to defend the rights of others, and certainly their honour does not depend on their doing so.

Case 10: Majid's 'brothel'

Majid is a pimp (*mordegau*). He summons women by sending his wife Tajbibi after them. She fixes them up and then he gets some money for it. I'm not joking, everybody knows, it is not only me saying it . . .

Majid doesn't arrange these things himself; if he is going to fix a meeting he sends his wife to fetch the woman. If a woman goes from house to house, people don't worry as they do if a man does. We call her *ruybar*, a woman sent by her husband to another man to fix it up between him and another woman. So she does *ruybari* for them and brings them face to face.

Majid and his wife use their own house, and when she has the woman inside she locks the door. Some women are not accustomed to this kind of business and get angry, but the man is stronger than her and he may cover her mouth, then what can the woman do?

If a woman isn't agreeable then either they will find some present to please her, or they won't approach her next time.

Majid takes money from the men: 50 or 100 Afs. a time. He may give half to the woman. We call it bribery [*mak*]. This is his occupation. [He also worked as a share-cropper for his father-in-law and was known as a money-lender.] He may give half to the woman; or the men will bring him a pound or two of meat or some rice on bazaar days. The important thing is that his cooking pot is full each evening.

This happens in the other villages too, but it is not so open that everybody knows about it. There it is done secretly, and only a few people know, not the whole population, not every share-cropper and labourer and shepherd and camel-herd and cow-herd. Of course the grey-beards talk about it, but Majid's eyes are like a locust's and he listens to no one. The elders have abused him and his father has beaten him with sticks and kicked him.

Majid swears on the Koran that he won't do it any more, but then it starts again a week later. Once a man has begun doing this, there is no end to it.

People say things to him, but if a girl's guardian doesn't talk, what can anyone else do? There have been five or six women under Majid and Tajbibi's control . . .

Mamadzi's father-in-law is a pathetic, weak man. If he doesn't do anything, what can anyone else do?

[This moderately wealthy man was so ineffectual that he was unable to prevent his wife from quarrelling violently with Mamadzi, the wife of his eldest and only married son. This quarrelling led to the son's separation from the household. Mamadzi's husband, nicknamed 'Mouse', was sickly and unable to work because of a deformed arm; his wife and four small children barely survived on his meagre earnings as village cow-herd. Mamadzi herself was strong and high-spirited and, being from another Ishaqzai subtribe, had no agnatic kin in the village.]

Sati's husband is young and people don't listen to him much; they don't care about him.

[Sati is sister of Tajbibi, Majid's wife. Her husband and his younger brother, neither of them yet in their twenties, had been orphaned as children and had barely been able to defend their own fairly considerable patrimony. Sati and her husband had been engaged in childhood (they were patrilateral parallel cousins) and the marriage had been completed some years before the husband reached puberty. Sati's own father, who might still have supervised her behaviour and thus helped his nephew, was however already so compromised by the behaviour of his son-in-law, Majid, and his daughter, Tajbibi, that he was unable or unwilling to intervene.]

As for Karim's engaged daughter Mastan . . . Karim is not here and her mother has now gone to an autumn camp and there is no one. Her FB and FBS have also gone, and now she herself is the head of the household. The other women can't stop her from going around. She will say, 'I'm going to such and such a house' and then she goes to Majid's.

[Mastan lives with her mother, a Maduzai woman, and her FB, one of the 'Sayyids'; her father Karim is said to be quite mad, having abandoned his family some time ago. The weakness of the 'Sayyid' households has been described (see p. 152). Mastan is engaged to a landless young man of the subtribe, by origin from another Durrani tribe; he had planned to wed her in 1972, but the previous winter had lost his only property, 200 sheep. Her brideprice has not been paid and he has been forced to take employment as a shepherd for others.]

And Sherap – in truth, she doesn't mind what either of her brothers says. She doesn't accept their authority and she says, they have nothing to do with me!

[Sherap has been a pawn in a major intra-lineage quarrel (see p. 266), and though she had many attractive suitors she was engaged by her brothers to the pre-pubertal son of an opposing house. She considers her brothers to have betrayed

her, and in the activities described here and in other ways she has shown her con-
tempt for them.]

We strongly disapprove of the house of Majid. We don't go there now. Majid isn't a man,
he is like a cow. It is not good or Muslim, he has become polluted and all his body is foul.
He is such a *mordagau* man, what can we do? Do you have such things too?

While 'non-Durrani' (by definition, from a Durrani point of view) male and
female prostitutes are available, both in the local towns and, Maduzai say, in the
camps of gypsies, Majid's 'brothel' was exceptional because villagers were
involved and because of the extent of its organization.

   Other extra-marital affairs certainly occur and women's disaffection from
their households is a clear element in their participation in such activities. To this
extent, Majid's house too has less the character of a brothel than a safe-house for
assignations. Though such affairs affect the personal honour of only the people
of the households immediately concerned, nonetheless, leading men of the
village hope to conceal the situation from outsiders and to avoid damaging the
wider reputation of the lineage and subtribe. But they had not managed to put a
stop to Majid's activities, and it would seem that none of them felt their personal
– or collective – honour to be threatened to the extent that they should override
the principle of household independence and risk a confrontation with the leaders
of the opposing village factions who were well known to be among the patrons
of the 'brothel'. Indeed, in some respects the villagers were fascinated by the situation and particularly by the possibility of profiting from the dishonour of the
households of the protagonists, reasoning that those who have shown themselves
to be incapable of controlling their women are likely to be equally incapable of
defending their other property.

Conclusions
In the Maduzai community few men or women are able to exercise much individual control over their lives. However, in the areas where scope for choice
exists, it is notable that the respective situations of men and women differ significantly. It is possible to argue that those who ultimately have the least freedom of
action within their defined sphere are not women, but rather those men who have
few close kinsmen to support their claims to economic and political resources.
These men are likely to be oppressed in a variety of ways, among which they may
lose control of their women to more powerful men who will 'steal' their sisters
or daughters, or respond to such women 'calling out', or meet their wives in illicit
affairs.

   The irony of the position of the weak man whose daughter or wife has
deceived him reveals the curious place of gender in the ideologies of responsibility and honour and shame. In spite of Durrani statements that the control of
women is the most important dimension of these ideologies, it is clear that claims

to an honourable status depend far more on the economic and political resources a man controls than on the behaviour of the women of his household. In the case of a weak household, a woman's disruptive behaviour is often little more than an index of a man's failure to provide economically and compete politically.

On the other hand, powerful men – those who may act as usurpers and oppressors – are also likely to be those who are able to control the sexual behaviour of their women most effectively. That is, the ideology of control becomes self-fulfilling. In part this is because wealth and power enable them to provide for the material and other needs of household members, and women with conventional expectations are likely to be well supported. Where the rights of a woman living in a relatively strong household are unfulfilled, she has very few strategies open to her to improve her situation.

Any immodest behaviour or threat of subversion on her part is likely to be severely suppressed by the men of the household, less because they fear for their honour than because they quite simply have the resources which make them relatively independent of any individual woman. Meanwhile her expressions of grievance remain unrecognized because of their tacit association with possession fits, whether authentic or fake. Only in the most unusual and rare cases may such a woman risk all and escape the household through a romantic liaison. If she succeeds, as Kaftar did, she will certainly be seen to dishonour the men who were responsible for her.

11

The marriages in the house of Hajji Adam

The cases described in chapter 10 show clearly that Maduzai households are now ruthlessly competitive. Evidence indicates that this was not always so. The particular character this competition now takes among the Maduzai is related to the increased value set on household independence, which in turn can be attributed to the considerable increase in population of the region over the last fifty years, the consequent pressure on land and pasture, and the process of settlement which the Maduzai have experienced. The tribespeople themselves recognize the importance of these factors. On the one hand, they recount with a certain amazement stories of how, in the old days, people could afford to be 'simple' and apparently casual in their marriage arrangements and the control of women, but on the other, they also see clearly that when there was an abundance of land and pasturage, 'everybody had adequate means, people were comfortable and had *qaumi*'.

We have seen how the control of marriages and of the sexual behaviour of members of a household may be usurped by others. The likelihood of such an infringement of their rights depends very much on their strength or weakness. The Maduzai accept that all outsiders to the subtribe present a potential threat to its resources, but they admit that among themselves too there are trouble makers, men who like to fight and won't hesitate to 'eat' the rights of other men, whether in women or in animals or land, if they think they can get away with it. As one young married man said:

Such men simply claim the women or property for their own. They see that the other people are poor and without means, and they make a fight – that is the way it is.

And such men know that even if they do not ultimately succeed in taking the woman or property of the other party, they may well gain from the dispute, if only by being paid to let it drop. Given the value attached to household independence and the extreme unwillingness of other households, even of close agnates, to support a weaker one, there is little a household can do against such 'thieves' (*haqq khor*), unless they are fortunate enough to persuade one of the village leaders to support their case.

A major implication of the cases discussed in chapter 10 was that the marriage policies of poor households are aimed basically at simple household survival, or at best at guaranteeing independence and freedom from interfering outsiders. The aims of wealthy householders are not fundamentally different, but wealthy households have far more choice in the marriages they make, and they are likely to be able to manipulate their choices to serve a variety of interests.

In this chapter I examine in detail the marriages made by a single family, one which was wealthy and remained so, while expanding over fifty years into five separate households. The circumstances of this family, and the marriages it contracted, are quite typical of similar Maduzai families towards one end of the wealth/power spectrum in the subtribe.

Maduzai marriages – a narrative history

I have fashioned the narrative history of the marriages of Hajji Adam's house from the accounts given to me by many different men and women. It is thus a collage and something of an experiment (cf. Munson 1984). My hope is that the description suggests something of the centrality of marriage in Maduzai social life by placing the protagonists and the complexities of marriage process on a wide canvas whose background is the demography and inter-ethnic relations in Turkistan and whose foreground is coloured by subtribe politics – in this respect, I take as given the earlier discussions of ethnicity, factionalism, household organization and gender. I am well aware that though my aim has been to give substance to the contexts of Maduzai marriage, I have inevitably simplified both my subjects and their world. I certainly did not learn all there was to learn about the marriages described, but equally, my informants certainly did not have perfect knowledge about the marriages or the motivation of the individuals concerned. The narrative is inevitably partial and incomplete.

However, the narrative seems to me an important way of uniting the variety of other perspectives through which we have viewed Maduzai marriage in the earlier chapters. It locates the marriage forms – of brideprice and exchange – with respect to each other; describes the contexts of other institutionalized aspects of marriage, such as *bazi* and trousseaux; relates issues of individual temperament to household demography and marriage; and shows the relation between household wealth and marriage policies. It also illustrates other aspects of Durrani marriage patterns whose interconnections can be demonstrated only by such detailed case material. These include, first, the extent to which qualitative differences between marriages (even of the same mode) must be taken into account if marriage as a social process is to be understood; and, second, the extent to which each marriage is a consequence of those which have preceded it and anticipates other marriages which follow.

The narrative is written from the point of view of the household heads and, in this respect, it can be said to be a narrative dominated by male voices and views. This should not be surprising if we remember that this is a history of wealthy households. We know that in general among the Maduzai the co-operation of all household members is highly valued and that men and women often share ideas and practical responsibilities in order to forward household interests. In successful, wealthy households the conventional expectations of women are often met and such women often have considerable say in protecting their children through good marriages, and as mediators between their kin and affines. Perhaps paradoxically, Maduzai wives and mothers who are secure and loved often seem very similar to the men of the household: they are strong-willed, articulate, and ruthlessly ambitious. In practice, they are the closest companions and confidants of household men and they can become more or less equal partners in determining household strategies.

But, as we have seen in chapter 10, women of wealthy, successful households who feel their interests do not coincide with household policy are likely to be muted by the very strength of the men of the household. Their grievances – of loveless marriages and co-wives; back-breaking domestic chores; childlessness, the demands of child-care or the heart-breaking sadness of a child's illness, unhappy marriage or death – find expression in illness and spirit possession fits and in private conversations with mothers, sisters or childhood friends. The grievances may also emerge in bitter quarrels with other women of the household.

As the narrative history makes very clear, among the Maduzai not only are women considered subordinate to men, but they are all ultimately pawns in the marriage process. Those who are favoured, or lucky, will share the men's view of marriage and can play a considerable role in marriage choices and arrangements. Those who are less fortunate can hardly make themselves heard, and what they say reveals almost nothing about the marriage process, and why and how women (and men) are thus controlled and oppressed.

The series of marriages I take as examples are from Section I of Lineage C: the descendants of Tella's eldest son Toman, who had three sons, Adam, Soleyman and Payz Mohammad. There is no space here to describe and analyse the marriages made by the whole section, so I shall present only – but all – those made by Adam and his descendants. This group of kin identify themselves, and are identified by others, as the *aulad* or *qaum* of Adam, or as Adam's house (*kor*). Throughout our fieldwork we were closest to this group of people, which included Maduzai protagonists the reader has met earlier: our host, Hajji Ibrahim, headman of Sinjit village and rival of the Maduzai Khan; and his father's brother, the wealthy but politically erratic Hajji Sultan. We follow the relations between Ibrahim's and Sultan's households: as we shall see, political and economic competition between them has grown over a period of many years,

Table 25. *Wealth and marriages made by households of Section I, Lineage C*

Ancestor	Present number of households	Household wealth				Number of marriages[a]
		I	II	III	IV	
Adam	5	3	1	0	1	56
Soleyman	8	2	5	0	1	46
Payz Mohammad	1	0	0	1	0	10

[a]Marriages within each house have been counted twice.

but its expression has been almost exclusively in terms of marriages. The narrative history thus links leadership and marriage and provides many examples of the ways in which such men can interfere in the lives and marriage strategies of agnates and clients from weaker but ostensively independent households; as we shall see, they do this by defining a wide variety of structural ambiguities to support their own interests and by coercing the agreement of others through various threats or bribes which often take the form of promises of women to be given in marriage.

The marriages made by Adam's house were much the same in pattern as those of Soleyman's house, while Payz Mohammad's house became poor and did not increase. Table 25 gives an indication of the present circumstances of the households of Toman's descendants.

The Kandahar marriages (see Figures 11, 12, 13)

On arrival in Turkistan in about 1915, the three brothers Adam, Soleyman and Payz Mohammad were already in separate households, their father having died many years before. I have little information on the circumstances of the marriage made before the migration, but I shall summarize what I know of them as a backdrop for the marriages of Adam's house which followed.

Adam's three wives were all Parsiwans, and all married before the (?re-alliance) of Lineages A and C in Kandahar (see p. 70). All three women came to Turkistan and Adam lost touch with his affines, who remained in Kandahar, though one wife's brother, a Baluch, is known to have moved later to northeastern Afghanistan.

Adam, the eldest brother, was a retiring man with no pretensions to anything but piety. Soleyman was the dominant brother, and indeed one of the leaders and senior elders of the whole of Lineage C until his death ten years ago. He married two wives in Kandahar: one was a Baluch whose kin still have ties with the Maduzai (members of one such Baluch household were clients of one of Soleyman's sons in 1972). His second wife was a $F^1/_2BD$. Shortly after arriving in Turkistan he fell in love with and married a girl of Lineage D, and then many years later married Adam's only surviving widow.

Payz Mohammad married his only wife in Kandahar: his F¹/₂BD, for whom
the brothers' only sister was given in exchange. He died soon after arrival in
Turkistan, leaving his wife with one son and two daughters. The widow hoped
that Soleyman would take her, but he was enamoured of the woman of Lineage
D and not interested; nor was Adam, and they remarried her for a token *sar* to a
poor agnate (Section III) as his first wife. Payz Mohammad's orphans remained

Figure 11   Skeleton genealogy of Lineage C

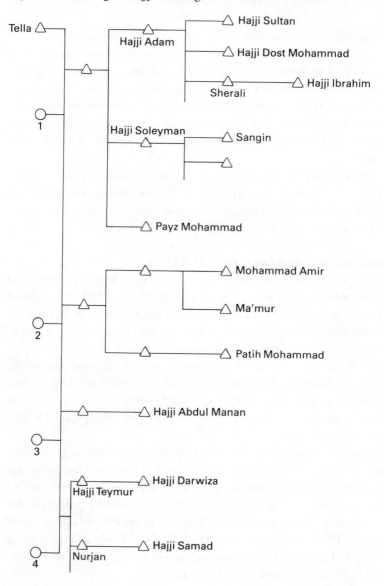

Figure 12 Adam's house (Section I, Lineage C)

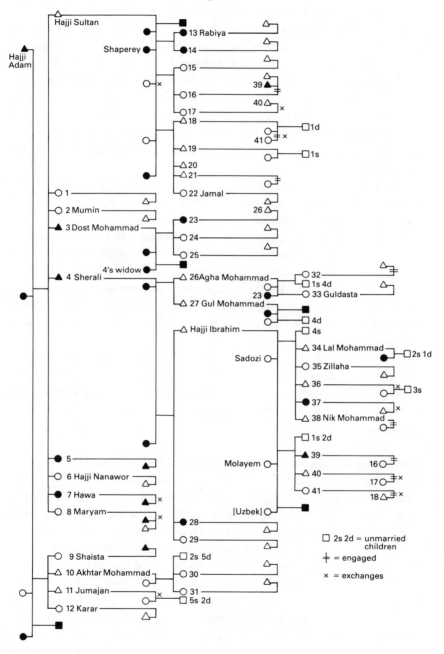

with Soleyman, who is said to have treated them as if they were his own children. He also held Payz Mohammad's property in trust for his son.

Two of Adam's daughters were married in Kandahar. The elder (1) went to a man of another Ishaqzai subtribe, and although she died young her agnates still maintain intermittent contact with her husband's family, who now live in the northeast of the country. Her younger sister Mumin (2) was married to an agnate (Section IV) who is now one of the wealthiest men in Sinjit. Mumin has borne him three sons and remains his only and much loved wife. She was due in 1971 to go to Mecca with her BS Ibrahim and her younger sister Nanawor (6), who is married to a leading man of Lineage A, but in the event only the other two made the pilgrimage.

The strength of Mumin's marriage has been of continuing importance in the relations between the Sinjit factions. Among other things, she personally arranged two marriages between her children and her brother's children (25 and 34). Though these marriages have created tensions between the households involved, they were certainly inspired by a sense of friendship and co-operation between close kin, and they have undoubtedly served to temper the hostility between the two factions. These marriages, explicitly arranged by a woman with her own close agnates, are quite different in kind from the other marriages which Section I made with the Upper Sinjit faction of Lineage C, all of which were exchange marriages following quarrels.

Adam's eldest son Sultan was also married in Kandahar, where he took a woman from Lineage A as part of one of the exchanges which united Lineages A and C. Adam's second son Dost Mohammad (3) also married in Kandahar, a girl from another Ishaqzai subtribe which is today a near neighbour of the Maduzai in Saripul.

Early years in Turkistan - relations between Lineages A and C

The brothers Adam and Soleyman were on the best of terms, the former being content to accept the latter's leadership. Sultan, who had separated from his father's household some time in the early 1920s, though he was never strong enough to want to challenge his uncle Soleyman's dominance, did nonetheless find himself on occasion the latter's rival. For some thirty years after their arrival in Turkistan these two men controlled the marriages of Section I.

When little more than twenty years old, Sultan made his mark by contracting the first marriage of any Maduzai in Turkistan, his second, since his first wife had died young without any surviving children. The marriage is remembered as having set a new standard for brideprice payments: in Kandahar these were said not to have exceeded some 500–600 Afs., but Sultan now paid the extraordinarily high sum of 7,000 Afs. for Shaperey, the daughter of a leading man of Lineage A.

People say that it was as if he had paid seven lacs (700,000 Afs.) today. Moreover, now the men of Sinjit say of the men of Section III of Lineage A (from which the girl came), 'all their money is polluted (*haram*) because it was taken unjustly from Hajji Sultan'. This was the first non-exchange marriage between Lineages A and C, and the girl's father and the men of Lineage A were determined to make Sultan pay for the privilege of being a Durrani and marrying one

Figure 13 Duration of marriages made by Adam's house (1917–1972)

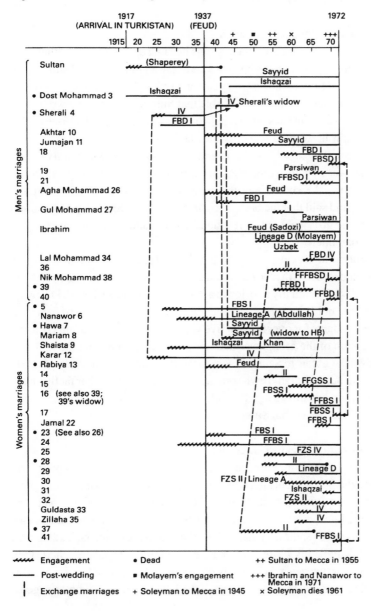

of their women for brideprice. At that time Adam's household was reasonably wealthy, certainly as compared with the household of Shaperey's father; however, 7,000 Afs. was a very large sum of money, and Sultan was fortunate in some trading activities which enabled him to meet the challenge. Today his close kin regard this marriage as of great symbolic importance and see his good fortune in collecting the money for the brideprice as a kind of mysterious blessing. Shaperey is said to have been both beautiful and wise, and she played a leading role in composing affairs after the Maduzai feud.

The origins of the Lineage C factions

Soon after Sultan's marriage to Shaperey, he became embroiled in another marriage (see Figure 14). Somehow, Nurjan, one of the leading men of Section IV of Lineage C, tricked Sultan into an engagement with his daughter. People say, 'he forced the girl on Sultan', and it is possible that Sultan was threatened or blackmailed in some way. Nurjan said that he would ask nothing in brideprice for his daughter, though he wanted some clothes and other items for her trousseau. Sultan was shamed by this proposition, and bought lavishly for her, only to find that her father was now insisting that since Sultan had paid 7,000 Afs. in brideprice for Shaperey he should pay the same amount for his daughter. Sultan became angry and said that the brideprice he had paid for Shaperey had nothing to do with it, that girls were only a few hundred Afs. and he would pay no more for Nurjan's daughter.

Nurjan refused to accept only a few hundred Afghanis, so Sultan broke the engagement and told him that he must find the girl another husband, but not from the *qaum*. She was eventually married to a Durrani living more than 80 km away. This dispute has not been forgotten: Section I made no further marriages with Nurjan's descendants for over twenty-five years, until Samad, Nurjan's son and now leading man of the group, was able to force Sultan into agreeing to marry one of his own daughters to Samad's son. In the event another girl, Sultan's BSD (33) was given, but as Sultan's own son said, 'those men of the other faction have got used to taking advantage of us', while others among Sultan's kin have said that 'they are like wolves, but Sultan was a frightened man'.

Land divisions and Lineage C factions

In the decade after the migration, several changes affected Adam's house. The Maduzai bought their present lands (though they did not settle on them until later) and one of the five shares was acquired by Soleyman on behalf of Section I. The division of the lineage into the present factions began at this time (see p. 84). After a first quarrel over the division of the valley lands, Teymur, the leading man of Section IV, took his closest agnates and left for Kandahar, where they remained for over two years. When they did return to Saripul, they were eventually reconciled with their agnates by one of the Ishaqzai Khans, who arranged a marriage exchange between Soleyman's son and daughter and the son and daughter of Teymur. However, these marriages did little to resolve the conflict, nor were they particularly successful in the long term, and within a few years a second dispute arose between Soleyman and Teymur.

Teymur again left Saripul, this time for the northeast of the country, taking not

Figure 14 Marriages between Section I (Lineage C) and Section IV (The Upper Sinjit faction of Lineage C)

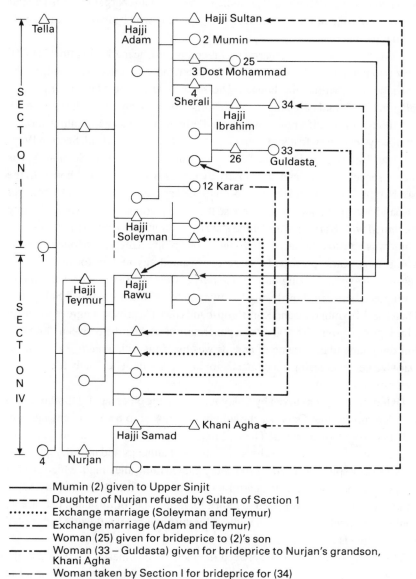

——————— Mumin (2) given to Upper Sinjit
– – – – Daughter of Nurjan refused by Sultan of Section 1
·········· Exchange marriage (Soleyman and Teymur)
—··— Exchange marriage (Adam and Teymur)
——————— Woman (25) given for brideprice to (2)'s son
—··— Woman (33 – Guldasta) given for brideprice to Nurjan's grandson, Khani Agha
– – – – Woman taken by Section I for brideprice for (34)

only his closest agnates but also two of Soleyman's sons and a man of Section II. This time when he returned, Soleyman was very anxious to keep him in Saripul for good. The settlement (c. 1924) proved difficult: Teymur was again given land, and a second pair of exchange marriages was arranged, this time between Adam's third son Sherali (4) and his half-sister Karar (12), and another son (Darwiza) and daughter of Teymur. Sherali's wife was considerably older than his sister Karar, and Adam paid a *sar* of 3,000 Afs. to Teymur so that Sherali could marry immediately. This payment of *sar* with the exchange marriage designed to make peace is a clear indication of the hard bargain which Teymur drove: it was one of the first of such *sar* payments which anyone in Lineage C could remember.

Soon after Sherali's first marriage was completed, he married again, his FBD, Payz Mohammad's eldest orphaned daughter; no brideprice was paid, as the marriage was 'within the house'. The second wife bore Sherali's first son, Ibrahim (1925) and two daughters. The first wife bore him two other sons who, to demonstrate the differences with their dominant half-brother Ibrahim, have in small ways carefully fostered their contacts with their *mamakhel*, Section IV.

Karar's marriage to Darwiza, who is now one of the leaders of Section IV, has been a successful one, and she closely identifies with her marital home. In the past her own closest agnates have been treated as neutral and separate from her husband and his agnates who compose the other faction of the lineage. Visiting continued with Karar in spite of the state of relations between the factions, and Karar was able to arrange the marriage of one of her daughters to one of Soleyman's sons. Karar promised that no one wanted any money for the girl, and because she was marrying into her *mamakhel* (her MFBS) a *mahr-e mosamma* was agreed between (now Hajji) Teymur and the son of his old rival Soleyman. Then Hajji Teymur died and Karar's husband Darwiza privately agreed to accept a brideprice of some 35,000 Afs., a generous one at the time between close kin. But the young man became ill and, as was his right with a *mahr-e mosamma*, Darwiza kept increasing his demands for brideprice until he finally took eleven *jeribs* of valley land.

Half of the land was given by Soleyman's son, the other half by Ibrahim, who was determined that Darwiza should not be allowed to break the engagement with his exorbitant demands. The wedding was completed, but has not been particularly successful, the bride herself being very unhappy and now thought to be possessed by spirits. Darwiza's treachery gained him valley land, which is what the two sections had begun to quarrel about decades before. But, ironically, some years later Darwiza was forced to return Ibrahim's half of this land, because he could not defend his claim to it without Ibrahim's support – the title is disputed by one of the Ishaqzai Khans.

The most recent outbreak between the factions of Lineage C erupted in the spring of 1972 when, during a quarrel over sheep, Darwiza fired a pistol at

Ibrahim's son. The shot missed, and the incident went no further, but I was astonished at the nature of the gossip then retailed about Karar by her agnates in Section I; no reference was made to the shooting, but I was several times told, quite out of the blue, that Karar and one of her daughters (married to Darwiza's brother's son) were both possessed by necrophagous spirits, and that they would haunt the graveyards at night to return home in the morning covered in blood – allegations quite unlike any I had heard before.

The marriages of Adam's daughters
In around 1921 Sultan separated his household from that of his father and brothers. A few years later Dost Mohammad (3) also separated, leaving the third brother Sherali (4) in charge of Adam's own household. Some time afterwards, Soleyman asked that the second of Dost Mohammad's three daughters (24) be engaged to one of his own sons. Dost Mohammad agreed, and asked no bride-price for the infant, being 'happy to give the girl free to her *qaumi*'.

Some time after the Maduzai began to winter in their valley lands, one of the Ishaqzai Khans saw Adam's daughters playing outside the camp. They were apparently very lovely girls, and the Khan approached Adam to ask to marry Nanawor (6). As she had already been promised to the son of a leading man of Lineage A, the Khan was offered her younger sister Shaista (9). The Khan is said to have been enchanted by the girl, and Sultan was able to drive a very hard bargain, taking more than 10,000 Afs. in cash and two camel-loads of cloth and other goods as brideprice. Adam and Sultan gained considerable prestige from the marriage, both because they had acquired the Khan as an affine and because they had extracted such a large brideprice from him. The Khan could easily afford the money (it was only because he was so wealthy that such a sum was demanded in the first place) and he involved himself in further conspicuous consumption by holding both a very large *khoshey* the next autumn at which *buzkashi* was played, and an equally lavish wedding a couple of years after (c. 1932). The marriage was fruitful, and when the Khan died in the early 1960s, Shaista's eldest son became leader of his branch of the Khan family; he remains in close contact with his *mamakhel*, where his mother continues to visit regularly.

Soon after Shaista's engagement (c. 1929), another marriage was completed. Years before, the two brothers Adam and Soleyman deliberately arranged it 'to keep their houses together': Adam was to give his third daughter (5) to Soley-man's eldest son. There was to be no brideprice because it was between brothers. By the time of the marriage, however, relations between the two households were somewhat frayed, though for what reasons I am not sure. Before the trousseau was finished, Soleyman demanded the girl, but Sherali (4) asked him to wait. Soleyman impatiently insisted on the wedding. A simple *nikah* ceremony was performed and Sherali, infuriated, left the girl and her trousseau on the ground and moved Adam's tent out of Soleyman's camp. Certainly, as he is portrayed now, Sherali was a very headstrong character – it was he who insisted on the violence which led to the feud, and to his own death.

The 'feud' and after

In about 1937, Adam went to Mecca with three friends from Lineage A, including Janshah, leader of all the Maduzai. In their absence the feud broke out and Sherali was killed (see p. 148). Sultan and Soleyman were responsible for negotiating the settlement on the part of Lineage C (see Figure 15).

Sherali's two eldest sons received wives, the third was born after Sherali's death. The oldest, Ibrahim, was only about twelve at the time, but he became head of Adam's household, which now included Adam's youngest sons (10) and (11), both younger than Ibraham. His bride, Sadozi, some five years older than he, was brought to the house the very night of the killing, with only one blanket and a pillow as trousseau (see pp. 74f., 154). She was later to bear Ibrahim seven sons, but he never treated her well, since 'her brother killed his father'. Hajji Adam, grief-stricken, died a few months after his return from Mecca. His only surviving widow was eventually married to Soleyman, some ten years after Adam's death.

Sherali's second widow stayed with her son Ibrahim but his first widow wanted to marry Sultan, Sherali's eldest brother. Sherali's other grown brother, Dost Mohammad (3) had no sons; he was a small man and ill with huge running sores, and Sherali's widow apparently joked rudely about marrying such a man. Sultan overheard her remarks, declared that she was a woman without shame (*bi-sharma*) and refused to marry her. In the end she was taken by his unfortunate brother, who, when he married her, promised to give in exchange his eldest daughter (23) free to the widow's eldest son Agha Mohammad (26).

Dost Mohammad's two wives now quarrelled continuously, for the widow was fertile and bore him two sons in quick succession. However, her second son lived for only a day after birth and she died soon after, less than two years after her marriage, leaving three orphaned sons. Dost Mohammad's first wife took care of the children but, angered by some naughtiness on the part of her tiny stepson, she hit the child, and he died soon afterwards. People say that the child's death put a curse on Dost Mohammad's house, and within a few weeks both Dost Mohammad and his wife were also dead. All of his property, his clothes, camels and two flocks of sheep, were taken by his elder brother Sultan, who also brought his three orphaned daughters (the two eldest already engaged) into his household.

Sherali's second son Agha Mohammad (26) was only five or six years old at the time of the feud settlement, and the bride whom he received in compensation for the death of his father was still younger. He and his infant brother went with their mother into the house of Dost Mohammad, who 'adopted' them and engaged his eldest daughter (23) to Agha Mohammad (26). After Dost Mohammad's death, Sherali's sons joined the household of their half-brother

Ibrahim. Agha Mohammad eventually began married life with his FBD (23) before the feud marriage arranged for him could be completed. When he was young, Sultan was known for his generosity and his willingness to use his wealth to smooth relations between people. So when Agha Mohammad's first bride grew up, Sultan told her father to ask whatever he wanted for her. 'The girl was given in the feud, for free, but Sultan wanted to do *qaumi* – to do good and make them his own. He was wealthy and didn't have to worry about money, so he didn't

Figure 15 Marriages between Section I (Lineage C) and the Durkhan faction (Lineage A)

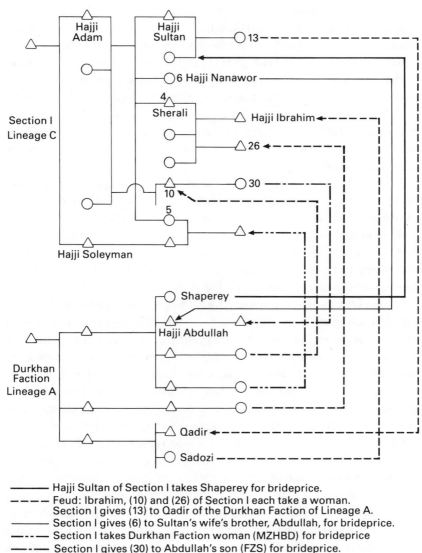

—————— Hajji Sultan of Section I takes Shaperey for brideprice.
– – – – Feud: Ibrahim, (10) and (26) of Section I each take a woman.
　　　　Section I gives (13) to Qadir of the Durkhan Faction of Lineage A.
—————— Section I gives (6) to Sultan's wife's brother, Abdullah, for brideprice.
—·· —·· — Section I takes Durkhan Faction woman (MZHBD) for brideprice
—·—·— Section I gives (30) to Abdullah's son (FZS) for brideprice.

hold back.' In fact he gave her father some 7,000 Afs. in order to buy the girl a proper trousseau. The wedding was completed in about 1946 with a small feast.

Sherali's half-brother Akhtar Mohammad (10) also received his wife as part of the feud settlement. He was younger than Ibrahim and both he and his wife were children at the time of their engagement, so the marriage was not completed for many years. Meanwhile relations between Lineages A and C improved, and when his bride reached puberty Akhtar Mohammad went to *bazi* with her. But she became pregnant, as her father discovered, and he furiously threatened to kill Akhtar Mohammad and revive the feud. However, Akhtar Mohammad's elder half-brother Sultan was able to pacify her father with a brideprice of some 5,000 Afs. and a *babirey* payment of an expensive gun worth some 3,000 Afs. In the end, Shaperey, Sultan's wife and FZ of the girl, completed all the arrangements; he gave some further money to cover the expenses and a small wedding was held.

Sultan also gave his eldest daughter (13) to the man wounded by Sherali at the beginning of the feud. She was young at the time of the settlement, and when she reached puberty her husband came to *bazi* where he was received by Shaperey, his WM and his own kinswoman. Though she too was given 'free', in fact a bride-price of some 5,000 Afs. was paid for her and in return she was provided with a large trousseau. As I was told by one woman, 'in a feud too, you take with one hand and give with the other'.

Structurally, Shaperey's marriage placed her in a good position to mediate between Lineages A and C after the feud. She certainly worked for the success of the marriages of the three women (all from her own Section III of Lineage A) given to men of Section I, and she tried to do the same for her daughter (13)'s marriage. However, it was another marriage in which she played an important role which had perhaps the most far-reaching consequences for relations between the two lineages (see Figure 15).

Shaperey's father had asked Adam for his daughter Nanawor (6) for his eldest son Abdullah, many years before, when she was still a tiny child. Adam agreed to the arrangement, but no formal engagement ceremony was performed. Nanawor grew into a very desirable young woman and many men (including one of the Ishaqzai Khans) wanted to marry her. Then during the feud her brother Sultan promised her to Patih Mohammad if the latter would slay Sherali's killer. Although Patih Mohammad killed another man instead, he nonetheless began to press Sultan for Nanawor. Her father Adam, who was now dying, learned of his son's murderous deal with Patih Mohammad and publicly repeated his promise to give the girl to Shaperey's brother Abdullah. Soon after Adam's death, Patih Mohammad also died and Shaperey was able to insist that her husband complete Nanawor's marriage (1938). Abdullah paid a brideprice of some 5,000 Afs., which was even then higher than most. Nanawor's marriage to Abdullah has in fact been a happy and successful one. Moreover, she was able to maintain close ties with her own agnates of Lineage C and has undoubtedly played a central role in relations between the two lineages, equivalent to that of Shaperey. Nanawor was taken to Mecca by her nephew Ibrahim in 1971 and became the first woman Hajji among the Maduzai. She personally arranged two marriages between the lineages, giving one of her HBD's to her sister (5)'s son (Soleyman's grandson), and taking her half-brother's daughter (30) for her own son.

Nanawor made the first of these two marriages out of friendship, and a bride-price of 40,000 Afs., a relatively small sum at the time (1955), was fixed for the girl because the mothers were sisters and because the girl was not particularly attractive. The marriage has been a success but the bride has never forgotten that she was married into the enemy camp, and she frequently uses the abusive term 'Torabi' to refer to her affines when they are out of hearing. The other marriage too was arranged when the spouses were very young. Nanawor's brother's daughter (30) was a pretty, fair-skinned child and Nanawor asked for her for her second son. Her brother Akhtar Mohammad agreed and a *mahr-e mosamma* was arranged. Nanawor and her husband expected to pay only 20–25,000 Afs. for the girl, though as the years passed before the wedding, her father began to make increasing demands for brideprice. Then, after her husband had come to *bazi*, she became pregnant, and though her father took no *babirey* he asked some 85,000 Afs. for the *mahr-e mosamma* before he would hold the wedding. His wife, however, was herself one of the women given by Lineage A in the feud, and she was determined to marry her eldest daughter into her own lineage in style, and she prepared a lavish trousseau for the girl. In the end, people agree, Akhtar Mohammad 'took little in brideprice, because he gave lots of clothes.'

The 'Sayyid' marriages
Soon after the feud and his father's death, Sultan arranged a series of marriages with the 'Sayyid' household which had recently joined the Sinjit *wolus* (p. 152; see Figure 16). Sultan married his youngest sister Maryam (8), then living in Ibrahim's household, to one of the three Sayyid brothers, and took a third wife for himself in exchange. He was anxious to bring his wife home quickly – he still had no sons – and secretly paid a *sar* for her. This payment, which is now publicly denied, was certainly part of the reason why a further marriage which Sultan had arranged (in which he promised Hawa (7), another of his sisters, as second wife for the eldest of the Sayyid brothers) before his own marriage was even completed, was converted at Ibrahim's insistence into a second exchange: the Sayyid would give his daughter by his first marriage to Sultan's youngest half-brother (11), then only a child. Only then was Ibrahim satisfied that people would not laugh at him for giving two girls in exchange for one. Hawa (7)'s wedding was held in about 1940; her brother Dost Mohammad (3), with whom she had been living, took a 3,000 Afs. *sar* for her because she was married so much earlier than the other girl, whose wedding was delayed for many years while she and her husband grew up.

Meanwhile one of the Sayyids had also made an exchange marriage with some Alikozai Durranis living near Mazar-e Sharif, whom the Maduzai had known from the time of their migration north. The girl exchanged there was soon widowed, and was to be remarried to a small child, a close agnate of her dead husband. Her brother then brought her to Saripul for a visit. Ibrahim saw her and wanted to marry her, and tried to persuade her brother to accept a brideprice for her and give some other girl to his affines in her place. The two men wanted the marriage but could not agree about how it could be arranged. While they were quarrelling, the widow eloped with another man. Initially, her dead husband's agnates, the Alikozais, blamed Ibrahim for what had happened: he was forced to flee to the summer pastures in the Hazarajat, while her brothers fled to the region of Mazar-e Sharif. There the Sayyids remained until 1948, when Hawa (7), her husband and Maryam (8)'s husband all died in a typhoid epidemic.

Though it was really none of their business, Sultan and Ibrahim decided that Sultan's sister Maryam should not remarry but return to Sinjit to live with them. They were particularly keen to prevent her from marrying her late husband's nephew, whom they considered wild and irresponsible, but the couple were married before Ibrahim could arrive to fetch Maryam back. Anar Gul, now head of the household, was only young and as yet unmarried himself, and it was Ibrahim who wound up the affairs of the Sayyid household and brought Hawa's caravan back to Saripul. With him came Anar Gul, Maryam and her second husband, and Anar Gul's young sister, (11)'s wife. Sultan and Ibrahim persuaded Anar Gul to stay in Sinjit where he already had many affinal links, and he married a granddaughter of Soleyman for a brideprice of 35,000 Afs. (higher than her own *qaum* would have paid for her) in about 1949. A further marriage soon followed: Anar Gul's younger sister was given to one of Soleyman's sons.

In this way, the members of Section I continued to benefit in various ways from the land owned by the 'Sayyids' along the migration route to the Hazarajat. More recently, however, this land has lost its value to the Durrani (in effect, it has been reclaimed by the local people for their own use) and the Sayyid households have become increasingly poor. At much the same time it was revealed publicly that the Sayyids were only Ghilzai who had falsely claimed a more prestigious identity, and there were no more marriages between them and Lineage C women. Contacts with the Alikozais have been maintained by Ibrahim and others, however. For example, Ibrahim engaged Payz Mohammad's grandson (Adam's BSS) to an Alikozai girl, while Sinjit villagers have sometimes gone to the Alikozai villages to find temporary work.

Sultan's marriage to the Sayyid girl did not bring him the sons he desperately wanted, while his second wife, the beloved Shaperey, was dying of tuberculosis. Right after her death in 1941 he took a further wife, an unattractive girl, but one who he hoped would prove fertile, from another Ishaqzai subtribe, several households of which were at that time Maduzai clients. Sultan paid some 8,000 Afs. as brideprice and the wedding was held a few months later. She at last bore him sons. Affinal ties through her proved unimportant, for her agnates grew further impoverished and moved away. Years later, when one of Sultan's sons wanted to marry a girl from his *mamakhel*, they refused him; partly because they

Figure 16 Section I and the 'Sayyids'

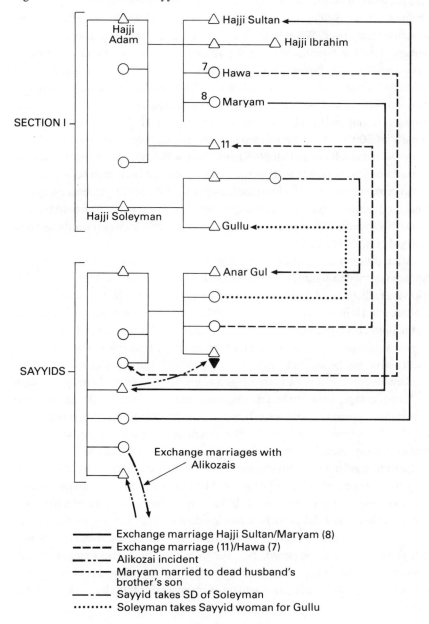

Exchange marriage Hajji Sultan/Maryam (8)
Exchange marriage (11)/Hawa (7)
Alikozai incident
Maryam married to dead husband's brother's son
Sayyid takes SD of Soleyman
Soleyman takes Sayyid woman for Gullu

disapproved of Sultan's various intrigues, and partly because the son, like his mother, was rather simple-minded.

Apart from his efforts to beget sons, Sultan was now active in attempting to establish his position as a leader to rival his uncle Soleyman. In 1946 Soleyman made a gesture of retirement by going on pilgrimage to Mecca. Sultan took the opportunity to do himself a service: he engaged one of Soleyman's sons, Shirin, to a daughter of his (Sultan's) friend, a wealthy man of another Ishaqzai subtribe from Maymana. Sultan argued that Shirin was wild and would cause trouble if he remained unmarried. When Soleyman returned, he apparently did not oppose the engagement, but determined to use the wedding as an occasion for a final fling in his own name. The brideprice paid was a substantial 30,000 Afs. and he spent many times that amount on the celebrations. The wedding was held in the steppe between Saripul and Maymana, and people came from both places, including the Ishaqzai Khans and the Hakim of Saripul; moreover, Hajji Soleyman organized a party of 300 women who formed a breath-taking procession on more than a hundred camels. It is said that the Khans' envy was aroused, while some people cursed Soleyman, saying that such a wedding had not been seen before. Sultan today remains in touch with his friend. They exchange costly presents every few years and recently, during a bad drought, Sultan's flocks were taken to Maymana to use his friend's pastures. The eldest son of the marriage was recently married to a girl of his *mamakhel*.

After this wedding, Hajji Soleyman retired as leader of Lineage C and apparently tried to assume the non-competitive role of respected Hajji and elder. However, there were continuing confrontations between him and his nephew Sultan, and Hajji Soleyman continued to be active in section affairs, as well as maintaining his reputation for lavish hospitality, until his death in 1961. Meanwhile, as one of the wealthiest men of the Lineage, Sultan was also one of the most active, but he was not a man of great political courage or cunning, and his nephew Ibrahim, whose early marriage and growing number of sons were much to his advantage, began to be known as the leader of Section I. Ibrahim's own career did not begin auspiciously, however, and he had to 'waste' two of his own children's marriages early, in the settlement of a sordid dispute, which also caused the first breach in the relationship between him and Sultan.

Ibrahim was friendly with the wife of an agnate from Section II, and in 1946 they were suspected of having an affair. Her father-in-law Seyf Jan questioned her about the rumours, whereupon she flew into a fury and struck at him with a knife, slashing his wrist. Somehow this incident became public knowledge, and Ibrahim was compromised. A *jirga* was assembled. Ibrahim denied all responsibility for what had happened, but Sultan bowed to public opinion, which favoured Seyf Jan, and gave Ibrahim's second daughter (37) to Seyf Jan's grandson, threatening to have Ibrahim sent on military service if he did not agree to the match.

Some years later, after Seyf Jan's death, his grandson went to *bazi* with his bride and his father Mohammad Amir asked for the wedding to be held. Ibrahim simply refused. Eventually another *jirga* was called, and the elders said that Ibrahim was right, 'the marriage would never have good taste' if he were forced to give his daughter away free. Mohammad Amir was a poor man and it was clear that he should give a girl to one of Ibrahim's sons. This he was most reluctant to do, and only after great efforts on the part of the elders was the second engagement arranged: one of Mohammad Amir's daughters, Mabi (see p. 219), was given to Ibrahim's second son (36). The first marriage was eventually completed in 1954, but the very small wedding was boycotted by Ibrahim himself. Some seven or eight years later the second couple reached puberty, and now Mohammad Amir refused to give his daughter, saying with some justice that his family were the injured party and yet they had received no compensation from Ibrahim: he insisted that a *sar* be paid for Mabi. This Ibrahim refused to pay, and in the end it was Sultan who paid the 10,000 Afs. which Mohammad Amir demanded. Ibrahim held the wedding for his second son (36) in 1962, and took the opportunity to put on a spectacular feast. Eighty *sirs* of rice were bought, a cow was killed to feed the guests, three pairs of pipes and drums announced the wedding, and *buzkashi* was played all afternoon. It remains the biggest wedding that any Maduzai has put on.

A few years after the original scandal occurred, another marriage was made which I think was related to it: in 1949, Sultan married Ibrahim's eldest sister (28) to one of Seyf Jan's sons for a small brideprice. Sultan gave the cash part of this (5,000 Afs.) to Ibrahim, but kept the sheep himself, further antagonizing Ibrahim and his mother.

Ibrahim never liked Sadozi, the woman he had married the night his father had been killed in the feud, and he sought a second wife. His plan to marry the Sayyid widow had been a fiasco (p. 256), but in 1950 he contracted a most extravagant second marriage. He fell in love with Molayem, the daughter of Mullah Daud, the leader of Lineage D, and arranged to pay a brideprice of 25,000 Afs. for the girl. But, before the engagement ceremony could be held, he learned that Purdil Khan, the Maduzai Khan, was himself going to bid for the girl and it was rumoured that the Khan was willing to pay up to 70–80,000 Afs. in brideprice. Ibrahim decided to go ahead with the engagement ceremony as planned; but he and his representatives were astonished when, once the ceremony had begun, Mullah Daud completely disregarded their previous negotiations and declared publicly that either he was given one lac in brideprice (100,000 Afs.) or the engagement was off. Shamed by the prospect of having his proposal rejected, Ibrahim immediately agreed to pay the quite unprecedented sum. When Sultan, who had been away at the time, returned to hear of the engagement, he was furious, both at the amount and because he had not been consulted as Ibrahim's senior agnate.

Soon afterwards Mullah Daud's son accidentally killed a Parsiwan servant, and Mullah Daud incurred huge expenses in his consequent dealing with the Ishaqzai Khans and the government. Even if, as is likely, he had intended to waive part of the brideprice, he was now obliged to demand it in full. Mullah Daud received 25 sheep, 3 guns (worth 5,000, 8,000, and 15,000 Afs. respectively) and 58,000 Afs. in cash from Ibrahim. Sultan came round to seeing the importance of supporting his nephew, and contributed a horse worth 5,000 Afs., while one of the Ishaqzai Khans applauded Ibrahim's audacity in the face of his own leader, Purdil Khan, and gave a *buzkashi* horse worth 10,000 Afs. In the end, Mullah Daud received some 101,000 Afs. as brideprice for Molayem. The wedding, held in early 1953, was a great celebration sponsored by Ibrahim's affines from the Ishaqzai Khan family. This extravagance was appropriate from Ibrahim as an emergent leader, particularly as his marriage to the girl was seen as a coup against the Maduzai Khan. Nonetheless the amount of brideprice paid was widely resented. Even though inflation in the previous thirty years meant that the 7,000 Afs. given by Sultan for his third wife was now considered a paltry sum, one lac was deemed greatly excessive, particularly for a girl who was neither distant nor judged to be beautiful. As one man said, 'At that time there were no one-lac women; for one lac a man could get or give six women.' Other people were now obliged to ask comparable amounts for their daughters or risk disparagement. In spite of further considerable inflation, brideprices nowadays are still based on the standard set by Ibrahim's second marriage, and the resentment remains.

A further consequence of Ibrahim's marriage, and of the negotiations and difficulties leading up to it, in which he had become involved on behalf of his new wife's father, Mullah Daud with both the Maduzai and the government, was that in 1955 Ibrahim was appointed official headman of Sinjit. When this happened it was clear that Ibrahim's public activities would dominate other concerns of his household, and that the partition of the household was overdue.

His uncles (10) and (11), both now married and with children, formed one new household; another was formed by his half-brothers (26) and (27), while Ibrahim and his family stayed with his mother and one unmarried sister in 'Adam's house'. In fact, at this time, Ibrahim moved out to a lone house on the far side of Chinar from Sinjit, where he cultivated lands he owned jointly with his uncles and half-brothers. A major advantage of this situation, he said, was that the house lay on the path along which any travellers between the Maduzai villages and the town of Saripul must pass, and indeed he entertained lavishly throughout the twelve or thirteen years he stayed in this spot, while not at all losing touch with affairs in Sinjit.

Sultan's retirement
Ibrahim's second marriage also marked his clear ascendancy both over his close agnates of Section I and indeed over the lineage as a whole. Sultan seems to have

accepted the prospect of Ibrahim's leadership with equanimity, for his was still much the wealthier household, and there was no doubt that his advice and support would be needed by his nephew.

Sultan turned to the task of completing a series of marriages of the young women living in his household. In 1945 his daughter (13), who had been engaged in the feud, was married. Some time shortly afterward, the daughter (24) of his brother Dost Mohammad (3), engaged in infancy to a son of Soleyman, was also married. Dost Mohammad had been determined to give his daughter without brideprice, but even among close kin it was now felt to be shaming to give or take a woman for nothing whatsoever, and a horse worth 1,000 Afs. was given for her. Sultan had raised Dost Mohammad's orphaned daughters but he had also taken all their patrimony and so he refused the animal, giving it to Ibrahim and his brothers. Then in 1953 Sultan engaged Dost Mohammad's last daughter (25), a lovely girl, to his own sister's son in section IV (p. 000). Sultan was wealthy and generous with his close kin, and he gave her for a token brideprice of only 15,000 Afs. of which he had taken only some 5,000 Afs. when the marriage was completed two years later.

At about this time too, he got Ibrahim's sister (29) married from his own house. Ibrahim's new bride Molayem fought fiercely with her mother-in-law, who received little sympathy from her love-struck son. When (10)'s wife produced twins, the old woman was asked to come and help nurse them, and she moved into (10)'s house where she lived until her death. When she left Ibrahim's house, her remaining unmarried daughter (29) was left there without support and she happily joined Sultan's household where there also lived two of Dost Mohammad's orphaned daughters. As she had left her brother's household in strained circumstances and as Sultan had no authority to marry her off, she had remained unwed for some seven or eight years after puberty. Then a once-wealthy man of Lineage D approached Sultan about her as a bride for his eldest son. Sultan spoke to the girl's mother, and together they eventually managed to persuade Ibrahim that the girl must marry. He agreed to a brideprice of 40,000 Afs. for her, and insisted on taking the whole amount in spite of the fact that Sultan was to marry her from his house.

Finally, Sultan engaged (14), the second of his own daughters by his beloved second wife Shaperey, to the eldest son of an agnate in Section II: he took some 40,000 Afs. in brideprice. In 1955, after these marriages were completed, Sultan made the pilgrimage to Mecca and people thought he would retire and join Soleyman as a respected senior elder of the lineage; but this did not happen.

Almost immediately after his return he had the opportunity to acquire a fifth wife, the widow of an agnate of Section IV. She was not young but was much respected, and Hajji Sultan hoped she would bear him more sons – his sons by his fourth wife seemed, to his great disappointment, to be taking after their somewhat weak-minded mother. The widow refused to marry her husband's brothers because of their poverty, and looked for support to her own brother, of Section III. Sultan paid the latter a *sar* of 8,000 Afs., giving only 3,000 Afs. to the men of Section IV. Soon after this confirmation of their weakness – no one was prepared to help them enforce their rights – they left the subtribe and migrated to a distant province. The widow however died only two years later of typhoid.

Then Hajji Sultan became involved as a mediator in a complicated dispute between men of Sections II and IV. To settle it he presumed on the goodwill, or malleability, of his own close agnates and usurped their right to control the marriages of women in their own households. The resentment and anger this provoked caused Hajji Sultan to be brought back squarely into the affairs of the section, and it marked a turning point in his own attitude to marriage and the control of women. Though he had in the past used his wealth through the idiom of marriage to validate his claims to high status *vis-à-vis* outsiders to Lineage C, within the group of his agnates he had in fact been quite consistent in his willingness to use his money and the marriages he controlled to facilitate good relations within the lineage. By the end of this dispute with his kinsmen, however, Hajji Sultan's attitude had changed and, as his kinsmen now say, he became tough and uncompromising in his affairs. I feel sure that his change in attitude reflected a much more widespread change in the importance of marriage in Maduzai politics at this time.

The dispute began with a question of inheritance (see Figure 17). When his younger brother Mamur died, Mohammad Amir, the leading man of Section II, took the widow as his third wife. As the woman was part of the patrimony which belonged properly to Mamur's young son, Darey, whom he had taken into his own household, Mohammad Amir promised to give the boy one of his own daughters, Mustan. After some years had passed, however, two brothers from Section IV approached Mohammad Amir for the girl, requesting that she should be married to Jamaluddin in exchange for his brother Kamaluddin's daughter Spin, who would be given to Darey. Since Mustan had reached puberty and Darey was still a child, this arrangement seemed a good one, and an engagement was planned for the two couples.

The very night before the ceremony was to be held, Padshah, brother of Jamaluddin and Kamaluddin, was discovered secretly visiting the widow of Patih Mohammad, FBS of Mohammad Amir. Padshah was caught and beaten, but in the excitement the widow managed to escape to Padshah's house, where she 'called out' for him, saying he was her husband.

All the latent hostility between the two Lineage C factions now came to the fore and only the swift intervention of Hajji Abdul Manan, leading man of Section III of the lineage, prevented them from fighting. Hajji Abdul Manan's intermediate position between the two factions, both genealogically and spatially, aided him as a peacemaker. But perhaps even more important were the roles of both Padshah's and Hajji Abdul Manan's wives. Padshah's wife

Figure 17 Kamaluddin and Zillaha

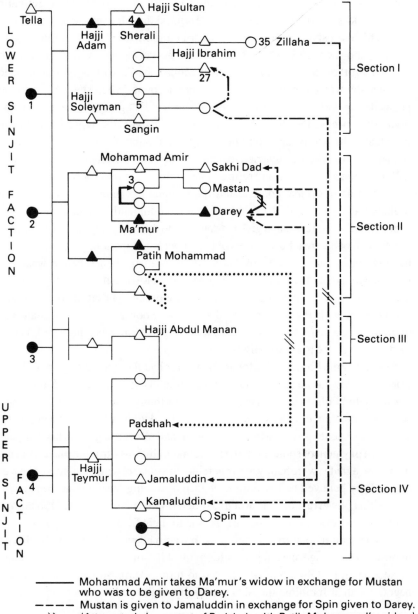

———— Mohammad Amir takes Ma'mur's widow in exchange for Mustan
who was to be given to Darey.
– – – – Mustan is given to Jamaluddin in exchange for Spin given to Darey.
•••\\\•••• (Attempted elopement of Padshah with Patih Mohammad's widow).
– – – – Darey dies, his widow Spin is given to Sakhi Dad.
—\\— Sangin's daughter promised to Kamaluddin by Hajji Sultan.
—••— Sangin's daughter given to (27)
—•— Hajji Ibrahim's daughter (35) given to Kamaluddin by Hajji Sultan.

belonged to the Lower Sinjit faction of the lineage and she was doubly eager, both to avoid having a co-wife and out of loyalty to her own kin, to get Patih Mohammad's widow out of her house. Hajji Abdul Manan's wife was in fact Padshah's own sister, several times described to me as a good and intelligent woman, and she seems to have been an ideal go-between between her husband and her brother. She approached Patih Mohammad's widow and demanded whether she wanted men to be killed on her account. When she was unable to persuade the widow to return to her dead husband's agnates in Section II, she invited her to leave Padshah's house and come and live with Hajji Abdul Manan. Eventually the widow agreed to this course, and a month later, in Hajji Abdul Manan's house, she was married to her dead husband's brother, though she was still frightened for her life and refused to go to live with him for over a year.

All of this of course complicated the original exchange planned between Mohammad Amir and the brothers Kamaluddin and Jamaluddin. At first Mohammad Amir refused to give his daughter to them at all, saying that this case was typical of the treachery of men of the Upper Sinjit faction, but after a year of negotiations, again directed by Hajji Abdul Manan, the exchange was confirmed. Mohammad Amir took 12,000 Afs. *sar* for Mustan, ostensibly because she was the older of the two girls, but in fact as some compensation for Padshah's involvement with Patih Mohammad's widow. Soon afterwards Mustan was married. Some years later, before his marriage to Spin was completed, Darey died. And then the trouble really began.

As head of the household, Mohammad Amir had the right to dispose of Spin, Darey's widow, as he chose, and he gave her to his own eldest son, Sakhi Dad. But Kamaluddin's own wife had died too and he thought he saw a way to get himself a second wife, or at least a brideprice for his daughter Spin, so he broke the terms of the exchange with Mohammad Amir and refused to give up his daughter without a payment of some 20,000 Afs. Kamaluddin was a trouble maker, but his own close agnates were happy to support him in a quarrel with members of Lower Sinjit. They believed he had a good chance of forcing Mohammad Amir, who was neither powerful nor of a particularly determined nature, to pay. Mohammad Amir too saw this was the case, and he sought help from other members of his faction. He could not turn to Ibrahim, with whom he was already involved in an unpleasant exchange marriage (the aftermath of Ibrahim's affair with the woman of Section II, p. 258), so he was forced to turn to Hajji Sultan, a far less able negotiator than Ibrahim, and also one easily frightened by determined opposition.

Sultan's intervention in the case was strikingly unsuccessful. First it would seem that Kamaluddin pleaded with Sultan that he be given Sultan's sister (5)'s daughter, the granddaughter of Soleyman, and Hajji Sultan eventually agreed, saying that Kamaluddin was *qaum*, not a stranger, and he could have her. After she was promised, Hajji Sultan apparently expected Kamaluddin to complete the exchange of his daughter Spin with Mohammad Amir's son without further ado. But not only did Kamaluddin continue to insist on the 20,000 Afs. *sar* for his daughter (which Mohammad Amir eventually had to pay) but he also seized on Sultan's promise of (5)'s daughter and pressed for the girl's proper engagement to him. The girl's father, Sangin, was furious with Sultan, saying, 'What right has he to give my daughter, just because she is his sister's daughter? I'm not going to give her up, she's mine.' And he promptly engaged the girl to Sherali's youngest son (27). At this, Kamaluddin became even more bellicose and uttered all kinds of threats which would lead to government involvement, while Sultan for his part became even more determined to placate Kamaluddin. To this end he promised him another girl, this time Ibrahim's eldest daughter (35). Ibrahim apparently agreed to this arrangement only with the greatest reluctance, out of 'respect' for his uncle, and he was furious with Kamaluddin and determined to take every Afghani of the *kotara* brideprice of 60,000 Afs. Even then, Ibrahim put off the wedding and started on the spring migration (1958), hoping to postpone it a few months longer, but Kamaluddin's caravan followed close behind. Ibrahim's anger was such that he delegated responsibility for the wedding to his eldest son and left for town. That very night the *nikah* ceremony was performed and the two caravans moved off in separate directions the next morning. People say, with hindsight, 'Kamaluddin was happy to have got a wife, but his house would never be lucky because of his behaviour.' After the bad winter of 1971–1972, his household was in fact reduced to real poverty.

Meanwhile Hajji Sultan also engaged his eldest son (18) to Soleyman's daughter by Adam's widow. The girl was beautiful and clever, and Hajji Sultan gave a brideprice worth 75,000 Afs. for her. Both the *khoshey* and the wedding were extravagant celebrations, and when the marriage was completed in 1961 Hajji Sultan again hoped to retire as an elderly Hajji, like Soleyman (who died the same year). He hoped that (18) would take over his duties as household head. This did not happen, and Hajji Sultan continued, as he does now, in the anomalous and resented position of an elderly man who is still politically active.

In the dispute just described, Hajji Sultan was clearly revealed as an ineffectual and easily frightened man, and soon men from Section IV tried to take advantage of him. Again the case was a complicated one in which Hajji Sultan interfered in the affairs of another household of close agnates, that of his brother's sons Agha Mohammad and Gul Mohammad (26 and 27), and increased his agnates' hostility towards him (see Figure 18).

As we have seen, Soleyman's son Sangin, in order to avoid giving his daughter to the rogue Kamaluddin of Section IV, had promised her to his WBS Gul Mohammad (27). Gul Mohammad and his brother Agha Mohammad (head of their household) decided that rather than pay brideprice for the girl they would give Agha Mohammad's young daughter Guldasta (33) to the girl's younger brother Nadir in an exchange, and pay 20,000 Afs. *sar* so that Gul Mohammad could marry his bride right away. This was arranged and Gul Mohammad was soon married (1956). But, in the meantime Hajji Samad from Section IV had been pressing Hajji Sultan to give his eldest daughter (15) by his third wife to his (Samad's) eldest son. Again as with Kamaluddin, Hajji Sultan casually agreed to consider the possibility of the marriage, while apparently never intending that it should be arranged, but Hajji Samad considered it a promise and began to threaten him. Hajji Sultan's wife, a very determined woman, refused to give the girl there and arranged with Sangin to give her to Nadir in place of Guldasta (33), giving the latter to Hajji Samad's son for a brideprice of only 12,000 Afs. Agha Mohammad was furious, but he was persuaded to accept this interference as the privilege of Hajji Sultan, his senior agnate. His daughter was married in 1963.

It later emerged that Hajji Sultan had never intended that his daughter (15) should be part of the exchange with Gul Mohammad's bride, and he refused to let her go unless his third son received in exchange Sherap, another daughter of Sangin. People were outraged at this subversion of the agreement, and Sangin's wife (Hajji Sultan's sister, 5) flatly refused to give her daughter to him, saying that she had anyway nursed Hajji Sultan's son, so the couple, as milk-siblings, could not marry. Hajji Sultan claimed he was giving (15) away free, since she had been part of an exchange involving another household and that anyway Sangin had already received a high *sar* for his own daughter.

If Soleyman had been alive, he might have forced a compromise, but at the *jirga* which was eventually convened the elders told Sangin's wife that she was behaving shamefully to her brother and that she should give her daughter to his youngest son (21) instead. Hajji Sultan was instructed to pay a brideprice for the girl. With much ill-feeling, the settlement was agreed.

Once his sister's daughter, Sherap, was engaged to his son (21), Hajji Sultan allowed his own daughter (15), to be married to Sangin's son Nadir. Since then, however, both his sister and Sangin have died, and Hajji Sultan tried to force their sons to give his niece free, as if it had been an exchange marriage with his daughter (15). Public opinion was strongly against him, but he avoided paying any brideprice for the girl, Sherap, who was approaching twenty years of age, while his son (21) was still a child. Sherap felt that her brothers cared nothing for her happiness, and she despised them for their inability to force Hajji Sultan to pay a brideprice for her.

Omar, Sherap's older brother and the household head, was due to leave for military service in the autumn of 1971, and was anxious to see her married before he left, for he was afraid that she might 'do a Kaftar' and elope once he had gone, and the household was left in the control of his weak younger brother Nadir. But he was equally determined to extract a brideprice from Hajji Sultan, who was of course in no hurry to marry his young son. In a way, Omar was right in his fears about Sherap's disloyalty to her brothers' household, for she became involved in the 'brothel' (p. 000) after he had gone. But worse, in Omar's absence Hajji Sultan decided to pay a brideprice and hold the wedding. First he got his daughter (15), Nadir's wife, to trick Sherap and bring her to Hajji Sultan's house; once she was thus compromised, he was able to shame her brother Nadir into an agreement. Hajji Sultan gave some 10,000 Afs. and some orchard land above Saripul as brideprice, and held the wedding quickly in spring 1972. His daughter has now realized that she and her weak husband Nadir were duped by Hajji Sultan and that, among other things, they had accepted the orchard they coveted without getting proper deeds for it. To secure any claim to it they will have to turn to Ibrahim, who has already demanded half of it if he is to help.

Figure 18 Khani Agha and Guldasta

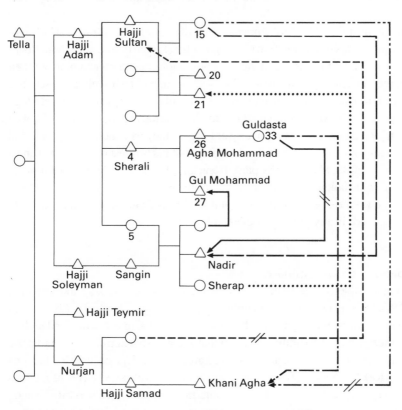

--- Samad's sister refused by Sultan.

——— Exchange marriage – 27/33 to a son and a daughter of Sangin, 33's marriage not completed.

—··— Samad wants 15.

—— In the exchange, 33 replaced by 15.

—·— 33 given to Samad's son, Khani Agha.

········ 21's wife Sherap claimed as exchange for 15 – small brideprice paid.

After the marriage which led to the dispute just described, Agha Mohammad and Gul Mohammad made two further marriages. Soon after he had been forced to accede to Hajji Sultan's arrangement for his first daughter's marriage to Hajji Samad's son of Section IV, an arrangement which he continues to resent deeply, Agha Mohammad's second daughter (32) was born. His sister soon arranged her engagement to her own infant son (FZS/MBD) for a very small brideprice. However, she soon died and the household became increasingly impoverished and her son turned out to be a feckless youth, while Agha Mohammad's daughter grew into an intelligent, beautiful and hard-working young woman. Agha Mohammad has been loath to let his daughter go to such an indigent household and an unattractive young man, while he and his father were desperate not to lose such an attractive bride; the situation, which led to machinations on the part of both households, was unresolved at the time of our departure (see N. Tapper 1979: 294ff.).

In the meantime Gul Mohammad's wife died after only a few years of marriage, and he had quickly to find himself another, for the brothers had both flocks and farmland and needed to divide the household in summer to manage their resources efficiently. The new bride was the daughter of an impoverished Ishaqzai from Maymana who had come to Saripul explicitly in order to get a high brideprice for his beautiful daughter. She had various suitors from Sinjit, who were rejected either for their poverty or because they were already married, and in the end Agha Mohammad's suit on behalf of his brother was accepted and a brideprice of 80,000 Afs. was paid. Ironically, her old father then went off to Kandahar and bought himself a virgin Durrani bride for a tenth of that sum. Since that time (1960) Agha Mohammad and his brother Gul Mohammad have not been involved in any more marriages.

Ibrahim's affairs, continued

Having completed the marriage exchange of his second son and daughter (p. 259), Ibrahim next acquired a wife for his eldest son (34). His FZ (2), married to a very wealthy man of Section IV (p. 218), made the match with her daughter Shiri (see also Case 5), telling Ibrahim that she was so determined on it that she 'would steal from her husband and give half of the brideprice herself'. In fact a brideprice of some 60,000 Afs. was fixed. The marriage was between the factions of Lineage C, but (2) was able to act as intermediary, and there was little tension during the year's engagement; as people say, 'the marriage was between close kin'. Ibrahim was let off paying some five sheep and 5,000 Afs. of the brideprice, and a very large trousseau was prepared for Shiri.

Ibrahim had probably planned to hold a lavish celebration, but Shiri became pregnant and the preparations had to be rushed. Only once the wedding celebrations had begun did Shiri's father make known his demand for *babirey*. He declared that he would not let her go unless he was given Ibrahim's expensive rifle or some 18,000 Afs. in lieu of it, and the wedding festivities were stopped until Ibrahim eventually produced the gun (he bought it back some years later for 14,000 Afs.). Shiri was then married, and she bore a son in her husband's house three days later. In fact her father was very fond of her and each year he gave her and her children presents of clothing and animals: and when her household separated from Ibrahim's, it was done with her father's encouragement and generous contributions to the household supplies; quite regularly he would send them rice, tea and other foodstuffs as well as cloth and other household goods – until Shiri's sudden death in 1971. Shiri's husband was away on military service when she died, and before he had even learned of her death his independent household was reabsorbed into the household of his father, Hajji Ibrahim.

Meanwhile, Ibrahim inadvertently acquired a third wife, an Uzbek widow from a village near Maduzai land in the Saripul piedmont. He had been a friend of her husband, after whose death he continued to visit their house. This was shocking to the Uzbeks, who met Ibrahim and a companion on one of their visits and threatened their lives, severely beating the companion and forcing Ibrahim to marry the widow, to whom he had 'given a bad name'. She knew no Pashtu, and was unhappy in her new home; eventually she returned to visit her agnates and was allowed to remain there. Ibrahim never sought her return, and the separation was considered permanent and tantamount to a divorce, though she was still spoken of as his wife.

Around the same time (about 1960) the first engagement to unite Ibrahim and his uncle Hajji Sultan was contracted (see Figure 19). Sultan gave a daughter (16) to Ibrahim's first son by his second wife, Molayem. The boy (39) died of small-pox a few years later, and Ibrahim wanted to transfer the bride to Nik, his third son (38) by his first wife, but this was not to be. On the one hand, the girl's mother flatly refused to give her daughter to one of the sons of Ibrahim's first wife, who she said was dirty (she was certainly unfavoured in Ibrahim's household), and on the other, the dead boy's mother Molayem insisted that the widow should either go to her second son, an infant, or be married far away. She too was adamant that 'her bride' should not be given to any of her co-wife's sons. Then, without con-sulting Ibrahim, Hajji Sultan engaged the girl without any brideprice to Hajji Soleyman's principal heir, Gullu, whose own wife had just died. The young girl was delighted with this arrangement, and the marriage was completed a year or so later (1965); and Hajji Sultan was, in fact, given some 10,000 Afs. and a pistol so that the girl couldn't be said to have been taken 'for free'. Ibrahim was incensed by this marriage, and re-opened a land dispute with Hajji Sultan, based on their patrimony in Adam's estate. Relations between uncle and nephew deteriorated, and they remained estranged for several years.

Ibrahim was accustomed to visiting and acting as scribe for one of the Ishaqzai Khans. A few years ago he managed to purloin some deeds from the latter and thus to transfer a large amount of his land in the Hazarajat to the Maduzai Khan, who with the support of the Maduzai *wolus* could probably defend this land against both the Ishaqzai Khans and the Hazaras. Also working for the Khan as his overseer was a Pashtu-speaking Parsiwan who learned about Hajji Sultan's wealth and prosperity from the Khan. The latter urged the overseer to marry his lovely daughter to one of Hajji Sultan's sons. The man agreed that it would be fine to have such people as affines, and he 'forced his daughter' on Hajji Sultan, offering her free to his second son (19). Hajji Sultan in fact paid a brideprice of 30,000 Afs. for her and decided to hold a lavish wedding celebration. Ironically, the deceived Khan's son, not yet aware of Ibrahim's theft, allowed the wedding to be held at his home and sponsored it generously (though I do not know what motive he had in so doing). This marriage (in 1969) was a success, and as a result Hajji Sultan tried to mend the differences between Ibrahim and himself. It was at this time that he and Ibrahim exchanged dwellings, so that Ibrahim now moved back into Sinjit village.

Hajji Sultan arranged for Hajji Soleyman's only remaining daughter to be married to Ibrahim's third son Nik (38), to whom he had earlier refused his own daughter. On the same day, Sultan's own daughter (17) was engaged to Ibrahim's second son by Molayem (40). The engagement ceremonies were thoroughly muddled, and witnesses are not at all clear what brideprices were promised by whom. Some say that Nik's marriage to Gullu's sister is an exchange with the marriage of Hajji Sultan's daughter (16) and Gullu (see above); while Gullu himself argues that his sister was given for a *mahr-e mosamma*. Ibrahim insists that he agreed to a *kotara* brideprice of 70,000 Afs., and taking advantage of Gullu's departure on two years' military service in 1970, he paid about half this amount for Gullu's sister and took his son to *bazi* in the summer. There was similar disagreement between Hajji Sultan and Ibrahim over the brideprice in the marriage of (17) and (40); then Ibrahim and Hajji Sultan's son (18) came to blows over a separate issue, whereupon Hajji Sultan absolutely refused to give (17) unless he were given another girl in exchange.

Early in 1971 at the age of 48, Ibrahim relinquished the post of headman and went on the pilgrimage to Mecca. On his return he expected to renounce competitive activities for the status of elder, and indeed practically the first move he made as a Hajji was to arrange the exchange marriage which Hajji Sultan wanted. Now the marriage of (17) and (40) forms part of an exchange by which Hajji Ibrahim's young daughter (41) is to go to Hajji Sultan's eldest son (18), whose first wife has failed to produce sons. Only with the greatest difficulty was this agreement reached: only Hajji Sultan's gift to Hajji Ibrahim of a *sar* (*sic* – actually a huge bribe) of some 21 *jeribs* of valley land, the ownership of which they had disputed, clinched the deal. Even then, to the astonishment of witnesses, Hajji Ibrahim asked 300,000 Afs.(!) as a brideprice for his daughter in case the other bride died, showing his continued resentment of Hajji Sultan. However, the importance given to this exchange was made clear by the numbers of men who came to witness the engagement, among them the Maduzai Khan. The ceremony was held in spring 1971, and a few weeks later, when the wedding celebrations were held for Hajji Sultan's daughter (22) to one of Hajji Soleyman's grandsons, members of the two households joined in the preparations.

The two houses are now said to be reconciled, though it is doubtful whether this will last. Among other things, Hajji Sultan is worried that he may die before his son (18)'s marriage is completed (his bride is only about nine years old), and that Hajji Ibrahim will take the opportunity to make further trouble. Hajji Sultan considered that a marriage for brideprice between his third son (20) and Hajji Ibrahim's next youngest daughter (42), who is about six or seven, would encourage Hajji Ibrahim to complete the exchange if he should die. Hajji Ibrahim,

Figure 19 Marriages between the households of Hajji Sultan and Hajji Ibrahim

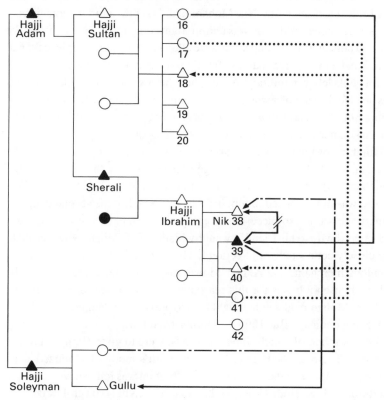

──────── 16 given to 39 for brideprice
          39 dies; the widow (16) is to be remarried to 38; Hajji Sultan breaks
          16's engagement and gives her to Gullu.
─ · ── Soleyman's daughter given to 38 in ?exchange for 16. Brideprice paid.
········· 17 given to 40 in exchange for 41 given to 18.

however, flatly refused this, saying he would never settle a dispute by giving two girls for one in return.

Hajji Ibrahim's son Nik (38)'s marriage with Gullu's sister is also likely to bring him into conflict with the Hajji Soleyman branch of Section I. Nik had separated from his father and joined his elder brother (34)'s household; then in summer 1971, soon after Shiri's death, he learned from his own bride that she was pregnant. Nik has been going to *bazi* less than a year, and without the approval of her brother and guardian Gullu, and moreover the terms of the brideprice were in dispute. Not only that, but Nik was himself due to go off on two years' military service in less than a month's time. Nik feared that both Hajji Ibrahim's and Gullu's anger would be formidable if the girl's condition were discovered. He told his mother of the pregnancy, and she pleaded with Hajji Ibrahim that their home had been desolated by Shiri's death and that Nik's bride should be brought into the household as quickly as possible. However, Hajji Ibrahim was unsympathetic to this argument, and Nik's mother said in desperation that she would help his bride abort the child. Nik Mohammad, his wife and his mother were firmly agreed that the child's life was unimportant compared with the shame, the expense and both guardians' anger if it were allowed to live; the couple reckoned they could make many more babies after they were married. The abortion was successful. Nik left for military service but the argument that his brother's orphans needed the care of a woman was genuine, and when we left at the end of the summer of 1972 Hajji Ibrahim was considering marrying Nik's bride 'to a gun' (p. 164), since Nik had another year's service to go.

Hajji Ibrahim meanwhile had antagonized his other uncles by attempting, like Hajji Sultan, to interfere in their marriage policies. Akhtar Mohammad (10)'s first daughter (30), promised in childhood to the son of her FZ Nanawor (6) in Lineage A, was duly married to him in 1970 (p. 255). But his second daughter (31)'s marriage was not so successful. Hajji Ibrahim arranged to give this attractive girl as third wife to his friend, a wealthy Maduzai of Chinar, who wished to become closely connected with Section I. The man had a bad reputation as an unscrupulous merchant, and Akhtar Mohammad's brother Jumajan (11), the head of the household, was for this reason strongly opposed to the marriage, while Akhtar Mohammad's wife fought hard to prevent her daughter from being married polygamously. But Hajji Ibrahim's friend was willing to pay over 100,000 Afs. for her, of which some 7,000 Afs. were to go to Hajji Ibrahim as match-maker. This was the twin girl Hajji Ibrahim's mother had nursed as an infant (see p. 261), and on these grounds Hajji Ibrahim was felt to have a claim to some of the brideprice. Both Akhtar Mohammad and his new son-in-law became worried that Hajji Ibrahim and Jumajan might insist on a higher brideprice, and the wedding was quickly completed in summer 1971 while both the latter were in the mountains.

Apart from the household of Hajji Ibrahim's eldest son, now in a very difficult position after Shiri's death, the other four households of Adam's descendants are now divided from each other by a history of quarrels over marriage and the division of their patrimony. In spite of his attempt to withdraw from active village politics after his pilgrimage to Mecca, Hajji Ibrahim is unlikely to do this for many years. Hajji Sultan is now very old and may not live much longer, while his sons remain ineffectual. Hajji Ibrahim's household should continue to grow and, particularly in view of the recent exchange marriages, Hajji Ibrahim will probably acquire control of Sultan's household and property. Meanwhile the two fraternal households, those of Hajji Ibrahim's uncles and his half-brothers, are unlikely to be partitioned for many years: so far the undoubted antagonisms between each pair of brothers have been kept under control and each household needs all the male labour available to it. Thus in Agha Mohammad's household there is so far only one son, and Agha Mohammad and his brother depend on each other's labour, while in the other household Akhtar Mohammad himself has five still unmarried daughters and his brother six sons, and they realize the strong position this combination of children puts them in. On the proceeds of his daughter (31)'s marriage, Akhtar Mohammad hopes to make the pilgrimage to Mecca and thus establish himself as an elder of equivalent status to Hajji Sultan and Hajji Ibrahim.

Personal biographies and intra-lineage competition
In the narrative, the careers of two men, Hajji Sultan and Hajji Ibrahim, are of particular importance. Sultan was already married before the Maduzai emigrated to Turkistan in about 1917. In the early years after their arrival, when the Maduzai generally had little interest in agriculture, Sultan shrewdly bought two mills and a number of tracts of farmland, and he soon became very wealthy; today his household is still the wealthiest of all in Lineage C.

Sultan was apparently never particularly ambitious politically, but his wealth established him as a leader in Lineage C and certainly in Section I. Very early he became known for his generous and conciliatory nature and his willingness to use his wealth to appease his opponents rather than confront them. Such attitudes were not inappropriate in the early decades in Turkistan when the population was small and resources accessible to all. But pressure on resources grew and the Maduzai became increasingly competitive, and this was reflected both in the greater use of marriage to focus economic and political competition and also in certain changes in marriage forms.

Sultan's own attitude to marriage did not change so quickly, and he was made to look foolish and weak on a number of occasions when he became involved in marriage arrangements. Not only did he allow himself to be taken advantage of, but he also assumed that the earlier openness between households of close agnates continued, and he blundered badly when he interfered with the marriage arrangements of other households. He did learn from his mistakes, however, and in recent decades has become known as hard and grasping, even to the extent of tricking his own daughter to gain his ends. I think there is no doubt that the change in Sultan's attitude to marriage, which others discussed quite explicitly, reflects, at the level of the individual, the increasing competitiveness the Maduzai in general now experience.

The second man, Hajji Ibrahim, is quite different in temperament and character from his uncle, and his career reflects this clearly. Before he reached puberty his father Sherali was killed, leaving him a married man and head of an independent household, and he fathered two sons before he was twenty. This early start in adult life was in many ways an undoubted advantage from which Ibrahim had the intelligence, ambition and ability to profit. As a young man he showed that he possessed diplomatic skills and courage and determination in the face of opposition; at the age of thirty he became headman of Sinjit village.

Nowadays people say that Sultan was a frightened man of whom every wolf took advantage. But, they say, when Ibrahim grew up and became known by the government officials, no one could take advantage of him. He became a strong man. As the Sinjit headman, Ibrahim is involved in a wide variety of political activities. He is leader of the Sinjit *wolus*, sometimes *vis-à-vis* the government, sometimes against the Chinar *wolus* led by the Maduzai Khan, though this latter kind of confrontation is just as often seen in lineage terms, in which Ibrahim represents Lineage C against the Khan and Lineage A. Within Lineage C, Ibrahim acts as the leader of the Lower Sinjit faction. In the winter settlement, Ibrahim's house is literally at one end of Sinjit village, the furthest from those of the opposing faction who live at the other end of Upper Sinjit. Ibrahim is nowadays the most powerful man within Section I.

In the early years of Ibrahim's rise to power, he and Sultan were allies. Then, when Ibrahim's involvement in a scandal became public, Sultan proved himself extremely sensitive to public opinion, and on the grounds of his seniority settled the quarrel by arranging an exchange marriage involving Ibrahim's son and daughter. Sultan's intrusion into Ibrahim's household arrangements began a quarrel which continues today. Behind the quarrel lie disputes over inheritance and the differences in wealth between the two households, but these issues have rarely been explicit, rather, relations between them have always been couched in the idiom of marriage. This became dramatically clear after an engagement arranged between children of the two houses was broken in 1964. From then until 1972, the four further marriages arranged between the two households simply cannot be understood without direct reference to the broken engagement and the grievances which grew out of it.

Marriage forms and political rivalry
The narrative demonstrates, first, the extent to which a marriage may be contingent on those which have preceded it, and secondly, the great variations in

content which may exist between marriages even of the same form. The first point is amply illustrated by sets of marriages – between Lineages A and C, between factions of Lineage C, and between households of Section I. In some, friendship and the most positive aspects of kinship and affinity have been stressed, while other sets began in an atmosphere of hostility which was perpetuated in further marriages.

The variation between marriages is also amply demonstrated. In this respect, four marriages are of particular note. Thus, two marriages which occurred over thirty years apart, in which Sultan and Ibrahim each keenly sought a particular bride for whom an unprecedentedly high brideprice was asked, not only confirmed the political leadership of our protagonists, Sultan and Ibrahim, and validated the Maduzai identity of Lineage C, but also set new standards of brideprice payments which lasted for decades. These two marriages were undoubtedly extraordinary in Maduzai eyes. To the outsider, they vividly demonstrate the relationship between personal biography, upward social mobility and marriage.

The first of these marriages was that of Sultan and Shaperey in the year the Maduzai arrived in Turkistan; the second was that of Ibrahim to Molayem, some thirty-five years later. For Sultan the brideprice was set as a challenge to prove his equality with his proposed affines, members of Lineage A. In effect, the successful completion of the marriage payments erased (for a considerable time) the stigma of Lineage C's possible Parsiwan origins and confirmed their status as a bonafide section of the Maduzai subtribe. Ibrahim's marriage was a further episode in the relations between Lineage C and Lineage A. Ibrahim was in competition with the Maduzai Khan for the girl and in his case too the high brideprice was to test his equality with his rival.

It is likely that neither of the brides' guardians ever imagined that the respective brideprices could be agreed to, let alone paid, but they were, and in each case wealth was converted to prestige by the groom and his family, and defined the groom as one of the leaders of both lineage and section. Ibrahim's marriage also led directly to his election as the headman of Sinjit village. In retrospect, each man is seen by others of Lineage C to have acted as representative for all men of Lineage C against their Lineage A rivals, who claimed for themselves superior status but who found this denied and the equality of the two lineages affirmed by these marriages.

But perhaps the most important and striking aspect of these two marriages is the way they set standards of brideprice payments which thereafter remained unchanged for many years. The information at hand, which is slight, indicates that over the half century since the arrival of the Maduzai in Turkistan, there has been a rise in average brideprices by a factor of about 100, and that prices of irrigated land, and of wheat, have risen by the same factor; though, people say, prices of animals have not risen quite so much. But, while land, grain and livestock prices have risen fairly smoothly and in line with national and international supply and demand, brideprices have been influenced by sudden radical changes in standards. Thus, on the Maduzai arrival, the standard brideprice is said to have been 500–600 Afs.; the new standard of 7,000 Afs. then set by Sultan was not exceeded until the rapid general inflation during the 1940s, leading to a general standard by the early 1950s of about 20,000 Afs. It was then that Ibrahim in turn, by paying one lac for the first time, set the new standard which was still observed in 1972.

Furthermore, the personal appearance and behaviour of Shaperey and Molayem had an effect on the ideals and practices relating brideprice to desirable qualities in a wife. Molayem at least also became a fashion leader among Maduzai women; for example, the clothes she wears reflect both her husband's wealth and status and her own high status within the household, and create new criteria by which honour may be evaluated.

Though each of these two marriages set standards of brideprice which lasted decades, the information I have on brideprices which were paid after Sultan's marriage suggests that there was far more variation and leeway in the definition of an acceptable brideprice in the earlier period than there was after Ibrahim's marriage to Molayem. Ibrahim's marriage occurred around the time that competition for resources within the subtribe began to become acute. As a reflection of this competition, brideprices too seem to have become more strictly managed to conform to a single standard. In these new and more precarious times, individual household heads sought, through brideprices, to confirm their equality with other households of the lineage, while revealing less of their differences. As we have seen, perhaps the most remarkable thing about the recent Lineage C brideprices is their relative uniformity. Nowadays, men constantly compare their situation with that of other households, and their daughters with those of other men, and they feel compelled to seek brideprices which express their commensurate status or risk ridicule and dishonour.

By the same token, it is possible that women's behaviour has also changed and become more circumspect. People describe Shaperey as fun-loving as well as clear-headed and articulate; she clearly had a considerable freedom to participate in the politics of the subtribe. In these respects, she seems far more like Kishmir, the women's headman, than Molayem, Shaperey's later counterpart. Today, however, Kishmir is exceptional, and her outspokenness and participation in the wider affairs of the subtribe are regarded as somewhat aberrant and due to her marginal status as an independent, widowed household head. By contrast, Molayem, though also clever and quick-witted, is not a dynamic personality in the public arena – whether at weddings or in mixed gatherings at home. Rather, her activities and interventions occur almost entirely on the domestic front, where she acts as Ibrahim's closest friend and advisor. It is possible that the increasing control of women in marriage has also led to a certain 'domestication' of women, such that secure and successful wives, like Molayem, find that acceptable personal power is best achieved through a discrete, matronly role.

Other kinds of variation relate to the festivities surrounding marriage, which may be either very extravagant or wholly absent. The feud marriages discussed in chapter 5 provide clear examples of the latter situation, while two other marriages, that of Hajji Adam's daughter Shaista (9) which was managed by Sultan, and that of Shirin, Hajji Soleyman's son, indicate the close connection between political claims and conspicuous consumption in marriage.

In the first of these two marriages, Sultan, acting for his father, insisted that the Ishaqzai Khan who fell in love with Shaista pay a very high brideprice for his sister. There was no question about the high status of the prospective groom, quite the contrary; the high brideprice was demanded to dispel any suggestion of the inferiority of Sultan and Lineage C in general. The large and impressive trousseau Shaista took with her was another way in which Sultan claimed high status for himself and his family. From the marriage Sultan gained both wealth and honour, and he and his family have fostered their affinal ties with the Khankhel with great care, and have been able to use them for specific economic and political ends.

Shirin's marriage, though different again in its arrangements and consequences, is fundamentally a variation on the same themes. Shirin's wedding is famous even today for the grand scale of the celebrations. These had nothing to do with the character of the relations between the parties to the marriage, but were provoked by the interference in the arrangement of the marriage by Shirin's FB Sultan. Shirin's father Hajji Soleyman financed the lavish celebrations and gained considerable regional renown. Like Hajjis Sultan and Ibrahim after him, Hajji Soleyman had apparently intended to retire from political life after his pilgrimage to Mecca, but in his case too his own close agnates were the first to attempt to exploit his wish to their own advantage and interfere with the affairs of his household. His reaction was a dramatic statement of his political autonomy and, indeed, the marriages which followed Shirin's were directly determined by the political role Soleyman continued to play, by exploiting both his wealth and his religious stature.

As is the case with these four notable marriages, the many other insights we may derive from the extended case history can, in the first instance, only be understood contextually. However, with sufficient detailed material of this kind, it is possible to generalize about the complex structure and process of Maduzai marriage and the ideology of control which informs it.

12

Durrani marriage – conclusions

In this ethnography of Durrani marriage I have treated marriage from a number of different angles. The variety of strategies I have employed in my presentation may be summarized in terms of three rather different emphases: first, a focus on the complexity of marriage choice and the specificity of each marriage; second, the nature of the ideology of control which embraces all aspects of Maduzai social relations; and third, the effects of the wider environment on competition among the Maduzai.

Each marriage makes a complex statement about social relations and involves a large number of people in many different kinds of social activity. This inevitably means that any discussion of marriage based on classification into particular modes (such as brideprice marriage or direct exchange) or in terms of the ties it creates within or between groups (cousin-marriage, intra-lineage marriage, interethnic marriage, etc.) is bound to be simplistic. For example, an exchange marriage between the houses of close agnates who are both poor and in need of wives differs greatly in both causes and implications from an exchange marriage arranged to settle a dispute between two powerful households. They differ in the way the exchange is arranged, in the quality of the affinal ties created, in the extent to which the marriage celebrations may be used to gain prestige, and so on.

In other ways too, each marriage differs from every other: in duration, in fertility and in terms of wider economic and political importance. Thus, a successful, fertile marriage which links opposing factions of a lineage and lasts twenty or thirty years will have a very different effect on the individuals involved and on lineage factionalism from, say, a marriage between close agnates which lasts only a few years and from which there is no issue.

Of course these differences are relevant to marriage in any society, but it seems clear that the more central the institution of marriage in a society as a vehicle for both engineering and symbolizing economic and political change, the more important these issues become. The extended narrative is intended to reveal just such subtle, and less subtle, variations in the form and content of different marriages and to examine their wider implications.

The second reason for turning to the extended narrative is perhaps more important, since it touches on an area in which marriage among the Maduzai is fundamentally different from marriage in many other societies. In my account, the historical perspective has been one of 'social change'. That is, I have discussed changes in marriage forms and practices which have taken place over the last fifty years and offered explanations for them in terms of other changes in social organization and environment which have taken place concurrently.

However, the extended narrative also allowed me to consider how history, in the sense of a sequence of specific perceived events, impinges directly on each marriage. In some societies – in parts of my own, for instance – most marriages can be treated as isolated events. The marriage choices of my siblings, cousins and friends may create an atmosphere which influences the type of marriage partner I will seek, but it is most unlikely that they will directly affect my choice of a specific individual. In other societies – especially those where marriage choices are prescribed or preferred – marriages, far from being isolable events, are all part of a much wider set of relations between social groups. In theory, and to a considerable degree in practice, they are themselves relatively uniform and predictable building blocks of such relations.

But marriage among the Maduzai fits neither of these models. Among the Maduzai, qualitative differences between individual marriages reflect and/or affect the political role of those marriages. Moreover, few marriages are isolable and lead to no subsequent marriages. And, finally, the patterns which build up from a series of marriages are not uniform but highly varied. This is partly because the Maduzai operate a complex system of marriage choice, but also because marriage is used to express many different kinds of values and facts of Maduzai social life. Each marriage is embedded in the particular social, and especially marital, histories of the households involved: disputes may lead to marriages and then to further disputes, or marriages may lead to friendship and then to further marriages, and so on (cf. Bourdieu 1977: 66f.). In other words, marriages are an integral part of on-going political relations at all levels of social organization from the household to the ethnic group, and they are as much the cause as the consequence of political activity.

Marriage and exchange

The ultimate goal of all social activity among the Maduzai may be seen as political and economic security (social production) and continuity (social reproduction). Members of each household seek freedom from extreme economic privation and political oppression in this world, religious merit enough to allow them hope for the next, and the prospect of immortality through legitimate descendants.

The heaviest expenses any household has to bear are those concerned with marriage. In other words, production is directed largely towards reproduction – towards acquiring wives, who will produce sons, who will produce labour and political support in defence of productive and reproductive resources, especially land and women. Daughters, though of less direct value to their natal household as producers and reproducers, are useful in exchange for wives, or for acquiring brideprices which help toward acquiring wives. Control of all resources is understood in terms of responsibility and honour. We can view the real inequality in this system as a spiral whereby the weak lose control of resources of all kinds, lose honour and become weaker still, while the strong gain control of resources, gain honour and become stronger. And yet this inequality and competition are balanced by an alternative ideology of religious and tribal equality, also seen in terms of responsibility and honour. Both equality and competition are expressed through the complex idiom of marriage. The various elements on which security depends can be related graphically, as in Figure 20.

This is of course a crude representation of a complex set of relations and suffers from two important faults. First, it does not illustrate the spiral of relations through time. The fierce competition between ethnic groups in Afghan Turkistan encourages Durrani, when considering relations among themselves, continuously to shift perspective between the alternative values of hierarchy and equality. Synchronically, it is this interplay between contradictory values which is of interest. Viewed diachronically, however, the alternative ideologies implicit in the structure may be realized, and the status and ethnic identity of both individuals and groups may change over time. Thus exchange marriages of recognition may be used to achieve and simultaneously to confirm Durrani identity, while the original Durrani migration to the north of the country, where the Durrani as a minority had to close ranks to establish their control of resources, seems directly to have encouraged an emphasis on the value of the equality (and hence unity) of all Durrani. The opposite pattern is also found – both individuals and groups can lose Durrani status. It seems that such identity is often lost when oppressed households leave an area and migrate to a distant part of the country. So too, I would argue, without interethnic rivalry in Turkistan, competition between Durrani would have long since led to the formation of a class division between Durrani landowners and a landless Durrani peasantry. There is historical evidence that, in some areas of southern Afghanistan where Durrani form a dominant majority, such classes have existed and are associated with a process whereby landless Durrani eventually lose effective Durrani identity (see N. Tapper 1981: 406 n. 7).

A second failure is that the flow diagram seems to suggest that all elements in the system are commensurate and that conversions between any two of them are of equal value. In fact, the different elements and the exchanges involving them are hierarchically ranked. That is, the four elements (men as producers; women as reproducers; productive resources and valuables; and produce) are ranked and form, analytically, four spheres of exchanges, while the element of cash is separate and anomalous (see N. Tapper 1981: 406 n. 8). Exchanges are correspondingly ranked; conveyances within each sphere rank according to the rank of the sphere, while conversions upwards bring honour and those downwards dishonour, depending on the distance between the spheres involved.

Men are ranked highest; direct exchanges between them include the most honourable and manly of all activities: vengeance and feud, political support and hospitality and the practice of sanctuary. These three activities are the basis of the famous code of Pashtunwali (cf. Janata and Hassas 1975) whose principles, though not formalized among the Maduzai, are nonetheless conceptual keys to honour and the ideology of control.

Women belong to the second sphere. Maduzai women are often treated exclusively as reproducers and pawns in economic and political exchanges. However, there are clear taboos on the explicit recognition of this fact; for example, it is virtually unthinkable that women might alienate resources from the household or ethnic group; similarly, the Durrani explanation of compensation

Figure 20 Household honour and control of resources

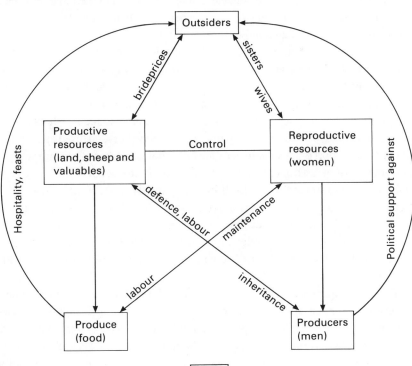

marriage does not include the idea that the women thus given bear 'replacement men' for the victim's group. By focusing on women's informal, day-to-day contacts with men, men and women soften the harsh, narrow view of women's position which they both explicitly accept. This view is in fact supported by an examination of the women's limited involvement in productive activities, by the stereotypes of women held by both sexes, and by certain aspects of the women's muted models of themselves, as in their susceptibility to spirit possession. Women are exchanged by men directly through the highly valued direct exchange forms of marriage. The other main conveyance within this sphere centres on the preparation of trousseaux, which is, in fact, the only productive work for which women of different households co-operate. The trousseau itself is the most important marriage prestation which women manage, securing status recognition both for themselves and for the bride in her marital home.

Exchanges of productive resources, especially of land and animals, and valuables, form a sphere in which the equivalence of various items has more to do with the social relations between givers and receivers than with market values. This is perhaps most appropriately shown in the composition of a brideprice. Sheep are frequently sold in the local market as a strictly economic activity. However, when sheep are accepted as part of a brideprice, it is usual for them to be given for a fixed cash value which is usually less than half their market value. Sometimes, however, the real value of a brideprice may be altered to benefit the groom by assigning a high relative value to the sheep.

Land and valuables are also treated in a special way. It is of the greatest importance to the subtribe that land should never be sold or mortgaged to outsiders, and indeed none has been alienated in this way, though individuals have bought considerable tracts of land from one another and from members of other ethnic groups. Similarly the loan or gift of expensive animals, such as horses and camels, and luxury goods, such as guns and even jewellery, are used as gestures of political support or friendship between households; all these items are acceptable for inclusion in a brideprice. Ideally, such items should not be, and only very infrequently are, traded in the local market. Equally, certain large items of a trousseau including some carpets and rugs may be bought in the bazaar, but they will not be sold again once they have been given as part of a marriage.

Finally, market values are relevant in direct exchanges in the fourth sphere – the barter of produce – which is a frequent but low status activity associated with the poor.

The only proper conversion between the first two spheres occurs when women are given in compensation for a killing or injury. The meaning is highly ambiguous, but essentially the honour goes to the killers who have 'taken' a man and 'given' only two women. Bride-service, though uncommon, is another form of conversion between the spheres of men and women: a household gives a man's labour in exchange for a woman. This may occur when a wealthy household with too little male labour agrees to marry a daughter to an impoverished but able young man prepared to work as a client. He may gain status, and perhaps wealth, through direct association with his affines. To the observer, brideservice provides a clear example of a status change effected through marriage. However, Maduzai themselves often instance such cases to support their belief in the basic equality of all Durrani, whether rich or poor, as potential marriage partners. Marriage for brideprice is among the more obvious forms of conversion between spheres. A woman is given in exchange for productive resources, valuables and cash, thus clearly compromising the honour of the wife-givers, who are very unwilling to take goods from the even lower sphere of produce (e.g. by accepting grain as a substitute for some part of the brideprice), while upward conversion redounds to the honour of the wife-takers. Other conversions present a consistent picture: it is dishonourable to sell one's labour for recompense in any form, while it is honourable to employ labour, to have clients and dependants, people to whom produce is given in return for their labour.

The anomalous factor in all this is cash. Strictly speaking it operates as a medium of exchange with all spheres and as a store and measure of any kind of value, but basically cash is low-status, and sometimes regarded as even lower than the sphere of produce. Thus exchanges of cash for cash, as in gambling and money-lending, are among the most dishonourable and stigmatized of activities. However, most of the time Maduzai treat cash as of two distinct kinds: 'small money' used in the sale and purchase of produce, and 'thousands' (literally 1,000-Afghani notes) used obligatorily whenever cash is given as part of a prestige exchange for productive or reproductive resources. Thus the cash portion of a brideprice is negotiated and paid in 'thousands' and though only women are acceptable as compensation in a Durrani homicide, 'thousands' may be given to compensate victims of other ethnic groups.

All the exchanges mentioned so far are evaluated in terms of that part of Durrani ideology which relates to competitive honour and status inequalities. Other exchanges may be deliberately removed from this context and placed explicitly in that of religious honour and tribal egalitarianism. Most typical of these are acts of charity and hospitality towards the weak, while most spectacular are the *mahr-e mosamma* marriage contracts, conceived in terms closely approximating Sahlins' notion (1974) of generalised reciprocity (just as *kotara* contracts resemble the negative form and exchange marriages the balanced form of reciprocity).

Virtually all but the simplest exchanges may be interpreted in a variety of contradictory ways, and there are many ways in which the meaning of an exchange may be modified – as by the time lapse between gift and counter-gift, or by the relative status of the parties involved. An elaborate sequence of exchanges, such as in marriage, provides many opportunities and many ways of making statements about social status. The fact that each household must control items from each sphere means that it must inevitably become involved in conversions from one sphere to another.

Every household is continually involved in competition for the control of resources and prestige, and its *de facto* independence from interfering outsiders (and thus its honour) is continually tested in exchanges. In fact no one but the socially or physically destitute convert their resources downward without a cogent explanation of their motives, and an account of their expectations and various gains. However, they will be believed by others only if there is no doubt that they are operating from strength, not weakness. When Durrani marriage is viewed as part of the exchange system as a whole, its centrality as an institution becomes clear; so too do the means and ends for which marriage can be manipulated. The variety of contextual interpretations of any Durrani marriage relate ultimately to the values given the items exchanged: men, women, productive resources and valuables, and intangibles such as prestige and political support. The relations between these items of exchange are the basic units of a language in which claims to status can be made and refuted, while the occasions of marriage provide frequent public opportunities for such dialogues.

Marriage, competition and the wider environment
Among the Maduzai, marriage and the control of women are defining criteria of only two specific groups in the society – the household and the Durrani ethnic group as a whole. These are not only the key elements ideologically, but they are also important units in the practical control of resources. In particular, there is a considerable degree of power located with the household head, while the degree to which a household is expected to control its women and the marriages of all its members is a fundamental element in the determination of prestige and the control of resources. However, Maduzai emphasis on individual, independent households, and the actual power of household heads, can be misleading, unless household relations are understood in a wider social context.

Thus, the idioms of responsibility and honour and shame, used to sum up all those elements which determine the total status of individuals and households, derive their meaning from the nexus of relations between households and the wider environment. In this respect, household autonomy is more apparent than real and the ideologically distinct unit of the 'household' owes its existence to external demographic, economic and political considerations. It also depends on the ideology of patrilineal descent and its relation to both customary inheritance patterns and the actual constitution of political groups. In this respect, the structure and process of Maduzai marriage as I have described it can be understood in terms of the relation of population to resources as refracted through three further cultural biases: first, the ego-centred networks of kin and affines which derive from non-exogamous lineage organization; second, the fragmentation of landholding which is associated with the rules of Islamic inheritance; and third, the tendency to social differentiation as expressed in marriages for brideprice. In these areas, we can see that the character of the institution of Maduzai marriage has changed over time.

A model of the past

Northwestern Afghanistan is generally acknowledged to be among the richest agricultural areas of the country, yet towards the end of the nineteenth century great stretches of fertile land there lay unused. The local communities had been weakened and depopulated by a long series of internecine wars before Afghan rule was established, by cholera epidemics and famine, especially in 1871–1873, but perhaps most drastically by the Turkmen slave raids which were continuous throughout much of the nineteenth century. By 1880, the northern frontier districts were virtually deserted and the once-populous settlements north and west of Maymana were abandoned. To the northeast, in the plains of Afghan Turkistan, there was a similar dearth of population, both in the cities and in the countryside, in which, according to Yate, 'the supply of water was far in excess of present requirements, and cultivators were the only thing wanting' (1888: 134–135). As Peacocke observed, 'granted only a sufficient population, a very few years would suffice to develop the plains of Afghan Turkistan into a granary that would quite eclipse that supposed to be afforded by the Herat Valley' (1907: iv). Amir Abd al-Rahman (1880–1901) determined to repopulate these waste-lands, and in this he succeeded. The history of the Maduzai migration to Afghan Turkistan and the process by which they became owners and then cultivators of irrigated land is part of this story. And during the ensuing decades, both the population of the subtribe and that of the region as a whole expanded apace.

Stirling has suggested two 'ideal-type' models of household developmental cycles in Turkish villages which can be adapted to help explicate the Maduzai case. The first model, 'Land in plenty', approximates the circumstances in the period when the Maduzai first began to settle and farm in Turkistan, when a land surplus was associated with social mobility within the community and marriage forms coincided with economic conditions in a way which facilitated the leadership of 'big-men'.

As sons grew up, the household was able to expand both its livestock and landholding. Male labour was the key to this expansion and as

the wealth controlled by the head increased, the surpluses produced by each constituent element were pooled in his hands, and the whole unit benefited by efficiency in proportion. The head might well join the village leaders . . . or even become the most influential among them (Stirling 1965: 136).

Sons tended to marry later, after which they separated from their father's household, the livestock they took as anticipatory inheritance enabling them to set up their own establishments. However, joint pasture-rights and co-operation in herding units allowed sons to continue to benefit from economies of size, while such agricultural land as they worked continued to be owned and controlled by their father. Yet on the father's death,

each son would inherit only approximately as much land as he himself had been plough-ing. Every new household, born out of the splitting of a large one, would thus start with the same amount of land, whether it sprang from a household with only one male heir, or one with ten. Each young household head would depend on his own procreative prowess, skill, hard work and luck to build for himself a position of prominence in his later years (p. 137).

Of course, things were never quite so simple. But in the early years in Saripul, inherited wealth counted for less among the Maduzai than did luck and skill. Indi-vidual men could improve the standing of their households. And, among other things, householders used exchange and brideprice marriages to recruit Durrani and non-Durrani clients respectively to the *wolus*.

In short, the Maduzai situation can be partly understood in terms of Chayanov's analysis of a peasant economy in which 'labour, proportionate to the size of the family, is the stable element which determines the change in the volume of capital and land'. Thus, 'any working family unit able to control the amount of land for use can increase its labour productivity' (Kerblay 1971: 154); as a family matures, the area it cultivates expands. Clearly, the stable, if cyclical, peasant economy described by Chayanov's model is particularly appro-priate for regions with a low population density where peasant households can buy or take more land. In turn the peasant economy, based on readily available land, determines other patterns of social intercourse which are culturally specific.

In the Maduzai case, this situation is related to the stress on egalitarian political forms whose locus was the ethnic group as a whole, an open, agonistic system of status competition expressed through the idioms of responsibility, honour and shame, and an absence of formalized leadership positions complemented by a system of *jirga* assemblies. It was also related to the relative latitude of brideprice payments and the absence of strict, formalized controls on the exchange of women between households, in addition to the use of marriage to recruit political support. Moreover, though the value of women was as reproductive resources, it seems likely that women themselves may have had a degree of freedom of move-ment and expression outside the domestic setting which reflected the relatively relaxed ethos of the early period.

However, as Sahlins puts it, 'each political organization harbors a coefficient of population density, thus, in conjunction with the ecological givens, a deter-minate intensity of land use' (1974: 131). With the natural increase of population in Turkistan came concomitant changes in economic and social relations.

Present competition

Boserup's (1965) model of economic development treats population growth as the independent variable which plays a major role in determining agricultural change as well as the intensification of other cultural features. As both the Maduzai and regional population expanded and the demand for irrigated valley land increased, Stirling's second model of household development helps to explain the new situation.

> ... sons are still as much desired as ever. They are still a source of prestige ... [and] form an armed guard for the defence of the household, and they enable father to take his ease. [Those who can] not be absorbed as extra labour on the household lands could increase household income as labourers, servants, shepherds or migrants. But when household land does not expand in proportion to the male labour force, fission leaves each son with less land than he is capable of working. One or two may succeed in acquiring extra ... by purchase or by simple appropriation. But over the whole village, in two or three generations, many households will be reduced to poverty (1965: 140–141).

Again, things are not so simple. But, in spite of Maduzai efforts to offset the new pressures, the development of the now great inequalities between Maduzai households owes much to the increased importance of landowning in conditions of land shortage. Among the Maduzai, land use intensified and diversified, subsistence techniques were refined, and migration to less populous areas of the country became a common default strategy of the landless poor. Moreover, in recent decades, other social dimensions of this process have become evident in both the external and internal relations of the subtribe.

As we have seen, Durrani have always defined the ethnic boundary between themselves and others in Turkistan in terms of the control of women and marriage. This cultural bias has grown in importance in recent years as inter-ethnic competition has increased. It is elaborated, for instance, in the way Durrani explain their uniformly high brideprices in terms of the ideal of Durrani equality and as a means of differentiating themselves from all other local ethnic groups.

Equally, as households have become more obviously enmeshed in increasingly complex exchange relations with other households, so marriage and the control of women have become more important as a means whereby a household can make a statement about its relative autonomy. Symbolic forms have been elaborated, but so too have practical marriage strategies evolved in the face of the increasing competition. Maduzai now stress the unity of the household, and arrange the earlier marriage of sons while no longer practising anticipatory inheritance: paternal or fraternal joint households have become a prominent residential pattern. Moreover, agnates, even those living in separate households, now make every effort to manage inherited land jointly and to avoid land divisions, but these have nonetheless occurred. Although exchange marriages, as expressions of equality, have become more frequent and brideprices more uniform, marriage choices are now often calculated to facilitate the appropriation of land. Further, brideprices and the complexities of marriage arrangements, as well as the opportunities marriage ceremonial offers for conspicuous consumption, are used to differentiate wealthier households from the poor. Ultimately, inherited wealth in land creates a differential which the poor cannot easily overcome.

Since the advent of the Maduzai to Turkistan, the Maduzai have experienced a change from a relatively egalitarian society based on an abundance of land to one in which social rank is increasingly determined by inherited wealth in land. Emergent local leaders have manipulated social forms, such as marriage, in a way which both sustains and increases their control of productive and reproductive resources, while simultaneously representing their interests as those of the Durrani group as a whole. Until the very recent period, it would seem that the brake on the incipient class consciousness and divisions which are entailed in this process was the virulent inter-ethnic competition in the region, and indeed the country, as a whole. Only at the very time of our fieldwork was an emergent system of stratification based on social class becoming evident in Saripul for the first time, and this transition was not yet reflected in the institution of marriage.

Rather, perhaps what emerges most vividly from the Maduzai ethnography is the extent to which they now use marriages to prevent the deterioration of agnatic and other relations between the households of political rivals. Most marriages between close agnatic cousins are of this kind and often represent rather desperate attempts to prevent the complete breakdown of the relationship. The Maduzai believe that open hostility between households of close agnates over a period of time renders them vulnerable to outside interference. But, paradoxically, they are also aware that such marriages also afford close kinsmen the opportunity to gain long term advantage in competitions for control over each other's household property, especially land.

The women who are given in such marriages do of course form a link between their households of birth and marriage. But the nature of the rights and duties which are transferred at marriage, the absence of divorce, and the lack of alternative strategies for women, dictate that a woman's best interests lie in giving her first loyalty to her husband and her marital home. In confrontations where women are forced to choose between brother and husband, it is almost invariably the latter they support.

Moreover, the increasing competition expressed through marriage has had a further consequence for women. Nowadays the circumstances which lead to marriage choices themselves may determine the nature of women's loyalty to their marital home. A marriage between close agnates is often arranged as a response to a quarrel, which means in effect that a woman has been used by her father and brothers as a pawn in a power struggle. In such cases it is clear to all, especially the woman herself, that consideration about her personal happiness has been of secondary importance. Women resent being used in this way and are often very ready to transfer their allegiance to their husband. Exceptionally, a woman whose marriage fits this pattern can insist on some reconciliation between the two households, which often takes the form of a further marriage between them, but this is only possible if she is wise, determined and well-respected by her husband, and if he himself is a man to be reckoned with. If not, the pressures a woman alone can exert towards a rapprochement are likely to be ignored in favour of political and economic gains.

It is quite possible that the locus of responsibility for the control of women was not always so unambiguous and that women's ties to their natal households as agnates afforded them a countervailing power against their husbands. If this was so, women have now lost this advantage. And not only have their marriages become even more tightly regulated, but they have also become, in the wealthier households at least, more 'domesticated'. It may be that the intensity of stereotypes of women as sexually active and unreliable is related to the intensity of competition among men. It is also true that as inequalities between households increase, women of the poorer households are indeed more likely to choose to improve their personal situation by creating their own ties with wealthier and more powerful men, whether through 'calling out' and elopement or illicit liaisons before or after marriage. If this occurs, they will indeed provide models of 'the irresponsible woman', which will certainly lead to an increase in men's control of women in affluent households.

Quarrels between more distant agnates, such as the two factions of Lineage C, also result in marriages between the households of the rivals themselves, or in the manipulation of marriages of close dependent households to the same end. In all marriages between households of rivals in an agnatic lineage, whatever the exact genealogical distance between them, the same kinds of factors are relevant: the marriages are arranged to allay fears of outside intrusion in the affairs of the lineage section, rather than for positive reasons related to the ideals of agnatic solidarity.

As we saw in chapter 10, the greatest threat to the independence of a weak and vulnerable household is likely to come from their closest agnates, who are well placed to usurp their farmland or pastures. Such close kin are likely to hold and exploit such immovable property jointly, and a change in its control is easily achieved. Though such changes may not be known publicly for some time, sooner or later outsiders will learn of the usurpation, which is often revealed in subsequent marriage arrangements. Public knowledge of weakness and a lack of agnatic support will lead to more general interference. Agnates can readily find excuses to justify intervention, not least because the ideals of agnatic solidarity generally contradict those relating to household independence. The authority of senior agnates may also be invoked, as may residual rights over daughters, or widows, of men who have once been members of the same household. Finally, agnates (or others) may use sheer force, or the threat of it, to gain control of the affairs of the very weak.

The counterweight to such machinations seems to be quite simply that the total destruction of a kinsman's household results in the loss of manpower to the lineage, whether through emigration or the extreme poverty which precludes a man's marriage. In the end, the Maduzai know that the strength of any single household depends on the number of men it can muster. So strong households must balance their greed for power and wealth gained at the expense of others, against the need for manpower and allies in confrontations with more distant groups.

The situation of dependant agnates is virtually identical to that of clients (*hamsaya*), even though the household head may be a separated son of the 'patron' himself. Often the marriages of a dependant household are controlled by the patron to suit his purposes, while, in so far as they do manage their own marriages, clients of the same patron household often intermarry. At this point, as we have seen, the ethnic boundary is permeable in both directions: Durrani clients may easily lose their Durrani status, while non-Durrani clients of a Durrani *wolus* can, over time, become assimilated as Durrani.

Clearly, this account does not describe a process which is unique to the Maduzai. Quite the contrary: it is a process which can be glimpsed throughout Durrani history, but which has not been described in any detail at all. My account is of the distinctive cultural responses of the Maduzai Durrani to external conditions related to land availability and population pressures. My aim has been to examine the ideology and practice of marriage among the Maduzai as a system which encompasses the contradictory values of hierarchy and equality in Durrani society and to show how marriage provides the means and motive for their expression both synchronically and diachronically.

Notes

Chapter 1

1 Since the time of our fieldwork other ethnographers have published material directly relevant to our study, which is the richer for this comparative dimension. Glatzer's monograph (1977), based on a field study of Durrani Pashtuns in Badghis province to the west, was the first to fill the ethnographic gap and provides material directly comparable to that which is presented here. Other studies of Durrani have followed: particularly those by Tavakolian (in the northwest, e.g. 1984a, 1984b and 1984c).

Studies of Pashtuns in other parts of Afghanistan are more numerous: see especially the various writings of Ferdinand (1959, 1962, 1963, and 1978), Janata and Hassas (especially 1975), Evans-von Krbek (1977) and Balikci (1981); Anderson's work with Ghilzai Pashtuns in the southeast has been particularly useful (1975, 1978a, 1978b, and 1983).

Other anthropological studies of Turkistan have been done by Davidov (1976), Dupaigne (1978), Rao (1988), Shalinsky (1979), Stucki (1978) and R. and M. Poulton (1979). Barfield has published a study of Arab nomads in the northeast (1981), while Azoy's fascinating monograph on the game of *buzkashi* (1982) is relevant to many aspects of Afghan culture. The Centlivres' work on many facets of Afghan culture and social life has been invaluable (see especially Centlivres and Centlivres-Demont 1988).

Many of the anthropologists who have worked most recently in Afghanistan have contributed to one or more of the following edited volumes, which together provide the best entrée to the literature on the country: see the Danish journal *Folk* (Vol. 24, 1982) on marriage in Afghanistan; contributions to R. Tapper (1983) are by both anthropologists and historians; Shahrani and Canfield (1984), J.-P. Digard (1988) and B. Huldt and E. Jansson (1988) all offer wide discussion of the social and political circumstances of the country.

On Pashtuns in Pakistan, see Ahmed (1980, 1983), Barth (1959, 1969, 1981), Lindholm (1982), and Grima (1986) among others, while aspects of the debate concerning the historical transformation of Pashtun society are dealt with in Barth (1959, 1981), Ahmed (1976), Asad (1972), Meeker (1980), Lindholm (1982).

Chapter 3

1 In March 1988, provincial boundaries were redrawn and Saripul became a separate province made up from the southern parts of the former provinces of Jouzjan and Balkh.

2 The use of the term 'tribe' is standard in the literature for a descent group (*tayfa, qaum*) at a particular level within the Durrani genealogy: it is generally agreed that the Durrani tribes include the Alikozai, Alizai, Atchakzai, Barakzai, Ishaqzai, Nurzai and Popalzai. In their southwestern homelands, these groups have a degree of political and perhaps territorial unity comparable to that of 'tribes' described elsewhere, even though in the north they might better be seen as 'clans' or 'maximal lineages'. See Glatzer (1977: 110–118) for genealogical tables relating to Pashtun and Durrani tribal organization based on widely known historical sources as well as some information from local informants. Caroe (1965) also gives much detailed information on Pathan genealogies. However, I consider the constructed relation between tribes and the Afghan state (cf. R. Tapper 1983, 1–75 and passim) to be far more interesting than the formal genealogies *per se*.

The problem of describing the relation between genealogical divisions at lower levels of segmentation and actual people on the ground is also knotty and made more difficult by the fact that Durrani use *tayfa* and *qaum* to refer to a wide variety of social groups which have some commonality based on an ideology of descent, including all the following which I distinguish in my discussion. Thus, I have chosen to use the term 'tribal division' for all genealogically defined divisions of a tribe, while the word 'lineage' is used as a synonym for 'a local descent group' in the sense defined by Leach (1951). In turn, lineages are subdivided into branches which I have called 'sections'. One or more lineages form the core of the local political groups which I term 'subtribes'.

Chapter 5

1 A ploughland (*juft*) is reckoned, on this land, at 88 *jerib*. Technically 2 *jeribs* equal 1 acre, and 5 *jeribs* equal 1 hectare. Actually, it is the water that goes with the land which is most important. On the canal from which the original Maduzai lands are watered, one hour in each cycle of 18 days goes to every 11 *jeribs* of land. Thus land is measured in three ways: areally, by *jeribs*, in the deeds and if ever the Government should register holdings; by water allocation (which can be sold temporarily separate from the land); and by labour/animal input, i.e. by ploughlands: one *juft* ('yoke of oxen') divides into two 'cows' (*gav*) of 44 *jeribs*.

References

Abu-Lughod, L. 1986. *Veiled Sentiments: Honor and Poetry in a Bedouin Society.*
  University of California Press, Berkeley.
  1987. 'Bedouin blues'. *Natural History*, 96 (7), 24–33.
Ahmed, A. S. 1975. *Mataloona: Pukhto Proverbs.* Oxford University Press, Karachi.
  1976. *Millenium and Charisma among Pathans.* Routledge and Kegan Paul, London.
  1980. *Pukhtun Economy and Society.* Routledge and Kegan Paul, London.
  1983. *Religion and Politics in Muslim Society: Order and Conflict in Pakistan.*
  Cambridge University Press.
Anderson, J. W. 1975. 'Tribe and community among Ghilzai Pashtuns'. *Anthropos*, 70,
  575–601.
  1978a. 'Introduction'. In J. W. Anderson and R. F. Strand, eds., *Ethnic Processes and
  Intergroup Relations in Contemporary Afghanistan.* Occasional Paper no. 15. Asia
  Society, Afghanistan Council, New York.
  1978b. 'There are no *khan*s any more: economic development and social change in
  tribal Afghanistan'. *Middle East Journal*, 32 (2), 167–183.
  1982a. 'Cousin marriage in context: constructing social relations in Afghanistan'.
  Folk, 24, 7–28.
  1982b. 'Social structure and the veil: comportment and the composition of interaction
  in Afghanistan'. *Anthropos*, 77 (3–4), 397–420.
  1983. 'Khan and khel: dialectics of Pakhtun tribalism'. In R. Tapper, ed., *The Conflict
  of Tribe and State in Iran and Afghanistan.* Croom Helm, London.
  1985. 'Sentimental ambivalence and the exegesis of "self" in Afghanistan'. *Anthropological Quarterly*, 58, 203–211.
Asad, T. 1972. 'Market model, class structure and consent: a reconsideration of Swat
  political organization'. *Man* (NS), 7, 74–94.
Aswad, B. 1971. *Property Control and Social Strategies in Settlers on a Middle Eastern
  Plain.* University of Michigan, Ann Arbor.
Azoy, G. W. 1982. *Buzkashi: Game and Power in Afghanistan.* University of Pennsyl-
  vania Press, Philadelphia.
Balikci, Asen. 1981. 'Stratification and pastoralism among the Lakenkhel'. In J. Galaty
  and P. C. Salzman, eds., *Change and Development in Nomadic and Pastoral
  Societies.* Special Issue, *Journal of Asian and African Studies*, 16 (1–2).
Balland, D. and C. M. Kieffer. 1979. 'Nomadisme et sécheresse en Afghanistan:

l'exemple des nomades Paštun du Dašt-e Nawor'. In Equipe Ecologie et Anthro-
pologie des Sociétés Nomades, eds., *Pastoral Production and Society*. Cambridge
University Press.
Barfield, T. J. 1981. *The Central Asian Arabs of Afghanistan*. University of Texas Press,
Austin.
Barry, M. 1972. 'Western Afghanistan's Outback'. Unpublished manuscript. Communi-
cation Media, USAID, Kabul.
Barth, F. 1959. *Political Leadership among Swat Pathans*. Athlone, London.
    1962. 'The system of social stratification in Swat, north Pakistan'. In E. R. Leach, ed.,
    Aspects of Caste in India, Ceylon and North West Pakistan. Cambridge University
    Press.
    1969. 'Pathan identity and its maintenance'. In F. Barth, ed., *Ethnic Groups and
    Boundaries*. Allen and Unwin, London.
    1973. 'Descent and marriage reconsidered'. In J. Goody, ed., *The Concept of Kinship*.
    Cambridge University Press.
    1981. *Features of Person and Society in Swat*. Routledge, London.
Bates, D. 1974. 'Normative and alternative forms of marriage among the Yörük of south-
    eastern Turkey'. *Anthropological Quarterly*, 47, 270–287.
Black-Michaud, J. 1975. *Cohesive Force*. Blackwell, Oxford.
Bloch, M. and J. Parry, eds. 1982. *Death and the Regeneration of Life*. Cambridge Uni-
    versity Press.
Boeson, I. 1983. 'Conflicts of solidarity in Pakhtun women's lives'. In B. Utas, ed.,
    Women in Islamic Societies. Curzon Press, London and Malmo.
Boserup, E. 1965. *The Conditions of Agricultural Growth*, Aldine, Chicago.
Bourdieu, P. 1977. *Outline of a Theory of Practice*. Cambridge University Press.
Bourne, A. 1966. 'Social Organization in a Pathan District'. Three Mimeo Papers, Uni-
    versity of London, School of Oriental and African Studies.
Bradburd, D. 1984. 'The rules and the game: the practice of marriage among the
    Komachi'. *American Ethnologist*, 11, 738–753.
Canfield, R. 1973. *Faction and Conversion in a Plural Society: Religious Alignments in
    the Hindu Kush*. University of Michigan, Ann Arbor.
Caroe, O. 1958. *The Pathans 550 BC–AD 1957*. 2nd edn. Macmillan, London.
Centlivres, P. and M. Centlivres-Demont. 1988. *Et si on parlait de l'Afghanistan?
    Terrains et Textes 1964–1980*. Institut d'Ethnologie, Neuchâtel, Maison des
    Sciences de l'Homme, Paris.
Cohen, A. 1965. *Arab Border-Villages in Israel*. Manchester University Press.
    1970. 'The politics of marriage in changing Middle Eastern stratification systems'. In
    L. Plotnicov and A. Tuden, eds. *Essays in Comparative Social Stratification*.
    Pittsburgh University Press, Pittsburgh.
Comaroff, J. L. 1980. 'Introduction'. In J. L. Comaroff, ed., *The Meaning of Marriage
    Payments*. Academic Press, London.
Compagnie d'Etudes Industrielles et d'Aménagement du Territoire (CINAM). 1973.
    Services for Children within Regional Development Zones. Research and Action,
    Experimental Activities at Village Level. 3 vols. Government of Afghanistan,
    Ministry of Planning, and UNICEF, Kabul.
Davidov, A. D. 1976. *Sotsialno-ekonomicheskaya Struktura Derevni Afghanistana:
    Osobennosti Evolutsii*. Akad. Nauk S.S.S.R., Institut Vostokovedeniya, Moscow.
Digard, J.-P., ed. 1988. *Le Fait Ethnique en Iran et en Afghanistan*. Centre National de la
    Recherche Scientifique, Paris.

Donnan, H. 1985. 'The rules and rhetoric of marriage negotiations among the Dhund Abbasi of northeast Pakistan'. *Ethnology*, 24 (3), 183–196.

1988. *Marriage among Muslims: Preference and Choice in Northern Pakistan.* Brill, Leiden.

Dupaigne, B. 1978. 'Une farce turkmène d'Afghanistan: comme on marie les jeunes gens'. In R. Dor and M. Nicolas, eds., *Quand le Crible était dans la Paille.* Maisonneuve et Larose, Paris.

Eickelman, D. 1989. *The Middle East: an Anthropological Approach.* 2nd edn. Prentice Hall, Englewood Cliffs.

Elphinstone, M. 1842. *An Account of the Kingdom of Caubul.* Richard Bentley, London.

Evans-von Krbek, J. H. P. 1977. 'The social structure and organization of a Pakhto-speaking community in Afghanistan'. Unpublished Ph.D. dissertation. University of Durham.

Fallers, L. 1957. 'Some determinants of marriage stability in Busoga'. *Africa*, 27, 106–123.

Ferdinand, K. 1959. 'Les nomades'. In J. Humlum, ed., *La Géographie de l'Afghanistan.* Gyldendal, Copenhagen.

1962. 'Nomad expansion and commerce in central Afghanistan'. *Folk*, 4, 123–159.

1963. 'Nomadisme'. *KUML*, 108–147.

1978. 'Marriage among Pakhtun nomads of Kabul-Laghman area'. *Pashto Quarterly*, 2 (2), 126–133.

Galt, A. 1982. 'The evil eye as synthetic image and its meaning on the island of Pantellena, Italy'. *American Ethnologist*, 9 (4), 664–681.

Gazetteer of Afghanistan. 4th edn, 1907. Vol. II. *Afghan Turkistan.* Calcutta.

Gazetteer of Afghanistan. 4th edn, 1908. Vol. VI. *Kandahar.* Calcutta.

Geertz, H. 1979. 'The meaning of family ties'. In C. Geertz, H. Geertz and L. Rosen, *Meaning and Order in Moroccan Society.* Cambridge University Press.

Gilmore, D., ed. 1987. *Honor and Shame and the Unity of the Mediterranean.* American Anthropological Association, Washington, DC.

Glatzer, B. 1977. *Nomaden von Gharjistan.* Steiner, Wiesbaden.

Gobar, A. H. 1970. 'Suicide in Afghanistan'. *British Journal of Psychiatry*, 116, 493–496.

Good, B. 1977. 'The heart of what's the matter: the structure of medical discourse in a provincial Iranian town'. Unpublished Ph.D. dissertation. University of Chicago.

Grima, B. 1986. 'Suffering as esthetic and ethic among Pashtun women'. *Women's Studies International Forum*, 9 (3), 235–242.

Hart, D. M. 1985. *Guardians of the Khaiber Pass.* Vanguard, Lahore.

Holy, L. 1989. *Kinship, Honour and Solidarity.* Manchester University Press.

Huldt, B. and E. Jansson, eds. 1988. *The Tragedy of Afghanistan.* Croom Helm, London.

Hunte, P. 1985. 'Indigenous methods of fertility regulation in Afghanistan'. In L. Newman, ed., *Women's Medicine: A Cross-Cultural Study in Indigenous Fertility Regulation.* Rutgers University Press, New Brunswick, New Jersey.

Jamous, R. 1981. *Honneur et Baraka.* Cambridge University Press.

Janata, A. and R. Hassas. 1975. 'Ghairatman – der gute Pashtune – Excurs über Grundlagen des Pashtunwali'. *Afghanistan Journal*, 2 (3), 83–97.

Jansen, W. 1987. *Women without Men.* Brill, Leiden.

Joseph, R. and T. B. Joseph. 1987. *The Rose and the Thorn: Semiotic Structures in Morocco.* University of Arizona Press, Tucson.

Kakar, H. 1971. *Afghanistan: a Study in Internal Political Developments, 1880–1896.* Kabul.

1979. *Government and Society in Afghanistan. The Reign of Amir ʿAbd al-Rahman Khan.* University of Texas Press, Austin.

Kerblay, B. 1971. 'Chayanov and the theory of peasantry as a specific type of economy'. In T. Shanin, ed., *Peasants and Peasant Societies.* Penguin, Harmondsworth.

Leach, E. R. 1951. 'The structural implications of matrilateral cross-cousin marriage'. *Journal of the Royal Anthropological Institute,* 81, 23–55.

1957. 'Aspects of bridewealth and marriage stability among the Kachin and Lakher'. *Man,* 57, 50–55.

Lewis, I. M. 1962. *Marriage and the Family in Northern Somaliland.* East African Studies, 15. Kampala.

1986. *Religions in Context.* Cambridge University Press.

Lindholm, C. and C. Lindholm. 1979. 'Marriage as warfare'. *Natural History,* October, 11–20.

Lindholm, C. 1982. *Generosity and Jealousy: the Swat Pakhtun of Northern Pakistan.* Columbia University Press, New York.

Marx, E. 1967. *The Bedouin of the Negev.* Manchester University Press.

Meeker, M. 1976. 'Meaning and society in the Near East: examples from the Black Sea Turks and the Levantine Arabs'. *International Journal of Middle East Studies,* 7, 243–270 and 383–422.

1980. 'The twilight of a south Asian heroic age: a rereading of Barth's study of Swat'. *Man* (NS), 15 (4), 682–701.

Munson, H. 1984. *The House of Si Abd-Allah.* Yale University Press, New Haven.

Needham, R. 1971. 'Remarks on the analysis of kinship and marriage'. In R. Needham, ed., *Rethinking Kinship and Marriage.* Tavistock, London.

Ortner, S. and H. Whitehead, eds. 1981. *Sexual Meanings.* Cambridge University Press.

Papanek, H. 1973. 'Purdah: separate worlds and symbolic shelter'. *Comparative Studies of Society and History,* 15, 289–325.

Pashtu Qamus, 1330–1333/1952–1954. Two volumes. Kabul.

Pehrson, R. 1966. *The Social Organization of the Marri Baluch.* Compiled and analyzed from his notes by F. Barth. Wenner-Gren, New York.

Peters, E. 1960. 'The proliferation of segments in the lineage of the Bedouin of Cyrenaica'. *Journal of the Royal Anthropological Institute,* 90, 29–53.

1963. 'Aspects of rank and status among Muslims in a Lebanese village'. In J. Pitt-Rivers, ed., *Mediterranean Countrymen.* Mouton, Paris.

1965. 'Aspects of the family among the Bedouin of Cyrenaica'. In M. Nimkoff, ed., *Comparative Family Systems.* Houghton Mifflin, Boston.

1967. 'Aspects of the feud among the camel-herding Bedouin of Cyrenaica'. *Africa,* 37, 261–282.

1976. 'Aspects of affinity in a Lebanese Maronite village'. In J. Peristiany, ed., *Mediterranean Family Structures.* Cambridge University Press.

1980. 'Aspects of Bedouin bridewealth among camel herders in Cyrenaica'. In J. Comaroff, ed., *The Meaning of Marriage Payments.* Academic Press, London.

Pitt-Rivers, J. 1965. 'Honour and social status'. In J. G. Peristiany, ed., *Honour and Shame.* Weidenfeld and Nicolson, London.

1977. *The Fate of Shechem or the Politics of Sex.* Cambridge University Press.

Poulton, M. and R. Poulton. 1979. 'Ri Jang: un Village Tajik dans le nord de l'Afghanistan'. Unpublished Ph.D. dissertation. 3 vols. Ecole des Hautes Etudes en Sciences Sociales, Paris.

Rabinow, P. 1977. *Reflections on Fieldwork in Morocco*. University of California Press, Berkeley.

Rao, A. 1982. *Les Gorbat d'Afghanistan*. Editions ADPF, Institut français d'iranologie de Téhéran, Paris.

Rawlinson, H. 1841. *Report on the Dooranee Tribes*. Political and Secret Memoranda – A2, India Office Library, London.

Rogers, S. C. 1975. 'Female forms of power and the myth of male dominance'. *American Ethnologist*, 2, 727–756.

Rosen, L. 1985. *Bargaining for Reality*. University of Chicago Press.

Sahlins, M. 1974. *Stone Age Economics*. Tavistock, London.

Salzman, P. C. 1978a. 'Does complementary opposition exist?' *American Anthropologist*, 80, 53–70.

1978b. 'Ideology and change in tribal society'. *Man* (NS), 13, 618–637.

Seddon, D. 1976. 'Aspects of kinship and family structure among the Ulad Stut of Zaio rural commune, Nador province, Morocco'. In J. Peristiany, ed., *Mediterranean Family Structures*. Cambridge University Press.

Shahrani, N. and R. Canfield, eds. 1984. *Revolutions and Rebellions in Afghanistan*. Institute of International Studies, Berkeley.

Shalinsky, A. 1979. *Central Asian Emigres in Afghanistan: Problems of Religious and Ethnic Identity*. Occasional Paper no. 19. Asia Society, Afghanistan Council, New York.

Shepherd, G. 1987. 'Rank, gender, and homosexuality: Mombasa as a key to understanding sexual options'. In P. Caplan, ed., *The Cultural Construction of Sexuality*. Tavistock, London.

Stirling, P. 1965. *Turkish Village*. Weidenfeld and Nicolson, London.

Stucki, A. 1978. 'Horses and women: some thoughts on the life cycle of Ersari Turkmen women'. *Afghanistan Journal*, 5 (4), 140–149.

Tapper, N. 1968. 'The role of women in selected Islamic pastoral societies'. Unpublished M.Phil. thesis. University of London.

1973. 'The advent of Pashtun *maldars* in Northwestern Afghanistan'. *Bulletin of the School of Oriental and African Studies*, 34 (1), 55–79.

1977. 'Pashtun nomad women in Afghanistan'. *Asian Affairs*, 8 (2), 163–170.

1978. 'The women's sub-society among the Shahsevan nomads of Iran'. In L. Beck and N. Keddie, eds., *Women in the Muslim World*. Harvard University Press.

1979. 'Marriage and social organization among Durrani Pashtuns in northern Afghanistan'. Unpublished Ph.D. dissertation. University of London.

1980. 'Matrons and mistresses: women and boundaries in two Middle Eastern societies'. *Archives Européennes de Sociologie*, 21, 58–78.

1981. 'Direct exchange and brideprice: alternative forms in a complex marriage system'. *Man* (NS), 16, 387–407.

1983. 'Acculturation in Afghan Turkistan: Pashtun and Uzbek women'. *Asian Affairs*, 14 (1), 35–44.

1984. 'Causes and consequences of the abolition of brideprice in Afghanistan'. In N. Shahrani and R. Canfield, eds., *Revolutions and Rebellions in Afghanistan*. Institute of International Studies, Berkeley.

1990. 'Women and power: a perspective on marriage among Durrani Pashtuns of Afghan Turkistan'. In S. Akiner, ed., *Cultural Change and Continuity in Central Asia*. Kegan Paul International, London.

Forthcoming a. '*Ziyarat*: Gender, movement and exchange in a Turkish community'.

In D. Eickelman and J. Piscatori, eds., *Muslim Travellers: Pilgrimages, Migration and Religious Imagination*. Routledge, London; University of California Press, Berkeley.

Forthcoming b. 'Romantic love and illicit sex: the Middle Eastern Case'.

Forthcoming c. 'Anthropology and the Study of Marriage in the Middle East'.

Tapper, N. and R. Tapper. 1982. 'Marriage preferences and ethnic relations among Durrani Pashtuns of Afghan Turkestan'. *Folk*, 24, 157–177.

1987. 'The birth of the Prophet: ritual and gender in Turkish Islam'. *Man* (NS), 22, 69–92.

1988. 'Concepts of personal, moral and social disorder among Durrani Pashtuns in Northern Afghanistan'. In N. Huldt and E. Janssen, eds., *The Tragedy of Afghanistan*. Croom Helm, London.

1989. 'A Marriage with Fieldwork'. In I. Ariens and R. Strijp, eds., *Focaal – Anthropological Couples*, 10, 54–60.

Tapper, R. 1974. 'Nomadism in modern Afghanistan: asset or anachronism?' In L. Dupree and L. Albert, eds., *Afghanistan in the 1970's*. Praeger, New York.

1979a. *Pasture and Politics: Economics, Conflict and Ritual among Shahsevan Nomads of Northwestern Iran*. Academic Press, London.

1979b. 'The organization of nomadic communities among pastoral societies of the Middle East'. In Equipe écologie et anthropologie des sociétés pastorales, eds., *Pastoral Production and Society*. Cambridge University Press.

1983. 'Introduction'. In R. Tapper, ed., *The Conflict of Tribe and State in Iran and Afghanistan*. Croom Helm, London.

1984a. 'Holier than thou: Islam in three tribal societies'. In A. S. Ahmed and D. M. Hart, eds., *Islam in Tribal Societies: From the Atlas to the Indus*. Routledge, London.

1984b. "Ethnicity and class: dimensions of intergroup conflict in north-central Afghanistan'. In N. Shahrani and R. Canfield, eds., *Revolutions and Rebellions in Afghanistan*. Institute of International Studies, Berkeley.

1988. 'Ethnicity, order and meaning in the anthropology of Iran and Afghanistan'. In J.-P. Digard, ed., *Le Fait Ethnique en Iran et en Afghanistan*. CNRS, Paris.

1989. 'Ethnic identities and social categories in Iran and Afghanistan'. In E. Tonkin, M. MacDonald, and M. Chapman, eds., *History and Ethnicity*. ASA Monographs 27. Routledge, London.

Forthcoming a. 'Felt huts, haired tents, scene changes and thought structures: reflections on nomad dwellings'. In P. A. Andrews, ed., volume on tents, *Tübinger Atlas des Vorderen Orients*.

Forthcoming b. 'Golden tent-pegs: settlement and change among nomads in Afghan Turkistan'. In S. Akiner, ed., *Cultural Change and Continuity in Central Asia*. Kegan Paul International, London.

Tapper, R. and N. Tapper. 1972. 'The role of nomads in a region of northern Afghanistan'. Final report on SSRC Project HR 1141. London.

1986. '"Eat this, it'll do you a power of good": food and commensality among Durrani Pashtuns'. *American Ethnologist*, 13 (1), 62–78.

1988. '"Thank God we're secular!" Aspects of fundamentalism in a Turkish town'. In L. Caplan, ed., *Studies in Religious Fundamentalism*. Macmillan, London.

Forthcoming a. 'Marriage, honour and responsibility: Islamic law, ideal and practice'.

Forthcoming b. 'Possession, insanity, responsibility and the self in northern Afghanistan'.

Tavakolian, B. 1984a. 'Women and socioeconomic change among Sheikhanzai nomads of Western Afghanistan'. *Middle East Journal*, 38 (3), 431–453.

1984b. 'Sheikhanzai nomads and the Afghan state: a study of indigenous authority and foreign rule'. In S. Shahrani and R. Canfield, eds., *Revolutions and Rebellions in Afghanistan*. Institute of International Studies, Berkeley.

1984c. 'Religiosity, values and economic change among Sheikhanzai nomads'. In A. S. Ahmed and D. M. Hart, eds., *Islam in Tribal Societies: From the Atlas to the Indus*. Routledge, London.

UNICEF. 1978. 'Statistical Profile of Children and Mothers in Afghanistan'. Unpublished manuscript. Kabul.

Vieille, P. 1978. 'Iranian women in family alliance and sexual politics'. In L. Beck and N. Keddie, eds., *Women in the Muslim World*. Harvard University Press.

Wright, S. 1985. 'Identity and influence: political organization in Doshman Ziari, Mamasani, Iran'. Unpublished D.Phil. thesis. Oxford University.

Yate, C. E. 1888. *Northern Afghanistan*. Blackwood, London.

Index

see also land
veiling of women, 105
village settlements, 3, 31, 36–7, 67, 79, 92
virginity, 163, 170, 182, 189, 223
viricide, 213–14, 221
visits by women, 104, 106, 126, 161, 167–8, 171, 220, 251

wealth, 73, 197, 274
  inherited, 286, 288
  validation of status claims, 262
  wolus membership, 51, 88
wedding (*wade*), 10, 17, 150, 157–8, 164–70, 172, 175–6, 224
  see also marriage festivities
wedding celebrations, 166, 251, 260, 265, 268, 270, 277
wedding songs (*babulale*), 106, 166, 180
widow(s), 45, 108, 156, 187, 234, 269
  as household head, 111, 119, 126, 183, 186, 276
  remarriage, 104, 183, 185–9
  see also widow inheritance
widow inheritance, 49, 104, 127, 172, 183–8, 189–90, 194, 199, 228, 243–4, 252, 256, 261–2, 264
  payment of *sar*, 151, 156
wife-givers, 53, 141–2, 148, 157, 176, 183, 196, 283
wife-takers, 53, 57, 141–2, 147–8, 157, 168, 174, 176, 183, 196, 283
wolus, 30, 32, 47, 50–2, 67–8, 72, 83–4, 196
  Chinar, 68, 274
  membership, 73, 83, 88, 286, 290
  Sinjit, 68, 86, 255, 274
  strength of ties, 90–1

wolusi, 47, 51, 86
women, 52, 122, 185–6, 210, 224–5, 269
  behaviour of, 103–4, 239, 276
  characteristics, 52, 209, 212
  dependence on others, 125, 208, 213, 221
  dissatisfaction with marriage, 213, 217–19, 231–3, 242, 250
  given as compensation, 48, 54, 63, 74–9, 148–9, 151, 154, 230, 252, 282–3
  given free, 74–8, 148–9, 156, 176, 248, 250–4, 258–9, 261, 266, 269–70
  irresponsibility, 215–21, 289
  passivity, 21, 208, 212–13, 215
  as pawns in marriage system, 104, 196, 224, 231, 237, 242, 281, 288
  power of, 22–3, 104, 106, 207–8, 277
  procreative role, 52, 54–6, 65, 125, 211
  as reproductive resource, 16, 20, 22, 52, 160, 196, 207, 216, 280–1, 286
  status, 103–4, 212, 282
  stereotypes, 52, 120, 208, 210, 221, 226–7, 282, 289
  subordination of, 12, 16, 21, 242
  subversive power of, 21–3, 61, 207–8, 220–2, 225, 228, 239
'women's headman', 229, 276
women's leaders, 104–5, 165

Yar Mohammad, 234–5

Zahir, 74, 76–7
-zai (tribal groups), 38–9, 46, 68
Zarip, 77–9, 84
Zarur, 228–32
Zeytun, 234–5

Cambridge Studies in Social and Cultural Anthropology

Editors: JACK GOODY, STEPHEN GUDEMAN, MICHAEL HERZFELD, JONATHAN PARRY

*available in paperback.

DATE DUE